Building Bridges
through Writing

Trixie G. Smith

Allison D. Smith

with Holly Hamby

D1065714

FOUNTAINHEAD
PRESS

Our green initiatives include:

Electronic Products
We deliver products in non-paper form whenever possible. This includes pdf downloadables, flash drives, and CDs.

Electronic Samples
We use Xample, a new electronic sampling system. Instructor samples are sent via a personalized Web page that links to pdf downloads.

FSC Certified Printers
All of our printers are certified by the Forest Service Council, which promotes environmentally and socially responsible management of the world's forests. This program allows consumer groups, individual consumers, and businesses to work together hand-in-hand to promote responsible use of the world's forests as a renewable and sustainable resource.

Recycled Paper
Most of our products are printed on a minimum of 30% post-consumer waste recycled paper.

Support of Green Causes
When we do print, we donate a portion of our revenue to green causes. Listed below are a few of the organizations that have received donations from Fountainhead Press. We welcome your feedback and suggestions for contributions, as we are always searching for worthy initiatives.
Rainforest 2 Reef
Environmental Working Group

Design by Susan Moore

Copyright © 2014 by Fountainhead Press

All rights reserved. No part of this book may be reproduced or utilized in any form or by any means, electronic or mechanical, including photocopying and recording, or by any informational storage and retrieval system without written permission from the publisher.

Books may be purchased for educational purposes.

For information, please call or write:

1-800-586-0330

Fountainhead Press
Southlake, TX 76092

Web Site: www.fountainheadpress.com
E-mail: customerservice@fountainheadpress.com

First Edition

ISBN: 978-1-59871-782-2

Printed in the United States of America

Instructor Preface

Welcome! We are delighted you have chosen to use *Building Bridges through Writing* with your students, whether it is for a freshman composition course, an advanced writing course in English, or a Writing Across the Curriculum (WAC) or Writing in the Disciplines (WID) course. The main purpose of this book—presenting writing in an innovative contextualized way—came from our experiences teaching writing in a variety of college and university programs across the country. In addition, we have presented to and learned from instructors at various levels who were interested in making writing instruction more real for their students. We learned quickly when we became writing teachers that talking about writing with students is not enough; we need to provide contextualized and discipline-specific assignments that encourage students to make the most of their writing and prior knowledge.

Recently, in the fields of composition studies and education, the notion of transfer has become not only important but crucial, as our students gain writing knowledge and skills that are effective both in their freshmen courses and in other general education courses and courses in their major. Preparing students for the successful transfer of their writing knowledge and skills to the workplace also has become critical. Keeping this in mind, we designed *Building Bridges through Writing* as a different kind of writing textbook—one that focuses students on the different types of writing they will do across the curriculum and in the workforce. As a writing instructor, you will find this approach helpful in one of two ways: as you teach a freshman composition course that provides students an opportunity to investigate who they are and what their major will be or as you teach an upper-level writing course that is specific to a particular discipline.

Writing Across the Curriculum (WAC) is a method of teaching and learning writing, one that has at its center the notion that writing and writing instruction should occur throughout students' entire undergraduate education and that all types of reading and writing enrich students' knowledge and better their overall writing skills. Instructors in programs such as this will expect students to write often, think critically, and engage deeply in their own learning. This textbook supports you as you ask your students to do all three of these. *Building Bridges through Writing* also reinforces successful strategies students can use to learn essential twenty-first century literacies that are necessary for their success.

Building Bridges through Writing = WAC = WTL + WID

In shaping *Bridges,* we brought together both writing-to-learn (WTL) activities and writing-in-the discipline (WID) activities. The WTL approach underscores the importance of writing as a way for students to comprehend and retain information more effectively. In the words of composition specialist Janet Emig, "Writing represents a unique mode of learning—not merely valuable, not merely special, but unique." This idea is the cornerstone of the WTL approach, and *Building Bridges through Writing* provides ample guidance and opportunities for you and your students to engage in WTL activities throughout the semester that can be used as a scaffold to more formal writing. The writing-in-the-disciplines (WID) approach, sometimes referred to as the learning-to-write (LTW) approach, highlights how each discipline has its own writing conventions, including specific genres. It is this combination of writing-to-learn and learning-to-write activities that makes *Building Bridges through Writing* an exciting and innovative text for you and your students. At the center of teaching students to become effective writers is the blend of having students write-to-learn, learn-to-write, and then transfer these skills to contexts (and courses) other than the course in which they are learned. Each discipline-specific chapter within *Building Bridges through Writing* offers this trio, offering information, direction, and activities that scaffold what students need to do to become more effective writers.

Building Bridges through Writing is a writing textbook that you and your students can effectively use as they learn to become more critical in their thinking and more skilled in their writing. The first four chapters provide an introduction to writing across the curriculum, the writing process, reading across the curriculum, and the research process. These four chapters provide a foundation for any course, whether you and your students continue your journey through all the discipline-specific chapters that follow or just one or a few of them.

Accompanying the foundational and discipline-specific chapters is the sustained theme of bridges: an interesting way to introduce students to writing concepts, and an idea that will take hold for your students as they leave the classroom and bridge or transfer their writing knowledge and skills to other classes and the workplace. In addition to this focus, students are also introduced to background or real-world information about writing through the **Did you know?** feature. This text element explains or contextualizes what they are learning, which helps them understand why writing is so important to them now and for their future.

Scott Timian, the president of Fountainhead Press, and all the employees of Fountainhead Press are not only eager to bring you and your students an affordable WAC textbook, they are passionate about it. The entire Fountainhead team worked tirelessly to keep costs to a minimum so that they could pass on the savings to your students. And unlike other academic publishers, Fountainhead is an entirely green company, printing textbooks on recycled paper and constantly searching for ways to conserve natural resources. We are proud to be part of the Fountainhead team, and we are excited to share this book with you.

Acknowledgements

Although our names are printed on the cover, there are also other important people who were part of the writing and production process. Our thanks go to everyone at Fountainhead Press, including Scott, Felix Frazier, and Susan Moore, for all the encouragement and support they have given for the project and over the years of our relationship with the company. We express gratitude to the reviewers of *Building Bridges through Writing*. Your insights and comments helped us refine both the framework and content. We truly appreciate your time in assisting us with this project.

Sarah Arroyo, California State University–Long Beach

Meagan Kittle Autry, University of North Carolina–Wilmington

Anis Bawarshi, University of Washington

Darren DeFrain, Wichita State University

Heather Shearer, University of California–Santa Cruz

Wendi Sierra, University North Carolina–Wilmington

—Trixie, Allison, and Holly

As a writing center director, I have worked with numerous faculty across the disciplines, listening to their struggles, helping them find new ways to think about and then create their writing assignments, as well as ways of identifying and then scaffolding the skills needed to achieve the goals of the course, the major, and possibly the field. I am indebted to all of these teachers for sharing their journeys with me and for helping me think about how diverse writing actually is across the academy, as well as how diverse writing is out in the world where our students encounter and produce a wide array of texts. Much of that work is evident in this text, and I hope it will help you and your students with your own journeys. In particular, I would like to say thank you to several of my colleagues who helped facilitate faculty workshops and seminars: Mike Orth, Terry Trupiano Barry, Bridget Behe, Suzanne Thiem, Dianna Baldwin, and Zeynep Ustunol, as well as graduate assistants Jason Wertz, Andrea Davis, Matthew Cox, and Daisy Levy, who are all spreading their knowledge at their own universities now. Special thanks as well go to numerous consultants at The Writing Center at MSU for sharing their experiences working with writers from across the curriculum, but particular thanks to Marilee Brooks Gillies, Elena Goodwin Garcia, and Shari Wolke. Finally, thanks to my writing group for reading numerous drafts of chapters in this text and offering insights from their various fields: Manuel Colunga, Eva Kassens, Wen Li, and Janice Molloy. I dedicate this text to all of the students who were willing to share their writing with us so that we could share it with you. For many of them it was a brave thing to do, so treat their writing with care and know that these are real-world examples and none of them are perfect.

—Trixie

A special thank you goes to my Spring 2013 graduate seminar students (Jonathan Bradley, Kayla McNabb, and Donna Swaner), who beta-tested and discussed many of the ideas in this book. The books I write always come from what my students and I discover in the classroom or from what I learn supervising teachers and graduate teaching assistants. My Spring 2013 class, plus many others, helped me discover a great deal about writing transfer as we wrote this book. Best of luck to all of them in their future teaching careers. A very special acknowledgement goes to my nephew Zack and my niece Molly—I hope that as you take your first steps into college classrooms, your instructors are already thinking about how you will be able to transfer your writing knowledge and skills to other contexts. My portion of this book is dedicated to Zack and Molly and all those other new college students writing to learn and learning to write.

—*Allison*

I am especially thankful to my co-authors and mentors, Allison and Trixie, for inviting me to work on this project with them. A special thank you also goes to my Fisk University colleagues, and to my composition students with whom I first tried several of the activities in this book. Many thanks also go to my in-laws, Jim and Joyce Hamby, who spent countless weekends caring for my son, Arley, so that I could focus on writing this book. Of course, I also thank my husband, Jim Hamby III, for his constant support and feedback.

—*Holly*

Table of Contents

chapter 1

Writing Across the Curriculum

Writing represents a unique mode of learning—not merely valuable, not merely special, but unique.

—Janet Emig

This handbook takes a Writing Across the Curriculum (WAC) approach to help you improve all your writing, including the writing you do in every one of your higher education courses, from your first freshman composition or general education course, to the senior-level courses in your major, to the writing you do postgraduation. WAC is a method of teaching and learning writing. At its center are the notions that writing and writing instruction should occur throughout your entire undergraduate education and that all types of reading and writing enrich you as a person and better your overall writing skills. Any program that uses the WAC approach asks you to write often, think critically, and engage deeply in your own learning. This handbook supports you as you do all three. However, your involvement in improving your writing is essential. You need to understand the importance of being an effective writer, and commit yourself to expanding your writing abilities and securing your future.

A focus on WAC supports the writing you do in your general education courses and develops your written communication and critical thinking skills. In addition, a focus on writing in the disciplines further expands the writing and thinking skills associated with the major you choose to pursue. Overall, what these types of writing classes and their assignments do is help you work on writing and thinking skills that are easily transferred to your life after college.

In addition, learning to write effectively for all occasions and especially for the specialized writing of your discipline and future career, is one of the keys to getting and keeping a job. In a recent survey by the Partnership for 21st Century Skills, when employers were asked what makes recent college graduates ready to hire, more than 90 percent of the employers said that writing and critical thinking are "very important" for success. In the same survey, however, these same employers described only 16 percent of their new hires as having excellent written communication skills and 28 percent as having excellent critical thinking skills. The 2004 College Board's National

Did you know?

A 2006 survey of employers and recent college graduates—sponsored by The Association of American Colleges and Universities—cites the following as the most important intellectual and practical skills a college-educated job applicant can have.

- Teamwork skills and the ability to collaborate with others in diverse group settings (76%)
- The ability to effectively communicate orally and in writing (73%)
- Critical thinking and analytical reasoning skills (73%)
- The ability to locate, organize, and evaluate information from multiple sources (70%)
- The ability to be innovative and think creatively (70%)
- The ability to solve complex problems (64%)
- The ability to work with numbers and understand statistics (60%)

Commission on Writing confirmed that writing is an entry-level skill that new employees are expected to have but that a third of workers fail to meet the writing requirements of their jobs, whatever that position or career is. Moreover, because these skills are now considered so essential, you should be prepared to have them tested at job interviews with problem-set writing questions, case-based interviews, mini-project assignments, and role-playing exercises, all of which require mastery of writing and critical thinking skills.

Thus, what the writing in a WAC-focused course does is prepare you for your future, including general education courses and your discipline-specific courses. To help you with this, your writing program may include one or both of these WAC fundamental concepts: writing to learn and writing in the disciplines.

WRITING TO LEARN

I never know what I think about something until I read what I've written about it.

—William Faulkner

The writing-to-learn (WTL) approach underscores the importance of writing as a way for you to comprehend and retain information more effectively. One of the key tenets of writing-to-learn is to use writing to make your thoughts more visible to yourself, so you can organize and analyze them. Your freshman composition instructor may use this approach to get you writing as often as possible, or you can use writing-to-learn to help you prepare for written exams, essays, or research papers in other courses. Typical writing-to-learn class activities are short and informal, such as journals, summaries, or reading responses, and can be done in or out of class. These types of assignments are usually considered low risk and are commonly evaluated on a global level, where you or your instructor concentrate on content. The main objective behind any of these assignments is for you to become more comfortable with critically thinking about key concepts or principles and sharing those thoughts with yourself, your instructor, or your classmates. A list of common writing-to-learn activities and assignments is provided in Box 1.1, and fuller descriptions of these and other types of assignments are also included in each discipline-specific chapter in this handbook. You will complete these activities either on paper or using technology, depending on the assignment.

Box 1.1

Common Writing-to-Learn Activities

Annotations: Summarize and evaluate readings using the style of the documentation system used in your class.

Dialogue Journals or Discussion Board Entries: Share your thoughts and questions with another writer or your instructor and receive a response.

Discourse Analyses: Analyze conventions and formats for assignments and projects.

Discussion Blogs or Logs: Summarize key discussion points from class.

Discussion Starters: Respond briefly to a short reading, quotation, or remark at the beginning of a class discussion.

Freewrites: Choose a topic, put pen to paper or fingers to keyboard for a short time, and do not stop writing. Use the freewriting to brainstorm ideas or narrow topics.

Graphic Organizers: Brainstorm supporting ideas by using a visual organizer.

Group Response Sheets: Evaluate presentations or readings with classmates.

Learning Logs: Record key terms and observations.

Letters: Use the letter format to share key ideas with a classmate or someone else.

Micro-Themes: Write short one-page arguments or explanations about a concept or issue being covered in class.

Oral Drafts: Present a short (two minutes to five minutes) talk to a small group about your paper, giving information about an essay in progress. Sometimes, you will be required to ask your listeners to answer questions, and sometimes your listeners will be required to ask you questions that you must be able to answer extemporaneously.

Outlines: Organize your thoughts or responses to cases, problems, or prompts.

Peer Review Forms: Use these comment or evaluation forms to review the writing of your classmates. Use their comments on your papers to help you revise and edit.

Pre-Test Warm-Ups: Stretch your writing skills by responding to questions similar to those found on a test.

Problem Analyses: Evaluate problems or cases that are provided by the instructor or classmates.

Problem Statements: Pose problems based on readings or class discussions where the answers may lead to an essay topic.

Progress Reports: Give a brief description of where you are in your project and what your next steps will be.

Project Notebooks: Track the progress of your project by including brainstorming and planning activities in one place.

Project Warm-Ups: Practice conventions and formats for assignments and projects.

Reading Journals: Summarize and respond informally to assigned readings, sometimes as homework or briefly in class prior to a class discussion. Highlight areas of interest or concern.

Reading Responses: Focus on one reading or a group of related readings, and respond within given guidelines. Use first person, if instructed.

Summaries: Describe key elements of a reading, lecture, or other form of research.

Writing Journals: Keep track of your writing process, from brainstorming activities, to outlining, to ideas for revising or editing drafts.

WRITING IN THE DISCIPLINES

The writing-in-the-disciplines (WID) approach highlights how each discipline has its own writing conventions, including specific formats and forms. WID class activities ask you to participate in the academic discourse of your particular disciplinary community, and they stress discipline-specific conventions and forms. Typical WID activities are focused on practicing writing that is specific to a discipline, such as learning how to structure a literature review in the humanities or a lab report in the sciences. These types of assignments are usually considered high-stakes or high-risk writing since the grades these assignments receive have an immense impact on the writer, helping to determine placement in a program or a final grade for a course. Your instructor or some evaluator will usually use high standards to assess the writing not just for content, but also for other writing qualities, such as organization, word use, grammar, and formatting. Normally, your WID assignments will be written over a longer period of time than a low-risk or writing-to-learn activity. A list of common writing-in-the-disciplines activities and assignments is provided in Box 1.2, and fuller descriptions of these and other types of assignments are also included in each discipline-specific chapter in this book. In the discipline-specific chapters, you will also find examples of student writing that demonstrate various students' approaches to the types of writing discussed. They are not perfect templates, but real-world examples from students just like you.

Did you know?

A survey of 120 major American corporations, which was sponsored by the College Board Advocacy and Policy Center, found that remedying deficiencies in writing may cost American firms as much as $3.1 billion annually.

- Annual cost of training new salaried employees in writing: $104,860,000

- Annual cost of training new hourly employees in writing: $98,670,000

- Annual cost of training current salaried employees in writing: $1,362,104,758

- Annual cost of training current hourly employees in writing: $1,525,308,436

- **Grand total: $3,090,943,194 annually**

Box 1.2

Common Writing-in-the-Disciplines Activities

Annotated Bibliographies: Prepare a citation list of articles, books, book chapters, essays, websites, and other documents. Depending on the document system for your discipline or the assignment for the course, add a brief paragraph after the citation that describes and evaluates the source.

Casebooks: Provide a review of cases (in law) or problems that support a response. Requires closely following the vocabulary, format, and layout conventions of the field.

Grant Proposals: Write a proposal or plan that explains a problem, suggests an answer, and requests funding to apply the answer. Requires closely following the vocabulary, format, and layout conventions of the field or grant agency.

Interpretative Essays: Write an essay using both fact and opinion as you attempt to understand something, usually a text.

Jargon Journals: Collect the common terminology of the discipline or field you will be joining.

Journal or Professional Articles: Write an article that follows the requirements of your discipline or the field you will be joining.

Lab or Field Reports: Present a description of an experiment or experience. Usually requires following the vocabulary, format, and layout conventions of the discipline or field.

Literature Reviews: Discuss previously published information (articles, books, essays, websites) on a particular subject. Summarize, synthesize, or do both, per the assignment guidelines.

Management Plans: Describe how a project will be managed. Include information about the goals and objectives, participants, timeline, funds, and whatever other information is required by the assignment or expected in the discipline.

Memos: Communicate your thoughts (informative memo) or requests (persuasive memo) in a brief and to-the-point format, following the format and conventions of your discipline or field.

Micro-themes: Write a short, one-page argument or explanation about a concept or issue being covered in class.

Oral Presentations: Present information, possibly with visual aids. Requires a knowledge of the audience, careful planning, and attention to delivery conventions of your discipline or field.

Popular Articles: Write an article about your discipline or field and present the information in a way that will be understandable to the common reader.

Position Papers: Discuss your topic and provide objective supporting evidence. Requires knowledge of the format and conventions of your discipline or field.

Project Proposals: Write a proposal or plan that explains how you plan to organize and manage your project. Requires closely following the vocabulary, format, and layout conventions of the field or grant agency.

Rhetorical Analyses: Use your critical reading skills to break down a text into its parts and purposes. Determine what objectives the writer has and what strategies the writer uses to achieve those objectives.

WTL + WID

Even though writing-to-learn and writing-in-the-disciplines (WID) activities differ, your teacher may ask you to use them together as you move through the writing process. When you break down assignments into smaller components, you use what is called a scaffolding approach, allowing you to be initiated into the discourse of your discipline step by step and ultimately become an insider who uses expert insider prose. For instance, writing-to-learn activities can help you think through key ideas, and then WID assignments can help you learn the academic language of your major or the writing conventions of your discipline and future field of employment. This handbook introduces and promotes the use of both WTL and WID activities in the writing classroom or on your own as you become a sophisticated writer who uses both the vocabulary and structure of an expert insider. This growth process does not occur overnight. The sequenced processes of both WTL and WID class assignments will allow you to evaluate the writing of your field and begin your quest to become an effective and successful member of your discipline's writing community.

Did you know?

Employers in all fields care about your writing ability. Some reasons given by employers in the 2004 National Commission on Writing report included the following:

- "In most cases, writing ability could be your ticket in . . . or it could be your ticket out."
- "All employees must have writing ability. Everything is tracked. All instructions are written out. Manufacturing documentation, operating procedures, reporting problems, lab safety, waste-disposal operations—all have to be crystal clear. Hourly and professional staff go through serious training. They must be able to communicate clearly, relay information, do postings, and the like. As a government contractor, *everything* must be documented."
- "Writing skills are fundamental in business. It's increasingly important to be able to convey content in a tight, logical, direct manner, particularly in a fast-paced technological environment."
- "My view is that good writing is a sign of good thinking. Writing that is persuasive, logical, and orderly is impressive. Writing that's not careful can be a signal of unclear thinking."
- "Scientific precision is required almost always for scientists and engineers responsible for preparing formal papers and technical reports."
- "Writing is integral in nearly every job. It's really not a promotion issue since you'd never get to the point of promotion without good communications skills. You can't move up without writing skills."
- "Business writing generally calls for clarity, brevity, accuracy, and an appropriate level of detail for documenting."

TRANSFER AND TWENTY-FIRST CENTURY LITERACIES

Students need to be prepared to make a living, to make a life, and . . . to make a difference.

—*Carol Jago*

Real writing is read—by customers, colleagues, officials, community members, and those we would win over with our words.

—*James Burke*

The way that writing is taught and learned has undergone a shift recently with the concept of transfer coming to the forefront of the many theories that underpin what happens in the everyday composition class. In its most basic sense, transfer is the application of skills or knowledge learned in one course to another course or from your academic reading and writing to the reading and writing that you do in the workplace after graduating. This transfer or application of skills or knowledge can be near or far. Near transfer includes the transfer of skills or knowledge from one context or class to another context or class, with both situations having many concrete overlapping features. For instance, if you learn how to write argumentative essays in one English class and then use the same skills you learned to write another argumentative essay in a different English class, the skills you use in both classes probably have many similarities. Far transfer includes the transfer of skills or knowledge from one context or class to another context or class with both situations having only some abstract or general overlapping features. For example, if you learn how to consider both sides of an argument in an English class and then use this same skill in a history class or in the first memo you write in a new job, that one intellectual maneuver shows a far transfer.

Near transfer and far transfer are called by various names in writing scholarship. Near transfer is sometimes referred to as *low-road transfer* or *hugging*, and far transfer is sometimes called *high-road transfer* or *bridging*. Both types of transfer are essential if you are to be a successful writer in school and after school. However, bridging—or how students make connections between different contexts is at the center of writing—across the curriculum programs and this text. It also influenced us to choose *Building Bridges through Writing* as the book's title.

When you write, both near and far transfers are usually part of your writing or writing process. Rebecca Nowacek, a composition scholar who researches writing transfer, describes transfer as both a cognitive (mental) and rhetorical (stylistic) act. She recommends that you learn to recontextualize what you have learned through previous writing experiences each time you attempt to write something new. When you learn writing strategies in your freshman composition class, use those strategies to focus on how to think about your topic and also how to choose the appropriate genre or language to present the topic. It is important that you make connections across disciplines, taking what you have learned and applying general knowledge or specific skills that may help you with any new writing task.

For many years, the assumption was always that transfer just happened through regular instruction and that students automatically remembered to shift what they learned in a writing class to different classes (or even the workplace). Now, though, most instructors will present strategies that will help you transfer the skills and knowledge from your freshman writing classes to other general education courses, courses in your major, or your future workplace. It is crucial that you, as a thinker and writer, learn how to extend what you have learned in one context to other new contexts. This will not only make you a better writer, it will help you succeed as a writer in the academic environment and the workplace.

Indeed, each chapter in this textbook, used as part of a course that focuses on writing across the university curriculum, shares strategies that will help you transfer the skills and knowledge that you gain from your writing class to other contexts, including courses in your major. Since strategies that are disciplinary specific are included in chapters throughout the book, this chapter focuses on the general strategies that you as a writer can follow to facilitate transfer, thus expanding both your academic and workplace literacies.

Strategies to Transfer Your Knowledge to New Situations:

1. **Become smart about texts (develop textual intelligence)**

   a. Learn how texts are structured, how different grammatical structures affect readers, what text format is needed, and how text can be in print, visual, or audio formats.

   b. Be knowledgeable about point of view, the verb tenses that are expected in different disciplines, and the influence of the text's organization on the reader.

2. **Look for contextual clues in your writing assignments**

   a. Contextualize: When you encounter a new writing assignment, reflect on how some of the tools or knowledge you used in past assignments can be applied to the current assignment.

   b. Decontextualize: After you complete a writing assignment, reflect on the tools you used and knowledge about writing you gained. Be prepared to access this information for future writing assignments.

3. **Think about thinking (develop metacognitive awareness)**

   a. After you complete a piece of writing, think about how you thought as you did your prewriting, writing, and postwriting.

   b. Keep a writer's log or workbook and jot down your reflections about how you discovered your thesis or found your research materials.

4. **Investigate all sides**

   a. Look at topics and arguments from multiple sides.

   b. Practice developing differing or conflicting interpretations and arguments, and then support these divergent ideas with well-structured support.

5. **Learn to identify genres (type of writing and format of writing)**

   a. Consider the type of writing that you are doing. Is it persuasive or argumentative? Informative or narrative?

   b. Also consider the form or shape your writing takes. Is there a particular format involved, such as memo form or research paper form, that is used in the discipline or in the work environment?

6. **Consider target audiences**

   a. As you write, identify the target audience. Investigate and keep track of the people who make up the discourse community (in-group) of your audience. Look at other writings that have been written for that audience. Are there particular terms or phrases that are used for them? Is writing aimed at them written in active (*The pilot flew the plane.*) or passive voice (*The plane was flown by the pilot.*)?

   b. When you write something new, look back at your previous writing projects and reflect on what you learned about the audience. Apply what you learned to the new writing, or if the audience is different, use similar strategies to reflect on who the new audience is.

   c. Keep track of what type of research or documentation is needed in each piece of writing you do. Return to earlier pieces to refresh your memory about the particular research or documentation necessary.

7. **Create writing goals that fit you and your future courses or workplaces**

   a. Figure out the big questions you want to explore through your education, and focus on these questions as you choose writing topics.

   b. Connect each assignment to where you are going next. Reflect on what you can carry with you from the current writing to the next step in your education.

8. **Revise, redo, repeat**

   a. Learn from everything you write. Reflect on the comments given to you about your writing, and use your new knowledge to revise, even if you will not turn in the revision for a grade.

   b. Collect your papers at the end of the semester. Keep them in a folder or binder, and return to them when you have a new writing assignment that is similar.

9. **Be an independent learner**

   a.   Whenever you complete a writing assignment or activity, reflect on what you learned and how that may relate to your future educational or work goals.

   b.   Write to learn. Whenever you read or think about something new, write about it as well.

   c.   Learn to write. Writing courses will never cover everything you need to know. Read your textbooks, and then independently study what was not covered.

   d.   Take notes, ask questions, and read a range of texts outside of your courses.

10. **Know your discipline**

   a.   How do members in your discipline find information? Where is the information available online? What research strategies are common?

   b.   Is collaboration common in your area of study? If so, how is that collaboration done, and how is writing credit usually shared?

ACADEMIC LITERACY

The writing that you learn about and do before you come to college and in your general education writing courses helps shape your academic literacy, and academic literacy is essential in order to achieve academic success. Academic literacy includes traditional educational elements such as reading, writing, listening, speaking, and critical thinking. It also includes habits of mind that will advance your academic success, such as curiosity and skepticism about new ideas, courage to embrace changing ideas, and participation in intellectual discussions. Being able to convey your ideas clearly and to listen and respond to the diverse views of others is also part of being academically literate.

However, the core requirements in the educational system of the United States have recently changed, and these changes have also added to what constitutes academic literacy. To be academically literate, you must be responsible for your own learning and engage in self-advocacy when what you have learned, or have not learned, does not meet the educational and workplace goals you have set for yourself. And, finally, academic literacy also includes basic and some advanced technological skills such as word processing, e-mail use, and the fundamentals of Web-based-research. Successful students know that their engagement with complex ideas underpins their membership in the academic community, and they also practice the twenty-first-century literacies that make up academic literacy as a whole.

Academic literacy includes your ability to engage in the following activities:

❏   Read and think critically

❏   Comprehend information presented in various modes, including print, visual, and audio

- ❏ Find, evaluate, incorporate, and acknowledge sources
- ❏ Identify, evaluate, and present arguments
- ❏ Paraphrase and summarize
- ❏ Write expository prose (e.g., argument, comparison, classification)
- ❏ Present information visually
- ❏ Develop and signal your own voice
- ❏ Work collaboratively with others
- ❏ Use a range of tools and strategies to solve the problems you encounter
- ❏ Self-advocate
- ❏ Participate in the ongoing intellectual dialogue that characterizes higher education
- ❏ Use basic (such as word processing software, e-mail, search engines) and any advanced technology used in your discipline (such as statistical or website design software)

It is you who determines how academically literate you are or will become, and this resolve determines your academic (and future workplace) success since a focus on the above core literacies is increasingly found not only in your freshman composition or general education courses, but also in courses across all disciplines. In addition to the core literacies, each discipline has its own customs and conventions. As a member of your chosen major or discipline, not only are you expected to acquire bodies of knowledge (facts, theories, and concepts), but you are also expected to learn and participate in your discipline's way of seeing, thinking, and communicating. When you decide on your major, you become an apprentice to that discipline, and as such, you need to become knowledgeable about all aspects of it.

In a way, then, you are responsible for acquiring multiple academic literacies—the core literacies and those literacies particular to your field. Judith Langer, an internationally known scholar of literacy education, summed up the current thinking of multiple academic literacies in a speech at the International Reading Association conference in 2004, when she stated students need to develop a literate mind, which she defined as involving "the kinds of thinking needed not only to do well in school, but outside as well. It's the kind of mind [students] need to get on in life and adults need to keep up with life. It involves the ability to use language and thought to gain knowledge, share it and reason with it. We do this when we read, write, and use the symbols and signs that permeate our society," including the society of your field.

Writing as a competency can range from writing-to-learn activities, such as journals or blogs, to learning to write in your discipline activities, such as creating treatment plans in health education courses or sketchbooks in art courses. Most writing that you do in your general education courses, courses in your major, or even in your future workplace can be divided into four major types: persuasive, explanatory, imaginative, and expressive. When you write to persuade, you try to convince your reader to believe something or take action. Explanatory writing allows you to share knowledge or ideas with your reader. Imaginative writing is creative in nature, and expressive writing allows you to share your personal opinion without necessarily requiring you to support that opinion with evidence. In the following table, you can see some common forms of these types of writing; these forms are discussed in detail in the disciplinary chapters that follow in this text.

TABLE 1.1

Common Types and Forms of Writing Across the Disciplines			
Persuasive	Explanatory	Imaginative	Expressive
advertisements	annotated	biographical	blogs/vlogs
analyses	bibliographies	narratives	e-mail
debates	articles	creative nonfiction	journals
editorials	business plans	designs	personal statements
essays	casebooks/case	digital stories	reader responses
letters	studies	fiction	reflections
position papers	charts	graphic fiction	reviews
presentations	diagnoses	mixed media	social network posts
proposals	essays	monologues	text messages
research papers	essay exams	personal narratives	
reviews	field or lab	plays	
speeches	instructions	poems	
	histories	scripts	
	literature reviews	sketchbooks	
	manuals		
	posters		
	presentations		
	reports		
	resumes		
	summaries		
	treatment plans		
	websites		
	wikis		

WORKPLACE LITERACY

In the workplace, the common core of literacies that make up academic literacy is also essential. How effectively you are able to transfer the skills and knowledge that you acquire in college to your workplace is key to your success in the workplace. As Deborah Brandt, a widely recognized literacy scholar, shares in her 2001 book, *Literacy in American Lives,* "Literacy is a valued commodity in the U.S. economy, a key resource in gaining profit and edge" (Brandt 21). So, to get a job and keep that job, literacy skills, general knowledge, and specific disciplinary knowledge all are necessary. The 2007 report, "Tough Choices or Tough Times," published by the National Center of Education and the Economy (NCEE), confirms that "this is a world in which a very high level of preparation in reading, writing, speaking, mathematics, science, literature, history, and the arts will be indispensable . . . in which comfort with ideas and abstractions is the passport to a good job, in which creativity and innovation are the keys to a good life."

In its 2006 "Are They Really Ready to Work?" report, The Conference Board—a distinguished business think tank—estimates that 85 percent of newly created jobs between 2006 and 2016 will require a college education. As a conclusion to its report, The Conference Board reveals that the future U.S. workforce is "woefully ill-prepared for the demands of today's (and tomorrow's) workplace," particularly in the following four areas:

- ❏ Critical thinking and problem solving
- ❏ Oral and written communication
- ❏ Professionalism and work ethic
- ❏ Teamwork and collaboration

In her book *The Flat World and Education: How America's Commitment to Equity Will Determine Our Future*, Linda Darling-Hammond, a Stanford professor of educational policy, lists the following competencies that represent the workplace literacy of the future.

Workplace literacy includes your ability to:

1. Design, evaluate, and manage one's own work so that it continually improves
2. Frame, investigate, and solve problems using a wide range of tools and resources
3. Collaborate strategically with others
4. Communicate effectively in many forms
5. Find, analyze, and use information for many purposes
6. Develop new products and ideas

Note how similar the list of academic literacy competencies presented earlier in this chapter is to these workplace competencies. Transfer of skills and knowledge, then, is not only important as you transition from your general education courses to courses in your major, it is also vitally significant as you transition into the workforce.

Being able to decontexualize what you learn in your classes and then recontextualize those skills and that knowledge into the new environment of your workplace will determine your future. Thus, you need to be constantly aware of what you are learning and how what you learn can be transferred as support for your life and work goals.

READ MORE ABOUT IT

Bamberg, Betty. "WAC in the 90's: Changing Contexts and Challenges." *Language and Learning Across the Disciplines* 4.2 (2000): 5–19. Print.

Bazerman, Charles, Joseph Little, Lisa Bethel, Teri Chavkin, Danielle Fouquette, and Janet Garufis. *Reference Guide to Writing Across the Curriculum*. West Lafayette, IN: Parlor Press. 2005. Print.

Bean, John. *Engaging Ideas: The Professor's Guide to Integrating Writing, Critical Thinking, and Active Learning in the Classroom*. 2nd ed. Hoboken, NJ: Jossey-Bass, 2011. Print.

Blevins-Knabe, Belinda. "Writing to Learn While Learning to Write." *Teaching of Psychology* 14.4 (1987): 239–41. Print.

Brandt, Deborah. *Literacy in American Lives*. Cambridge: Cambridge, UP, 2001. Print.

Britton, James. "Writing to Learn and Learning to Write." *The Humanity of English: NCTE Distinguished Lectures*, ed. NCTE. Urbana, IL: 1972. Print.

Crowhurst, Marion. "The Role of Writing in Subject-area Learning." (1989). *ERIC Document Reproduction Service*, ED 303 805. Web.

Fulwiler, Toby. "The Politics of Writing Across the Curriculum." (1986). *ERIC Document Reproduction Service*, ED 276 061. Web.

Gray, Donald J. (1988). "Writing Across the College Curriculum." *Phi Delta Kappa* 69.10 (1988): 729–33. Print.

Griffin, C. W. "A Process of Critical Thinking: Using Writing to Teach Many Disciplines." *Improving College and University Teaching* 31.3 (1983): 121–28. Print.

Hall, Jonathan. "Toward a Unified Writing Curriculum: Integrating WAC/WID with Freshman Composition." *WAC Journal* 17 (2006): 5–22. Print.

Herrington, Anne J. "Writing to Learn: Writing Across the Disciplines." *College English* 43.4 (1981): 379–87. Print.

Hill, Charles A. Writing-to-learn as a Rationale for Writing Across the Curriculum. (1994). *ERIC Document Reproduction Service*, ED 370 108. Web.

Hill, M. "Writing Summaries Promotes Thinking and Learning Across the Curriculum—But Why are They so Difficult to Write?" *Journal of Reading* 34.7 (1991): 536–39. Print.

Hobson, Eric H., and K. W. Schafermeyer. "Writing and Critical Thinking: Writing-to-learn in Large Classes." *American Journal of Pharmaceutical Education* 58 (1994): 423–27. Print.

Johnson, Julie, Melinda Holcombe, Gloria Simms, and David Wilson. "Writing to Learn in a Content Area." *Clearing House* 66.3 (1993): 155–58. Print.

Knoblauch, C. H., and Lil Brannon. "Writing as Learning Through the Curriculum." *College English* 45.5 (1983): 465–74. Print.

Langer, Judith. "Developing the Literate Mind." International Reading Association. Speech. 4 May 2004. Web. 8 Aug 2013.

Larson, Richard. *Writing in the Academic and Professional Disciplines.* New York: Herbert Lehman College, 1983. Print.

Madigan, Chris. "Writing as a Means, Not an End." *Journal of College Science Teaching* 16 (1987): 245–49. Print.

National Center on Education and the Economy. *Tough Choices for Tough Times.* 2007. Web. Skillscommission.org. 10 Aug 2013.

Parker, Robert P., and Vera H. Goodkin. *The Consequences of Writing: Enhancing Learning in the Disciplines.* Upper Montclair, NJ: Boynton/Cook, 1987. Print.

Reese, Diane J., and Paula S. Zielonka. "Writing to Comprehend in the Content Areas." (1989). *ERIC Document Reproduction Service*, ED 315 767. Web.

Ruszkiewicz, John J. "Writing 'In' and 'Across' the Disciplines: The Historical Background." (1982). *ERIC Document Reproduction Service*, ED 224 024. Web.

Soven, Margot K. *Write to Learn: A Guide to Writing Across the Curriculum.* Cincinnati, OH: South-Western College Publishing, 1996. Print.

The Conference Board, et al. "Are They Really Ready to Work?" No City: The Conference Board, 2006. Print. www.conference-board.org. Web. 8 Aug 2013.

Watkins, Beverly T. "More and More Professors in Many Academic Disciplines Routinely Require Students to do Extensive Writing." *Chronicle of Higher Education* 36.44 (July 18, 1990), A13–A14, A16. Print.

Young, Art. "The Wonder of Writing Across the Curriculum." *Language and Learning Across the Disciplines* 1.1 (1994): 58–71. Print.

Zinsser, William. *Writing to Learn.* New York: Harper & Row, 1988. Print.

chapter 2

The Writing Process

When something can be read without effort, great effort has gone into its writing.

—Enrique Jardiel Poncela

WHY IS WRITING IMPORTANT?

Writing is power. It is the power to write successful essays and test answers in school and the power to write effective memos and reports in business. It is the power to present your own point of view or to disagree with someone else's. We are all writers; we write e-mails, blog posts, job applications, proposals, reviews, and requests. We answer important requests in writing; we respond to complaints in writing. And, overall, life is just easier for those who can write well.

Writing helps us to do the following:

- ❑ Communicate our thoughts and feelings
- ❑ Think more deeply and critically
- ❑ Discover and shape new ideas
- ❑ Consider ethical issues
- ❑ Improve our performance in the classroom and the workplace
- ❑ Prepare us for what comes after school
- ❑ Map out a meaningful life (see Figure 2.1)

Figure 2.1 Image of a Mapped-Out Life

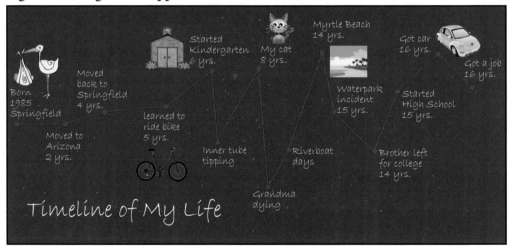

HOW DO COLLEGE WRITERS SUCCEED?

As a college student, your instructors will assume that you are already a proficient writer, and are able to both think critically about the topics you read about or discuss in class and skillfully present your knowledge and viewpoints. Even though your instructors may talk about the writing process or successful writing traits, they will often consider this review material. You can be proactive and take control of your writing class experience if you follow the steps below.

1. **Read the syllabus and each assignment thoroughly.** Highlight due dates and other important clues tthat will help you. Invest in a printed calendar just for your writing class, or create one on your computer and print it out. Build a writing process schedule that allows at least two to three weeks of incremental work leading up to each assigned essay. See Box 2.1 for suggestions on deconstructing the assignment sheet so you stay on task.

Box 2.1

Deconstructing the Assignment Sheet

- Read the assignment sheet more than once, highlighting different types of information with different colors. Be sure to highlight due dates, genre/media requirements, and formatting requirements.

- Return to the assignment sheet at various times throughout the writing process, double-checking that you are on task.

- If the assignment gives information about required writing process steps (such as brainstorming activities, multiple drafts, revising or editing workshops), note these on your calendar immediately.

- Pay close attention to important words (such as "requirement," "tip,""note,""NB," or "hint") that are used to focus your attention on particular tasks.

- Be sure to ask for explanations if you do not understand something about the assignment.

2. **Know your instructor and yourself.** On the first day of class, ask your instructor about his or her writing pet peeves. Write these down, and look them over each time you turn in a writing assignment. If you are a morning person, take a morning class. If not, try to sign up for class at a time that fits most effectively into your schedule. Writing classes require a lot of reading, excellent attendance and participation, and a knack for sticking to schedules. Anticipate early on which of these requirements might cause problems, and rework your schedule accordingly.

3. **Trust yourself.** Academic papers may be formal, but they still should reflect your own voice and views. Do not pretend to be someone you are not when you write.

4. **Be sure to use all the resources available to you.** In the first week of class, find out where your instructor's office is and what his or her office hours are. Find the writing center, if your campus has one. Locate a 24-hour computer lab. Take a tour of the library. Locate a copier that is close to your classroom.

5. **Do not procrastinate.** Do your reading when it is assigned or earlier than that if possible. In most writing classes, writing is viewed as a process, and instructors grade both process material and your final essay draft. Be sure to complete each step of the writing process on time, as this will help you arrive at a final essay draft before or by the due date.

6. **Attend all classes and participate in class discussions.** This seems obvious, but after years of being in high school writing classes, you might embrace the freedom of the college class too much and run your absences to the limit allowed. Not being in class is the easiest way to ruin your class grade even if attendance and participation are a small percentage of the total grade. Being in class allows you to learn the instructor's pet peeves, tackle small parts of writing assignments with your peers, and learn more about topics through class discussion.

7. **Keep track of instructor and peer comments.** Use a grid or a small notebook to collect instructor or peer comments about your writing, whether the comments are about content, logic, organization, vocabulary, or grammar. After a few assignments, you will be able to analyze your own writing, and you will know what you need to work on to improve the next essay.

8. **Be flexible.** Each writing instructor and class of students has a combined different experience than another. Understand that the advice given to you by your eighth grade teacher or advanced placement tutor is not the only good advice you may receive. Build up your writing knowledge base with each piece of writing advice you are given. Sometimes this means that you will have to consider opposing viewpoints—there is not just one way to become a good writer.

9. **Build up your reading muscle.** Complete assigned readings carefully before participating in class discussions or writing text analysis essays. If you do not read much outside of your classwork, now is the time to begin reading the newspaper once a day, making your way through a bestselling nonfiction or fiction book over the break, and/or dedicating yourself to reading a reporter's blog each day or week. Do not restrict your reading— the more you read, the more tools you will have to write.

10. **Write, write, write, and write some more.** Any type of writing will help you become a better writer, so do not limit yourself to essay assignments. Work through all the process assignments for your writing class, and use these same tools for other classes as well. Respond to prompts or questions given on class management software or outside blogs or news stories. Write a letter home once a month. Each time you work on your global writing skills—content, organization, and vocabulary—and your local writing skills—grammar, mechanics, and formatting—you help yourself become a better writer.

WRITING IN COLLEGE
WHAT IS ACADEMIC WRITING?

You may hear the term academic writing in your writing class or other courses. Although different instructors may expect different things when using this term, it is a good idea for you to become familiar with some general expectations or conventions that are common to writing classes or other courses.

Use your writing to show that you trust your own opinion. Use phrasing that shows this, and do not weaken it with wordy or empty phrases, such as *In my opinion, I think, I feel, I believe*, or *It is my belief that*. Read the two sentences that follow and notice how the second sentence comes across much more strongly than the first.

❏ It is my belief that the signs on the US 97 highway are always changing.

❏ The signs on the US 97 highway are always changing.

Create a strong thesis, continue it throughout the essay, and support it thoroughly with primary and secondary support. Be sure to use narrative examples, quotations from authorities, and factual data, when appropriate, and do not forget to check the assigned readings for supporting information. As you put together your argument and supporting information, look for the strongest rhetorical strategies that will help you organize your ideas for the best effect. If you use sources, be sure to document each one of them accurately in parenthetical (in-text) and works cited documentation (see Chapter 12).

Know the audience and the purpose of each essay you write. Ask your instructor if you are unsure about how a writing assignment is structured or to whom your argument should be addressed. Use a level of formality that is appropriate for your audience.

Take control of your words and sentence structure. Know the appropriate standards for the type of essay you are writing, and if you vary from them for effect, do so with a concrete plan. Learn the difference between grammar/mechanics and usage/style.

Finally, take one last look at the writing assignment, and follow all formatting requirements. Turn in the essay on the due date, and hand in the document with all required materials.

As you can see, academic writing includes more than the writing itself. It also incorporates all parts of the writing process and the way in which a document is prepared.

COLLEGE WRITING ASSIGNMENTS

Writing assignments can vary from a five-minute prewriting activity to a long research essay to a multimedia document.

Process work

Most writing classes will include process work that will be graded or counted in some way; instructors in other academic classes may not grade process work but still expect you to do such work as a precursor to meeting with them about a writing project. Process work may include any activity that helps you brainstorm, organize, review, revise, edit, or proofread your essay. Many of these activities may take place during class time, making good attendance necessary and worthwhile.

In-class or timed writing assignments

Writing assignments may include in-class or timed essays, which are often given as a get-to-know-you-writing activity or on the last day of class as a final activity. In-class writing usually does not allow time for substantial revision and editing time. If given an in-class essay, break the time allowed into short blocks that mimic the parts of the process for an out-of-class essay. If you have 60 minutes, use 5–10 minutes to brainstorm and outline, 30–40 minutes to write the first draft, 5–10 minutes to revise for global concerns, and 5–10 minutes to edit for local concerns. If you are writing on a computer, print out a copy of the  paper if possible, to revise and edit offline. Then, add changes, correct spelling and typos, and print your final draft. Even in a tight writing situation, it always pays to make time for both revising and editing.

Out-of-class essay assignments

The typical essay associated with a writing class is the out-of-class essay assignment that is given to you about two or three weeks before the essay is due or possibly months in advance for an extended research project. It is important to work out a writing plan and analyze the assignment sheet in depth as soon as you receive it. Often, this assignment sheet will also detail writing process step-by-step activities, such as due dates for drafts or revision/editing workshops. Mark these dates on your calendar, and make each deadline a way to ensure good process marks.

Multimedia assignments

A writing class may also include activities that you might not automatically associate with writing. However, writing is an important component of some process assignments, such as presenting or responding to ideas in e-mails, class discussion boards, and social networking sites. Multimedia assignments in a writing class can also include designing Web documents and oral presentations.

UNDERSTANDING THE RHETORICAL TRIANGLE

Reading widely and getting as much information as possible exposes you to small pieces of a giant jigsaw puzzle, and even if the information is not 100 percent clear at the time, by shuffling it around in your mind, ideas eventually come to you.

—James Portman

The visual of a triangle is often used by writing instructors to illustrate the most important parts of a writing assignment. As shown in Figure 2.2, all of the parts taken together represent the rhetorical situation that you, as the writer, should consider as you begin to write.

WHAT ARE ETHOS, LOGOS, AND PATHOS?

Classical rhetorician Aristotle argued that there are three types of appeals to the audience that are necessary for a successful persuasive or argumentative communication. These three types of appeals are *ethos, logos,* and *pathos.*

Ethos

Ethos demonstrates the authority and credibility of the speaker or writer. Writers will want to demonstrate their credibility to an audience, and this credibility can be determined by the answers to the following questions. Is this writer a well-known figure or expert in the subject of the argument? Does the writer have well-reasoned and legitimate *logos* (see below) that proves to the audience that the writer is knowledgeable about the issues? Does this person have other aspects that may demonstrate to the audience that she or he is dependable in this context, such as being a religious or political figure? The rhetorical situation, specifically the audience being appealed to, will guide which characteristics can establish a writer's *ethos.*

Figure 2.2 The Rhetorical Triangle

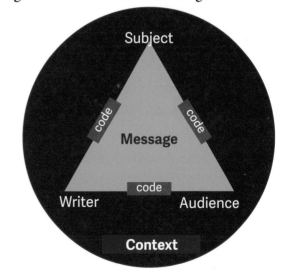

Logos

Appeals classified as *logos* are those which focus on logic, either by argumentative structure or proof/evidence for the writer's claims. Modern *logos*, particularly used in researched argumentative writing, focuses on the use of credible evidence to support a thesis. This evidence includes texts, graphic evidence, quantitative data, interviews, and other qualitative data. In many fields, the *logos* necessary to convince a particular audience will differ based on the genre of the writing and the caliber of the audience. Not only is successful *logos* important to substantiate a writer's argument, but it also supports *ethos* by enhancing the writer's credibility.

Pathos

Pathos is an appeal made to an audience's emotions. The types of emotions the writer should appeal to for a successful argument will depend on the rhetorical situation. Often, a writer will want to demonstrate a similarity to the audience, either as people sharing a common bond or sharing the same view of the subject at hand. This can include appealing to an audience's shared dreams or dilemmas. Sometimes the author may choose to appeal to an audience's fears; while this is negative on the surface, it can be necessary to sway an audience to agree with the speaker (such as with some literature in public health which encourages readers to make a lifestyle change in order to save their lives). Narrative techniques, such as use of metaphor and simile, and emotional delivery of the text by the writer, are some ways to enhance *pathos*.

THE SUBJECT

Your instructor may give you the subject or topic of your essay, you may be asked to choose from a list of possible topics, or you may be asked to choose your own topic. If you are given a subject area, consider narrowing it down to a subtopic that calls to you in some way, whether it is something you are strongly for, strongly against, or very interested in learning more about. Use brainstorming techniques (see page 27) to help you engage with the subject or narrow it down to a topic of interest.

- ✓ What topics always interest you?
- ✓ What topics do you want to know more about?
- ✓ Who else might be interested in the topics?
- ✓ Do you know enough about the topic to write about it? If not, where can you find more information?

THE AUDIENCE

Your instructor may specify an audience for your essay, or he or she may ask you to provide one of your choosing. Either way, be sure to think carefully about who this audience is, including their likes, dislikes, language use, power, and status. This will help you work out the formality level of your language, the arguments you may want to include or exclude, and the examples that will appeal to your readers.

- ✓ What do you know about the members of your audience? In what way are you similar to or different from them?

✓ What does your audience know about your topic? What type of information do you need to share with them to make your argument stronger?

✓ How might your audience react to your argument? What is the best strategy to get your audience to agree with your argument?

Have you ever thought about how you structure an argument? A traditional academic essay has an introduction with thesis statement, an adequate number of main points that relate to and support the thesis directly, and a conclusion with a restated thesis or innovative closing. This linear structure is common in the United States and other western countries, but not everyone in the world writes this way. Some cultures do not explicitly state the thesis until the very end of the essay, if at all. The important thing to remember, though, is to write in a way that your audience expects and will clearly understand.

THE WRITER

As the writer, you connect all other aspects of the rhetorical situation, so the choices you make significantly impact how successful the overall essay will be. You must know yourself and your topic well or be willing to learn more about both as you progress through the writing of the essay. Your choices will establish your *ethos*, or credibility as an expert on the topic.

✓ What do you know about the topic? What do you need to learn about the topic?

✓ How strongly do you believe in your topic? What interests you the most about your topic? What is a narrow argument within the topic that you can support?

✓ How similar are you to your audience in your beliefs, language use, and background?

✓ What will you use to lay a foundation for your *ethos* or credibility?

THE CODE

Notice that the line that forms the rhetorical triangle represents the code, or language that you will use to inform your audience about the topic or persuade them to agree with your argument (see illustration on page 23). The language that you use is an important aspect of essay writing, but its importance is often overlooked by writers. You need to consider the dialect or language backgrounds of your audience, and also make an informed decision about the level of formality needed for the essay.

Every code is a kind of language

✓ Will the audience understand the language of the argument or the terms used in the background information?

✓ Will the audience appreciate the support provided by visuals? If so, do the visuals and the text work well together?

✓ Is the level of formality of the language used appropriate for the audience and the purpose?

THE MESSAGE

In the rhetorical triangle, the message is placed within the triangle, representing the specific argument or thesis that the writer is sharing with the reader. Note that the message is at the center of everything else included in the image; if all other parts of the rhetorical situation are met, your writing should allow the reader to receive the specific message you are trying to get across.

✓ What is your specific argument or point?

✓ What do you want your reader to take from your essay in addition to the specific argument or point you are making?

✓ How do your code (language) and context fit with your specific message?

THE CONTEXT

Many other things come into play when you are writing an essay for a class assignment, including items that may be decided for you by the assignment itself. Pay particular attention to how the length of the assignment may influence what you write about or how you write about it. In addition, instructors may also call for a particular type or genre of essay, ranging from a particular rhetorical strategy to a particular type of media.

✓ If you are writing an essay for an assignment, what limitations or liberties have been given?

✓ If your topic or message requires research, how much time have you been given to accomplish this?

✓ Which genre or medium is your instructor expecting, and what are its requirements?

✓ Are there extra design or media elements that you would like to include? Have you discussed this with your instructor?

UNDERSTANDING THE WRITING PROCESS

Meaning is not what you start with, but what you end up with.

—Peter Elbow

Peter Elbow is a well-known researcher who writes about college-level writing. He calls trying to write an essay correctly the first time *the dangerous method* "because it puts more pressure on you and depends for its success on everything running smoothly." Let's face it, though. Most writing tasks do *not* run smoothly, and turning in an essay that you just wrote overnight is definitely a dangerous method, especially when it comes to grades. In the late 1960s, many composition instructors began to treat writing an essay as a process, rather than just as a product to be assigned, collected, and graded. Process writing classes give you the time needed to plan, draft, revise, edit, and proofread your essay before turning it in for a grade.

The process of writing, though, is not a simple linear activity; it is often cyclical and recursive, with writers returning to various stages in the writing process before arriving at the final draft. Each writer has a unique writing process, so even though you will be introduced to the different stages of the writing process, you may use them differently from another student writer in your class. This is one of the reasons why every writer is unique.

Writing is a process that involves planning (or brainstorming), drafting, revising, and editing, though not necessarily in that order. But did you know that this approach to teaching writing has been in use only over the last 30 to 40 years? Understanding writing as a process occurred when psychology was brought into the study of writing and researchers became interested in the writing strategies of individual writers.

Planning and Brainstorming

Good fortune is what happens when opportunity meets with planning.
—Thomas Edison

We write best when we write about topics that we are interested in and familiar with. Writing is like painting in that it is a very individualized process. Someone can show us how to apply paint to a canvas but, eventually, we must make these acts our own by adding our own touches.

You can come up with ideas for essays in many ways; however, if you are stuck and cannot find a topic to use, brainstorming, as part of the prewriting or planning you do, can help narrow down general ideas into a focused topic and then help you decide what to use as supporting detail. You may already have your own style of prewriting; however, you should experiment with different methods of brainstorming to find what best suits your style.

Some of the most basic components of effective writing are also some of the oldest. What we often call *brainstorming* Aristotle called *inventio* around 350 BCE, referring to the process of discovering and developing ideas as a precursor to writing an argument. Even the classic five-paragraph essay dates back to 100 CE, when Quintilian wrote about the basic structure of an argument.

Freewriting

You should think of freewriting as a "no holds barred" type of brainstorming. When you freewrite, begin by allotting yourself a specific amount of time, such as 10 to 15 minutes. This technique is more constructive when you already have an idea for your topic. However, freewriting also can be used to generate ideas for topics. Begin by simply writing. Write whatever comes into your mind. Do not be concerned with punctuation, grammar, or complete sentences. Use symbols or question marks in place of words that you cannot come up with automatically. If you cannot think of anything to write, simply jot down the phrase "I don't know" until you begin writing other words. Remember, this does not have to make sense to anyone else. This should be as stress-free as possible.

Here is an example done in three minutes with the topic of "peace":

> I only have three minutes to come up with something decent to write about. This is stupid. This is not peaceful this is stressful. Peace is not writing under pressure. Peace is being barefoot on grass by a lake or hearing people laugh. Besides, who can think of peace with all of the atrocities in the world? Peace is not war. Peace is the absence of war, but maybe it is more than what it isn't. Peace is represented by doves, white flags, smiles, and happiness. Peace is also represented by a peace sign or holding up two fingers. But I guess peace doesn't have to be related to war. It can be associated with one's mindset, one's life, or anything that we come into contact with in our daily lives.

Once your time is up, sit back, and look at what you have written. Separate out the promising phrases, organize these ideas, and then expand them.

Go back, and read your freewriting paragraph again, underlining potential topics and subtopics.

Looping

Looping is a variation of freewriting. It can be a more constructive brainstorming exercise for those who need a little more focus than freewriting provides. This technique works best when you already have a general topic in mind.

For example, you have been assigned to write on your definition of war. Take out several sheets of paper and begin to freewrite as defined earlier. When time is up, read over what you have written, and try to pinpoint a central idea that has emerged from it. Perhaps it is the idea that you liked best for whatever reason. It may simply be an idea that stands out to you. Put this thought or idea in one sentence below the freewriting. This is called your center of gravity statement. This completes loop number one.

To begin loop number two, begin freewriting from the previous "center of gravity" statement. Freewrite for another 10 minutes. Upon completion of this freewriting session, you will once again assess what you have written and extract a compelling or important idea that emerged from your writing. Write this main idea below your freewriting. This is your second "center of gravity" statement. Now you begin freewriting from the second center of gravity statement.

Example of Loop Number 1:

> War is chaos, fighting, and mental anguish. Our traditional definition of war encompasses historical "wars" such as the Revolutionary war, the Civil War, World War I, World War II, and Vietnam just to name a few. War has been a massive part of societies for centuries. War is death, destruction, and bombing. However, I don't think war has to be defined in terms of actual countries physically fighting one another. <u>Wars are waged every day in people's hearts, minds, and lives.</u>

Example of Loop Number 2:

> Wars are waged every day in people's hearts, minds, and lives. The definition of war exceeds beyond the boundaries of our usual definition. War is loneliness, heartbreak, mental illness, daily adversity, and struggles. We normally think of war as having heroes and fantastic stories of bravery. <u>However, if war is defined as doing battle against a foe that is challenging one's established way of life, then loneliness, heartbreak, mental illness, disease, adversity, and struggles can fit easily within the definition of war.</u>

You should continue this looping process until you are satisfied and comfortable with the topic you have generated.

Journaling

Journal writing is a voyage to the interior.

—Christina Baldwin

Sometimes, instructors will lead you toward a topic by assigning journals. These are informal writings that allow you to take a vague idea and write about it. These journals allow you to follow an idea or a hunch without worrying about penalty. Think of these journals as a more controlled version of freewriting. Once you complete a journal entry, you can set it aside for a time and come back to it at a later date when you are rested and ready to approach the topic once again. Revisiting your journal after a break, you may find that you have new ideas or a different take.

Example of a Journal assignment: Write your initial impressions of Faulkner's "A Rose for Emily."

> When I read Faulkner's "A Rose for Emily," I was initially appalled. Miss Emily is clearly sick as she murdered Homer Baron and kept his body in the upper room locked away from the rest of the world. However, I was looking through a scrapbook today and was shocked at what I found. There, in that scrapbook were pressed flowers, pictures, ticket stubs, and other mementos. Only then did it occur to me that I was acting as Miss Emily had acted. I saved mementos and pictures of a special time that would otherwise be lost forever with nothing to show for it but a memory. I was, just as Miss Emily did, capturing a moment. I suppose it should be noted that Miss Emily had suffered some tragic events in her life and did not have the proper outlets by which to express her heartbreak and loneliness. She merely acts in the only manner she finds effective. In this respect, Faulkner's story demonstrates Miss Emily as a profoundly sympathetic character.

After writing a journal entry, you may want to further explore your topic by using other brainstorming exercises or even discussing it with your instructor and other classmates. Then you can revisit your topic in your journal.

Clustering or mapping

Another technique you can use for brainstorming is clustering, sometimes referred to as mapping. You can cluster in two different ways.

- ❏ Start with possible topic ideas, and then cluster them by drawing circles around them and organizing them into clusters.
- ❏ Start with a clustering grid, and then fill in the circles with ideas.

Whatever way you decide to cluster, start by putting your general topic in the middle of a blank page. If you want to use the first clustering method, jot down possible subtopics and details all around the central circle. After you have written down as many subtopics or details as you can, locate the more general subtopics, circle them, and attach these circles to the middle circle that holds the general topic. After this, find details that will support the subtopics, circle them, and attach these circles to the subtopic circles. When you have circled enough subtopics and details to start outlining or writing your paper, erase or cross out all the extra, unconnected information.

Figure 2.3 Example of a Cluster Map

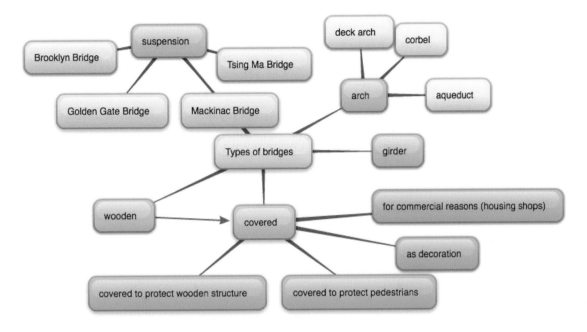

If you want to try the second clustering method, write your general topic in the middle of a blank page and draw lines from this circle to five or six circles (these will hold your subtopics). Then draw lines from the subtopic circles to three or four other circles (these will be your supporting details). Regardless of the clustering method you choose, you should allot 10 to 20 minutes for this brainstorming process. What you end up with might look something like the cluster/map shown in Figure 2.3, which uses the types of bridges as the general topic.

Cubing

Yet another way to generate ideas is by cubing your topic. Imagine a cube with six sides, or use a die from a game set you have around your house. Next, imagine the numbers for the commands given below are written on each side of the cube, or attach the commands to the sides of a die. Picture yourself rolling the cube (or roll the actual die), and write according to the commands that come up.

Listed below are the commands you should visualize on your cube.

1. **Describe it:** What does the subject look like? Sound like? Engage all five senses if possible.

2. **Compare and contrast it:** What is the subject similar to? What is it different from? How so?

3. **Free associate with it:** What does the subject remind you of? Any particular memories?

4. **Analyze it:** How does it work? What is its significance?

5. **Argue for or against it:** What advantages and disadvantages does it have?

6. **Apply it:** What are the uses of your subject? What can you do with it?

Write whatever comes to your mind for 10 minutes or so. When you have finished cubing, take the topics and subtopics you have generated and organize them by clustering or outlining them.

Listing

Another way to brainstorm is to simply create a list of any ideas that pop into your head for about 10 minutes. After you have finished your list, look for connections between ideas, or look for one main idea that encompasses several small ones.

Here is an example for the general topic of television:

Entertaining	Usually 30-minute programs
Informative	Media
Corrupting	Listen
Poisoning	Corporate sponsorship
News	Music television
Comedy	Home shopping
Drama	"Boob tube"
Sports	Game shows
Educational	Remote control
Biased	Mind-numbing
Commercials	Weight gain
People	Possible contributor to "dumbing down" of society

After examining the list, do you make any connections? Does anything stand out that you might want to write about? If so, try clustering or outlining the idea to see if it can be developed.

Interviewing and discussing

Sometimes a topic or an idea may seem unclear at first. In this case, discussing the topic with someone else can help to make it more clear. Perhaps the other person is able to offer a perspective that you had not thought of previously.

As you are discussing your idea with a classmate or a friend, think of the subject as your friend or classmate asks questions that would naturally come up in conversation. Your "interviewer" might ask you what are termed *journalist questions*, such as the following:

Who?	Who believes X? Who is involved?
When?	When did it happen? When did you change?
Why?	Why did X do Y? Why is this interesting?
What?	What happened? What did you do?
Where?	Where did it happen? Where were you?
How?	How did you become involved? How is it interesting?

Make sure you listen to what you are saying as you are being "interviewed." Was there a particular part of the subject that you were most interested in talking about? If so, why? You may find that you have discussed your way into an interesting topic. However, this may not prove fruitful. If you are still without a clear subject by the end of the "interview" session, change roles and ask your classmate or friend to respond to the questions. If your friend had to write an essay based on the information you had just discussed, what would he or she write about? Why?

Questioning

Sometimes, no one is available for interviewing. If this type of brainstorming works best for you, try questioning yourself about the subject. Think of your favorite attorney on television or in books. How would he or she cross-examine a witness? You should model your cross-examination of yourself in this manner. You could ask yourself a million questions about your subject. However, below is a list of five categories to help you start narrowing your subject.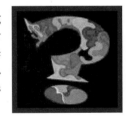

Definition: How does the dictionary define the word or subject? How do most people define it? What is its history? Where did it come from? Give some examples.

Compare and contrast: What is it similar to? What is it different from? Think also along the lines of synonyms (likes) and antonyms (opposites).

Relationship: What are its causes and effects?

Circumstance: Is it possible or impossible? When has it happened before? Are there any ways to prevent it?

Testimony: What do people say about it? What has been written about it? Have you had any experience with it? Has any relevant research been done on the subject?

Outlining

Outlining can help you brainstorm for subtopics, or it can be used as a method for organizing the material that other brainstorming techniques have helped you generate. Either way, the value of the outline is its ability to help you plan, see logical connections between your ideas, and recognize obvious places to add new ideas and details.

An informal outline can be just a map of paragraphs that you plan to use. For example, here is a short, informal outline for the topic of effective study practices.

> Body paragraph one: discussion of free services
> Body paragraph two: discussion of writing assistants
> Body paragraph three: discussion of learning aids

You can also add examples and supporting details and construct a more detailed informal outline.

I. Free services
   A. Mini-course on improving study skills
   B. Writing assistance
      a. Composition
      b. Foreign language
   C. Weekly seminars
      a. Stress management
      b. Test anxiety
II. Writing assistants
   A. Top graduate students in their field
   B. Experienced teachers
III. Learning aids
   A. Supplemental texts
   B. Workbooks

Note that the above is not a formal outline, which would have strictly parallel parts and would be expressed in complete sentences. Unless your instructor requests a formal outline, do not feel you must construct one. An informal or working outline helps you get to the drafting stage, but it should not restrict you from changing subtopics or details to make your essay topic stronger.

Drawing or creating word pictures

Try brainstorming without words by sketching out your topic. What pictures do you immediately associate with your topic? Look at size, color, and juxtaposition of the pictures you sketch out or color in. What do these pictures and the way you sketch them tell you about your topic?

You can also try *drawing* word pictures. Begin by writing your topic in the center of the paper, drawing pictures and adding words. Consider this as freewriting with pictures—keep drawing until you find something in your images that you can use to narrow down your topic. Or you can create pictures just out of words that come to you as you think about your topic.

> *I even shower with my pen, in case any ideas drip out of the waterhead.*
> —*Graycie Harmon*

Practice exercise

Directions: Choose one of the practice topics below, and practice different techniques for brainstorming until you find the technique that works best for you.

- ❏ The signs of friendship.
- ❏ Differences between high school and college.
- ❏ Legalization of drugs.
- ❏ What does *peace* mean to you?
- ❏ Heroes.
- ❏ What is the most significant event of your life up to this point?
- ❏ Should there be dress codes in schools?
- ❏ Analyze your favorite song, book, or film. Why is it significant?
- ❏ What constitutes *good* and *evil*?
- ❏ Should there be censorship?

COMPOSING THE ROUGH OR FIRST DRAFT

Take the ideas that you have generated through brainstorming and organize them into a preliminary order for your first (or rough) draft. At this time, you should decide on a specific thesis or argument and choose details from your brainstorming that support both the organization and the supporting points of your essay. As you compose your first draft, you may find that you do not have enough supporting details or that you are unable to support your thesis effectively. At this point, remember that writing is cyclical, and it may be time to return to one or more brainstorming activities to help narrow down your topic some more and find more supporting detail.

The writing process never begins with the opening paragraph and never ends with the final punctuation mark in the last paragraph. The writing process extends beyond the actual paper itself. Brainstorming is the first of many steps that comprise the writing process. If you examine the time it takes to brainstorm and effectively produce a topic for an essay, you will soon realize it is never a good idea to wait until the night before to begin writing a paper. In fact, it is best to begin as soon as it is assigned. This does not mean that you must work on the paper exclusively. By getting started early, you allow yourself time to ponder your idea, exhaust all possible angles, write, live your life, rewrite, focus on other things, and have someone else look over your essay before you revise it once again.

Below we present the first draft of a student essay on the significance of signs. Pay attention to the instructor's comments. What did they focus on? Why do you think the instructor commented on only these things and not the grammar, punctuation, and style? Compare this draft with the second one that begins on page 46.

Brian Jones

Jones 1

Professor Walker

English 1010

02 February 2009

Significance of Signs

In today's society, there are many signs around us. From restaurants to road signs to advertisements we are surrounded. My family and me saw alot of signs when we made the regular family trip from Indianapolis to Destin, FL, which required a thirteen hour car drive. If I was lucky, my parents would decide to leave at night, allowing my sister and I to sleep for almost the entire trip. But this wasn't very easy for my parents to do, we would usually pack up the van early in the morning and spend the day on the road. Considering that we made the trip at least three times a year from the time I was born until I graduated from high school. I got to know the route pretty well.

> Remember that your intro should establish the purpose or main idea of your essay. Where is your thesis statement? Try to distill the main idea into one sentence and add it to the introduction. Also, avoid starting with vague statements; try to get your reader's attention!

Jones 2

LOUISVILLE 100 miles. NASHVILLE 60 miles. Huntsville. Birmingham. Montgomery…ah, Montgomery. Once I saw that sign, I really got excited, because that meant that we were about to get off I-65 to take the back

roads to our final destination. Those signs are embedded in my mind, even now, not having made that drive for several years, I can recite those major cities in order and visualize their distance from each other. But really, those signs were the boring ones. Each one only represented a check mark to make on my mental list of cities we had to get through before I could go to the beach. The good signs were ones that meant we were going to stop (and probably eat lol). Cracker Barrel signs were pretty good, it usually meant some candy or maybe a cheap toy. One of my favorites was for a peach farm in Alabama. We always stopped at the peach farm no matter what to get fresh produce and some home made ice cream. On the back roads past Montgomery we'd watch for signs for another of our favorite stops, a little country cookin' restaurant called Annie's. Though we stopped eating there in later years, I always had an eye out for that sign, reminding me not only of past trips, but also of how close we were getting to the end of the long drive.

We always knew when we got to Alabama without any signs because there is a huge rocket at the rest stop just passed the state line. You can't miss it. My parents always talk about how excited I would get when the rocket came into sight, and when I was little that rest stop was not only the highlight of the trip, but a required stop. Once I remember even losing a shoe at that stop. Even today I get a little excited still on the few occasions I get to drive that way and see the spaceship.

In order to pass the time, we usually played a round or two of the ABC game. I'm sure you know the game, so you know that it can last a really long time, sometimes even the whole trip. Especially because of

> Don't forget about topic sentences, which help guide the reader through your essay by telling the main idea of each paragraph. This paragraph, however, seems to have more than one idea in it. You might want to split it into two separate paragraphs: one describing the road signs and one describing the places you stop at.

> This paragraph doesn't seem to fit with the rest of your essay, which focuses primarily on the signs you saw along the way. You might consider removing this paragraph altogether.

> I like this paragraph, but can you describe the game more clearly? Not everyone might be familiar with it. In general, you want to avoid using 2nd person for this very reason.

Jones 3

the long stretches between major cities with no signs and cuz its hard to find words with Q and Z. (X, by the way, was allowed to be anywhere in the word, or else the game would never end). Not many businesses or restaurants started with these letters, so when you finally saw one, you have to make sure you saw it first and could yell it out before someone else did. Z was especially hard, and if you saw signs for construction zones or speed zones, the game was yours. The winner was declared to have the sharpest vision and would receive bragging rights for the rest of the trip, but really all that mattered is that we had made part of the trip go by a little faster.

OK! This idea of memories in connection with the signs is very good. You just need to make sure this concept is clear throughout your essay and especially in your introduction. And overall, add more description and detail so your readers feel like they were there with you.

"It's about the journey, not the destination." I think I really understand this old saying because of the long drives. Though we really hated those long drives I guess they gave us alot of good times. Many family stories were created along the route between Indy and Destin. And while the roads have been repaved and the signs have changed with the times, the memories are remembered still.

REVISING

Write your first draft with your heart. Rewrite with your head.

—From the movie *Finding Forrester*

To revise means to read, review, and change with the aim of improving your writing. Revising is the part of the writing process that focuses on the global characteristics of writing or those elements that contribute to the rhetorical situation—content, organization, and style.

Writers who revise often discover and develop new or better ideas through the revision process. Revision is changing the paper, hopefully for the better. Most professional or skilled writers view revision as a necessary part of their writing because it is useful for generating new ideas, focusing and reorganizing ideas, and polishing the overall paper. A draft is a work in progress, and it is a good idea to write multiple drafts for each essay in order to write the best paper and get the best grade possible.

You can add, delete, and substitute material during the revision process. For example, if a sentence is unclear, you can add information to clarify your point, delete ambiguous words or phrases, or substitute a new sentence that has more clarity.

Focus on revision

When you begin to revise, be sure to focus on global characteristics or overall elements that influence the rhetorical situation or context of your essay. Examining these rhetorical elements—content, organization, and style—also gives you the opportunity to pay closer attention to the topic, the context, your audience, and to yourself as a writer.

Content

Focusing on content for revision purposes involves looking at the central message of your essay. Look at the big picture. What is your central message? Everything in your essay (from words to paragraphs to graphics) should revolve around this central idea.

Organization

Focusing on organization means that you are checking whether the main and supporting ideas clearly relate to your thesis or argument. Good organization is the glue that holds the central message and all supporting content together. Examining the organization on its own helps you to see whether you have included all the important points or whether you have added something tangential that needs to be removed. Sometimes, an outline is the best way to see whether or not everything in your essay relates back to the main idea or thesis.

Style

Focusing on style gives you the time to examine whether your words and sentences are appropriate for your topic and your audience. Look at the formality of your language. Does it fit with your thesis, audience, and purpose? As a writer, you want to choose your words and sentence patterns to fit both yourself and your audience. Dressing up your essay with words you have found in the thesaurus but normally do not use is a sure way to lose authority and sincerity.

Did you know?

The first usage of the word *revise* is recorded in the *Oxford English Dictionary* as occurring in 1589. It literally meant "the act of being seen again."

Rhetorical situation or context

Be sure to take into consideration all the elements of the rhetorical situation or context (see page 23) as you put together your balanced essay. Especially at the revising stage, looking at how the audience will view your message in context, not just in a vacuum, will help you identify supporting evidence that does not fit or sentences that do not sound appropriate. If you are trying to persuade your audience of something, have you taken the time to understand them? The interplay between audience and purpose is a delicate one; adding in the need for a style that will allow you to share your message in a way that is neither too strong nor too weak is an even greater balancing act.

SOME REVISING TIPS

I'm not a very good writer, but I'm an excellent rewriter.

—*James Michener*

The following tips on how to revise effectively are given as choices to consider. Not all writers will need to do all of them, and not all essays require all of them. Revision is a part of the writing process that is unique to the writer, and knowing your writing strengths and weaknesses will help you decide which of these steps will help you improve your paper on the global level in regard to content, organization, and style.

Read a printed copy

Although we live in a computerized world, using a printed version of your writing for revision enables you to make quick margin notes as ideas occur to you. Hard copies are also easy to read and reduce any tendency you may have to edit or "correct" as you read.

Ideally, you have written your draft well in advance of any deadline and have allowed it to rest a few days before beginning the revision process. In this circumstance, reading reminds you of what you have written. On the other hand, college life is often less than ideal, and you may find yourself moving immediately from drafting to revising. So if you have just written your draft, why take the time to read it? Regardless of how clearly you outline, how logically you think, or how quickly you type, you must read your writing to discover areas that might be improved through revision.

Annotate your draft

Circle, highlight, or note any issues that surface as you read. Perhaps a paragraph seems out of place or a sentence no longer makes sense. You may realize that your writing does not support your thesis or that you have strayed from your thesis statement completely. Maybe your enthusiasm for the topic has led you to include a few well-intentioned but unrelated rants. Whatever the concern, identify it and keep reading. You should not begin expanding, condensing, honing, or opting for a different course of action until you have read completely through your draft and identified areas that might benefit from revision.

Assess your essay

Using a worksheet such as the one shown in Figure 2.4, review your essay as though you were the reader or audience. As you answer the questions, highlight and annotate places in your essay that need some more work.

Figure 2.4 Self-assessment Worksheet

1. What is the purpose of your paper (to analyze, to inform, to entertain, to persuade)?

2. What is the subject of this paper? Why did you decide on this topic?

3. Who is your audience? What does the audience likely know about this subject? What are the expectations of your audience?

4. What type of brainstorming did you do for this paper? How did it help with writing?

5. What is your thesis statement?

6. What are the supporting points for your thesis?

7. What were the most difficult things about this assignment?

8. What do you like best about your essay?

9. Which parts of your paper still need the most work?

10. What questions or problems do you have about your paper? For which parts do you think you need your reader's help or advice?

Create a reverse outline

An easy way to determine if you have organization issues is to create a reverse outline. Instead of outlining what you intend to write, you can use a reverse outline to clearly tell you what you have written, using one short statement to describe the main point of each paragraph. Now you can quickly identify whether you may have omitted any important points or repeated yourself.

The reverse outline also works well when applied to paragraph organization. However, when working with paragraph organization, do not outline what each sentence says; outline what each sentence does. For example, a reverse outline of the previous paragraph might look like this:

a. Introduces reverse outline

b. Explains reverse outline

c. Lists benefits of reverse outline

If you need to expand your details, condense or clarify your ideas, or rearrange your sentences, a reverse outline will help you determine where to start.

Color-code your draft

Use highlighters to clearly show the different parts of your essay. If you use one color for main points, one for transition statements, another for definitions, and still another for explanations or details, you will begin to recognize issues with organization, repetition, and balance.

This technique is particularly useful when writing compare/contrast essays, position papers, and arguments or when using source material. For example, when you color-code your writing in a compare/contrast essay, you should detect frequently alternating colors if you have used a point-by-point organization or large sections of each color if you have used a block arrangement. Highlighting sourced material used in any writing can help you recognize whether you have relied too heavily on the words of others.

Cut up your draft

A great way to check transitions and the organization of an essay is to cut it into pieces, literally. With each paragraph becoming a separate piece, you can discover overlooked problems and play with the arrangement of your essay. If after cutting your essay into separate pieces you are unable to reassemble it, then revise transitions or the organization to help put the essay back together more easily. For an even more revealing exercise, you might have a friend attempt the reconstruction. If he or she is unable to put your essay back in order, it is time to revise.

Create a paragraph essay

You can check the coherence and organization of an essay by creating a paragraph paper. To begin, simply create a paragraph by copying your thesis statement and then each succeeding topic sentence from your draft into a single paragraph. If your paragraph is well organized, coherent, and reflective of the substance of your essay, you have written well. If, on the other hand, your paragraph seems disordered, vague, or untidy, it is time to expand, condense, fine-tune, and consider your options.

This technique also works well for reviewing paragraph organization. Write each sentence on a separate note card and then arrange the cards into a paragraph. You may discover issues that need attention, find that your initial arrangement is sufficient, or realize that an alternative organization works better than the original.

Read your essay aloud

Read your essay aloud to a friend, and be sure to read exactly what you have written. As you read, use a highlighter to note places where you stumble or think there is a problem. Ask your friend to use a marker on his or her copy and to write question marks next to elements that do not make sense or need further clarification.

You can also have someone else read your paper to you. Be sure to adopt the role of the reader or audience as you listen, and use a marker to put checks or question marks next to words or sentences you will want to go back to after the reader finishes your essay.

Share your paper

Having a friend or classmate read your essay is always a good idea. However, do not simply hand the essay to someone and expect constructive comments. Use an assessment sheet similar to the one shown in Figure 2.4 page 40, and ask your friend to fill it out as he or she reads your paper.

If your instructor asks you to participate in a revision workshop, be sure to take full advantage of the opportunity. Come to class prepared that day with the correct number of copies to share with your peers. Your instructor will probably give you an evaluation form to complete for a peer's paper; be a good reading partner and fill it out completely and constructively. Your willingness to do this will be a model for others reading and reviewing your paper.

Whatever way you share your paper with others, be selective in the comments you choose to guide your revision. Be sure that the changes strengthen your paper's content, organization, and style.

DIFFERENT LEVELS OF REVISION

Global characteristics of writing can be found on different levels in your essay. Be sure to revise on all levels: the overall essay, the paragraphs, the sentences, and the words. It is best to divide these levels of revision and work on them separately since a good revision plan involves an examination of all levels.

Revising on the essay level

When you revise at the essay level, focus on large-scale changes that will improve the overall essay. Here is a list of essay-level concerns that you should consider each time you write and revise an essay.

- ✓ Look first at the central idea of the essay. If all sentences in the essay do not support this main idea, you will need to either revise the main idea or revise the support in the essay. Although it is not necessary to have an explicit thesis statement, it is a good idea to include one in a college essay. A clearly defined central idea will help you write the essay—and it will help the audience reading your essay as well.

- ✓ Make sure that you have an audience in mind when writing and revising the essay. If a reader cannot see himself or herself as the audience, then you need to revise and pay more attention to the audience of the essay.

- ✓ Check the introduction and the rest of the essay to make sure that all of it relates to your underlying purpose in writing the essay. If any of the support given throughout the essay does not support your purpose, you will need to revise the support.

✓ Review the overall organization of the essay. Does each body paragraph support the central idea of the essay? Are the paragraphs ordered in a way that will make sense to the reader?

✓ Check the balance inside the essay. Are any of the supporting paragraphs out of balance with the rest of the essay? If so, consider splitting large paragraphs or combining short paragraphs.

✓ Make sure that your essay flows well. Use transitions between body paragraphs so your reader will not get confused when you change topics.

✓ Review your central idea if it is an argument, making sure that you have addressed counterarguments at some point in the essay.

✓ Be sure to use an interesting title that will encourage your reader to take the time to read your essay.

Revising on the paragraph level

After revising on the essay level, you need to check whether the paragraphs in your essay are effective. Here is a list of paragraph-level concerns that you should consider each time you write and revise an essay.

✓ Reread the introductory paragraph. Does it include an effective lead-in to the central idea? Will the introductory material capture your reader's interest? Be sure to stay away from overused introductory strategies, such as providing a dictionary definition or general statements such as *today's society*.

✓ Focus on topic sentences. Read only the first sentence of each paragraph in order; do they give a good indication of the central idea of the essay and the supporting evidence?

✓ Add more examples and details to weakly developed paragraphs. Stay away from generalizations.

> For example, instead of saying *Nurses are not easy to find*, say, *In 2003, Tennessee is experiencing a shortage of 154,000 nurses* and cite the source of the information.

✓ Check summarized, paraphrased, or quoted material that you use for support. See **Chapter 12** for more information about citing sources.

✓ Check for coherence within body paragraphs. If you provide multiple supporting sentences, use transitions to join them together. Review and perhaps rewrite the introduction and conclusion.

✓ Reread your concluding paragraph. In addition to reinforcing key ideas from the body of the essay, try to conclude in a way that makes your reader want to read more. Making a prediction or inviting a response are techniques that work well. However, be careful not to introduce new information.

Revising on the sentence level

Writers often check for sentence grammar and punctuation and forget to check for sentence-level changes that would clarify content or organization. Here are some sentence-level strategies to use when you revise your essays.

✓ Check for sentence clarity. Does each sentence make sense? Check for ambiguity.

> For instance, a sentence such as *Visiting relatives can be bothersome* has multiple meanings and needs clarification.

> Changing this sentence to *My relatives who visit often can be bothersome* or *I do not like to visit relatives* clears up the ambiguity.

✓ Try not to use long introductory phrases or clauses. These usually distract the reader from what you are trying to emphasize in the sentence.

> A sentence such as *Before I left for work that day and caught the bus on the corner of Main Street and Jones Boulevard, I broke my leg in the shower* has a long, unnecessary introductory clause that de-emphasizes the main point of the sentence.

✓ Use sentence-combining techniques to provide more sentence variety in the essay. Readers get bored reading the same structure over and over again. Balancing short, simple sentences with compound or complex sentences works best.

Revising on the word level

Choosing your words well helps your reader understand the central point more easily. Revising on the word level improves not only the content of your essay, but also the way the paper flows. Here are some word-level strategies you can use when revising your essay.

✓ Look for wordiness. Cut empty phrases, such as *there are, it is, I feel that, I know that, you will understand that, I think, in today's society*, and so on.

✓ Use concrete nouns for subjects, and avoid overusing pronouns, especially at the beginning of sentences.

✓ Ask your instructor about his or her policy on using first person (*I, me, my*) and second person (*you, your, yours*).

✓ Be sure to use *you* appropriately if you use it. *You* can only be used if the reader is actually the *you* referent.

✓ Change passive verbs to active ones when possible.

✓ Read aloud for unnecessary repetition. Replace overused words with synonyms, but be careful that you clearly understand how to use words you find in a thesaurus.

✓ Check the tone of your essay and be aware that word choice plays a role in creating the overall tone. If your instructor asks you to use an academic tone, do not use conversational-type word choices, such as *Well, I then went to the bus stop on the corner and then got on the bus and then took it downtown* or *I was chillin' in my crib*.

✓ Review transitions used throughout the essay. Pay particular attention to using transitions used between body paragraphs and within body paragraphs when switching from one supporting point to another. See the list of transitions in Box 2.2 at the end of this chapter.

Read over Brian Jones's revised essay about the significance of signs. Go back to **page 36**, and compare the first draft with this revised draft. What has he changed? How has that strengthened the essay? Are there any other revision suggestions that you would give to this writer?

Now look over the margin comments—how will these suggested editing changes strengthen the essay?

Brian Jones

Jones 1

Professor Walker

English 1010

09 February 2009

Significance of Signs

The regular family trip from Indianapolis to Destin, FL required a monotonous thirteen hour car drive. If I was lucky, my parents would decide to leave at night, allowing my sister and I to sleep for almost the entire trip. But this wasn't very easy for my parents to do, we would usually pack up the van early in the morning and spend the day on the road. Considering that we made the trip at least three times a year from the time I was born until I graduated from high school. I got to know the route pretty well. The familiar road signs and billboards along the way not only indicated our path, but also became an integral part of the trip. I can't think about our family trips without recalling that long drive and the signs along the way.

> Good revision on the introduction! You start right off into your story, and you lead into the main idea of your essay—that signs recall memories of your family trip. Watch out for comma splices and fragments, though.

I must have learned early not to ask my parents that famous question, "Are we there yet?" Instead, I got used to keeping an eye on the giant green and white signs that kept passing by and learned to figure out our progress on my own. LOUISVILLE one hundred miles. NASHVILLE sixty miles. Huntsville. Birmingham. Montgomery. Ah, Montgomery. Once I saw that sign, I really got excited, because that meant that we were about to get off I-65 to take the back roads to our final destination. Those signs are embedded in my mind even now, not having made that drive for several years, I can

> Well done. The purpose of this paragraph is much clearer with the new topic sentence. I see a run-on sentence!

Jones 2

recite those major cities in order and visualize their distance from each other. But really, those signs were the boring ones. Each one only represented a check mark to make on my mental list of cities we had to get through before I could go to the beach.

The good signs were ones that meant we were going to stop (and probably eat). Cracker Barrel signs were pretty good, they usually meant some old-fashioned candy or maybe a cheap toy. One of my favorite signs was for a peach farm in Alabama. Next to the sign there was a water tower shaped and painted like a giant peach. We always stopped at the peach farm, no matter what, to get fresh produce and some home made ice cream. On the back roads past Montgomery, we'd watch for signs for another of our favorite stops, a little country cookin' restaurant called Annie's, famous for their fried catfish. Though we stopped eating there in later years, I always had an eye out for that familiar and comforting sign, reminding me not only of past trips, but also of how close we were getting to the end of the long drive.

> You have a lot of great description in this paragraph! Check for comma splices.

The signs along the way had an important function for us, too. In order to pass the time, we usually played a round or two of the ABC game. Finding a word for every letter of the alphabet turned into a competitive game for my family, sometimes lasting the majority of the thirteen hours. Especially because of the long stretches between major cities with no signs and cuz its hard to find words with Q and Z. (X, by the way, was allowed to be anywhere in the word, or else the game would never end). Dairy Queens and La Quinta Inns were few and far between, and construction zones or speed zones were the only hope for winning the game. The winner was declared to have the sharpest vision and would receive bragging rights for the rest of the trip, but really all that mattered is that we had made part of the trip go by a little faster—and had fun doing it.

> I'm glad you took out the 2nd person here and explained the game more. It's much more interesting to read.

We really hated those terribly long trips and complained about the distance, but in some ways they exemplify that old cliché that it's about the journey, not the destination. Though we really hated those long drives I guess they gave us alot of good times. Many family stories were created along the route between Indy and Destin. And while the roads have been repaved and

> Much stronger conclusion. You might consider rewording the end of the first sentence, though, to emphasize your point about the importance of the journey.

> Jones 3
>
> the signs have changed with the times, the memories persist, as clear and
>
> sharp in my mind as the signs that we carefully watched out for—either to
>
> lead the way, entice us to stop, or pass the time.

Editing

The time to begin writing an article is when you have finished it to your satisfaction. By that time you begin to clearly and logically perceive what it is you really want to say.

—Mark Twain

Editing and proofreading are additional steps in the writing process. Many writers make the mistake of focusing on error correction and proofreading before taking the time to develop, clarify, and organize ideas fully through drafting and revision. Although the parts of the writing process are not finite and often overlap, editing and proofreading should be treated as separate activities designed to address what writing specialists call local issues, such as grammar, sentence variety, mechanics, spelling, and formatting.

Some editing tips

Editing comes after you feel confident about the choices you have made in content, organization, and style. You might compare editing and proofreading to washing, waxing, and polishing your car. It would be absurd to take the time to do these things to a vehicle that does not run! Drafting and revising ensures that your writing is first fine-tuned. Then you edit to make it shine on the surface.

Set the work aside after revising

After you complete a revised draft, put your essay aside for a while. This allows you to use fresh eyes when you pick up the essay again to look for mechanics or spelling. Invest in a calendar that is only used for your writing class. Each time you receive an assignment, start with the due date and work your way back in the calendar, marking personal deadlines for a rough draft, revised draft, and edited draft. This will help you save enough time at the end of the writing process for editing and proofreading.

Participate in editing workshops

Some instructors will ask you to participate in editing workshops in class. Take full advantage of this opportunity, asking your peers to pay close attention to your work. Be prepared when you come to workshop day with the number of copies that you need, and also bring a variety of colored highlighters. After you receive your essay copies back, ask questions of your peers or instructor if you do not understand a comment or correction.

Use available tools and resources

When you edit, be sure to have a dictionary, thesaurus, and grammar handbook available. Do not postpone looking something up, and if you cannot find assistance by yourself, be sure to take advantage of your university's writing center and your instructor's office hours.

Read your essay aloud

Read your essay aloud to yourself, highlighting anything that does not seem correct. Check your resources for assistance or reword in a way that you know is correct. Have a friend listen to your essay, just so you have an audience; the friend may not be able to help with spelling or punctuation but should be able to hear other types of writing problems, such as wrong word choice, incorrect subject/verb agreement, incorrect pronoun/antecedent agreement, and so on.

Have someone else read your essay aloud

Have a friend read your essay to you, and immediately mark any places where the reader stumbles or hesitates. This may be a clue that a comma is misplaced or a word is misspelled. After your friend completes the reading, go back and check out those places that you marked.

Read backwards

Read the last sentence of your essay first, then the second-to-the-last sentence, and continue on in this order until you have reached the first sentence of your essay. As you read each sentence, you will be focused on the sentence itself, rather than the content or topic of the entire paper, which may help you notice some spelling or punctuation errors that you did not notice previously.

Keep track of your editing problem areas

Use a chart such as the essay grid shown in Figure 2.5 to note the two or three most common problems your instructor or peers marked. Then, use the grid to check each essay before you turn it in. As you progress through the semester, note if you have been successful in eliminating these problem areas, and add other problem areas that pop up in later essays.

Figure 2.5 Essay Grid

Essay	Area #1	Area #2	Area #3	Area #4	Area #5	Area #6
1						
2						
3						
4						
5						

Levels of editing

Similar to the revision process, you can edit on different levels, including the paragraph, sentence, and word levels.

Editing on the paragraph level

The first step in editing is to check your paragraphing. Think of paragraphs as larger forms of punctuation that broaden the connections shown by traditional punctuation marks, such as commas, semicolons, and periods. Punctuation marks indicate pauses, relationships, and connections within and between sentences. Likewise, paragraph indentations and lengths provide readers with visual guidance to relationships and connections between major ideas.

- ✓ What does each paragraph say (main idea) and do (introduce, provide proof or support, give an example, illustrate, connect, conclude)? Check that each paragraph begins a new idea.

- ✓ Are sentences within paragraphs unified and consistent? Check for unrelated ideas, illogical sequences and series, mixed metaphors and/or confusing comparisons, and mismatched subjects and verbs, (e.g., *butter reads* or *books believe*). Make sure transitional words or phrases are used correctly.

Editing on the sentence level

- ✓ Are the connections between ideas effectively communicated through subordination and coordination? Check for short, choppy sentences or excessively long, hard-to-follow sentences. Make sure that subordination is done correctly.

- ✓ Is the structure of each sentence clear and easy? Check for misplaced parts, modifiers that have no referent in the sentence, and modifiers that are too far from the words they modify.

- ✓ Are ideas balanced through the use of parallel elements?

- ✓ Do sentences vary in length and construction?

- ✓ Are sentences concise and free of deadweight or unnecessary words? Check for empty placeholders such as *there, it, this,* and *these.* Also look for excessive use of forms of the verb *to be,* and replace these with strong, specific verbs.

- ✓ Are there any fragments, comma splices, or fused sentences?

Editing on the word level

- ✓ Do all subjects and verbs agree? Do all pronouns agree with their antecedents? Are all verb forms correct?

- ✓ Are there any sudden shifts in grammatical structures? Check for consistent use of verb tense and consistency in person and number.

✓ Are words clear and direct? Check for consistent use of active voice—where the subject performs the action of the sentence (e.g., *The registrar misplaced your transcripts*). Also, be sure that use of passive voice is intentional and accurate, for example, to avoid assigning blame or for emphasis (e.g., *Your transcripts were misplaced*).

✓ Are any words vague? Check for vague or general nouns—and replace them with specific or concrete nouns (e.g., replace *school* with *Yale* or *vehicle* with *Jeep Wrangler*). Also check for vague or general verbs—and replace them with specific, active verbs (e.g., replace *says* with *argues* or replace *ran* with *sprinted*).

✓ Are any words or phrases overused? Check for repeated words at beginnings of sentences and overused phrases or clichés.

✓ Have necessary words been left out? Have unnecessary words or phrases (especially prepositional phrases) been left in?

✓ Does your vocabulary reflect sensitivity to audience, purpose, and context? Check for stereotypes, biased language, unintentional connotations associated with words, and jargon.

✓ Does your choice of words or tone reflect assumptions about the readers or their beliefs?

✓ Have you used *you* or *I* when your assignment asks you to avoid them?

PROOFREADING

In the final step of the writing process, be sure to take the time to proofread your essay carefully before turning it in. Use this step to focus on punctuation, spelling, capitalization, italics, and formatting.

Proofreading for punctuation

✓ Do sentences have the correct closing punctuation?

✓ Are commas, semicolons, dashes, apostrophes, and other internal punctuation marks used correctly?

✓ Are quotations correctly introduced, punctuated, and carefully cited? Are quotation marks turned the right way, toward the quoted material?

✓ Are in-text citations correctly punctuated?

Proofreading for spelling

✓ Are all words spelled correctly? Remember that spell-checkers are not foolproof! Check for commonly confused words.

✓ Have you used the correct forms? Double-check any abbreviations, contractions, or possessive nouns.

✓ Have you used hyphens correctly? Double-check any hyphenated adjectives.

Proofreading for capitalization and italics

- ✓ Are words capitalized appropriately?
- ✓ Are quotations capitalized correctly?
- ✓ Are proper names and titles distinguished with appropriate capitalization and punctuation?
- ✓ Are titles punctuated correctly, using either italics or quotation marks as appropriate?

Proofreading for formatting

Formatting an essay correctly shows that you care about the presentation of all your hard work. However, looks can be deceiving; a paper that looks good can still contain serious errors. Computers have made it much easier to produce a professional-looking document, but proofreading is still essential.

- ✓ Have you followed all of your instructor's directions about formatting?
- ✓ Are the margins correct?
- ✓ Is the spacing correct between words, sentences, and paragraphs?
- ✓ Is the assignment block (with information about you, your class, and your instructor) present and correct? Does it contain all of the required information in the correct order and form?
- ✓ Do you have a title that is centered and spaced correctly, and not underlined, italicized, bolded, in quotation marks, or in a different font?
- ✓ Have you included a header with your name and the page number?
- ✓ If needed, do you have a Works Cited page that follows the required documentation style?

I'd rather be caught holding up a bank than stealing so much as a two-word phrase from another writer.

—Jack Smith

Take a look at Brian Jones's final draft, and compare it to the two other drafts on **pages 36 and 46**. For this draft, what has he changed? How has his editing strengthened the essay? Are there any other editing or proofreading suggestions that you would recommend?

SAMPLE STUDENT ESSAY
FINAL DRAFT

Brian Jones   Jones 1

Professor Walker

English 1010

16 February 2009

The Signs Along the Way

The regular family trip from Indianapolis to Destin, Florida required a thirteen hour car drive. If I were lucky, my parents would decide to leave at night, allowing my sister and me to sleep for almost the entire trip. But this wasn't very easy for my parents to do, so we would usually pack up the van early in the morning and spend the day on the road. Considering that we made the trip at least three times a year from the time I was born until I graduated from high school, I got to know the route pretty well. The familiar road signs and billboards along the way not only indicated our path, but also became an integral part of the trip. I can't think about our family trips without recalling that long drive and the familiar signs along the way.

I must have learned early not to ask my parents that famous question, "Are we there yet?" Instead, I got used to keeping an eye on the giant green and white signs that kept passing by and learned to figure out our progress on my own. LOUISVILLE one hundred miles. NASHVILLE sixty miles. Huntsville. Birmingham. Montgomery. Ah, Montgomery. Once I saw that sign, I really got excited, because that meant that we were about to get off the seemingly endless, always boring I-65 to take the much more interesting back roads to our final destination. But those signs were embedded in my mind; even now, not having made that drive for several years, I can recite those major cities in order and visualize their distance from each other. However, those green and white signs were really the boring ones. Each one only represented a check mark to make on my mental list of cities we had to get through before I could go to the beach.

The best signs were the ones that meant we were going to stop (and probably eat). Cracker Barrel signs were pretty good; they usually meant some old-fashioned candy or maybe a cheap toy. One of my favorites was for a peach farm in Alabama. Next to the sign there was a water tower shaped and painted like a giant peach. We always stopped at the peach farm, no matter what, to get fresh produce and some home made ice cream. On the back roads past Montgomery, we'd watch for signs for another of our favorite stops, a little country cookin' restaurant called Annie's, famous for their fried catfish. Though we stopped eating there in later years, I always had an eye out for that familiar and comforting sign, reminding me not only of past trips, but also of how close we were getting to the end of the long drive.

The signs along the way had an important function for us, too. In order to pass the time, we usually played a round or two of the ABC game. Finding a word for every letter of the alphabet turned into a competitive game for my family, sometimes lasting the majority of the thirteen hours due to the dwindling number of signs and billboards between major cities and the inevitable difficulty of finding words beginning with Q or Z (X, by the way, was allowed to be anywhere in the word, or else the  game would never end). Dairy Queens and La Quinta Inns were few and far between, and construction zones or speed zones were the only hope for winning the game. The winner was declared to have the sharpest vision and would receive bragging rights for the rest of the trip, which wasn't such a big deal, but really all that mattered is that we had made part of the trip go by a little faster—and had fun doing it.

We really hated those terribly long trips and complained about the distance, but in some ways they exemplify that old cliché that the journey is more important than the destination. Many of our family stories find their origins along the route between Indy and Destin, and now that my sister and I are grown up and have moved to different states, we often talk about all those trips we made down I-65 together as a family. While the roads have been repaved and the signs have changed with the times, the memories persist, as clear and sharp in my mind as the signs that we carefully watched out for—either to lead the way, entice us to stop, or pass the time.

SHARING, PRESENTING, AND PUBLISHING

Motivation is key to becoming a good writer, but motivation can prove elusive when someone else is requiring you to write. One way to help yourself become a better writer is to go beyond writing for a class grade. Find a way to share your writing in other venues. Sometimes, an instructor will build this type of incentive into a writing class syllabus by asking you to read your final draft to others in the class or by posting the final draft online for others—your classmates or outsiders—to read. If this is not available to you, consider some other ways to share your writing outside of class:

❑ Ask your instructor to allow you and your peers to each share one essay aloud in class on the final day.

❑ Ask your instructor if you can take up essays from those who volunteer and publish them in bound-copy form at your university's printing office or a local copy shop.

❑ Submit your essay to an English Department student-published journal or magazine.

❑ Submit your argumentative essay to the Letters to the Editor section of a local newspaper or to the "My View" column in magazines such as *Time* or *Newsweek*.

❑ Ask your high school English teacher if you and some of your peers can visit his or her class to share your writing as samples of the writing students should expect in college.

Box 2.2

Transitional Expressions

Addition➔ moreover, furthermore, besides, likewise, also, too, finally, second, third, last, additionally

Cause➔ since, because

Comparison➔ similarly, likewise

Concession➔ although, though, despite

Condition➔ unless, provided that, if

Contrast➔ but, yet, however, nevertheless, in contrast, on the contrary, nonetheless, whereas, even though, although, otherwise, on the other hand

Exception➔ except

Exemplification➔ for example, for instance

Intensification➔ indeed, in fact

Place➔ where, here, near, beyond

Purpose➔ (in order) to, to this end

Repetition➔ in other words, as I have said, as previously mentioned, as stated above

Result➔ therefore, thus, consequently, as a result, hence

Summary➔ in conclusion, in short, all in all, overall, finally

Time➔ when, after, before, until, as long as, meanwhile, while, immediately, soon, afterward, then, henceforth

READ MORE ABOUT IT

Elbow, Peter. *Writing with Power: Techniques for Mastering the Writing Process*. New York: Oxford UP, 1998. Print.

---. *Writing without Teachers*. New York: Oxford UP, 1998. Print,

Graff, Gerald. *They Say, I Say: The Moves that Matter in Academic Writing*, 2nd ed. W.W. Norton, 2009. Print.

Hacker, Diane, and Nancy Sommers. *A Writer's Reference*, 7th ed. Boston: Bedford/St. Martin's, 2010. Print

King, Stephen. *On Writing: A Memoir of The Craft*. New York: Pocket Books, 2002. Print.

Lamott, Anne. *Bird by Bird: Some Instructions on Writing and Life*. New York: Anchor Books, 1995. Print.

Strunk, William, Jr., E. B. White, and Roger Angell. *The Elements of Style*, 4th ed. Boston: Allyn and Bacon, 1999. Print.

Truss, Lynne. *Eats, Shoots and Leaves: The Zero Tolerance Approach to Punctuation*. New York: Gotham Books, 2006. Print.

Zinsser, William K. *On Writing Well: The Classic Guide to Writing Nonfiction*. New York: Collins, 2006. Print.

chapter 3

Reading Across the Curriculum

Let us read with method, and propose to ourselves an end to which our studies may point. The use of reading is to aid us in thinking.

—Edward Gibbon

The more that you read, the more things you will know. The more that you learn, the more places you'll go.

—Dr. Seuss, I Can Read With My Eyes Shut!

Reading is essential for learning—in more ways than you may think. Reading provides you with an understanding of vocabulary, grammar, sentence structure, and text structure. The more you read and the more varied you are in your reading, the more authentic language input you give your brain to absorb and process, allowing you to foster the development of a broader vocabulary, richer sentence variety, and rhetorical maturity. Reading also provides you with opportunities for cultural inquiry and awareness, including an introduction to the specialized writing you will be reading in your chosen field. Most of all, though, reading allows you to obtain content information about subjects that you are studying in depth.

Did you know?

The 2008 ACT's High School Profile Report noted only 53 percent of the students who took the ACT were ready for college-level reading requirements. In addition to reading readiness for college, employers identified reading and writing as top deficiencies of new employees.

—James Pelech and Susan T. Hibbard, *Evaluating the Effectiveness of Reading Strategies for College Students: An Action Research Approach*

Just as with writing, reading can be broken down into two areas that will help you focus on becoming the best college-level reader that you can be: reading to learn and learning to read. The reading-to-learn approach focuses on how you, as a reader, can locate and analyze complex ideas and then use this knowledge to craft your opinion. The learning-to-read approach involves basic strategies that you may have learned in high school or other courses; however, the focus at this stage is learning which of these strategies is most useful for each assigned reading and which ones work best for you.

READING TO LEARN

When you read to learn, you are reading to comprehend and retain information more effectively than when you read for fun. Just as with the writing-to-learn approach discussed in Chapter 1, one of the tenets of reading to learn is for you to use reading to make your thoughts more visible to yourself, so you can organize and analyze them effectively. Whether it is a general education course or a course in your major, your instructor will usually assign reading to help you understand lecture material or prepare you for writing assignments or exams.

To be a successful writer or test-taker, you need to be able to read varied and extensive material with a high command of understanding. Some reading assignments may be low risk, such as previewing material prior to a lecture, and some may be of a higher risk, such as reading research essays that you will critically evaluate in terms of their usefulness for your own research paper. Whatever the risk, the main purpose behind any assigned course reading is to make you more comfortable with thinking critically about key concepts. How you share these ideas with yourself, your instructor, your classmates, or any other type of audience is discussed more fully in Chapters 1 and 2, which focus on writing.

To be an effective reader, you should be an active reader. You need to bring all your knowledge to the forefront and use it as you process new material for understanding. Good readers engage with the text as if in a conversation, asking questions and searching for answers as they read. They observe how they are interacting with the text by taking notes or keeping track of main concepts and important information.

One of the most important ways for you to become an effective reader—one who is able to observe details, recall facts, and come to conclusions—is to learn and apply strategies that will help you process what you read. These reading strategies are critical if you are to become an active and effective reader.

LEARNING TO READ EFFECTIVELY

Reading is not magic. It is the consistent application of a range of comprehension strategies.

—Erika Daniels, The Power of Strategies Instruction

Different disciplines may have diverse classes, distinct types of information, and discipline-specific types of writing, but they all include reading. When you are assigned reading in a course, you are a scholar, and scholarly reading is quite different from reading for pleasure. You must become a critical reader to be an effective scholarly reader. One component of being critical involves asking questions about not only the assigned reading, but also about why the reading was assigned. The first step to becoming a critical reader is to engage with the reading by being an active reader. Be sure to understand why your instructor has assigned this particular reading. The following questions will help you understand the purpose.

- ❏   How does this reading fit in with the objectives of the course?
- ❏   How does this reading address the themes of the course?
- ❏   How does this reading relate to what is currently being covered in the course?
- ❏   Is the reading a critical part of an assignment that will follow?

Once you understand why a reading has been assigned, consider how your instructor wants you to read, process, and analyze the reading. If you are not certain, it is a good idea to ask your instructor how you should manage the assigned reading and process it for understanding. The time you allocate to the reading will depend on how much you want to absorb from the reading. Use these questions to determine how you want to read; the further down the list, the more time it will take you to process the reading for full understanding:

- ❑ Was this reading assigned for entertainment?
- ❑ Was this reading assigned to grasp a certain message?
- ❑ Was this reading assigned to find an important detail?
- ❑ Was this reading assigned to answer a specific question?
- ❑ Was this reading assigned to be evaluated?
- ❑ Was this reading assigned to apply its concepts to something else?

You must also be an active reader to be an effective reader. To think as you read, use active reading strategies, which improve comprehension, retention, and recall. Your high school teachers may have shared some strategies with you for becoming an active, engaged reader; therefore, some of these strategies may be familiar to you. Whether the following are new to you or not, it is a good idea to have an arsenal of strategies that work for you when you are assigned a reading in class. Consider the reading process to be like the writing process, with a separation into three primary areas: prereading, reading, and postreading. Depending on what kind of reader you are, you should be able to choose at least a few strategies in each area to improve your critical reading skills.

The research shows that [readers] who struggle tend not to ask questions at any time as they read—before, during, or after. . . . They're inert as they read. They read—or I should say they submit to the text—never questioning its content, style, or the intent of the author.

—Ellin Oliver Keene and Susan Zimmermann,
Mosaic of Thought

Strategies for Prereading

1. **Know your discipline's common organization for articles and books.** Each field has its own practice, and knowing yours will help you know where to find abstracts or conclusions that will help you review the material.

2. **Read the preface and introduction.** Oftentimes, the author or editor will present or review important points or even each chapter for you.

3. **Preview and predict what the reading will be about.**

   a. <u>Look</u> at the table of contents, and review the headings and subheadings for the assigned reading.

   b. <u>Write</u> a short journal entry that describes what you know about the topics that are listed in the headings.

c.   Draft some questions you have about the topic.

d.   Use a K-W-L chart by creating columns headed with "What I Know," "What I Want to Know," and "What I have Learned." Fill in the first two columns prior to reading and the last after you finish.

4.   **Skim and scan the reading before you start fully reading.** Look at how many pages the reading is, how many sections there are, how long the sections are, and what types of headings and subheadings there are.

5.   **Create reading goals and develop a plan to split up what you need to read or what has been assigned.** You can do this in a journal, on notebook paper, on your calendar, or in the table of contents.

6.   **Choose specific times to read that work for you, and plan enough time to finish a full section.** Find out how many pages you can read in an hour, count up your assigned reading, and then make a realistic plan.

STRATEGIES AS YOU READ

1.   **Read for 30 to 45 minutes, and then review what you have read before taking a short break.** An effective strategy is to read for 30–45 minutes, review for 5 minutes, and take a break for 5 minutes.

2.   **Read section by section.** It is best to stop when there is a natural break in the reading material. This will help later when you organize your notes, since they will already be focused on one section at a time.

3.   **Circle new terms and underline their definitions.** Use a circle or some other graphic tool to help you note new terms as you read and note them later as you return to review the reading. If the term is not defined in the text, look it up and note the definition near the term in the reading, if possible. Consider creating a "terms" page at the beginning of your notebook or binder, and note both the term and its definition when you first encounter them.

4.   **Annotate your text.** Draw attention to main ideas or important points by underlining, highlighting, circling, or using asterisks or other graphic reminders. Use a pen or pencil, rather than a highlighter; you'll have less chance of marking excessively.

 If you are marking too much, it means you aren't able to select main points and important details. Highlighting more than 20 percent of the text means highlighting isn't working for you.

5.   **Read difficult sections out loud, or take turns reading out loud with a classmate.** This will help you process the important information in more than just one way since it adds the audio element to the visual.

6. **Create a bulleted list of main ideas as you read, or use an informal or formal outline method.** You might also use a cluster approach to keep notes about related ideas together.

7. **Create a timeline to keep track of dates, especially when reading literature or when reading about history.**

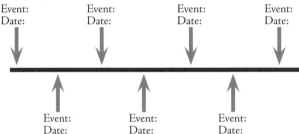

8. **Draw helpful pictures or diagrams in your notes, especially when you want to depict relationships between one character or idea to another.**

9. **Visualize different sections or ideas by using different colored pens, pencils, or highlighters.** Take notes as you read.

10. **Write down questions next to the material as you read.** Or keep a detailed Reader's Notebook with questions, and be sure to include the page number of the material to which they refer.

11. **Use information management software to take notes, add tags to highlight related ideas, and then organize your notes into folders.** Information management software is available for most computer platforms and is an easy way to search through your notes. (See Box 3.1.)

Box 3.1

Information Management Software		
AllMyNotes Organizer	KeyNote	Qiqqa
AudioNote-Notepad	KNote	SilverNote
BasKet Note Pads	Memonic	Tiddly-Wiki
Catch Notes	Microsoft OneNote	Tomboy
CintaNotes	MyInfo	TreeDBNotes
Evernote	MyNotex	WikidPad
Gnote	Notee	Windows Journal
Jarnal	Okular	XLnotes
Keeppy	PDF Studio	Xournal
KeepNote	Personal Knowbase	Zim

STRATEGIES FOR POSTREADING

1. After reading, write to learn by using journals, graphic organizers, or other options described in Chapter 2.

2. Read particularly challenging sections again, or reread as needed to answer study questions.

3. Answer reading questions that your instructor has given you, or check the end of the chapter or the book's website for helpful questions.

4. Mark information in your notes that connects to your instructor's lectures or other class materials. Bring your reading notes to class, and highlight any information from the book that your instructor covers again in class or asks questions about.

5. Turn your linear notes into a chart, table, outline, or any other graphic that will help you process the information more quickly. Check out the many different types of graphic organizers at http://www.thinkport.org/technology/template.tp. See Figure 3.1 for one example of a Venn diagram.

Figure 3.1 Venn diagram

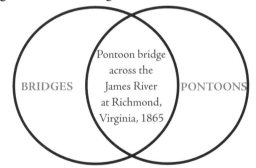

BRIDGES | Pontoon bridge across the James River at Richmond, Virginia, 1865 | PONTOONS

6. Use the *shrinking outline* method. Immediately after reading, write in a journal as much information as you remember or think is important. Then, go through what you've described, making it more concise by taking out things you've repeated or that are not as important as others. Then, go through the information one more time, and create a concise, abstract-like description of what you read (see Chapter 9, p. 243).

7. Create a concise statement about the reading topic. While riding on an elevator for a few floors, try to come up with a brief statement of what the reading was about before the elevator stops, or you might apply this strategy as you walk up a few flights of stairs.

8. **Use special strategies for difficult material.**

   a. <u>Reread</u>. Sometimes rereading is all it takes to grasp something you didn't understand the first time.

   b. <u>Stop</u> reading after each paragraph or section, and write your notes or rephrase what you have read using your own words.

   c. <u>Discuss</u> the reading with a classmate, create a study group, or go see your instructor during office hours.

   d. <u>Create</u> a flow chart of how ideas in each section or paragraph relate to each other.

   e. <u>Take</u> a break from your reading and return when you are refreshed. Sometimes, a cup of coffee or a good night's sleep will help you understand what was eluding you.

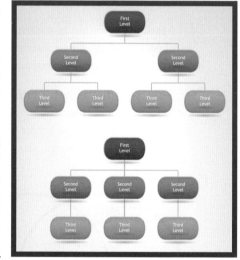

You may have also learned a reading and studying technique in high school that constructed all of the reading steps into one model, such as the SQ3R, SQ4R, or PQRST methods. If you break down these models, they follow the same prereading, reading, and postreading pattern described earlier, but you may want to add other strategies from the list above when you build your own reading model. Here's a brief breakdown of these methods:

S ➙ SURVEY
Q ➙ QUESTION
3R ➙ READ, RECITE, REVIEW

S ➙ SURVEY
Q ➙ QUESTION
4R ➙ READ, RECITE, RELATE, REVIEW

P ➙ PREVIEW
Q ➙ QUESTION
R ➙ READ
S ➙ SELF-RECITE
T ➙ TEST

Reading researchers stress that students should choose reading strategies that fit their personalities, reading levels, and time constraints. Once you choose what strategies work for you, it is best to make using them a habit as you read for your courses. Use an organizer like the one in Figure 3.2 to track your reading strategies.

Did you know?

Students who fail to employ reading strategies tend to experience difficulty inferring conceptual meaning, relating to what they have read, self-monitoring their learning and understanding, and evaluating texts for clarity and consistency.
—Kathrynn Di Tommaso
from her research study described in *Strategies to Facilitate Reading Comprehension among College Transition Students*

Figure 3.2 Sample Strategies Organizer

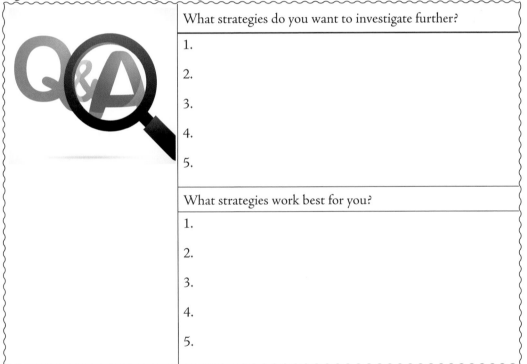

Q&A	What strategies do you want to investigate further?
	1.
	2.
	3.
	4.
	5.
	What strategies work best for you?
	1.
	2.
	3.
	4.
	5.

READ MORE ABOUT IT

Adler, Mortimer J. *How to Read a Book*. New York, NY: Touchstone, 1972. Print.

Buckner, Aimee. *Notebook Connections: Strategies for the Reader's Notebook*. Portland, ME: Stenhouse, 2009. Print.

Eagleton, Terry. *How to Read a Poem*. Indianapolis, IN: Wiley-Blackwell, 2006. Print.

Frank, Marjorie. *Graphic Organizers for Any Subject: Any Level*. Nashville, TN: Incentive Publications, 2007. Print.

Hennings, Dorothy Grant. *Reading with Meaning: Strategies for College Reading*. New York, NY: Longman, 2004. Print.

Smith, Brenda D. *The Reader's Handbook: Reading Strategies for College and Everyday Life*. New York, NY: Longman, 2009. Print.

chapter 4

The Research Process

Research has been called good business, a necessity, a gamble, a game. It is none of these—it's a state of mind.

> —Martin H. Fischer, Howard Fabing (ed.) and Ray Marr (ed.),
> *Fischerisms*

Research is formalized curiosity. It is poking and prying with a purpose.

> —Zora Neale Hurston, Robert Hemenway,
> *Dust Tracks on a Road: an Autobiography*

I think that the thing I most want you to remember is that research is a ceremony. And so is life. Everything that we do shares in the ongoing creation of our universe.

> —Shawn Wilson,
> *Research Is Ceremony: Indigenous Research Methods*

WHY IS RESEARCH IMPORTANT?

Research is part of most writing, especially writing for academic purposes. But why? What does research do for you the writer or for your writing? What does it do for your reader? For one, it can help you learn more about your topic, showing you facts and opinions about your subject matter. It can help you support your claims and illustrate your points. It also helps you learn what others have already said about your topic so that you can become part of an ongoing conversation. It helps show your readers that you're a credible author whose writing can be believed or trusted. More importantly, it can help you answer your questions and satisfy your curiosity, no matter the subject or discipline. In fact, effective research starts with a good research question and is driven by your pursuit of the answer to that question. You may be trying to figure out weather patterns along the Gulf Coast in the last five years, patterns of use for different types of Facebook users, or the symbolism used in the Dickinson poem you just read; they all require research. The question then becomes what kind of research do you need to do? This chapter will discuss various types of research you might use as you write for your different classes and disciplines and will give you some guidelines for deciding which type(s) of research you need for your assigned or chosen project. It will also give an overview of the research process; you'll see that the research process bridges with the writing process, so refer back to Chapter 2, The Writing Process, as needed.

THE RESEARCH PROCESS

Basically, I'm not interested in doing research and I never have been. I'm interested in understanding, which is quite a different thing.
—David Blackwell

Being a scientist means living on the borderline between your competence and your incompetence. If you always feel competent, you aren't doing your job.
—Carlos Bustamante (Molecular Biologist, UC-Berkeley)

Where do you start when you want to learn something you don't know or when you've been assigned to research something for class? How do you even decide what to research? You start with what interests you. You start with your questions, your curiosity. You can also start with some explorations that will help you form your research questions.

Questions: What questions do you have about the topic or the subject matter of the class? What questions do you have in general; can they be connected to your assignment? What would you like to know more about?

Interests: What are you interested in? What bugs you? What makes you angry? What gets you excited? How does this topic relate to your major or your career plans? What's happening in the news right now and how might it affect you or your friends and family? How might this class connect to topics or issues from another class you're taking?

Go surfing: Search the Web for ideas of interest to you. Look at research databases related to your topic, class, or interests (you should use the databases provided by your school library for this). Read your local newspaper. Talk to your friends and family members; what is on their minds? What interesting questions do they have?

 Encyclopedias, including Wikipedia, often aren't allowed as a final resource in your paper, but they can be a good place to start as they give an overview of a particular subject and can point you in a fruitful direction.

Pay attention: What is happening on your campus or in your town? How might these issues affect you or people you know? What have you read, listened to, or seen on television lately that sparked your interest or led you to questions?

As you formulate your research questions—the questions that will guide your project—it is also important to consult your assignment. Sometimes topics or a range of topics are assigned, so you want to work within these parameters in order to be successful in class. If you have unlimited options, use the methods above, as well as the brainstorming techniques described in Chapter 2, to help you determine your focus. Research projects take a lot of time and energy, so you need a research question and topic that that will work for the assignment and that you want to spend time on.

In *The Curious Researcher*, Bruce Ballenger gives a list of the characteristics that make a question researchable:

- ❏ It's not too big or too small.
- ❏ It focuses on some aspect of a topic about which something has been said.
- ❏ It interests the researcher.
- ❏ Some people have a stake in the answer. It has something to do with how we live or might live, what we care about, or what might be important for people to know.
- ❏ It implies an approach or various means of answering it.
- ❏ It raises more questions, the answers to which might not be simple.

As you have been determining your topic, you have already been conducting research; however, once you have a focused research question, you can begin more focused research and you can decide which method or methods will best help you answer your research question. It is important to remember that effective research doesn't happen overnight. It takes time. In fact, most projects will require many hours of research throughout the researching and writing process, so you don't want to waste time. Starting as soon as you get an assignment and planning ahead for all that you have to do will help you be more successful.

You may need to incorporate intermediate deadlines into your timeline. Sometimes these middle steps or deadlines have been assigned by your professor, and sometimes you have to set them up for yourself. For example, you may have a topic due, then a working bibliography a few weeks later, then an outline or plan, followed by a research draft. These deadlines along the way are designed to help you move through the process and prevent you from waiting till the last minute to complete your project.

PRIMARY AND SECONDARY RESEARCH

Upon hearing the term research, some students may picture opening up a computer to Google and putting in a search term or two. Others may picture going to the library and sorting through books and journals. Still others may think of experiments in the lab or out in the field. Research is all of these things.

In some classes, you'll be asked to conduct primary research. Primary research involves the researchers collecting the data themselves. This may be done in a variety of ways, but some of the more popular methods include surveying participants, interviewing informants, and observing subjects and phenomena.

Surveying: Surveys are useful when you want to learn what a large number of people think about a topic. They are also useful when you want to limit the ways respondents can answer. Surveys may use multiple-choice responses or ask open-ended questions in which participants fill in the blanks or have space to tell their own stories. Another strength of the survey is that it can be anonymous, making it easier for some people to talk about difficult or controversial topics.

Interviewing: Interviews are usually conducted one on one or in small groups (including focus groups). They have fewer respondents than surveys, but can provide you with much more in-depth information. A large advantage of the interview is that it allows you to ask follow-up questions for clarification and expansion. A disadvantage is that interviews are not anonymous and can sometimes shut down people's responses. Interviews require very careful note taking because this moment in time cannot be recreated; even if you interview the same person again and ask the same questions, you will get different information. Often interviewers video and/or audio record their interviews; however, you must have the interview subject's permission first.

Observing: Observations allow you to watch and study a particular event, location, group of people, or phenomena. They usually involve a set span of time and extensive note taking. Observers may also utilize video and audio equipment to help with their observations (see note taking tips in relevant content chapters).

Closely tied to primary research is the idea of primary sources. Primary sources are original, uninterpreted documents. This may include novels, poems, plays, newspapers, government documents, student papers and other print documents such as memos, receipts, flyers, and posters. Media such as films, television shows, radio broadcasts, musical recordings, podcasts, and TED talks are also primary sources. You may also include original three-dimensional artifacts such as woven baskets, sculptures, couture clothing, paintings, photographs, and other items of study (pretty much anything you wish to research). A common research method used with primary sources is analysis or close reading.

Analysis: When analyzing a primary document, you read or look at it closely, usually multiple times. You will usually look for patterns or for things that stand out for some reason. Various theoretical frames are often used to conduct this kind of analysis, such as a feminist frame to look at gender in television commercials, a native studies frame to analyze beadwork, a strengths model to analyze patients' charts, or a queer theory frame to analyze HIV/AIDS educational pamphlets.

Often, primary research requires a mixture of methods and approaches. For example, you may conduct a survey to get a broad understanding of a topic, and then interview a few of your respondents (usually those who have volunteered through the survey) to get a more in-depth understanding of the topic. Or you may analyze a primary document then ask others their opinion about the same artifact.

You may also be asked to utilize secondary research. In fact, you may conduct secondary research first in order to better understand your topic before you start surveying or interviewing subject/participants. Secondary research relies on secondary resources, which are those with the interpretations, analyses, and opinions of others. These kinds of sources often provide historical context, summaries of other sources, and critical perspectives. They may be found in a variety of places, including books, journal and magazine articles, blog posts, and newspapers. Reference texts such as encyclopedias, including online versions like Wikipedia, are usually secondary sources as they collect and organize other reported research (often synthesizing primary research reports).

Both types of research are valid and important for the research process and both have their place in writing and researching across the curriculum. It is important to know what kind of research is being asked of you with any given assignment. It's also important to know what kind of research is valued in the discipline or major you're working within. If your assignment asks you to conduct "original" research, then you need to pursue a primary research methodology, but remember you will probably need to consult secondary sources when you develop your research plan and design your surveys or interview questions, and even when you interpret your results.

LIBRARY RESEARCH

In this age of smartphones and tablet computers, most of us to turn to our favorite Internet search engine any time we have a question. If we don't know something, we "google" it. This approach is useful for the small facts we want to know or verify on a daily basis; however, larger projects, especially those for class or work, require more. Going to the library first makes sense because working with your library is like fishing in a stocked pond; you're much more likely to get useful, appropriate results. One reason is that your library probably subscribes to numerous electronic databases on a variety of subjects, which means you can go to the library through the Internet (this is especially important for distance education and online courses or students). In these databases, information has already been verified, sorted, and tagged. You can then search for items using key words and subject terms (more on this later). And with many of these databases you can download PDF versions of the resources you want.

Of course, some items may only be available in your library; knowing where to find this information before you go will make your physical trip to the library more successful. Use your library's catalog to search for books, journals, and general reference works you may want to consult; the catalog information should include the call number, which will help you locate the materials within the library. Consult a map of the library or a reference librarian if you are unsure of how materials and call numbers are arranged on your campus. Some materials are still electronic but must be used within the library. For example, a library might offer a subscription to a great database of grant funders, but the database can only be searched from within the library on one of their hardwired computers.

Libraries offer a wide range of materials and services designed to make research easier and more successful for you, so learn what your library has to offer then take advantage of these services.

SPECIALIZED INDEXES AND DATABASES

As mentioned previously, libraries often subscribe to a wide range of electronic databases. General databases such as Academic OneFile, Project Muse, JSTOR, and LexisNexis index and store a range of sources including newspapers, magazines, journals, broadcast transcripts, photos, maps, and even blogs and book chapters. Other databases may be specific to different disciplines or research areas such as ERIC in education or the Web of Science in the sciences. The library also has electronic and print indexes for older materials. Sometimes these have to be located in hard copy or they may have been entered into a database as well. Early English Books is one such index, as is America's Historical Newspapers. These indexes can help you locate both primary and secondary resources.

Box 4.1

Boolean Logic and Electronic Databases

- Most online search engines rely on Boolean logic, including electronic databases and indexes. Boolean logic uses the terms AND (+), OR, NOT (−) to indicate relationships between desired information. Quotation marks are also used to show how terms fit together.

- Bridges AND Suspension: this search will give you sources that pertain to both bridges and suspension, but there are multiple types of bridges and multiple types of suspension.

  NOTE: Many search engines assume AND if you input two terms together.

- "Suspension Bridges": this search will give you sources that have these two terms together, so you aren't likely to get items about in-school suspension

- "Suspension Bridges" OR "Cable-Stayed Bridge": this search will give you sources on both of these types of bridges

- "Suspension Bridges" NOT "Golden Gate": this search will give you sources about suspension bridges but will leave out the Golden Gate Bridge.

- You can also look for the Advanced Search feature of the program you are using. It will explain how to narrow your search in that particular database and will often give you a fill-in-the-blank form to help you search.

GOVERNMENT DOCUMENTS

One set of resources often overlooked is government documents—both online and in federal depository libraries. The U.S. government makes available information from all of its various organizations including census data, statistics about agriculture, the weather, crime, the military, science, and technology, to name a few. Official depositories have copies of government issued pamphlets, books, guides, and other print and video materials. You can access many of these resources through portals at your local library. You can also find many of them online.

 Official government Web sites end with .gov (census.gov or fbi.gov, for example).

INTERLIBRARY LOAN

Most school libraries are part of a wide network of academic libraries that operate an interlibrary loan system. Through this system, you can request a book or document your library does not actually own. Your library borrows the book from another library and checks it out to you. This is a great way to expand the possibilities of your research, but it does require some advance planning. In addition, because these books are on loan, they often have a shorter checkout time and are not eligible for renewal. Make sure you know your library's policies.

ONLINE RESEARCH

Your school library is a great place to start your research, but as you probably noted above, sometimes this research will take you straight to the Web. And, yes, the Web is also a good place to do research—if you know how to look and how to evaluate what you find. One key to effective online research is to be as narrow and specific as possible so you do not find yourself sidetracked by information that may be interesting but not useful for your present project. You should also understand how search engines like Google or Yahoo work. The fact that a source pops up on the first page of results does not mean it's the best source; this just means it had the most key words or tags in common with your search. Often tags are wrong or misleading. You may want to use advanced search features that will enable you to look for certain types of sources such as those ending in .gov or .org or those that have been updated in the last six months. See Box 4.1 for more information about conducting effective online searches.

Did you know?

Anyone can visit a federal depository library. There are more than 1,200 locations throughout the United States and access is free. These libraries are staffed by knowledgeable reference librarians who are there to help you locate and access these free materials. You can find the federal depository library in your area by consulting their online directory.

There are also a number of archives online that may be useful to your research. Some of these are operated by libraries, museums, professors, and interested collectors. They may also be operated by related businesses or organizations. It is important to look at who set up the archive, what its stated purpose is, how often it is updated or maintained, and how reliable its materials are (see the CARS checklist on the next page).

You may also find blogs and wikis that are related to your topic; again, it is important to look at who created this material and why. You may find it easier to get to useful blogs if you go through a portal where the material has already been vetted or organized, such as scienceblogs. com or academicblogs.org.

EVALUATING SOURCES

When faced with such a wealth of materials, how do you decide what you can use and what you shouldn't? One step is to look at your assignment. Were you asked to use essays from peer-reviewed journals, magazine articles, primary documents such as newspaper clippings or television advertisements? Were you asked to use readings from class or to use materials found outside of class? Another step is to evaluate what you have found and compare it with other materials. Your findings should triangulate, or verify each other, not contradict each other on the basic facts (although, they may have different opinions and interpretations of primary source material).

CARS is a mnemonic device for remembering how to check the validity of materials, and it is especially useful for Web sites. It represents a set of questions that will help you eliminate sources that are biased, inaccurate, or not authoritative.

- ❏ **Credibility:** Is the information from a source you can trust? What are the author's credentials or qualifications? Is there evidence of quality control and/or fair reporting? Are multiple points of view represented? Is the author a known or respected authority in this area? Is there organizational support for this work? Can the author be contacted through this Web site?

- ❏ **Accuracy:** Is the information up to date, factual, detailed, exact, and comprehensive? Do the links work? Are there obvious grammatical or spelling errors?

- ❏ **Reasonableness:** Is the account fair, balanced, objective, and reasoned? Are there any conflicts of interest? In particular, follow the money trail: is someone trying to sell a product or service connected to this information? Is the source free of fallacies or slanted tone? Who is the site's intended audience?

- ❏ **Support:** Are supporting sources listed? Is there contact information or a way to ask questions? Is corroboration or a bibliography available? Are all claims supported and is documentation supplied?

As you review your resources, whether you are reading, watching, listening, or some combination of these, take detailed notes, being sure to include bibliographic information (see Chapter 12, Documentation, for more information on this topic). This includes the notes you may take while conducting your primary research. As you read and take notes, think about the most useful way to organize your thoughts, annotations, and quotes, using some system that works for you and your writing process and project: chronological order, points in your argument, or sources. Organized notes will make your writing easier (not easy, just easier).

Did you know?

Journals	versus	Magazines
Contain original research		Contain secondhand accounts
Are written by researchers and experts in the field		Are usually written by reporters who are not experts in the field
Have references cited at the end of articles (i.e., Works Cited or References)		Usually do not have references cited at end of article
Usually do not have glossy pages and photographs; appearance is not the goal		Are designed to look good with glossy paper, numerous photos or images
Are supported through subscriptions and organization affiliations, including universities		Are supported through advertisements
Are often refereed or undergo a process of peer review before being published		Limit the review process to the editorial staff

You may consider one of the many online programs designed to help with note taking and organizing. Zotero, for example, is a free application that allows you to build a library of your saved research materials. Endnote is a program you can buy that helps you collect materials, work collaboratively with group members, and create documents for sharing. Similarly, Scrivener bills itself as a project management tool that allows you to plan, collect materials, build storyboards, and write. All of these programs have features that help you create Works Cited and/or Reference pages in various documentation systems. See Box 3.1 in Chapter 3 for a more comprehensive list of software programs designed to help with note taking and annotating.

If you are conducting primary research, you will have additional note-taking needs for recording experiments, interview questions and responses, observations, and other first-hand data. You may want to use a log or double-entry notebook as described in Writing in the Sciences, Chapter 10. You may also want to use audio and video recording devices, once you have obtained permission from your project leader and your participants. No matter what kinds of notes you are taking, it is important to always record the date and time and to distinguish between your own thoughts or observations and exact quotes that are a part of your research, including the resources you read.

 Be sure to follow your instructor's guidelines for recording and turning in notes (whether on cards, papers, or electronic files), as well as the documentation style necessary for the class, assignment, or discipline in which you are working.

DISCIPLINARY DOCUMENTATION STYLES

Any time you complete research, you need to document the sources you used, whether they are the people you talked to, the location you observed, the books you read, or the Web sites you studied. However, the style used to document these sources and refer to them within your text will vary, depending on the discipline or subject matter. At times it will also depend on your instructor or the journal editors. It is important to learn which documentation system or systems are used in your field and then acquaint yourself with how the style system works. In **Chapter 12**, you'll find examples of various systems. Within the content chapters, you'll also find references to the common systems used in each field.

Most systems have two parts, parenthetical citation and the Works Cited or Reference page. Both parts are needed in order to avoid plagiarism and properly document your sources. The goal is to give your readers enough information to find your writing and arguments credible and to be able to find these resources if they want to read more or follow up on your work.

1. A parenthetical citation is located within the actual text, usually in parentheses right after a direct quote. With some systems, such as MLA, a parenthetical citation is also used after summaries and paraphrases. The parenthetical citation usually gives the author's last

name and the page number for the quote. It may also give publication year and other information required by the style guide.

MLA: The Golden Gate Bridge is "unquestionably an American icon" (McDonald and Nadel 7).

APA: The idea that "complexity is a constant in biology" is not an innovative one (Sole & Goodwin, 1997, p. 63).

2. The Works Cited or References page is located at the end of the text and is an alphabetical listing of *all* of the sources used in a given essay or piece of writing. The exact arrangement of each entry is dictated by the style guide for each individual system (or by the journal).

Avoiding Plagiarism

Throughout the research and writing process it is important to avoid plagiarism. Plagiarism is often defined as the intentional or unintentional use of another's words, ideas, or structures in your own work without crediting the original source. Plagiarism can have far-reaching effects, including legal action and being expelled from school. In addition, when you plagiarize, you are not learning what you came to school to learn.

Box 4.2

Tips for Avoiding Plagiarism

- *Know what plagiarism is.*
  Although definitions of plagiarism vary slightly, they all usually contain the same basic ideas. Plagiarism occurs when a student presents another's words or ideas as his or her own, using them in some parts of the paper or for the entire paper—it may be intentional or it may not be. Recently, the most common types of plagiarism occur from Internet use: Either the student cuts and pastes from one or more documents/Web sites, or the student purchases the entire paper from a Web site that sells documents.

  Although the Internet has become the most common source of plagiarism, plagiarism can also occur when a student incorrectly uses print sources in part or in their entirety. Additionally, a student who copies a paper topic, point, or wording from a peer, a parent, or some other source is generally subject to the same consequences as a student who plagiarizes from an Internet or print source. Be sure to check your school's rules about what constitutes plagiarism. You might be surprised at how some actions—such as turning the same paper in for two different assignments in two different classes—can also be considered plagiarism.

- *Plan ahead and give yourself time to write the paper.*
  Plagiarism often occurs when students run out of time and become desperate just to have something to turn in.

- *Properly document your sources.*
  If you are unclear about citing sources, use an electronic program, consult your instructor, your textbook, your school writing center, or a librarian at the reference desk. If you do not ensure that your source material is documented correctly, you have *intentionally* plagiarized. Also, remember that these rules apply to all source materials, including images, maps, factographs, videos, and audio recordings. All of these sources must be documented.

- *Take careful notes as you research.*
  - ◆ Save the PDF files you use in a folder on your computer or in the cloud. You can also make photocopies of your sources. Always write down all of the bibliographic information, including the URL, database, or index, as well as the date of access if researching online.
  - ◆ If you take notes instead of making photocopies, write down the information in direct quotes and give the necessary information, such as page numbers, as well as the bibliographic information.
  - ◆ Save paraphrasing and summarizing for the actual writing process. Do not paraphrase or summarize in the note-taking stage of research, or you may inadvertently plagiarize later on. If you absolutely must summarize, make sure you note this and don't mix direct quotes with summaries in your notes.
- *Learn how to paraphrase correctly.*
  Write as if you are explaining the material to someone else using your own words and sentence structures. Be careful, however, not to misrepresent or distort the author's meaning. Your own opinion does not belong in the paraphrase. Also, a paraphrase should be approximately the same length as the original.

Example of Paraphrasing

Original Quote:
Irving Morrow was responsible for the iconic features and architectural enhancements which define the Golden Gate Bridge's Art Deco form. These are admired the world over and contribute to people's view of the bridge as a sculpture ("Art Deco Style" online).

Paraphrase:
Irving Morrow turned the Golden Gate Bridge into a well-known sculpture by incorporating Art Deco style and features into the bridge's design and decoration ("Art Deco Style" online).

- *Like a paraphrase, a summary puts the original passage into your own words and sentence structure without changing the meaning.*
  Since a summary shortens the original passage and focuses on its main points, partial quotes may be used along with your own words to highlight the most important information.

Example of Summarizing

Original Quote:
The era of reckless daredevilry among "bridgemen" came to an end with the construction of the Golden Gate Bridge, as Chief Engineer Joseph Strauss insisted on a rigid safety code, supported by the latest safety innovations. Despite the high winds, churning currents, and towering heights that challenged the work, Strauss was determined to buck the industry's deadly average of one fatality per million dollars spent on a construction project. ("Cheating Death: Worker Safety During Construction" online)

Summary without Quotes:
Joseph Strauss, Chief Engineer for the construction of the Golden Gate Bridge, maintained a strict set of safety codes and lowered fatality averages during construction despite the dangerous conditions. ("'Cheating Death': Worker Safety During Construction" online)

Summary with Partial Quote:
Joseph Strauss, Chief Engineer for the construction of the Golden Gate Bridge, "insisted on

a rigid safety code" to "buck the industry's deadly [fatality] average" despite the dangerous conditions. ("Cheating Death: Worker Safety During Construction" online)

■ *Use your resources.*
Take your work to your school's writing center. Set up a meeting with your instructor during office hours. Talk to your reference librarian. Ask for help if you are unsure or need help at any stage of the researching and writing process. This type of assignment is given as a learning experience, so speak up and advance your own skills. Also, if your instructor offers peer review workshops, make sure you go prepared and then listen to the advice of your peers; you can't judge what is useful and what is not until you have heard what they have to say.

PUTTING IT ALL TOGETHER: EVIDENCE-BASED WRITING

A common phrase you may hear from instructors or see on assignment sheets is *evidence-based writing*; others may call it *thesis-driven writing*. Evidence-based writing is what this whole chapter has been about. You use the facts, data, and evidence you collect through your research to support your thesis or your argument. Whether it's something you read in a reliable source, information you gathered from surveys or interviews, or evidence you recorded through experiments in the lab or the field, you pull this information together to note patterns or similarities, argue for causes and effects, explain differences, or illustrate how something works. The evidence is used to support your conclusion and to show your reader that your argument is logical and valid.

Previously in this chapter, you read about ways to use source materials—from both primary and secondary sources—using direct quotes, partial quotes, summaries, and paraphrases. You can also integrate facts, figures, and statistics into the body of the text or use charts, graphs, and other figures (the type of visual used depends on your data and your purposes, as well as accepted methods in your discipline). However, as you write in various courses, it is important to learn what is accepted evidence in each discipline and for a given genre. Look at what kinds of evidence are used in the model papers you read for class, in your textbook, even in your professors' lectures. Also pay attention to what kinds of evidence or support are asked for in a given assignment and what is acceptable with regard to primary versus secondary sources and what is acceptable. In some fields, secondary source material is used to back up or help explain primary data. In other fields, primary data may be used to illustrate a point you are explaining or arguing against from a secondary source.

It is important to remember, however, that your writing should reflect your thinking, your conclusion, *your argument*. An evidence-based paper is not a string of quotes from other sources. It is your argument with the judicious use of evidence gathered in your research to illustrate and support what *you* are saying. The writing you do for class, for your job, or for your community is one way you have to show what you have learned and what you are thinking. It is a method for contributing to the overall conversation in a particular field or area and for answering the questions that started your research.

A RESEARCH CASE STUDY

You have been asked to create a handout that can be used in a high school biology class. First, you'll need to consider the various topics covered in high school biology, which may lead you to look at area textbooks or talk with a couple of local biology teachers to see what they think is important or what their students have difficulty with. You may even decide to interview high school students to see what they want help with. This information might lead you to write about Mendel's rules of heredity. You may even want to narrow your topic still further by showing students how to complete Punnett squares.

Figure 4.1
Punnett Square

	B	b
B	BB	Bb
b	Bb	bb

Your assignment may ask you to rely on secondary sources. At this point, you'll want to look at a number of different sources that explain how Punnett squares work, what their purpose is, how they are used, and why students should learn how to do them. You can then synthesize this information to create your own explanation of the purpose and process of Punnett squares. You may design a handout or brochure that explains the information. If you have the freedom, you may decide that your audience of high school students would be better served by a video that demonstrates how the squares are completed and used or by an interactive website that allows them to complete their own Punnett squares.

Perhaps, you need to (or have the freedom to) complete primary research for this project. You might design a test or survey that can show what kinds of problems students encounter when they try to complete Punnett Squares. Or you might interview a group of students and have them explain the problems they are having with the concept. You can then use the data, along with the information you have gathered from secondary resources, to design a resource that will help with the problem area(s) you have discovered through your primary research. Again, both types of research are accurate and valid, but the two different approaches will most likely lead you to design two different projects.

READ MORE ABOUT IT

Ballenger, Bruce. *The Curious Researcher*, 7th ed. New York: Longman, 2011. Print.

Booth, Wayne, Gregory G. Columb, and Joseph M. Williams. *The Craft of Research*, 3rd ed. Chicago: U Chicago P, 2008. Print.

Gibaldi, Joseph. *MLA Handbook for Writers of Research Papers*. 7th ed. New York: Modern Language Association, 2009. Print.

Publication Manual of the American Psychological Association. 6th ed. Washington, D.C.: APA, 2009. Print.

University of Chicago Press. *Chicago Manual of Style*. 16th ed. Chicago: U of Chicago P, 2010. Print

Wilson, Shawn. *Research is Ceremony: Indigenous Research Methods*. Winnipeg: Fernwood Publishing, 2009. Print.

chapter 5

Writing in Arts and Humanities

ARCHITECTURE, ART, ENGLISH, FILM, HISTORY,
MUSIC, PHILOSOPHY, THEATER, AND THEOLOGY

*Good composition is like a suspension bridge—each line adds strength
and takes none away.*

—*Robert Henri*

PURPOSES OF WRITING IN THE ARTS AND HUMANITIES

Arts and *humanities* are general terms representing a variety of academic disciplines that focus on questions that have preoccupied us as humans since the dawn of thought. Even without absolute answers, these questions may concern us on a daily basis: What is love? How is love depicted? Is there a higher being? Why are there hate and pain in this world? Is there a place in the world for everyone? Writers in the arts and humanities pose and try to answer such questions of human existence, and the answers are not like the definitive ones that might occur in other disciplines such as the sciences or business.

Four general types of writing are used in the arts and humanities: creative, theoretical, interpretive, and analytical. Those who do creative writing place their focus on narrative and character development for fictional works, such as novels (*Bridge to Terabithia*), plays (*A View from the Bridge*), poetry ("The Bridge Builder"), and short stories ("An Occurrence at Owl Bridge"). Those who do theoretical writing attempt to create generalized and abstract overarching views of how or why something is true, such as Milton literary scholar Robert Bridges's prosodic analysis of Milton's *Paradise Lost* and other works, which helped him create a theory about Milton's work. Those who do interpretive writing try to discover meaning in a text or in the process of reading a text, such as a student who writes about how the erratic time sequencing in "An Occurrence at Owl Creek Bridge" creates a special meaning of its own. And those who do analytical writing examine the components or form of the text by breaking it down into its parts, such as an architect describing how the octagonal bridge over London's Grand Union Canal works.

©wikimediacommons.org

The Rolling Bridge by Thomas Heatherwick

Interpretive writing and analytical writing overlap in many ways since both interpretive and analytical writers are interested in examining texts for patterns, looking at how language is used, and searching for clues that are in the text as well as clues that are missing in the text.

As a writer in the arts and humanities, you may be asked to do any of these types of writing; however, the majority of the writing done in the humanities is motivated by interpreting and analyzing texts. In most writing situations, you will be asked to closely and critically read whatever text you are studying and then draw your own conclusions based on your interpretations. The arts and humanities text you will be studying may be oral, visual, or written. It may be a piece of music or a poem, a film or a painting, a play or a novel. It may be an architectural artifact, such as a bridge, or a theological event, such as a sermon.

When you write about the arts or humanities, you may be writing for many different types of courses within this discipline. This chapter is designed to help you meet your writing goal as you consider the purpose behind your communication and what conventions of the field are expected as you investigate the text or artifact under consideration. In addition, this chapter offers guidelines that you can transfer to any writing you do after you graduate. Remember, most employers today are looking for new hires who can communicate effectively through oral and written language. Knowing the conventions of your field can help you secure employment, as well as help you showcase your communication skills throughout your career.

TYPES OF WRITING ASSIGNMENTS IN THE ARTS AND HUMANITIES

A word after a word after a word is power.

—*Margaret Atwood*

In the arts and humanities, choosing the appropriate form or format is often the first step in beginning your writing. Since various types of writing assignments exist, learning those that are appropriate for the fields within the arts and humanities discipline is essential. This section

Did you know?

Genre knowledge = A knowledge not only of a genre's formal features but also of what and whose purposes the genre serves, how to negotiate one's intentions in relation to the genre's social expectations and motives, what reader/writer relationships the genre maintains, and how the genre relates to other genres in the coordination of social life.

—Melanie Kill, in *Genre: An Introduction to History, Theory, Research, and Pedagogy*

includes some common genres of writing assignments you may be asked to use in an arts and humanities course and some additional types of writing genres that you may be asked to create in a job related to the arts and humanities. First, though, review Table 5.1, which highlights some common writing activities and genres for a variety of fields within the discipline of arts and humanities.

TABLE 5.1

Common Writing Genres in Arts and Humanities Fields	Art	Architecture	English	Film	History	Music	Philosophy	Theater	Theology
Class notes	√	√	√	√	√	√	√	√	√
Journals	√	√	√	√		√	√	√	√
Peer reviews or responses	√	√	√	√		√		√	
Summaries			√		√		√		√
Book reviews			√		√		√		√
Writing-to-Learn invention exercises			√						
Sketchbook	√	√							
Exhibition design	√								
Statement of directorial concept						√		√	
Fiction			√						
Poetry			√					√	
Plays			√					√	
Proposals	√	√	√	√		√		√	
Editorials			√						

	Art	Architecture	English	Film	History	Music	Philosophy	Theater	Theology
Oral presentations	√	√	√	√	√	√	√	√	√
PowerPoint, Prezi, or other digital presentations	√	√	√	√	√	√	√	√	√
Professional reports	√	√		√		√		√	
Response/ Reflection essays	√	√	√	√		√	√	√	√
Review or critique	√	√	√	√		√		√	√
Descriptive essays	√	√	√			√	√	√	√
Narrative essays			√	√			√		√
Comparative essays	√	√	√	√	√	√	√	√	√
Interpretative essays	√	√	√	√		√		√	√
Analysis essays	√	√	√	√	√	√	√	√	√
Argumentative essays	√	√	√	√	√	√	√	√	√
Visual essays	√	√	√	√	√			√	
Primary source analysis	√	√	√	√	√	√	√	√	√
Research notes			√		√		√		√
Literature reviews			√		√		√		√
Annotated bibliographies			√		√		√		√
Research papers	√	√	√	√	√	√	√	√	√
Essay exams	√	√	√	√	√	√	√	√	√
websites			√						
Conference presentations			√		√		√		√

Below we discuss some of the most common writing assignments and genres for the arts and humanities. This is not an exhaustive list, and your instructor or employer might ask you to write in a genre that is not given here. If so, use that form or genre, and read the section in this chapter on Writing Effectively in the Arts and Humanities on page 98.

REVIEW OR CRITIQUE

A review or critique briefly describes a text and explains its merits for readers so they can decide whether they want to experience the text for themselves. Remember that a text can be written, visual, or oral—this means that this genre can be useful in most subfields of the arts and humanities. As a student in an art or architecture course, you might critique a painting or a building; in a history or philosophy course, you might review a book in the subject area of a research paper; in a film or theater course, you might review a movie or a play that you have seen for class, and so on. In presenting your review or critique, be sure to go beyond the first impression you take from reading, viewing, or listening to the text. In your review, you will discuss a few key points about the text, rather than describe everything that the author or artist created. No matter the academic field, you should always include these three pieces of information: (a) identify the text and its creator, (b) include a brief summary of the text, and (c) include your evaluation. Depending on the assignment or your field, the review or critique might also expand to include some or all of the following parts:

- ❏ An informative title that identifies the title of the text or work and its creator
- ❏ A summary of essential content and main ideas
- ❏ A description of the creator's theme, purpose, and methods of development
- ❏ A brief biography of the creator, including information about other texts or works
- ❏ A description of how the text or work relates to other texts or works in the field
- ❏ Your evaluation of the text or work, with evidence supporting your opinions
- ❏ Short quotations or visuals from the text or work that represent the theme of the piece and the creator's style and tone

Most reviews or critiques are shorter than essays, around one to two pages. Some instructors might ask you to write a review or critique essay, in which case you will want to look at both this section and the section on writing essays in this chapter.

ORAL PRESENTATION FOR CLASS OR A CONFERENCE

Most fields in the arts and humanities will require you to give an oral presentation at some point. If you have never given an oral presentation before, you might be quite anxious. To alleviate any anxiety, prepare for your presentation effectively by clearly identifying the content you want to present, organizing it into a well-defined outline, and creating a handout for your audience (if the assignment, your instructor, or your employer permits). Your first step in the process of developing the oral presentation is to recognize and organize the content you want to present. Here are some questions that will help as you think about the preparation and content of your talk.

- ❑ How much time do I have for my talk, and how much information will fit within my time limit?

- ❑ What types of supporting materials can I use? This might be restricted by the assignment or your instructor.

- ❑ What types of technology and software are available for me to use?

- ❑ What is the thesis, main idea, or main argument of my presentation?

- ❑ What are the key points related to my thesis, main idea, or main argument?

- ❑ How can I limit my focus to only three or four key points to help my audience process all the information?

- ❑ What examples (oral, written, or visual) will I use to support the key points? How will I present these examples?

- ❑ What examples will be the most relevant for my particular audience?

- ❑ What strategies will I use to help the audience follow my presentation?

TIP **Use signposts within your presentation to guide the reader through key points, supporting ideas, and different segments. Common signposts include the following:**

- ■ **Using numbers, such as *First*, *The first point*, *My third example*, and so on**

- ■ **Using parallel structures, such as *My first quotation comes from*, *My second quotation comes from*, and later in the talk, *My last quotation comes from***

- ■ **Using strict chronological order when presenting information, such as giving supporting evidence that is organized from oldest to newest or vice versa**

- ■ **Using organizational words—such as *In conclusion*—to remind your audience where you are in your presentation**

After clarifying the content you will cover in your presentation, you will want to carefully organize the material. Here are some hints to assist you in preparing the introduction, body, and conclusion of your oral presentation.

Introduction

- ❑ Begin with an attention getter, such as an interesting quotation or statistic.
- ❑ State the focused topic or intention of your presentation (e.g., *I will be discussing two philosophical movements today*).

❑ Provide an outline or plan of what you will discuss (e.g., *I will be comparing these two movements by focusing on three elements: X, Y, and Z*).

❑ Pass on any significant background information that might be needed to process the material you will be discussing.

Body

❑ Present the information, following the outline or plan you presented in the introduction.

❑ Include just enough evidence to clearly support your points and not overburden your audience.

❑ Use signposts that help your audience process the information you present.

Conclusion

❑ Announce clearly to your audience that you are beginning your conclusion (e.g., *In conclusion, . . .*).

❑ Restate the main points very briefly.

❑ State the importance of the information you have presented.

❑ Ask your audience to imagine themselves taking action, or invite them to ask you questions or share their ideas.

Finally, you will need to decide whether you will memorize your talk, read your material from a script, or use an outline to help you deliver your information. If you are preparing an oral presentation for a class, read the assignment thoroughly to see if you do indeed, have a choice or if your instructor requires only one of these options. If you are presenting at a conference, make sure you understand the conventions of your field. For example, if you present on a literary topic either in English or foreign language studies at the annual Modern Language Association conference, you most likely will be expected to read from a script. However, if you present at the same conference on a linguistics or composition topic, you most likely will be expected to have a helpful handout and a presentation using technology, such as PowerPoint slides or a Prezi demonstration.

All three types of oral presentation methods can be effective, but each has its pros and cons, so if you have a choice, it is up to you to decide which one feels the most comfortable for you. Memorizing your talk can make it seem that you are an expert in your field, but it can also be uncomfortable if you experience anxiety or forget your material. Reading from a previously written script will ensure that you do not forget to discuss all the points you planned on, but it might also prevent you from interacting effectively with your audience since your eyes will be down when you read. Using an outline to guide your talk showcases your expertise and allows you to make eye contact with your audience, but it also requires you to memorize a great deal of the material. Whichever delivery method you choose, be sure to practice your presentation multiple times, by yourself and in front of a practice audience, so you will be more fully in control of the timing and delivery of your material.

DIGITAL PRESENTATION

Oral presentations can often be more effective and interesting if you use technology to support the delivery of your information. If you are giving an oral presentation for a class, check the assignment to see whether you can use technology within your presentation. Some instructors may even assign a digital presentation on its own, rather than an oral presentation, especially if they are preparing you to share information with peers at conferences or workshops. Two of the more common digital visual aids in the arts and humanities are PowerPoint and Prezi.

PowerPoint

Using Microsoft PowerPoint is an easy and helpful way to add a professional touch to a presentation. PowerPoint provides a variety of templates that can be used to quickly format your presentation, or you can design your own templates or slides. Figure 5.1 presents a typical PowerPoint slide. If you choose to use PowerPoint, use it wisely by following some of these important guidelines:

Learn how to compose slides effectively
- ❏ Keep the design basic so it does not distract from the content.
- ❏ Create a slide template that allows room for visuals or website addresses.
- ❏ Choose an easy-to-read font size and type.
- ❏ Decorate slides in a professional manner.
- ❏ Decide that content is always the primary concern. Do not let the design restrict or distract from your message.

Be consistent
- ❏ Use the same font type on all slides.
- ❏ Use the same font size for headings/subheadings/examples.
- ❏ Use no more than five or six colors for the entire presentation.
- ❏ Create a frame for images, and use this frame throughout the presentation.
- ❏ Choose a way of highlighting important information (such as bolding, underlining, changing font color), and do it the same way throughout the presentation.

Figure 5.1 Sample PowerPoint Slide

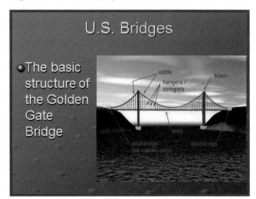

Add text
- ❏ Use key words only. Do not use full sentences.
- ❏ Use the text as an outline or supplement to your oral presentation. Do not read from your slides.
- ❏ Balance text with images, and do not overwhelm the slide.

Add images

❏ Use images to help your audience visualize the material. Do not decorate with them.

❏ Create your own images, rather than overusing stock or comedic clip art.

❏ Balance images with text, and do not overwhelm the slide.

Consider your audience

❏ Use text and images that fit their expertise and expectations.

❏ Highlight the material you are introducing to them.

❏ Use font types and sizes that will be viewable by all in the audience.

❏ Provide a handout of printed slides and enough room for the audience to take notes.

❏ Avoid "Death by PowerPoint"—be sure that what you choose to present is of interest to your audience.

Practice your presentation

❏ Use a timer so your talk will fit within the required time limit.

❏ Know the technology you will be using, and try it out in the room in which you will be presenting.

❏ Use the PowerPoint presentation as an outline to help present your ideas smoothly.

❏ Maintain eye contact with the audience.

❏ Speak naturally—not too quickly or slowly.

Prezi

Prezi (http://prezi.com) is online presentation software. Like PowerPoint, it allows you to present information digitally to an audience by using template designs. However, by using Prezi, you can also highlight information more by using its nonlinear presentation functions that allow you to zoom in and out, embed multimedia elements, and graphically organize your material. Prezi is available online for free if you want to use only its basic functions. Be sure to check out the upgraded version if you want to have even more options. By using the same basic guidelines as given above for PowerPoint presentations, especially those related to design and audience, you can create an informative and interesting presentation. For a sample Prezi presentation, that covers how to create an effective Prezi presentation, visit http://prezi.com/c9pdlrpx3pr6/copy-of-presentation-on-presentations. A sample Prezi slide is shown in Figure 5.2.

Figure 5.2 Sample Prezi

ESSAY OR RESEARCH PAPER

A variety of long-form genres are used across the fields of arts and humanities. You might be assigned a critical analysis essay in a music, art, or theater course in which you must choose an element or some elements to analyze and discuss. In a history course, you might be assigned a comparative essay, in which you are asked to compare two events or two time periods. Or you might be asked in a film or English course to write a response essay, in which you use a film to trigger personal memories that you then relate. Whatever essay type or genre you are asked to write, the basic structure includes an introduction, body, and conclusion with the presentation of an explicit or implied thesis in the introduction. In a personal essay, your thesis can be informational or argumentative; in this type of essay, your own personal experience is given as support throughout the essay. In an essay that requires you to engage with a primary source or text, such as a song or a short story, your thesis can be informational or argumentative, depending on what essay genre you are writing. In this type of essay, you can use your own experience, ideas from the primary source, or quotations from the primary source as support for your thesis. For an essay that requires you to form your thesis or argument and use evidence as support, you use primary or secondary sources within the body of your essay to support the thesis with evidence, take at least a small part of the essay body to engage with some counter-evidence, and then conclude the essay. See the section on Writing Effectively in the Arts and Humanities (page 103) for more details on how to write different types of essays and what types of evidence you might want to use in your essay.

Personal essay genres, as described above, most likely include only your own thoughts or opinions. Generally, these types of essays are shorter because the support you include comes from your own experiences, rather than from sources outside yourself. Although we can describe some essay genres as personal, these same genres can also be used with primary or secondary sources. Table 5.2 illustrates how some essay genres can be used with personal experience alone or in combination with primary or secondary sources. Since many

Did you know?

Case-study research suggests that university students read much more than they are assigned to write. But when novice writers are confronted with a large—and alien—body of material on new topics, especially library research, they often postpone writing their assignment until they have finished the reading. In contrast, professionals start to formulate what they want to say while they are gathering their material, the fundamental expert move that, again and again, students across the disciplines neglect. Often, then, students end up transporting chunks of material from sources to their papers, creating "the book report" genre Vivian Allen described that lacks an evaluative point of view.

—Mary Soliday, in *Everyday Genres: Writing Assignments Across the Disciplines* fields of study exist within the arts and humanities, it is best to consult with your instructor about any essay genre that is assigned.

TABLE 5.2

How Essay Genres Can Be Used			
	Personal experience	Primary source	Secondary source
Descriptive essay	√	√	
Narrative essay	√		
Reflection/Response essay	√	√	
Review or Critique essay	√	√	√
Summary essay		√	√
Comparison/Contrast essay	√	√	√
Interpretive essay	√	√	√
Analysis essay	√	√	√
Argumentative essay	√	√	√
Visual essay	√	√	√
Research paper (informative or argumentative)		√	√

The research paper is a longer form of the essay, and it requires a much longer and in-depth research process, along with a sophisticated and critical level of inquiry. As part of the research paper process, you locate and use secondary sources, such as peer-reviewed articles, in order to assess and support your own thesis or argument. Research papers can be informational, such as a 15-page paper in a philosophy course, in which you present the life and theories of a particular philosopher. Research papers can also be argumentative, such as a 10-page paper in a different philosophy course, in which you make an argument that the film *The Bridge* is an inaccurate representation of the philosophical trolley problem. The format of the research paper parallels that of an academic essay. Thus the format described below represents both short essays and longer research papers. For more information on using primary and secondary sources for essays and research papers, see the section later in this chapter entitled Know the Kinds of Evidence Used in the Arts and Humanities. Additionally, you can review what the research process entails by reading Chapter 4.

Basic structure of an essay or research paper in the arts and humanities

Introduction

❑ Use an attention getter or hook, such as a quotation or a startling statistic to engage the reader immediately.

❑ Appeal to the reader's *ethos* (emotional side) or *logos* (logical side).

❑ Provide a frame or context for your topic by narrowing it down to a specific point by the end of the introduction.

❑ (Optional) Provide a question that relates to the specific topic of your essay, setting up the answer to this question as the thesis of the essay.

❑ Provide a thesis or argument (this can be written or implied).

Body

❑ Provide evidence that supports your thesis or argument.

❑ If there might be an opposing view to your argument or thesis, present it here, but also include some evidence against the opposing argument.

Conclusion

❑ Give the essay a sense of completeness by doing the following:

» Stressing the importance of the thesis

» Answering the question, "So what?"

» Showing how the points and evidence you have presented strongly support the thesis

» Echoing the introduction and reminding readers that you have brought them full circle

» Giving the reader something to remember

» Inviting the reader to apply something from the essay to herself or her own life

» Raising a question that the reader can think about after he finishes your essay

» Asking the reader to use the information from your essay and make a prediction for the future

LITERATURE REVIEW

The literature review paper is used to show the reader that you have read and understand the major published works (also known as the *literature*) within a particular field or about a particular question. Some instructors give a literature review as a stand-alone assignment, but it is often assigned in conjunction with a longer work, such as a research paper or thesis. What we provide here is appropriate for many fields within the arts and humanities, but be sure to consult the assignment and your instructor about which specific format to use and which types of sources are acceptable.

Before you begin to gather sources to review, be sure to have a specific topic that you are researching or a clear argument for which you are gathering sources. Treat the literature review as a formal assignment and use a clear and academic voice and tone. Here are some hints to follow as you collect sources and prepare to create the literature review:

- ❏ Focus your research by narrowing your topic and creating an in-progress thesis. The thesis may change as you do your research and read your sources, but having one at the start of the literature review will help you collect only relevant sources.

- ❏ Read your sources critically, keeping careful and complete notes on the important information you want to include in the literature review. Be sure to use a system that allows you to mark summaries, paraphrases, and quotations you want to use.

- ❏ Choose effective sources that will fit both the literature review and any further assignment:

    - » Avoid duplication of information.
    - » Identify areas of controversy.
    - » Record additional questions your sources raise.
    - » Highlight gaps in sources and find other sources that fill in the missing information.

In the literature review, be sure to synthesize sources and information. Do not just describe what one source says and then what the next source says and so on.

The format for the literature review may be specialized according to your field or your teacher's instructions. However, what follows is a basic outline of what a literature review includes. Design your literature review in a way that reflects topics or subtopics on which the source authors (dis)agree, or relates these topics back to your argument. Use signposts that show relationships among the sources or between the sources and your argument. Transitional expressions such as these can be useful as signposts: again, also, conversely, however, in addition, moreover, nevertheless, on the other hand, and similarly.

Basic structure of the literature review in the arts and humanities

Introduction

- ❏ Make it short and clear, giving a blueprint to what main topics and arguments will be covered.
- ❏ Explain the order in which you will present the literature and why you have selected this order. Typical organizational patterns include:
    - » Moving from general to specific.
    - » Arranging according to topics.

» Classifying via type of theory, research, or research method.
» Structuring with an organizational pattern that fits your sources, thesis, topic, or field.
❑ Give the purpose of the review.

Body

❑ Group authors who share opinions or views.
❑ Compare and contrast authors with different views.
❑ Discuss and critique author methodology.
❑ Highlight excellent studies.
❑ Highlight gaps in research done previously.
❑ Show how your study relates to previous studies.
❑ Show how your study relates to the literature in general.

Conclusion

❑ Give an overall summary of what the literature says.
❑ Recap sources or studies that are significantly related to your own research or argument.
❑ Show an understanding of how the sources you have reviewed relate to your original argument, the overall field of your research, or any future research you plan on doing or would consider doing.

ANNOTATED BIBLIOGRAPHY

The annotated bibliography is an organized list of sources (articles, books, journals, periodicals, websites, and so on) with each source having a brief note or annotation that follows. In the annotations, you summarize the content of the source, remark on the source's usefulness for your research, evaluate the validity and reliability of the source's method or conclusions, and present your reactions to the source.

The format of an annotated bibliography can vary across fields, courses, and instructors. If you are required to prepare an annotated bibliography for a course, be sure to read the assignment thoroughly and ask your instructor about the specific format required. Generally, in the arts and humanities, the bibliographic information of the source is written in Modern Language Association (MLA) documentation style; for more information on MLA documentation style, see **Chapter 12**. The annotations for each source are written in paragraphs, and the length can vary from a few sentences to a few pages, depending on the course assignment and how the annotated bibliography will ultimately be used. If you are asked to write only summaries, the annotations will be rather short; if you are asked to add an evaluation for each source, the annotation will be longer.

Chin-Cheng Eric Lin   Lin 1

Dr. Dubek

English 1020

3 August 2011

Annotated Bibliography

Beef: It's What's For Dinner. Beef Industry Council and Beef Board-Commercial. 1993.
Youtube.com. Youtube, 2005. Web. 31 July 2011. Subtle advertising is the key in this
commercial. While the focus is a tight shot around the dishes made from beef, the hands
and headless bodies tell of the gender assigned to the specific dishes. From these brief
images we associate the kabob and the steak sandwich as man food whereas the sirloin
citrus salad is associated with women and children's food. These subtle imageries linger
and form our subconscious so that as men or women, we are then prone to look for these
offerings at our next dining experience.

"Mein Coming Out." *Happy Endings*. ABC. WKRN, Nashville, 20 April 2011. Television.
The exploits of six friends in their late twenties is the premise of the sitcom. In this
particular episode, the gay character, Max, is in a quandary over whether to continue to
lie to his parents or face the music and come out. Deciding to enlist the help of Jane, a
married female friend within the group, Max and Dave, another single male character in
the group, attends dinner with Max's parents. As they approach Max's parents, we are told
that they actually think that Dave is the gay one. This misunderstanding is backed just as
Dave is about to deny his homosexuality; the waiter brings the drinks to the table with 2
scotches and a daiquiri. Dave then responds, "Really guy? That's your timing?" The intent
here, following the stereotype that men drink scotch while women, or in this case gays,
drink daiquiris.

Sobal, Jeffrey. "Men, Meat, and Marriage: Models of Masculinity." *Food & Foodways* 13
(2005): 135-158. *Academic Search Premier*. Sun. 31 July 2011.
In exploring the differences between food choices, Sobal relates to the complexities
derived especially in terms of marriage. As food influences our identity, we come to
identify foods as either masculine or feminine. Where men identify with a meat-centric
diet, women do not. As such, in marriage, a compromise must be formed. Focusing on
the selection of meat in dining, Sobal explores what it is to be a man culturally. She then
applies that definition to marriage and how it then creates turmoil as the two sexes attempt
at a compromise. This singular masculinity is defined and in compromise, Sobal attempts
to expand on masculinity and define "Multiple Masculinity" to the meat-centric man.

"To See or Not to See?" Science Channel. July 24, 2011. Television.

Focused on our sense of sight, the program explores the various situations and circumstances where sight affects us. In particular, we are introduced to the physiology of sight and the processes by which our brain adapts its information to memory. We also see research into the extraordinary, where lack of sight is replaced by other senses such as sound. Of particular interest is the closeness to which we associate color with taste. In this segment, the researchers introduce a group of highly trained culinary students to color liquids with contrasting tastes that are not commonly associated with their familiar colors. Some examples of these pairings are yellow liquid to strawberry flavor or red liquid to lime flavor. Upon tasting these liquids, the student-chefs are asked to identify these liquids. The results are surprising. Even with the refined tastes of the chefs, the liquids are all misidentified. Where yellow should have been strawberry, it is identified as lime or citrus in flavor. This experiment shows that our sense of sight not only influences our senses and memory, it is in fact dominant over our sense of taste.

When Harry Met Sally . . . by Nora Ephron. Dir. Rob Reiner. 1989. MGM, 2001. DVD.

A film about the meeting and relationship turmoil between two individuals different in occupation and life is the main focus of the story line. The question of what makes a man so different from a woman is explored. We see the male character Harry Burns, played by a rough and unrefined Billy Crystal, an active, on-the-go basketball referee walking through life living the typical man's dream—with pragmatic social commentaries in love and life to physical activities of batting cages and poker nights with the guys. While the female character Sally Albright, played by the always lovable and refined Meg Ryan, embodies the typical emotional and cunning yet seductive woman. The film is filled with gender stereotypes and has produced many iconic scenes, one of which is the restaurant scene in which we see Sally act out a scene of sexual climax. It is at this scene which we see the epitome of social stereotypes not only in life but also more subtly in food. On the table, we see the typical meal of the man, Harry, which is a heavily stacked pastrami sandwich of which he is engulfing with gusto. Meanwhile, Sally's meal consists of an equally heavily stacked turkey sandwich except, wait; she removes most of the meat prior to eating it diminutively. This scene subconsciously encourages us to further identify and empathize with our respective gender characters.

WRITING EFFECTIVELY IN THE ARTS AND HUMANITIES

To make our communications more effective, we need to shift our thinking from "What information do I need to convey?" to "What questions do I want my audience to ask?

—*Chip Heath*

KNOW THE AUDIENCE(S) IN THE ARTS AND HUMANITIES

Many people writing in the arts and humanities are writing for their peers or colleagues: peers in university courses, fellow researchers, employers and employees, team members, and project managers. They may be presenting at conferences or workshops, writing journal or magazine articles, or sharing through newsletters, blogs, and websites. They may be communicating with more general, inexpert audiences through their websites and blogs, newsletters, newspaper articles and editorials, and community talks or presentations. It is important to always know who you are writing for in order to determine whether your narrative should be written in the first or third person (See Figure 5.3). Before you begin to write, ask yourself the following questions:

❑ Who are your primary readers?

❑ Who else might read your writing or listen to your presentation?

❑ What will the members of your audience already know about your topic or text?

❑ What will you need to define or explain?

❑ Will your audience be predisposed to agree or disagree with your point of view?

Figure 5.3 Point of View Flow Chart

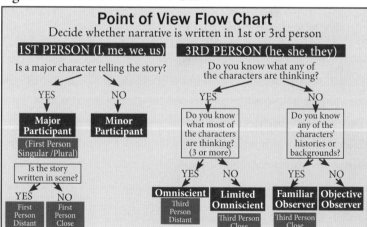

❏   What do you want this audience to do or believe?

❏   What kinds of evidence will be most convincing for this audience?

In addition, if you are writing for a course, you need to be aware that your instructor is also part of your audience. It is always best to consult your instructor about whether she wants to be included as part of your knowledgeable audience—and if that is the case, it is a good idea to learn how much your instructor knows about the topic. Likewise, if you are writing for your job, you need to be aware that your employer is also part of your audience.

KNOW THE QUESTIONS TO ASK IN THE ARTS AND HUMANITIES

A prudent question is one-half of wisdom.

—Francis Bacon

As a student, you may be assigned research questions or writing goals. Often, however, you will have to make a decision about these questions or goals. You can begin your writing preparation by asking yourself what you want to know more about and what you need to understand better in order to complete the assigned task or goal. One of the first factors you should consider is the type of arts and humanities writing you will be doing. Be sure to fulfill the assignment by providing the type of writing required.

Questions for interpretive writing

1.   **Why** did the events occur? Or, **why** was the artifact created?

2.   **Why** is the event or artifact significant to the author/creator or reader?

In interpretative writing, you are seeking to explain something, usually an event or an artifact. Your answers to these questions about your interpretations will show how you have explored your own thoughts or delved into the thoughts or mind of the creator of the text or artifact. In interpreting a piece of literature, music, or art, you try to determine the meaning of the piece, as though you are explaining it to yourself.

Questions for analytical writing

1.   **What** is the issue (question, or problem) addressed by the author? Or, **what** is the artifact made by the creator?

2.   **Why** is the issue (question, problem) or artifact important to the author/creator or reader?

3.   **Who** does the issue or artifact impact?

4.   **How** does the issue or artifact impact those affected?

Basically, in analytical writing, you are preparing a detailed examination or study of an issue, question, problem, or artifact that impacts others or yourself. The goal of the writing is to determine the issue's or artifact's nature, structure, or essential features. Your analysis should be systematic and methodical; in effect, you are breaking up a complex whole into its basic elements, such as analyzing a piece of music by breaking it down into its verses, bridges, and chorus. In an analytical paper written for an English class, you can use an ordered, logical structure to break down or resolve an argument. You can use the same type of logical structure for a paper in a philosophy, history, theology, or language class. In a music, architecture, or art class, you most likely will give a critical description of the piece under consideration by focusing on its structure and giving a synopsis of the piece.

If you find yourself in analysis paralysis with an inability to analyze a situation or issue effectively, you are most likely using an overly analytical approach or have an excess of information. Possible cures for analysis paralysis include simplifying your thesis or argument or outlining your paper to determine which information is the most important to use and which information can be discarded.

KNOW THE KINDS OF EVIDENCE USED IN THE ARTS AND HUMANITIES

Doing research [only] on the Web is like using a library assembled piecemeal by pack rats and vandalized nightly.

—Roger Ebert

A common organizational pattern of interpretative or analytical writing includes presenting your claim, providing support from the text or artifact, and then discussing how the support corroborates or proves your claim. This type of organization can be repeated multiple times, depending on how many claims

Did you know?

The classification of sources as either primary or secondary began in historiography—a field of historical research—in the nineteenth century as historians tried to identify and organize historical writing sources.

you make in your interpretation or analysis. For instance, if you want to break a text down into two parts for your analysis, you might decide to have two major parts of your essay. However, you might also take that same text and decide to take the piece as a whole but discuss five different possible interpretations of the piece.

Using primary sources

Since most arts and humanities writing is either interpretive, analytical, or a combination of both, and since the supporting evidence for this type of writing is most often textual or visual, your

Write what you know... **Research the rest.**

main focus will usually be on the text or artifact you are interpreting or analyzing. The text or artifact about which you are writing is considered your primary source, and this primary source can be presented in a written, visual, or audio format. Common primary sources in the arts and humanities are provided in Table 5.3.

TABLE 5.3

Common Primary Sources in the Arts and Humanities	
Art	Paintings, sculptures, folk art, quilts, blown glass, drawings, prints, sketches, photographs, carvings, computer and digital graphics, architecture, ceramics, mosaics, silk screens, lithographs, collages, furniture
English	Plays, poems, short stories, novels, nonfiction, creative nonfiction, autobiographies, biographies, fables, myths, folktales, fantasies, legends, ballads, jokes, satires, parodies, farces, monologues, essays, literary criticism, diaries, journals, travel literature, newspapers, magazines, comic books, graphic novels
Film	Scripts, recordings, photographs, feature films, television movies, media industry trade papers, film reviews, fan magazines, editorials, advertisements, film trailers, press kits, lobby cards, film clips, prints, slides, scene shots, publicity stills, archives, background music, documentaries, mockumentaries, filmographies, festival and exhibition programs, interviews
History	Archives, birth certificates, obituaries, marriage certificates, death certificates, political papers (such as the Declaration of Independence), census records, military records, diaries, letters, personal papers, coins, stamps, photographs, reports, literature, maps, advertisements, pamphlets, posters, laws, family Bibles, wills, deeds, school report cards, financial records, ledgers, board meeting minutes, tax and voter lists, department reports, police records, court records, oral histories, stories, anecdotes, films, paintings
Modern languages	Plays, poems, short stories, novels, nonfiction, creative nonfiction, autobiographies, biographies, fables, myths, folktales, fantasies, legends, ballads, jokes, satires, parodies, farces, monologues, essays, literary criticism, diaries, journals, travel literature, newspapers, magazines, comic books, graphic novels
Music	Songs, raps, opera, symphonies, suites, overtures, concertos, background, canons, ballads, carols, fugues, etudes, impromptu, marches, oratorios, sonatas, rondos, requiems, serenades, verses, refrains, choruses, hymns, variations, cycles, movements
Philosophy	Religious texts, pamphlets, letters, diaries, scholarly works, lectures, contemporary criticism, archives, journals, memos, manuscripts, newspaper articles, photographs, minutes of conferences or agencies
Theology	Religious texts or theological works in original language, translated religious texts or theological works, scholarly works, church records, lectures, contemporary criticism, archives, diaries, letters, journals, memos, manuscripts, newspaper articles of current events, photographs, government records, birth and death certificates, minutes of conferences or agencies

Using Secondary Sources

Anyone else who has written about your primary source or topic is considered a secondary source. Your instructor, usually through the assignment, will indicate whether you should focus only on the primary source or also use secondary ones. You should also think about how and where you can locate secondary source information. The type of writing you do to achieve your communication goals should guide your research approach and topics.

The key to writing an effective interpretation or analysis in the arts and humanities is to cite enough evidence to make your point but not to overload the paper with massive amounts of material from secondary sources. By focusing your topic and providing support in a concise manner, you will retain your own voice but also show that you are able to uphold your thesis or argument through the use of examples from the primary text or secondary sources. A good rule of thumb is not to use more sources than the number of pages in your essay or research paper.

Secondary sources include both general and specific sources. It is often wise to consult general sources as you brainstorm and then focus on a specific thesis or argument. General secondary sources such as dictionaries and encyclopedias, either in print or online, are a good place to begin brainstorming about your topic, but they are typically not considered valuable secondary sources to use within an essay or research paper.

In fact, these types of sources are sometimes referred to as *tertiary sources* (see Figure 5.4) to distinguish them from the types of secondary sources that are most useful in supporting arguments. In the arts and humanities, secondary sources that can be used successfully as effective supporting evidence include scholarly books and journals, which should preferably be peer reviewed, which means the article has been read

Figure 5.4 Example of a Tertiary Source

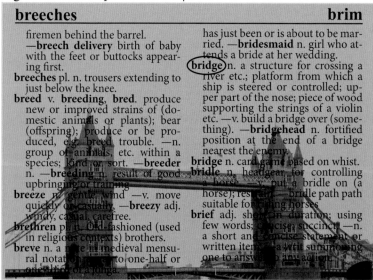

breeches	brim
firemen behind the barrel. —**breech delivery** birth of baby with the feet or buttocks appearing first. **breeches** pl. n. trousers extending to just below the knee. **breed** v. **breeding**, **bred**. produce new or improved strains of (domestic animals or plants); bear (offspring); produce or be produced, e.g. **breed** trouble. —n. group of animals, etc. within a species; kind or sort. —**breeder** n. —**breeding** n. result of good upbringing or training **breeze** n. gentle wind —v. move quickly or casually. —**breezy** adj. windy, casual, carefree. **brethren** pl. n. Old-fashioned (used in religious contexts) brothers. **breve** n. a note in medieval mensural notation equal to one-half or one-third of a longa.	has just been or is about to be married. —**bridesmaid** n. girl who attends a bride at her wedding. **bridge** n. a structure for crossing a river etc.; platform from which a ship is steered or controlled; upper part of the nose; piece of wood supporting the strings of a violin etc. —v. build a bridge over (something). —**bridgehead** n. fortified position at the end of a bridge nearest the enemy. **bridge** n. card game based on whist. **bridle** n. headgear for controlling a horse —v. put a bridle on (a horse); restrain —**bridle path** path suitable for riding horses **brief** adj. short in duration; using few words; concise, succinct —n. a short and concise statement or written item; a writ summoning one to answer in any action.

and reviewed by others in the field. Secondary sources are written by authors who evaluate, analyze, or interpret original information. For instance, if you are writing a three-page essay about the novel, *The Monkey Bridge*, you might list the following sources in your Works Cited.

Works Cited

Cao, Lan. *The Monkey Bridge*. New York: Penguin Books, 1998. Print.

Coward, Harold G. "Psychology and Karma." *Philosophy East and West* 33.1 (1983): 49–60. Print.

Reichenbach, Bruce R. "Karma, Causation and Divine Intervention." *Philosophy East and West*. 14.1 (1989): 135–149. Print.

Schinto, Jeanne. "Review: Invisible Scars." *The Women's Review of Works* 14.10 (1997): 26–27. Print.

Primary versus secondary sources

Although you might think that sources can always be clearly categorized as either primary or secondary, the distinction can sometimes be subjective and based on the context in which you are using the source. For example, an archive of letters from Benjamin Franklin may be considered a primary source for a historian to study in detail, interpreting or analyzing the content and form of the letters. However, that same archive of letters could also be considered a secondary source for someone in literature to study how Franklin responded to Thomas Paine's work *Common Sense*.

> *Facts are stubborn things; and whatever may be our wishes, our inclinations, or the dictates of our passions, they cannot alter the state of facts and evidence.*
>
> —*John Adams*

Qualitative versus quantitative supporting evidence

Although writers in the various fields of arts and humanities can use both quantitative and qualitative data in order to make arguments or support their claims, qualitative data are more the norm when interpreting or analyzing a text. Quantitative data, though not as common, can also be used to make arguments or support claims, especially in humanities areas other than English. Both types of data come from primary research regarding the text or artifact in question, as well as secondary research from other published resources. Common types of qualitative evidence used in arts and humanities writing include textual or other examples, definitions, testimonies, and stories or narratives. For example, if you are writing about the painting *Scholar on the Bridge*, you might use a quotation from Maxwell Hearn, the author of *How to Read Chinese Paintings*, to support your own ideas. Common types of quantitative evidence include facts and figures presented as numbers within the text or a combination of numbers, and visuals, such as charts and graphs in the text or in appendixes. If you are writing about patterns within a text or are attempting to demonstrate causal relationships, you need to present the methods you used to arrive at the quantitative data that you are presenting, including any mathematical formula used for transcribing or coding of the text. If statistical or quantitative analysis is used in arts and humanities writing, the mathematical component is often simple arithmetic or percentages. For example, you might want to compare two bridges in the San Francisco area: the Bay Bridge and the Golden Gate Bridge. In this case, you could use a simple pie chart to provide a comparison of the number of cars driving over each bridge daily. As the pie chart in Figure 5.5 clearly reveals, the Bay Bridge has much more traffic.

Figure 5.5 Quantitative Analysis

Comparison of car travel across two San Francisco bridges

■ Golden Gate Bridge
■ Bay Bridge

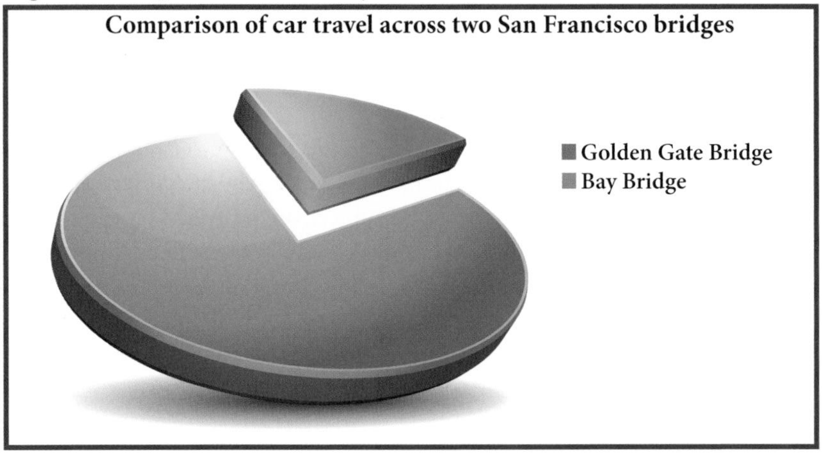

If you use established statistical tests to present quantitative data, be sure to acquaint yourself with the statistical packages available at your institution or required in your field. Two statistical packages used in the arts and humanities are SAS (Statistical Analysis System) and SPSS (Statistical Package for the Social Sciences), which are usually more familiar to social scientists. And, finally, always double-check the accuracy of your data before using it to support your arguments.

The most common type of qualitative data used in the arts and humanities to support an argument is a summary, paraphrase, or quotation from a secondary source. Qualitative data are nonnumerical and may include introspective evidence; testimonials from authors or critics; comments from focus groups, interviews, and surveys; or stories and observations from experts or ordinary people acquainted with the topic. Expert testimony often carries more weight with readers, so be prepared to explain an expert's credentials or qualifications. Ethnography is another type of qualitative research that arts and humanities writers might use to reflect the knowledge or systems within a particular (sub)cultural group. This type of research might be used by a compositionist (one who studies writing) who is investigating how certain groups create or organize their writings, or it might be useful to an historian who is interested in analyzing the artifacts of a particular group or time period. The resulting field report is descriptive in nature and allows the researcher/writer to explore cultural aspects of the humanities.

You may also use a combination of both quantitative and qualitative data—for example, percentages (quantitative) that show how often a particular word or phrase is used in a text alongside comments (qualitative) from readers that indicate how this amount of use affects their interpretation of the text. When possible, use multiple sources and types of evidence. The most important question to ask yourself is this: What kind of evidence is needed to support my claim or to make it persuasive to my intended audience?

You must be careful to present both qualitative and quantitative evidence in an ethical manner. Withholding evidence or not giving the full picture because you think it hurts your argument is unethical and presents inaccurate results. You should make sure that the evidence you use, no matter what kind, actually supports the claim you are making. For example, the evidence you present should avoid leaps in logic and inaccurate cause-and-effect arguments. See Table 5.4 for a summary of the different types of qualitative and quantitative supporting evidence.

TABLE 5.4

Types of Supporting Evidence	
Qualitative	Quantitative
Analogical	Physical
Anecdotes	Scientific results
Intuition	Statistics
Judgment of an expert	
Personal experience	
Testimonials	

KNOW THE WRITING AND STYLE CONVENTIONS USED IN THE ARTS AND HUMANITIES

Persistent, disciplined study can be shown as well in a personal narrative as in a lab report, so . . . academic writing is not restricted in style or voice, although disciplines and subfields of disciplines do vary in customary ways of thought and in traditional modes of expression.

—Chris Thaiss and Terry Myers Zawacki,
in Engaged Writers, Dynamic Disciplines

The writing genres and hints that we have shared so far are appropriate across many fields within the arts and humanities. Other general writing guidelines and stylistic conventions are shared across the entire discipline, and we give some of these here to help you recognize them. However, as you review the following guidelines, be aware that when you take specific courses, you always need to follow the assignments or consult with your instructors, in case the specialized writing or genre guidelines vary from the general norm presented here.

A good writer in the arts and humanities presents relevant content to the reader in a format that is easy to understand and appropriate to the field. To achieve this, you need to be attentive to both global elements of writing (content, organization, and style) and local characteristics of writing (format, grammar, and mechanics). The following guidelines present suggestions that will strengthen your writing on both the global and local levels.

Conventions about Content

Rhetorical triangle: As a writer, you always want to situate the message you are presenting through your writing. This means that whenever you write, you are aware of who your audience (the reader) is, what you want them to understand (the message), why you are presenting your message (the purpose), and what field you are presenting your message in (the context). At the university level, most of the writing you will do is academic in nature. For more information on the rhetorical triangle and the conventions associated with academic writing, see Chapter 2.

Thesis: The type of writing that you do helps determine what type of thesis you will write. Academic genres, such as the ones presented earlier in this chapter, tend to have a strong thesis at their center. Most of the common genres in the arts and humanities include either interpretative writing or analytical writing, and using a strong thesis makes each of these types of writing stronger. As well-known composition scholar Andrea Lunsford suggests, everything is an argument. However, a strong thesis (or argument)—one that shows clearly what is at the center of the entire paper—can be either implied or explicit in the introduction.

Support: Whether you write a personal essay or one that includes primary or secondary sources, you will always include supporting evidence for whatever thesis or argument you make. In a personal essay, such as for an assignment that asks you to reflect on your favorite piece of art or music, you will make your claim(s) and then provide support with specific and vivid details from either your life or the piece to which you are reacting. In an argumentative research paper, such as for an assignment that asks you to use five sources, you will make your claim and then provide support with specific details from your primary or secondary sources. For more information on using primary and secondary sources, see the section Know the Kinds of Evidence Used in the Arts and Humanities earlier in this chapter.

Conventions about organization

Title: Since using a title on a piece of writing is an arts and humanities convention, creating a good one is often overlooked. Do not make that mistake. In your courses, a good title is important because it can catch the reader's interest, help the reader predict what the content of the paper is, and reflect the tone of the writing or the voice of the writer. In addition, as you transfer your writing to upper-level courses or to the workplace, having an effective title with key terms that enable a quick computer or Web search makes your writing much more accessible to your intended audience.

Always create your own titles. Do not use the titles of other works as the title of your paper. For instance, if you write a paper about the book *Intelligent Design: The Bridge Between Science and Theology*, do not use the book title as your paper's title. Add something about the topic of your paper, such as "Investigating the politics of *Intelligent Design: The Bridge Between Science and Theology*."

Attention getter: Always include an attention getter in the introduction to your review, essay, or research paper. This is an arts and humanities convention that gives you a chance to entice the reader into reading your paper thoroughly and with interest. An attention getter is usually a few sentences near the beginning of the introduction; it should lead smoothly into introductory information that then leads into the thesis. One of the best strategies for creating an effective attention getter is to give a startling anecdote, fact, or statistic. The more you can surprise, shock, or scare your reader, the more likely it is that he will want to continue to read your paper. Another common and effective strategy is to give a quotation from an expert or someone who you are betting will either interest your reader or make your reader mad. Some writers make the mistake of using a question as their attention getter. A question is a good lead-in to a thesis, but usually it is not striking or interesting enough to be used as an attention getter.

Introduction, body, and conclusion: In the arts and humanities, a recognized format of most genres is to have an understood introduction, body, and conclusion. For more information on what to include in these sections, please see page 92-93.

Conventions about style

Across the arts and humanities, it is most common to use style and documentation conventions that are from the Modern Language Association (MLA), which publishes the *MLA Handbook for Writers of Research Papers*, now in its seventh edition. Be sure to have a copy on hand for those times when you may have a style or documentation question. Below are some style questions that might arise as you write in the arts and humanities.

In some fields, such as history, style and documentation information from *The Chicago Manual of Style*, 16th edition, is more relevant than the *MLA Handbook*.

Q: What general writing style is common in the arts and humanities?

A: In formal assignments, use a formal objective writing style, rather than a conversational style. Avoid slang and contractions, and be concise in your descriptions. However, you should also avoid the other extreme of using overblown or pompous language that may alienate your reader or make your writing hard to understand. Avoid giving human feelings or actions to nonhuman beings, especially written elements. For example, rather than saying, *The chapter states that the bridge was faulty*, say: *In 1981, Thompson stated that the bridge was faulty.*

Q: Which verb tense should I use?

A: In general, use the appropriate tense for the appropriate action: use present tense for present actions, past tense for past actions, and future tense for future actions. Pay attention to verb tenses, and be consistent. However, when referring to authors and their words or quotations, use the present tense: *C. B. Bridges says that it is important to cross the bridge when he comes to it.* or *C. B. Bridges suggests, "Crossing a bridge when I come to it is always an interesting prospect."* And, when referring to the narrative or storyline (for a literary text, film, or television show) in a paper for an English course, use what is called the <u>literary present tense</u> to describe what is happening: *Then, Nash Bridges takes the bandit by the arm and throws him into the San Francisco Bay.*

Q: When should I use third person?

A: When writing formal academic papers, in general, use third person (she, he, her, him, they, them) unless the assignment asks you for your personal opinion or story. For personal stories, or if the assignment or teacher instructs you to do so, use first person (I, me, my). Research papers are usually written in third person.

Q: Should I use active or passive voice?

A: It is conventional wisdom to use active voice to a greater extent in the arts and humanities. For instance, use *Moby Dick chased down the boat* rather than *The boat was chased down by Moby Dick*. However, use passive voice if it is appropriate for the context or if you are not sure who the subject of the sentence is. For example, use *The house was sold* instead of *Someone sold the house.*

Q: Is there a list of words or phrases I should avoid when writing academic pieces in the arts and humanities?

A: Stylistically, be as concise as you can when writing academic papers by avoiding weasel words, such as *I think, I believe, In my opinion, I know that it is true that,* and *Being that*; vague words, such as *good, bad, incredible, literally, people, they,* and *there*; or clichés or overused expressions, such as *a stitch in time saves nine, life is for the living,* and *as easy as pie.*

Q: How should I refer to authors within my essays?

A: The first time you present an author or his or her work, give the author's full name, such as *Thomas H. Winters proposes that we see the rose as a living being.* After that, use only the author's last name: *Winters also sees the bedroom as a symbol for a lonely death.*

Q: How can I avoid sexist language in my writing?

A: You can avoid language that marginalizes your reader by avoiding gendered pronouns, such as *she, he, him,* and *her,* and making them plural (*they, them*) instead. Also, do not assume that a job can be filled by only one gender or another; you can do this by avoiding labels such as *stewardesses, mailmen,* and *chairman,* and changing them to more neutral descriptions: *flight attendants, mail carriers,* and *chair.*

Conventions about Formatting

The format of your essays or other genres can vary across fields, so it is best to check with your instructor or refer to your textbook for the appropriate format for your assigned writing. That way, you will know whether an essay needs a cover page, preferred margins, and so on.

Conventions about Using Sources

In the arts and humanities, it is common and appropriate to use summaries, paraphrases, and quotations from primary and secondary sources as supporting evidence in your papers. A good rule of thumb is to use one source per page assigned. That is, if you are assigned a paper that is about 10 pages long, use around 10 sources. However, check the assignment carefully for any restrictions or requirements for sources. If you are using the *MLA Handbook* as your guide for documentation style, you will cite each summary, paraphrase, and quotation you use. Using the MLA documentation style involves using parenthetical (in-text) citations and a Works Cited page. When you want to add bibliographic or explanatory notes to a paper, MLA allows footnotes and endnotes but discourages extensive use of them. For more information on using sources and following MLA format, please see Chapter 12.

Conventions about Grammar, Spelling, and Mechanics

To be a successful writer, not only do you need to follow the stylistic and format conventions for your field, but you must also be aware of grammatical issues that can distract your reader from your message. The most common problems in writing involve a lack of sentence variety and an inadequate grasp of how to punctuate different types of sentences. Readers can become bored or irritated if they have to wade through sentences that they have difficulty understanding. Learning about the four different types of sentences (simple, compound, complex, and compound-complex) and how to punctuate them correctly can improve the flow of your paper and enhance the delivery of the content you want the reader to understand.

Spelling words correctly and using the appropriate word form are also important cues to your readers that you care about the topic, the paper, and them. Spend some time looking up correct spellings or word forms when you edit your work, and do not automatically accept everything your computer grammar and spell checkers tell you to do. You ultimately want your words to represent *you,* and leaving choices to your computer does not always represent you well.

KNOW THE APPROPRIATE DOCUMENTATION STYLE USED IN THE ARTS AND HUMANITIES

MLA, the documentation style recommended by the Modern Language Association, is typically used by scholars in the arts and humanities. However, instructors in some fields, such as history, may use *The Chicago Manual of Style*. Knowing which documentation style is preferred in a course or in your field is an important first step in knowing how to choose, incorporate, and cite sources. Always follow the guidelines dictated by your assignment, by your employer, or by the academic journal to which you are submitting your work.

The Internet and You: Using Internet Videos in First-Year Composition
Holly T. Hamby, Middle Tennessee State University

What: A variety of Internet video resources can invigorate your teaching practices and provide new avenues for critical inquiry, particularly as these videos can be considered as multimodal texts, which students can reflect upon and analyze and then respond to in writing. Included in this presentation: Internet-only animation, archived media from America's past (including propaganda cartoons), music videos, video collages (mash-ups) unique to the Internet, and the "reality" YouTube video phenomenon. These videos also utilize students' familiarity with some Internet characters (and retro characters in these videos, such as Bugs Bunny) and forms of text, which can be a gateway to teach students to understand, interpret, and analyze American issues and varieties of rhetoric.

Why: Internet videos in a variety of genres can be used in low-risk writing activities that segue into class discussions about global course concerns. These videos have distinct pedagogical purposes for both expository writing and research and argumentative writing.

- The videos can help students understand the importance of the rhetorical triangle and certain rhetorical strategies in their own writing/creation of a multitude of "texts."

- The videos often highlight dialectical and language concerns students have in writing, and more specifically, finding their writing voice(s).

- These videos also often present various arguments, both sound and not so sound, which help students to understand the principles of argument, and move into persuasive writing techniques in expository writing and later progress to argumentative strategies in research and argument.

Theoretical Support:
Mary Louise Pratt's Contact Zone theory (and the adapted Pop Culture Zone theory). These Internet videos, as a part of popular Internet culture, provide a contact zone for students and teacher to explore and grapple with language and writing, which in turn leads to practical writing techniques students use on high-risk writing assignments, as well as to the larger global concerns of the expository writing course.

But, I *can't* use this! I don't have a Master, Smart, or Computer Classroom:
Solution: Send the link/URL to students through e-mail, or post on D2L. Then, transform these in-class writing assignments to homework writing assignments. The students can watch these videos at their own leisure and come to class with their written responses, prepared for class discussion.

I. "You're my best friend" description activity
Based on a clip from the show *The Marvelous Misadventures of Flapjack*.
Clipped on YouTube: <http://www.youtube.com watch?v=um1wt5UDdY0>

__Summary:__ In this clip, Flapjack sings a short and sweet song to his best friend, Cap'n Knuckles, followed by a little ditty composed for a random "little old lady" who is in the audience. While this is a current cartoon on Cartoon Network that is apparently intended for children, it is very offbeat and populated with often grotesque characters that embody the "other." (For example, in another episode, Flapjack apparently falls in love with a girl, but it turns out he just has a parasitic infection of heart-shaped tick creatures that make him think he's in love). It proves both familiar and unfamiliar to students, who are sometimes unsettled by the characterization.

(I'm including this, although it's available on DVD, because this particular clip has been edited for the Internet to highlight one part. Also, it brings up questions of plagiarism, ownership of texts, and how that works with the Internet).

__Activity:__ This cartoon could be used to teach students how to write descriptions, which I would generally present near the start of my expository writing course.

1. Students are asked to view the cartoon and write down what phrases Flapjack uses to describe both characters.

2. Then, each student pulls from a container a slip of paper on which a noun is written. They are then given 5–10 minutes to compose their own short song in homage of their noun. They are asked to try and describe the most important characteristics of their noun in their song.

3. The students can then be put in small groups, where they share their songs with each other! As the group hears each person's song, they are asked to write down what descriptions the songwriter is using. Often the students are eager to perform their songs for the whole class, and the teacher uses the group's impressions of how their group-mates described their nouns to segue into a broader discussion of how to use description in more formal writing.

II. "My Humps" Style and Tone Comparison Activity
Original, by the Black Eyed Peas:
      http://www.youtube.com/watch?v=iEe_eraFWWs
Parody, by Alanis Morissette:
      http://www.youtube.com/watch?v=pRmYfVCH2UA

This activity engages students about style and tone, not to mention irony, in either model writing or their own writing. First, the teacher would need to define and discuss what we mean by *style* and *tone* in writing, and how we can analyze our own writing to determine what types of style and tone we are using and should perhaps use in future writings. These videos also usually lead to discussions of rhetoric, particularly what arguments are being made in each about appropriate behavior for men and women a'courtin.

Students should listen to a snippet of the original song and respond with a description of the style and tone (in writing). Then, the second version is played, and the students are asked to repeat the exercise (once again, by in-class writing). Then the whole class shares their observations. The point of this fun exercise is to clue students in to how to "read" style and tone differences, why these characteristics are important to understanding/interpreting texts, and how to use these style and tone changes in their writing for different audiences and purposes.

Elizabeth Burton

Burton 1

Dr. Laura Dubek

English 3000

15 December 2010

"Put a Ring on It":

Female (Dis)Empowerment in The Taming of the Shrew and

American Popular Culture

Gazing through the cultural lens of the increasingly malleable

gender roles of modern society, it may be difficult to imagine a

world similar to that of Shakespeare's *The Taming of the Shrew*—a

world where gender roles are non-negotiable. In Shakespeare's day,

the domestic life was the domain of the "submissive wife," while

the external world of commerce was the domain of the "masterful

husband" (Dolan 13). A woman knew "her place" and a man

monitored her closely to ensure that she remained there. The two

spheres and their keepers traditionally were never to be intermingled

or exchanged. Such mingling of spheres only occurred when

a woman's failure to fulfill her "wifely duties" necessitated her

husband's use of authority, which commonly manifested itself in the

form of physical violence or verbal abuse, in order to restore her to

her rightful subservient position within the relationship, household

and community (Dolan 13).

This set of disturbing social norms perhaps comes as a

shock to modern minds that, since infancy, have benefitted from

Name/Instructor/
Course/Date—
double space,
align at left and
top margin

Title—centered

Note that the
author puts quota-
tions around this
part of the title
because it is the
name of a song.
Normally, titles
will not take quo-
tation marks.

Attention-getter
opens the essay

Burton 2

movements toward racial and gender equality in mid-twentieth century America. In the current "progressive" culture, women can do anything from working as CEOs of Fortune Five Hundred companies to burning their undergarments in protest against traditional patriarchal values—or both concurrently. These women frequently work outside the home in occupations of their own choosing, raise children without the aid of "father figures," and hold authoritative positions within their families regardless of their marital statuses. However, these two seemingly contradictory societies may not be as far removed from each other as they initially appear. Katharina Minola of Shakespeare's *Shrew* has quite possibly met her match in the most unlikely of places—twenty-first century American popular culture. Within the presently overpopulated constellation of homogenous female pop stars, there is one, Beyoncé Knowles, who shines above the rest. Although these two women come from seemingly dissimilar cultures, they share a common goal and, more importantly, a common means by which they seek to obtain this goal: Both Katharina and Beyoncé benefit from artfully employing the male-constructed feminine stereotypes of their respective societies in order to acquire power within those societies.

> Thesis statement—this sets up the paper up as a literary analysis that compares and contrasts two works.

Within her community, there is little debate regarding Katharina's long-standing status as a shrew. Her demeanor

> Topic sentence that provides the overall focus of the following paragraph.

Burton 3

satisfies all of the necessary requirements: she is excessively talkative, loud, assertive, and often hostile. In short, she is the stereotypical "bossy woman" (9). However, as Frances Dolan reveals, a shrew is more than just an outspoken woman; she is "a woman refusing to submit to a man's authority and aggressively asserting her independence"—a woman who "strive[s] for mastery" (10). Although Katharina aims for mastery, her straightforward approach is unsuccessful because her overt assertion of dominance only serves to perpetuate her own submission. She fails to realize that her reputation within her patriarchal society is dependent on the reports of men with whom she interacts. In this way, Katharina unintentionally bestows upon men the power to turn their personal opinions of her into public facts. As a result, men portray her as "the devil," the enemy of her society, because her ideals, and thus her behavior, threaten the highly regarded patriarchal tradition (*Shr* 3.2.146).

After the utter failure of Katharina's initial approach, she finds her "occasion for revenge" by turning to her only other option—marriage (2.1.35-36). When Hortensio taunts her about the unlikelihood that she should ever find a willing mate, she boldly asserts:

> I' faith, sir, you shall never need to fear;
>
> Iwis it is not halfway to her heart.

The author uses a block-by-block comparison, discussing *Taming of the Shrew* first and then "Put a Ring on It" next, both in blocks of multiple paragraphs.

The author uses a short quotation from *Taming of the Shrew* and incorporates it effectively into a sentence that begins with her own words. Note how the line from a play is documented in the parenthetical citation at the end of the line.

Compare this long quotation and how the documentation is placed to the short quotation in the previous paragraph.

Burton 4

But if it were, doubt not her care should be

To comb your noddle with a three-legged stool,

And paint your face, and use you like a fool.

(1.1.61-65)

If Katharina must resort to marriage, she will triumph over her new

husband and make a fool of him by whatever means necessary.

Her plan of attack can best be evidenced by her first encounter with

the unfortunate "fool" Petruchio (2.1.250).

PETRUCHIO: Myself am moved to woo thee for

my wife.

KATHARINA: Moved? In good time! Let him that

moved   you hither

Remove you hence. I knew you at

the first

You were a movable.

PETRUCHIO: Why, what's a movable?

KATHARINA: A joint stool. (2.1.190-194)

In this exchange, the adaptations of the word *move* seem to

emphasize physical action; however, Katharina's wordplay actually

hints at the refinement of her strategy. Rather than attempting

to physically dominate her husband, she will mentally mold him

into her desired product. For instance, the noun *movable* may be

interpreted as both "one easily changed or dissuaded" and "an

The author italicizes any particular word that she is defining or discussing.

article of furniture" (Dolan 79). In this case, Katharina claims ownership of both meanings. She employs the interpretation that a *moveable* is a joint stool in order to outwardly insult Petruchio by comparing him to furniture while she secretly divulges her scheme to carefully whittle him down into a stool (or fool)—a joint stool being a "well-fitted stool made by an expert craftsman" (79). Katharina, the craftsman, utilizes Petruchio, that which is crafted, as a prop in order to enhance the believability of her performance.

Once married, Petruchio delivers his notorious "She is my goods, my chattels" proclamation and announces to his servants that he has "politicly begun [his] reign" over Katharina, which will undoubtedly be a success (*Shr* 3.2.219-4.1.157). Although Petruchio intends to kill his wife "with kindness" by depriving her of basic sustenance, Katharina finally demonstrates her mastery over him during the "sun and moon" confrontation when she tames him with her amiable disposition: "And be it moon, or sun, or what you please;/And if you please to call it a rush candle,/Henceforth I vow it shall be so for me" (4.2.177-4.5.13-15). By submitting to Petruchio, Katharina gains her independence through the guise of dependence. Petruchio believes he has successfully changed her into the ideal gentlewoman when, in fact, she has tricked him into accepting the authenticity of her reformation.

Katharina's subtle, yet satisfying victory culminates in her final Oscar-worthy performance at Bianca's wedding reception.

Burton 6

> Fie, fie! Unknit that threatening, unkind brow,
>
> And dart not scornful glances from those eyes
>
> To wound thy lord, thy king, thy governor.
>
> It blots thy beauty as frosts do bite the meads,
>
> Confounds thy fame as whirlwinds shake fair buds,
>
> And in no sense is meet or amiable.
>
> A woman moved is like a fountain troubled,
>
> Muddy, ill-seeming, thick, bereft of beauty;

(5.2.140-147)

The focus of this speech has traditionally been placed on Katharina's complete lack of shrewish qualities, on her obedience to Petruchio, and on her instruction of other women to follow the example she has set with her own behavior. Although the latter may be correct, Katharina's behavior, and consequently her instruction, is often misinterpreted as the promotion of submission. In this context, *moved* is commonly interpreted as a synonym for *angry*, which suggests that Katharina intends to criticize the supposed hostility of her female audience (Dolan 137); however, the reemergence of the word *moved* implies Katharina's continuation of her previous wordplay. In her speech, Katharina furtively hints that a woman changed, or altered, is not a thing of beauty. As she dominates her clueless audience with her captivating tongue, which was once considered only to

> Notice how the author supports her argument (underlined) with examples of particular wordplay within the play. She not only uses quotations, but also uses a summary of information from the play to make her point.

Burton 7

emit "meaningless noise," she instructs the other women not to begrudgingly submit to their husbands but instead to apply her method in order to obtain subliminal control (17). Thus, Katharina reveals Petruchio's perceived taming of her as a farce cleverly orchestrated by her via the usage of time-honored social traditions to her own advantage. Simply stated, Katharina succumbs under her own terms.

Observe the last sentence of the previous paragraph and how it sets up the transition from the Katharina block to the Beyoncé block.

Much like Katharina, Beyoncé Knowles has obtained power in modern culture by way of her own devices; however, unlike Katharina, Beyoncé has managed to escape the stigma of being labeled a shrew. Although she appears to be an unlikely candidate for "shrewhood," a quick review of Dolan's definition of a shrew will prove most enlightening because Beyoncé *is* "a woman refusing to submit to a man's authority and aggressively asserting her independence." Throughout the first decade of the twenty-first century, Beyoncé achieved success by relentlessly promoting herself as *the* image of modern female empowerment and independence—as a "Survivor" ("Survivor"). Even Beyoncé's public abandonment of her surname—forced upon her at birth in compliance with an archaic patriarchal practice—exudes defiance against a male-centered society. One superficial glance at her song lyrics clues the reader into the explicit nature of her message: I am a self-sufficient woman, and you can (and should) be one too.

Her song "Independent Women Part I" is quite possibly her most obvious assertion of dominance.

> I buy my own diamonds and I buy my own rings
>
> Only ring your celly when I'm feelin' lonely
>
> When it's all over please get up and leave
>
> Question: Tell me how you feel about this
>
> Try to control me, boy, you get dismissed
>
> Pay my own fun, oh, I pay my own bills

> ("Independent")

In order to extinguish any doubts listeners might still harbor about the legitimacy of her declaration of independence, she then proceeds to list her material possessions and continually brags, "I've bought it" and "I depend on me" ("Independent"). In the form of a conveniently concise and catchy phrase, Beyoncé has effectively armed the modern shrews of the world with their newest mantra: "I've bought it" (also known as the lengthier and less popular "I don't need a man to provide for me").

Perhaps more puzzling than Beyoncé's success as an updated version of Shakespeare's shrew is her simultaneous compliance with and perpetuation of the male-conceived standards of feminine beauty and behavior. In addition to her provocative clothing, voluminous hair and overstated makeup, her songs "Bills, Bills, Bills" and "Crazy in Love" reveal Beyoncé's submission to gender-biased ideals. In the former, she warns a potential suitor that he has no chance to date her unless he can pay her "telephone" and "automo' bills" ("Bills"); while in the latter, she confesses to a man, "Got me hoping you'll page me right now, your kiss/Got me hoping you'll save me right now" ("Crazy in Love"). This embarrassingly intimate confession begs the question, "Save you from *what*, Beyoncé? His own *absence*?" Her plea for a man to "save" her supports the classic view of woman as damsel-in-distress who not only desires but needs a prince to ensure her continued existence. At this point, one might ask, "What happened to your previous "Survivor" mentality?" Just as Katharina betrays her coveted principles by allowing Petruchio to publicly tame her, Beyoncé contradicts her own image of female empowerment in order to reinforce sexist ideologies by claiming that a woman's financial and emotional successes are dependent on the presence of a capable man in her life. Meanwhile, without so much as the appearance of a skeptically elevated eyebrow, her devoted female followers digest this blatant inconsistency in personal beliefs, and Beyoncé gains an entirely new set of listeners or, perhaps more accurately described, viewers from the male population.

The author refers back to the previous block about Katharina here to link this section of the paper to the last.

Although Beyoncé's two attitudes about gender roles appear to be incompatible, her identification with these patriarchal ideals allows her to manipulate her audience in order to advance

Burton 10

her independent lifestyle and to assert her dominance over the aforementioned audience as it grows larger and larger each year. Once again, she returns to her initial status as an undercover shrew. In one of her latest successes, "Single Ladies (Put a Ring on It)," Beyoncé embraces her incongruous, yet simultaneous roles as both empowered individual and objectified sex symbol. While repetitively expressing admiration for "all the single ladies," or independent women of the world, she informs the men of the world, "If you liked it, then you should have put a ring on it" ("Single Ladies"). Beyoncé's mastery of her audience is evident in her ability to praise self-sufficient women while also encouraging their compliance with the cultural institution of marriage. Furthermore, remaining true to her ambiguous form, she *demands* that men take the dominant role in relationships by putting "a ring on it." In this respect, Beyoncé takes her cues from Katharina by taming men while allowing them to think they possess absolute power. They remain oblivious to the fact that, in actuality, she *bestows upon them* this power. Inadvertently paying tribute to Katharina's wordplay, Beyoncé's use of "ring" also suggests ambiguity in meaning because the word may be understood literally as a wedding ring or figuratively as a means by which men seek to trap or tie down women. Beyoncé also seems to imply a third kind of ring—the metaphorical circus ring in which she performs daily her delicate balancing act between sovereignty and acquiescence.

> Once again, notice how the author inserts a direct comparison back to the previous section of the paper, so the reader does not lose track of what two things are being compared.

Burton 11

Although their cultures come wrapped in different packages, when the casings are removed, Katharina Minola of Shakespeare's *The Taming of the Shrew* and Beyoncé Knowles, the shining star of American popular culture, undoubtedly confront the same fundamental societal injustices. Once the motives behind their manipulative behaviors have been established, the focus must necessarily shift from *why they* do it to *what it* does to them. What are the effects of this deception on the deceiver? By using the patriarchal system against itself in order to reclaim their own individuality, these women actually risk losing themselves because they compromise their own belief systems in defense of those very same beliefs. It is no coincidence that only until Katharina relinquishes her right to speak can she finally be heard. Consequently, as Hortensio appropriately proclaims, "The field has been won," but who declares the victory (*Shr* 4.5.23)? The women who covertly control a sexist system by submitting to it? Or the men who retain their precious patriarchal practices, ironically assisted by the women who seek to control that system rather than to dismantle it? By playing the puppet, the shrew becomes the puppeteer; however, confined by the necessity to conceal her duality, she creates a new form of oppression for herself as she is destined to perform the traditional show of the previous master and thus to preserve the interests of those whom she claims to despise.

After completing the two blocks of material about Katharina and Beyoncé, the author now makes a direct comparison to conclude the paper.

Observe how the author ends the essay not with only a summary, but also with a final statement about how both Katharina and Beyoncé are caught in the roles they choose to portray.

Burton 12

Works Cited —

> **Heading centered**

Dolan, Frances E. *The Taming of the Shrew: Texts and Contexts*.

    Boston, Massachusetts: Bedford Books of St. Martin's

    Press, 1996. Print.

> **This entry is for a print book and follows the MLA format.**

Knowles, Beyoncé. "Bills, Bills, Bills." *The Writing's on the Wall*.

    Columbia, 1999. CD.

---. "Crazy in Love." *Dangerously in Love*. Columbia, 2003. CD.

---. "Independent Women, Part I." *Survivor*. Columbia, 2001. CD.

---. "Single Ladies (Put a Ring on It)." *I Am... Sasha Fierce*.

    Columbia, 2008. CD.

---. "Survivor." *Survivor*. Columbia, 2001. CD.

> **This entry is for a song from a CD and follows the MLA format. Be sure to put the type of recording (CD, MP3 file, or LP).**

Shakespeare, William. *The Taming of the Shrew. The Taming of the*

    Shrew: Texts and Contexts. Ed. Frances E. Dolan. Boston,

    Massachusetts: Bedford Books of St. Martin's Press, 1996.

    Print.

> **When two (or more) entries in a row are by the same person or group, use three hyphens in a row followed by a period in all entries after the first.**

1. Place the first line of each entry flush to the left margin. Each line after that in the entry will be indented.

2. Do not forget to alphabetize the list of sources.

3. Double space all entries.

WORTH A THOUSAND WORDS:

The Impact of the Brady Photographs in the Civil War

Patrick Murphy

HST 304: The American Civil War

Dr. Peter Knupfer

August 18, 2011

Murphy 1

It is the iconic picture of Gettysburg: the dead Confederate sniper in Devil's Den. The deceased is lying on his back, almost as if he were asleep. His rifle is standing where he fell, behind the tall rock wall sandwiched between two massive boulders. His hat has fallen by his feet. It is a haunting, moving scene. It is also a blatantly staged one. The body's position is parallel to the wall; for the hat to have fallen where it did, the body's angle would have had to have been different. Moreover, the rifle would not have been neatly leaning against the wall so much as fallen over the body. Finally, the rock wall is considerably taller than the man appears to be. He could not, under any circumstances, have died where he is photographed.[1] But accuracy was of little importance to Alexander Gardner, the cameraman. In the Civil War, photographers were not motivated to document the results of engagements, though their pictures served that purpose to an extent. Instead, it seems they were far more interested in capturing the emotions and spirit of the battles.

Currently, any news photographer or photojournalist who "doctors" a photo taken of an event immediately loses credibility, possibly their job, and their chances of restoring either. The idea of "posing" smacks of falseness and separation from reality rather than a reflection of it—studio photographers use it to make people look more attractive or intelligent or professional than they actually are. News photographers are supposed to take snapshots of reality, so that the audience can understand the truth about the subject being captured on camera. And yet, we find Mathew Brady and his team of photographers taking staged photos of the dead and passing them off as authentic at every battlefield they were at, save Antietam. Further, judging from the fact that they constitute a large and important collection in the National Archives, not only were they not stigmatized, they were applauded. How is it that these three fathers of photojournalism (Brady, Gardner, and Timothy O'Sullivan) were elevated for work that would get a modern photographer fired from the news circuit?

Perhaps, to the 19th century audience, Brady's men did capture a certain reality of war that had not been in the public eye. The dominant American mindset early in the war was that combat was a grand game, a test of values. Officers, especially Southern ones, were culled from the upper classes and thought of as highly chivalrous.

---

1. Alexander Gardner. *Dead Confederate Soldier in Devil's Den.* July 1863. Photograph. Library of Congress, Washington, D.C. http://memory.loc.gov/ (accessed June 21, 2011).

Among the 14 rebel generals listed by the New York Times in July 1861 were an Episcopal bishop, a former Secretary of War, a former governor, a Congressman, and a former ambassador.[2] Those who died, without exception, did so bravely and for the "right reasons," and each side was convinced that the righteousness of their respective causes would be enough to win the war.[3]

Newspaper articles reinforced these beliefs. Reporters following the Army asserted at Bull Run that a mere 20,000 Federal troops were gallantly engaged against a swarm of 90,000 rebels, and nearly carried the day anyway (actual combat strengths were less lopsided: 28,450 Union, 32,230 Confederate). Every Federal action was done "gallantly," as was every death of a Union soldier. The tone of these articles from Northern reporters insinuates the Confederates, who frequently hid behind cover, were less masculine, less heroic, and less noble than their Union counterparts.[4]

This kind of reporting had two effects on the public mind. First, readers were given a simple, "us vs. them" slant to the war, which allowed the audience to dehumanize the opposing side. Second, it fed the belief that chivalry and a worthy cause could, on the battlefield, trump an enemy's superior numbers, firepower, and generalship. This reporting style continued unchallenged for over a year, until a group of men, armed with cameras, began following the Army.

The images they took altered the course of public opinion and changed the way news was reported. Brady and his photographers, through the posed pictures of casualties, were able to drain romanticism out of the conflict and subdue its glorification. The tragedy of the conflict, blithely skipped over by the newspapers, screams out from the Brady photographs. Photographers like Brady were able to balance the nobility of the Federal cause found in the papers with the raw realism of combat and the underlying heartbreak of civil war. They illustrated the gruesome side of war while the papers, especially the Republican ones, reminded readers of what it all was supposedly for. The effect was that two different messages were

2. Thomas Summerhill. "Week Two: Amateurs at War." History 304: The American Civil War, Online. Accessed May 23, 2011; "Generals in the Rebel Army," *New York Times,* July 21, 1861, http://www.proquest.com.
3. Thomas Summerhill. "Week Two: Amateurs at War." History 304: The American Civil War, Online. Accessed May 23, 2011.
4. "Retreat of Gen. McDowell's Command from Mannassas: Full Details of the Engagement," *New York Times,* July 23, 1861, http://www.proquest.com.

communicated—one romantic, the other realistic. By 1864, this turn to realism was beginning to have an effect on the public's perception of the war. This was also true of northern sentiment toward southerners in general, making Lincoln's reconciliation plans more palatable in contrast to those of the revenge-hungry Republican Congress.

The photograph taken by O'Sullivan of the dead near McPherson's Woods is a fine example of bringing the war's brutality to the public's attention. Four Union soldiers lay close together on the ground, mangled by musket balls, as if they fell while advancing in formation.[5] Up through the end of the war, infantry tactics had hardly changed since Napoleon. Men fought shoulder to shoulder in the open, or on horseback. Such tactics were viewed as proper and manly. However, they also led to alarmingly high casualty rates. After Bull Run, one Union officer reported that of the one thousand men and officers of his regiment, only he and 200 others survived the engagement.[6] The photograph helps give the statistics a horrifying visual. For the audience, chivalry and a righteous cause provided little solace when the visuals were so graphic.

A similar photo by Gardner gives us another haunting visual. Taken near the "Slaughter Pen" by Little Round Top, Southern infantrymen, presumably of Hood's division, are strewn across the boulders and cuts at the base of the hill, gunned down as they advanced against what was left of Sickles's corps.[7] Picturing what a battle may look like can be difficult, but photographers were able to give the audience a visual reference point to contrast with the melodramatic newspaper descriptions. Consequentially, those same papers began reporting more accurately.

The battle at Peach Tree Creek in 1864, as reported by the once-hyperbolic *New York Times*, recorded the attack by Hardee's corps in a more modest manner when compared to earlier accounts. Here the *Times* actually gives credit to Southern soldiers for a "furious charge." The reporter also telegraphed more accurate casualty figures: 3,000 Confederate dead and wounded to 1,500 Union.[8] The sober, factual

---

5. Timothy O'Sullivan. *Bodies of Federal Soldiers, Killed on July 1, near the McPherson Woods.* Photograph. Library of Congress, Washington D.C. http://memory.loc.gov/ (accessed June 22, 2011).
6. "Retreat of Gen. McDowell's Command from Mannassas: Full Details of the Engagement," *New York Times,* July 23, 1861, http://www.proquest.com.
7. Gardner. *Slaughter Pen at the Foot of Little Round Top.*
8. "Details of the Battle: From Sherman's Army," *New York Times,* July 27, 1864. http://www.proquest.com.

reporting is more like what we would see today, and nothing like the reports from Bull Run a mere three years before.

At the battle of Franklin in November 1864, southern newspapers were still running melodramatic articles where the rebels nearly carried the day with a mere handful of casualties, in spite of being grossly outnumbered. This suggests a discrepancy between the papers each side had published.[9] The northern papers were growing more realistic in their reporting as more of Brady's battlefield photographs were displayed, while the southern ones remained essentially propaganda. It is also important to note that the South did not have a corps of battlefield photographers following their armies, where the Union armies had Brady's men in the camps. Thus the impact of civil war photographers cannot be overlooked because as northern newsmen continued to produce battlefield accounts they were inevitably held accountable by the existence of visual evidence.

The photographs of the Confederate dead, especially in such areas as Spotsylvania Court House and Gettysburg, had an effect on northern attitudes toward the Administration's reconstruction plans by the end of the war. These gruesome pictures of "the enemy" possibly were key to softening the North's stance towards the South as the war was concluding. Looking at the photographs of the dead, only the caption enables the reader to tell which side the deceased was on. This served to further engender sympathy for southern soldiers. The various photos O'Sullivan took at Spotsylvania Court House of a dead Confederate feature a body dressed in a uniform so dark it could well have been blue as easily as gray. His rifle changes position in the photos, as does the camera angle, but the man is just as difficult to identify.[10] A Gardner photograph of a dead Confederate at the foot of Round Top is also only identifiable as Southern by its caption.[11] These photographs were intentionally designed to inspire feelings of pity and pathos in its viewers—the pictured dead could just as easily have been one's son or nephew or neighbor, thus strengthening the link between the rank and file southerner with one's own flesh and

---

9. "The Battle of Franklin—Hood's Army," *Daily Richmond Examiner,* December 7, 1864. http://infotrac.galegroup.com.
10. O'Sullivan. *Bodies of Confederate Soldiers near Mrs. Alsop's House.*
11. Gardner. *Dead Confederate Sharpshooter at the Foot of Round Top.*

Murphy 5

blood. The "us vs. them" dynamic that defined the war's reporting for four years was in this way almost totally transformed by the end of 1864.

The *New York Times* noted in 1865 that the "common people of the South… are deserting the standards of the perjured traitors who betrayed them . . ." and demonstrates how many northern papers later accepted the southern people (in contrast to southern leadership).[12] As a result, in combination with the relative success of the Free State constitutions signed in Arkansas and Louisiana, there was a sense in the North that the Southern people were returning to the Union voluntarily—even if their state governments were not.[13]

By humanizing the South through photos of the dead, Brady's outfit contributed to making Lincoln's plan for post-war reconciliation more acceptable to Northern civilians. Harsher methods of reconstruction, such as the Wade-Davis bill, were increasingly seen as gratuitous torture of a beaten people. The *New York Times* stated that this particular bill and its sponsors intended " . . . to satisfy wounded arrogance, and to destroy [the Southern people]."[14] The paper also points out that Lincoln thought it unconstitutional as well. Until the president's death in 1865, there was little call for more suffering—there was enough death captured by Brady's photographs.

In a way, then, it seems that staging photos of the dead as Brady's men repeatedly did was an act of service to the country. They shook the civilian population out of the sort of careless romanticism that made throwing away the lives of soldiers seem acceptable. They reminded the viewer that even our wartime enemies are human and should be treated with dignity, not ground into a humiliating submission to make ourselves feel better. While neither Brady, O'Sullivan, or Gardner would probably retain a photojournalist's or publisher's position with a news organization today, they did bring home certain realities of the conflict that simply photographing the end results of battles may have missed. They told the story of the war in terms of its emotions, its high drama, and its deep tragedy. Robert E. Lee famously commented that "it is well that war is so terrible, lest we grow too fond of it." Brady's photographs made viewers agree.

12. "Jeff Davis' Army," *New York Times,* January 18, 1865. http://www.proquest.com.
13. "From Washington: Proclamation by President Lincoln. His View on Reconstruction," *New York Times,* July 10, 1864. http://www.proquest.com.
14. "The Wade Manifesto: The President's Action on the Reconstruction Bill of Congress," *New York Times,* August 18, 1864. http://www.proquest.com.

Bibliography

"Details of the Battle.: From Sherman's Army," *New York Times*, July 27, 1864. http://www.proquest.com.

"From Washington.: Proclamation by President Lincoln. His View on Reconstruction," *New York Times*, July 10, 1864. http://www.proquest.com.

Gardner, Alexander. *Dead Confederate Sharpshooter at the Foot of Round Top*. July 1863. Photograph. Library of Congress, Washington, D.C. http://memory. loc.gov/ (accessed June 21, 2011).

---. *Dead Confederate Soldier in Devil's Den*. July 1863. Photograph. Library of Congress, Washington, D.C. http://memory.loc.gov/ (accessed June 21, 2011).

---. *Slaughter Pen at the Foot of Little Round Top*. July 1863. Photograph. Library of Congress, Washington, D.C. http://memory.loc.gov/ (accessed June 21, 2011).

"Generals in the Rebel Army," *New York Times*, July 21, 1861, http://www.proquest.com.

"Jeff Davis' Army," *New York Times*, January 18, 1865. http://www.proquest.com.

O'Sullivan, Timothy. *Bodies of Confederate Soldiers near Mrs. Alsop's House*. Photograph. Library of Congress, Washington D.C. http://memory.loc.gov/ (accessed June 22, 2011).

---. *Bodies of Federal Soldiers, Killed on July 1, near the McPherson Woods*. Photograph. Library of Congress, Washington D.C. http://memory.loc.gov/ (accessed June 22, 2011).

"Retreat of Gen. McDowell's Command from Mannassas: Full Details of the Engagement," *New York Times*, July 23, 1861, http://www.proquest.com.

Summerhill, Thomas. "Week Two: Amateurs at War." History 304: The American Civil War, Online. Accessed May 23, 2011.

"The Battle of Franklin—Hood's Army," *Daily Richmond Examiner*, December 7, 1864. http://infotrac.galegroup.com

"The Wade Manifesto: The President's Action on the Reconstruction Bill of Congress," *New York Times,* August 18, 1864. http://www.proquest.com.

Kallstrom 1

Emma Kallstrom

Dr. Charles Wolfe

English 4440

13 April 2010

"They knew how to live with nature and get along with nature": The Martian Secret to a Successful Civilization

Twentieth-century Americans witnessed stunning scientific discoveries, such as the atomic bomb and the space age, frightening political maneuvering stemming from America's sense of superiority and the Cold War, and continued social strife in racial tension and religious intolerance. These scientific, political, and social phenomena clearly influenced Ray Bradbury's *The Martian Chronicles*. The development of the V-2 weapon, capable of reaching heights of 100 miles, during World War II marked the beginning of the space age. After the war ended, rocket-powered weapons development led naturally to space exploration programs ("History"). In addition, the Cold War ensued due to the rivalry and weapons buildup between the United States with its Western allies and the Soviet Union with its communist supporters (Snead). In *The Martian Chronicles*, Bradbury takes rocket technology and space exploration, combines them with the power struggle between the atomic-weapon-wielding superpowers, and imagines potential consequences played out in both the Earth and Martian arenas. Although the novel treats a variety of social and political ills, often bizarrely juxtaposed, a discernible story arc emerges regarding the relationship between successful civilizations, living in harmony with the environment, and careful management of technology. *The Martian Chronicles* travels from the Martians' harmonious coexistence with nature and technology through mankind's destructive and self-destructive disregard for such harmony to the final realization that humans must adopt the Martian philosophy in order to survive and succeed as a civilization.

The standard for living in harmony with nature and science is established in the second chapter, "Ylla," in which the lifestyle of a typical Martian couple is described. The description of the house evokes a serene, peaceful environment of fruit-bearing walls and creek-inlaid floors. Everything about the house has been designed to complement the Martian climate. For example, being farther from the Sun than Earth, the Martians have found a way to get as much sunlight as possible: The house "turned and followed the sun, flower-like" throughout the day, but to withstand the cold of night, it "clos[ed] itself in, like a giant flower, with the passing of light" (Bradbury 2, 5). Because the climate is also mostly dry, the Martians have invented ingenious ways to harness their limited water supply to provide necessary humidity: Within the home, a "gentle rain sprang from the fluted pillar tops, cooling the scorched air, falling gently on [Ylla]. On hot days it was like walking in a creek. The floors of the house glittered with cool streams" (Bradbury 2-3). The Martians have remained in control of their technology, using their impressive technological advances to enhance their harmonious relationship with nature. They sleep on clouds of chemicals that support and conform to their bodies overnight and gently lower them down to the floor in the morning. Books are fashioned from durable metal, eliminating the need for wasteful, polluting paper production. One of Mr. K's books sings of "ancient men [who] had carried clouds of metal insects and electric spiders into battle" (Bradbury 2), which reveals that at one time, Martian history had resembled that of war-prone Earth. However, at some point, Martians took control of their destiny, and the civilization as a whole endured successfully as indicated by the fact that the Ks' ancestors had lived in that same house before them for the past ten centuries.

Unlike their Martian counterparts, few Earth men appreciate the advantages of a peaceful, natural existence as illustrated in chapter seven, "—And the Moon Be Still as Bright." After three failed missions before them, the fourth expedition lands on Mars only to find a dead planet. The crew's cavalier attitude clearly shows the typical Earthman's, or more specifically, the typical American's, insensitivity to the loss of life or culture as long as their goal is achieved. They revel in their success despite the discovery that a nearby Martian city's population was decimated as recently as a week ago. Crewmember Biggs especially lacks respect for Mars or its lost civilization: he pollutes a canal by throwing wine bottles into it and later vomits the effects of that wine all over the beautiful ancient tile in the Martian city the team investigates. Of the sixteen surviving crewmembers only Spender and Captain Wilder understand the reverence that Mars deserves.

Spender, an archaeologist, is keenly interested in learning as much as possible about the Martians and their culture. His mind reels at the news that the Martians were senselessly destroyed by chicken pox:

Chicken pox, God, chicken pox, think of it! A race builds itself for a million
years, refines itself, erects cities like those out there, does everything it can to

give itself respect and beauty and then it dies. . . . [I]t has to be chicken pox, a child's disease, a disease that doesn't even kill *children* on Earth! It's not right and it's not fair. . . . It doesn't fit the architecture; it doesn't fit this entire world! (Bradbury 51)

Having rejected the mission, Spender wanders off to study the Martian artifacts on his own and begins to feel a connection with them. Through his research, he discovers the key to the Martians' way of life and the point at which the Mars and Earth philosophies diverge:

They knew how to live with nature and get along with nature. . . . Man had become too much man and not enough animal on Mars too. And the men of Mars realized that in order to survive they would have to forgo asking that one question any longer: *Why live?* Life was its own answer. Life was the propagation of more life and the living of as good a life as possible. . . . They quit trying too hard to destroy everything, to humble everything. They blended religion and art and science because, at base, science is no more than an investigation of a miracle we can never explain, and art is an interpretation of that miracle. They never let science crush the aesthetic and the beautiful. (Bradbury 66-67)

Spender recognizes the value of living in harmony with nature and science. He anticipates and loathes the effect colonists from Earth will have on Mars, knowing that they will destroy Mars just as they have been destroying and continue to destroy Earth.

While Capt. Wilder understands Spender's argument, he feels more responsibility to the mission and adopts a more optimistic attitude about Earth's relationship with Mars. He openly hopes that Earth will learn from Mars and use the knowledge to improve its civilization: "[O]ne day Earth will be as Mars is today. This will sober us. It's an object lesson in civilizations. We'll learn from Mars" (Bradbury 55). His doubt and inner struggle become apparent, however, during his pursuit of Spender through the Martian wilderness. During their temporary truce-protected discussion, Spender tries to sway Wilder to his point of view, but Wilder keeps his focus on the mission. Nevertheless, he swears to do all he can to provide future archaeologists with adequate opportunity to investigate thoroughly the Martian ruins in order to preserve the culture as much as possible. Apparently, he does try to keep his promise because in chapter 24, it is revealed that Wilder had been shipped off to

Saturn, Neptune, and Pluto for the twenty years following the fourth expedition to prevent his interference in the colonization program on Mars.

Following the success of the fourth expedition, colonization of Mars begins in earnest, confirming the Earthmen's insistence on molding the environment to suit them instead of learning to adapt to their surroundings. In chapter nine, "The Green Morning," colonist Benjamin Driscoll, having fainted upon arrival because of the thin air, vows to fight "a private horticultural war with Mars" (Bradbury 75) and plants thousands of tree seeds and sprouts. By doing so, he effectively changes the climate of Mars, adding rich oxygen to the atmosphere. The next chapter, "The Locusts," finds 90,000 colonists "beat[ing] the strange world into a shape that was familiar to the eye, . . . bludgeon[ing] away all the strangeness" (Bradbury 78). The transformation of Mars to adhere to Earth standards is evident in chapter 13, "Interim," in which Tenth City, built of imported Oregon pine and California redwood, so accurately resembles a replica of an Iowa town that one might believe "a whirlwind twister of Oz-like proportions had carried the entire town off to Mars to set it down without a bump" (Bradbury 88). Spender's prophecy that "We'll rip [Mars] up, rip the skin off, and change it to fit ourselves" (Bradbury 54) has been fulfilled; Earthmen have changed the face of Mars. The physical landscape is not the only item on the Earthmen's agenda; soon, their ideology takes over as well, further emphasizing their disharmony with their new surroundings. They begin with the basics—renaming towns with familiar Earth names:

> The old Martian names were names of water and air and hills. They were the names of snows that emptied south in stone canals to fill the empty seas. . . . And the rockets struck at the names like hammers, breaking away the marble into shale, shattering the crockery milestones that named the old towns, in the rubble of which great pylons were plunged with new names . . . , all the mechanical names and the metal names from Earth. (Bradbury 102-03)

This renaming of places had also been predicted by Spender: "[W]e'll give them new names, but the old names are there, somewhere in time, and the mountains were shaped and seen under those names. The names we'll give to the canals and mountains and cities will fall like so much water on the back of a mallard" (Bradbury 54). After the renaming is accomplished and Mars becomes comfortably familiar, officials arrive to impose the same laws and regulations that govern Earth's society. The Earthmen take complete control of Mars despite the existence of real Martians as confirmed by sporadic sightings of a few who have survived the Disease (chicken pox epidemic). In this way, amid the frenzy of colonization, the Martian culture is eradicated by the settlers from Earth.

The Earthmen's vision dominates Mars; however, an occasional settler understands the uniqueness of Mars and feels a natural harmony with it. Pop, the gas station owner in chapter eleven, "The Night Meeting," has the right attitude towards his strange new home:

> We've got to forget Earth and how things were. We've got to look at what we're in here, and how *different* it is. I get a hell of a lot of fun out of just the weather here. It's *Martian* weather. Hot as hell daytimes, cold as hell nights. I get a big kick out of the different flowers and different rain. . . . I'm just experiencing. If you can't take Mars for what she is, you might as well go back to Earth. Everything's crazy up here, the soil, the air, the canals, the natives . . . . Well, that's Mars. Enjoy it. Don't ask it to be nothing else but what it is. (Bradbury 79)

Pop's acceptance of Mars is so rare that it is not equaled again until the end of the book. Before then, however, the colonists witness the distant explosions and depart en masse for Earth, leaving a few individuals stranded on Mars. Genevieve Selsor, introduced in chapter 23 ("The Silent Towns"), willfully chooses to stay behind. She finds solace in her isolation on deserted Mars—she can eat whatever and whenever she wants without facing society's criticism for being overweight. Eventually, Genevieve meets Walter Gripp, who was left behind unintentionally. Although he is desperately lonely, Walter cannot accept Genevieve—the last woman on Mars—as a companion and opts instead for a life of isolation. By the time Capt. Wilder returns in chapter 24 ("The Long Years"), Walter has become so acclimated to Mars that he refuses passage back to Earth. Capt. Wilder encounters another forgotten colonist, former crewmember Hathaway from the fourth expedition. Even though Hathaway cannot bear the loneliness of his existence and creates a robotic family to keep him company, he does choose to live in the Martian wilderness instead of in the town built by the Earthlings. This handful of individuals represents the very small minority of people who accept Mars for what it is.

Finally, one family rejects Earth values permanently and embraces the Martian way of life unequivocally. They have seen the destruction caused by letting technology get out of control in the form of atomic war on Earth: The desolation following the Great War is depicted in Chapter 25, "There Will Come Soft Rains," which coincides with the family's emigration. This family determines to shed all vestiges of Earth—its technology, laws, and ideals—and start a new, improved civilization on Mars. They choose an authentic ancient Martian city in which to dwell and start their new lives. The father symbolically burns his important papers from Earth (government documents, religious doctrines, financial records, war propaganda, and world map) as he explains to his young sons what went wrong with Earth:

> I'm burning a way of life. . . . Life on Earth never settled down to doing anything
> very good. Science ran too far ahead of us too quickly, and the people got lost
> in a mechanical wilderness, like children making over pretty things, gadgets,
> helicopters, rockets; emphasizing the wrong items, emphasizing machines
> instead of how to run the machines. Wars got bigger and bigger and finally killed
> Earth . . . [T]hat way of life proved itself wrong and strangled itself with its own
> hands. (Bradbury 179-80)

Their capitulation to the Martian way of life is complete when the children ask their father when they will see real Martians, and he poignantly shows them their own reflections in the canal.

In *The Martian Chronicles*, Ray Bradbury explores the future of mankind if it were to follow its current course of space exploration, the development of atomic weapons, and international power struggles. His fictional hypothesis emphasizes the destructive tendencies of humans and warns them of the disastrous outcome that is likely to occur. He does offer a glimmer of hope, however, suggesting that by learning to live in harmony with the environment, effectively blending nature and science, mankind may yet save itself.

Works Cited

Bradbury, Ray. *The Martian Chronicles*. New York: Bantam, 1979. Print.

"History of Technology." *Encyclopaedia Britannica Online*. Encyclopaedia Britannica, 2010.
     Web. 30 Mar. 2010.

Snead, David L. "Cold War." *Dictionary of American History*. Ed. Stanley I. Cutler. 3rd ed.
     Vol. 2. New York: Scribner's, 2003. N. pag. *Gale U. S. History in Context*. Web. 4
     Apr. 2010.

ACTIVITIES

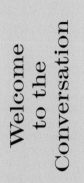

Discuss these questions with your classmates in class or via a class wiki or shared blog.

1. In general, what four types of writing are used in the arts and humanities?

2. What are the types of writing that are used most often in the arts and humanities?

3. If you have knowledge about a genre, what do you know?

4. What should you have before you begin your research and writing for a literature review?

1. **Summary**: Write a summary of an article or book chapter that deals with a topic related to an argument you are interested in using for a future research paper.

2. **Dialogue journal**: Create a dialogue journal page by drawing a vertical line from the top to the bottom of a piece of notebook paper. On the left, write three facts about an argumentative topic that you are interested in pursuing. For example, one of the facts you could write is "The Zhaozhou Bridge is the oldest standing bridge in China and the world's oldest stone segmental arch bridge." Now trade your dialogue journal with someone in class, and that person will write two questions about each of the facts you have written. For instance, next to the fact about the Zhaozhou Bridge, your classmate could write these questions: "When was the bridge built? What is the oldest bridge in the United States?"

3. **Reading journal**: Focus on a reading that you have done for class. In one page or less, summarize key ideas and people, and then respond to the reading's main points.

Learning to Write

1. **Annotated bibliography:** Choose a general area of research and narrow your topic down to one about which you can make an argument. Find at least ten sources that you may be able to use to research your topic. Prepare a citation list of at least ten articles, books, book chapters, websites, and other documents. For each citation, add one or two paragraphs that describe, summarize, and evaluate the source.

2. **Literature review:** Focus your preliminary research for a research paper by narrowing down your topic and creating an in-progress thesis (that is, an argument that may be changed later after you do your literature review). Read at least five sources critically, taking notes on important information you may want to include in the literature review. Following the literature review genre format for your field, write a literature review.

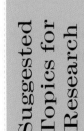

Suggested Topics for Research

1. **Digital presentation:** Choose a type of primary source that is commonly used in your particular arts and humanities field. For example, if you are a history major, you might choose census records or voter lists. Create a Prezi or PowerPoint presentation that introduces this type of primary source to your class/audience.

2. **Review, critique, or review essay:** Choose a primary text/source form your field, and write a review, critique, or review essay. Be sure to briefly describe the text/source before you explain its merits for your readers, so they can decide whether they want to experience the text for themselves. Remember to focus on a few key points rather than including everything that you know about the text/source.

READ MORE ABOUT IT

Allosso, Salvatore F., and Dan Allosso. *A Short Handbook for Writing Essays in the Humanities and Social Sciences.* No City: Stay Outside the Box Publishing, 2011. Print.

Barnet, Sylvan. *A Short Guide to Writing About Art.* 10th ed. New York: Longman, 2010. Print.

Barnet, Sylvan, and William E. Cain. *A Short Guide to Writing About Literature.* 12th ed. New York: Longman, 2011. Print.

DeVoss, Danielle Nicole. *Understanding and Composing Multimodal Projects.* Boston: Bedford/St. Martin's, 2013. Print.

Ferguson, Marcia L. *A Short Guide to Writing About Theatre.* New York: Longman, 2007. Print.

Goodson, Patricia. *Becoming an Academic Writer: 50 Exercises for Paced, Productive, and Powerful Writing.* Los Angeles: Sage, 2013. Print.

Herbert, Trevor. *Music in Words: A Guide to Researching & Writing About Music.* New York: Oxford UP, 2009. Print.

Lange, Alexandra. *Writing About Architecture.* New York: Princeton Architectural Press, 2012. Print.

Marius, Richard, and Melvin E. Page. *A Short Guide to Writing About History.* 7th ed. New York: Pearson, 2010. Print.

O'Hair, Dan, Hannah Rubenstein, and Rob Stewart. *A Pocket Guide to Public Speaking.* 3rd ed. Boston: Bedford/St. Martin's, 2010. Print.

Rampolla, Mary Lynn. *A Pocket Guide to Writing in History.* 7th ed. Boston, MA: Bedford/St. Martin's, 2012. Print.

Vyhmesiter, Nancy Jean. *Your Guide to Writing Quality Research Papers: For Students of Religion and Theology.* 2nd ed. Grand Rapids, MI: Zondervan, 2008. Print.

chapter 6

Writing in Business

MANAGEMENT, MARKETING, ADVERTISING, ACCOUNTING, AND HUMAN RESOURCES

Creating written documents reveals so much about you and your business skills. Your writing tells the reader about your educational background, pride in your work, and business expertise. The emergence of the paperless office, e-mail, the Internet and Web pages only increases the power of the written word. Any company with employees who can write clearly and concisely has a competitive edge over others who are still struggling to communicate.

—Gloria Pincu
"The Importance of Writing Clearly for Business"

PURPOSES OF WRITING IN BUSINESS

Whether you are writing for a class or on the job, your goal should be to communicate effectively. Consequently, you need to know the purpose behind your communication. Perhaps you are writing to inform, as a human resources officer sharing basic information in an e-mail or newsletter. Perhaps you are writing to get results, as a team leader sharing project goals or a technical writer composing a set of instructions. Maybe you are writing to persuade, as a salesperson writing up a proposal for a possible client or a manager submitting a bid for a project. Or you may be sharing bad news, telling an applicant that he did not get the job or explaining profit losses to shareholders. No matter what form you are using or what message you want to send, your message will be more effective if your writing is clear, to the point, and written according to the conventions of the format you have chosen or been assigned. From short memos to lengthy reports and proposals, you want to be understood, and this chapter is designed to help you achieve that goal.

TYPES OF WRITING ASSIGNMENTS IN BUSINESS

We each are a crazy quilt of characteristics, talents, ideas and ideals, sewn together by our experiences, our families and our own hands.

Yet some fabric patches are more sought after by employers. Which pieces are like royal blue velvet to a hiring manager, beautiful to look at and almost impossible to resist? Which deserve to show up again and again?

The American Management Association weighed in with the 4Cs— communications, critical thinking, creativity and collaboration—as increasingly in demand by employers.

Sew these all into some of my own thoughts on the crazy quilt of talents and values and I've come up with five traits most hiring managers seek: communication skills, integrity, adaptability and creativity, thoughtfulness and kindness, and critical thinking.

—Vickie Elmer
"Five Traits Employers Really Want"

Business writing takes on many different forms, depending on audience, purpose, context, and field. Similarly, learning objectives, programmatic goals, and even accreditation requirements may affect the types of assignments you receive in class, just as various factors may influence what you are asked to create on the job. Below are some common types of writing assignments that you may see, but keep in mind that this is not an exhaustive list and that you may be asked to create other types of documents or communication; likewise, you may know of alternative forms that may be effective for your audience, purpose, and context—if so, you should discuss these additional forms with your instructor.

MEMOS, LETTERS, AND E-MAILS

In the workplace, and thus in classes preparing you for the workplace, correspondence will be a key tool for getting things done. Memos and letters, both of which may be written as e-mails, are used every day to relay information, make requests, report findings, deliver good and bad news, accompany other files and reports, and solicit business, and the list goes on. This correspondence is often your professional face, so it is important for your writing to be professional—well written, organized, accurate, following the conventions of the genre, appropriate for the intended audience, proofread, and to the point.

We communicate more and more through e-mail, but that medium is not always used in a way that promotes civil correspondence between people. Make no mistake: e-mail is an extraordinary tool for communication, but it is also rife with potential pitfalls. Table 6.1 shows some guidelines for e-mail use that will help ensure you use it to maximum effect while also remaining civil in the tone of what you write.

TABLE 6.1

Some Things to Consider When Writing an E-mail
In General
1. Use e-mail to request or provide succinct pieces of objective information
2. Avoid discussing sensitive issues through e-mail
3. Use e-mail to publicly praise, but not to blame employees
4. Use e-mail to share insights, not to instigate confrontation
5. Judiciously use blind copy function
As Sender
1. Give e-mail a clear and direct subject heading
2. Get to the point
3. Avoid hedgers and qualifiers as phrases
4. If asking a question, be sure to ask the question (don't issue evaluation)
5. Specify who should respond
6. Be clear about when you need a response
7. Provide relevant context
8. Limit each message to one topic
9. Provide brief summary when sending an "FYI" or forward e-mail
10. Don't use sarcasm

As Receiver
1. Don't make assumptions about sender's emotional state
2. Don't escalate by sending an emotionally charged response (sleep on it; perhaps don't reply by e-mail)
3. Don't respond right away
4. Be careful when quoting e-mails out of context in a reply

Typically, memos are written to be distributed within an organization and can serve a variety of functions. The standard form, whether printed on paper or put in an e-mail, is to have a heading that includes *To:, From:, Date:,* and *Subject:.* The memo may be put on company letterhead or special memo letterhead to convey more formality and authority. Memos are usually short, but if you do require a second page, use a page header that includes an abbreviated title, the page number, and the date—either across the page or in the left-hand corner. See the Sample Business Project Plan that follows for an example of a memo.

Letters are written to those outside the organization and should be printed on company letterhead. The letter itself should be centered on the page, so adjust your margins accordingly. Many businesses use the full-block style, which aligns everything in the letter on the left margin: the date, inside address, salutation, body of the letter, complimentary closing, signature, signature block, and end notations, if applicable (see the sample business letter that follows). In the modified-block style, which is often used when no letterhead exists, the return address, date, complimentary closing, and signature block are aligned in the center while the inside address, salutation, and body are aligned on the left.

SAMPLE BUSINESS PROJECT PLAN

To: Jeff Grabill
From: Robin Stremlow, Laurel Sutherland, Kelly Washburn
Date: 11/3/2009
Re: Mice and Elephants Project Plan

MEMO

Problem
Michigan has been hit especially hard by the current economic crisis, and that fact is particularly evident in the Lansing area. Businesses are shutting their doors and people are moving away at alarming rates. It is time that we do something about it.

We are going to research a local organization called The Allen Neighborhood Center (ANC), which is a prime example of a small group with a mission that turned into an influential and prosperous "elephant." We are going to evaluate our findings and develop a strategic plan for another local group that could help stimulate the area.

Audience
Ultimately, everyone in the Lansing community benefits from this project. For this memo's purposes, however, we will assume our audience is two-fold. The primary audience is the local group that we will present a strategic plan for. We will tailor our recommendations to suit their specific needs, and we will present the information in a way that is suitable given their background.

The secondary audience is composed of our classroom peers. As we all will share research with each other in hopes of bettering our projects, we need to make sure to present those findings in a logical method.

Goals
Our main goals are:
- to understand the ANC's original mission and vision for the group
- to learn in what ways the group has changed over time
- to learn what made the ANC become what it is today
  - what communication tactics did group leaders use to promote their message
  - what stumbling blocks did the group have to overcome, and how did they do it
  - in what ways has the group changed over time
- to transform our findings into an abstract plan for success and implement our ideas into a tangible strategic plan for a small group

Solution Strategies

For the first leg of this project, we are dividing the primary research tasks into two groups. The first will be completed primarily by Kelly, who will conduct Internet research on the ANC. She will be compiling data from the ANC's website, as well as from newspapers, magazines, and other online tools that house information about the group and its history.

The second group will be completed by Robin and Laurel, and will consist of in-person, phone, and e-mail interviews and informal communications with past and present leaders and workers of the ANC. We will compile a listing of people we believe will be beneficial to our understanding of the group, and will welcome any recommendations from you and others we encounter during our research.

There are many unknowns in the second leg of this research project, but we are planning to divide up the tasks in a similar way. As we progress in this project, we will determine our needs and strategies for this portion.

Communication Plan

The three of us will communicate via group e-mail messages and text messaging to ensure each team member is aware of the project's progress, and to propose questions and feedback about our various sections of this project. We will use Googledocs as a way of housing our group's research findings so that each of us has access to all project information. We will conduct project update "meetings" in class each week that will be informal and strictly informational to further understand the progress of our group.

After the initial research is conducted in phase one we will have a brainstorming meeting to share information and propose ways of creating our report. After the report is created, we will use Google-docs to revise and share each other's work.

When we start the second phase we will meet to decide where we are going to take our findings, presumably in another brainstorming session. We will adopt the same revision and collaboration process described above for our final proposal.

Roles

We are all willing and able to switch roles from time to time if the need is recognized. For now, our assigned roles are as follows:

Project manager: Robin Stremlow
Background researcher: Kelly Washburn
In-person researchers: Robin Stremlow, Laurel Sutherland
Project plan writer: Robin Stremlow
Project plan editors: Kelly Washburn, Laurel Sutherland
Report writers: Kelly Washburn, Laurel Sutherland
Report editor: Robin Stremlow

Document designer: Robin Stremlow
Speakers: Robin Stremlow, Kelly Washburn, Laurel Sutherland

Timeline

DATES	ACTIONS	MILESTONES
Week 1 (November 1–7)	List of potential contacts Get and watch movie website research	List done
Week 2 (November 8–14)	Conduct all interviews and on-site research Finish virtual research Brainstorming/Information Sharing meeting	Virtual research done
Week 3 (November 15–21)	Identify mouse characteristics Draft report Write report	Write report
Week 4 (November 22–28)	Edit, polish, design report Virtual meeting to review report Last-minute changes	Present report
Week 5 (Nov 29–Dec 5)	Research Lansing group Brainstorm ideas	Phase 2 research done
Week 6 (December 6–12)	Write proposal	Write proposal
Week 7 (December 13–?)	Write, edit, polish, review final proposal	Present proposal

MICHIGAN STATE
U N I V E R S I T Y

Date

Organization Name
Organization Address

Dear _____:

As you may or may not be aware, the MSU Writing Center will be celebrating its 20th anniversary in the next academic year. The center has had an exciting couple of decades, growing and changing shape to its recent configuration, which includes the home center in Bessey Hall, as well as 7 other satellite centers in MSU Library, Holden Hall, Hubbard Hall, Brody Hall, SASS, the Business College Complex, and our online space in Second Life. In addition, we are anticipating three new satellites in MSU neighborhoods in 2012-13.

To commemorate the Writing Center's thriving connection to the MSU community, we are planning a year-long series of events for MSU students, faculty, and alumni. We're writing now to invite you to join us in co-sponsoring one of these events. In particular we're proposing (name the specific event we want to propose here). We'd like to collaborate with you in the following ways (list how we want them to be a part of the event – provide space? publication? help pay for speakers? etc).

COLLEGE OF
***ARKS AND
LETTERS***
The Writing Center
Michigan State University
300 Bessey Hall
East Lansing, MIchigan
48824-1033

517/432-3610
FAX: 517/432-3828

We aim to have all events confirmed by the beginning of March 2012 in order to facilitate advertising at spring and summer alumni events. Consequently, we'll be discussing options with potential partners in December and January.

Through these partnerships, we're hoping to highlight the interconnectedness between the MSU Writing Center and other organizations and departments in the college and across campus.

Thank you so much for your time, and we look forward to working with you!

Sincerely,
Trixie Smith and the 20/20 Celebration Committee

REPORTS

When you organize information to present to someone else, either within or outside of the company (or classroom), you create a report. Reports may be formal or informal, long or short, but no matter what type, you should consider the purpose of the report and the audience who will be receiving it. You should also consider whether or not a format already exists for this kind of report. For example, your workplace may always require a travel report after you return from a work-related trip. If this is mandatory, chances are that a form or format exists, which probably includes items such as trip date and destination, activities or people visited, accomplishments, and a budget. If a form or required format exists, you should always follow it. Otherwise, short reports are often given as memo reports with the needed information. Other types of reports you may be asked to write include progress reports, investigative or trouble reports, feasibility reports, and usability reports.

The progress report, also known as the activity report or status report, is often sent to team members on collaborative projects as well as the project manager; it may also go on to other stakeholders. Status reports are also a common classroom assignment for project groups. These are typically used with multistep projects that cover a large amount of time. The reports are written at regular intervals to update clients, managers, or other stakeholders, and they report what has been done and what remains to be done. They may include reports about employees on the project, supplies, equipment, permits, budgets, problems encountered, and projected completion date. The status report often ends with recommendations about future steps, especially if these steps differ from the original plan.

The investigative or trouble report analyzes a workplace problem or issue and may call for a recommendation as a result of your research. You may be asked to investigate ways to solve a recurring problem or issue, or you may be asked to analyze a specific accident or problem that occurred. Keep in mind that investigations into specific problems may become part of legal cases, so be clear when you are reporting facts and speculating about possible causes or issues. Again, internal forms or formats may exist for both progress and investigative reports, but if not, these reports should be clearly organized with an introductory statement of purpose, a body that uses headings to organize its various components, and a conclusion that outlines next steps or recommendations.

Another common report is the feasibility report, which is used in considering new projects or programs, developing new products or services, expanding the company in some way, or making some other large-scale change. The feasibility report examines not only the actual costs but also the ramifications in areas such as customer satisfaction, workplace morale, community relations, and legalities. It weighs the costs against the benefits in order to make a recommendation. It may suggest steps to minimize damage or prepare for change if the company decides to move forward with the change. Depending on the magnitude of the change, this report may be short and informal or quite lengthy and formal, perhaps going out to large numbers of stakeholders, such as stockholders, trustees, and boards of directors.

The **usability report** is produced after you have conducted usability testing to see if users or readers can easily use a document, manual, or website. Usability testing helps create products that are functional, easy to use, and reflect well on the company. After conducting tests with users or potential users, which may include interviews, comprehension tests, surveys, and focus groups, testers write a usability report to explain what is working and what is not and to recommend revisions or changes.

Formal reports, such as large-scale feasibility or recommendation reports, as well as internal proposals and client proposals, follow a typical pattern (see the sample business report). Not all reports will have all of these parts, but they typically come in the following order:

Front matter

1. **Title page**: The title page may include the title of the report, the person preparing the report, the company for which the writer works, the date, and the person or company to whom the report is being submitted.

2. **Abstract**: The abstract summarizes what is in the report, highlighting the main points in 200–250 words. It should actually be written last so that it accurately reflects the contents of the report.

3. **Table of contents (TOC)**: The TOC lists all of the major headings in the report, in order, along with their respective page numbers.

4. **List of figures, list of tables**: Figures include all drawings, photographs, maps, charts, and graphs. If a report contains more than five, they should be listed in the front matter, along with their page numbers. Likewise, if a report includes more than five tables, they should be listed in the front matter along with their page numbers. All figures and tables should be numbered consecutively with Arabic numerals (e.g., Fig. 1, Fig. 2, Table 1, Table 2).

5. **Foreword**: The foreword is a type of introduction that is written by someone other than the author of the report, such as the executive sponsoring the report or an expert in the field.

6. **Preface**: The preface is an introduction written by the author. It may discuss purpose and scope and offer tips for the readers. It may also contain acknowledgments for those who helped with the report and credit permissions for copyrighted materials used in the report.

7. **List of abbreviations and symbols**: If a report uses a large number of abbreviations and/or symbols that may not be familiar to the readers, the author may want to list them (and explain them) in the front matter.

Body

8. **Executive summary**: The executive summary is different from the abstract in that it provides a more complete overview of the entire text; in fact, it is written in the same order as the report and is typically about 10 percent of the length of the final report. Many people may read only the executive summary, so it should be written in a way that can be read independently of the full report. Never introduce information in the executive summary that is not in the full report.

9. **Introduction**: The introduction gives readers the general context for the report, including its purpose and scope, and often includes an overview of the main points.

10. **Text**: This is the main body of the report. It is organized using informative but short headings, and discusses how the topic was researched or investigated, what methods were used, what information was considered, and how problems were solved or choices were made. The text is usually enhanced by the use of visuals or graphics and is also supported by the use of valid references and supporting evidence, as appropriate.

11. **Conclusion**: The conclusion pulls together the information in the report and interprets the findings for the reader.

12. **Recommendations**: The recommendations, which may be combined with the conclusion, state what actions should or should not be taken based on the research findings.

Back matter

13. **Notes**: Reports may contain notes that further expand lines of thinking or provide additional background information. They may appear as footnotes or as endnotes to the text.

14. **References**: A list of References or a Works Cited page should appear at the end of the report, documenting sources used directly in the report.

15. **Appendixes**: An appendix supplements the report with information that is too detailed or lengthy for the body of the report. Often this information or level of detail is only of interest to certain segments of the intended audience.

16. **Bibliography**: The bibliography differs from the References section in that it includes all works consulted during the research, not just those cited in the report.

17. **Glossary**: At times you may need to give an alphabetical list of specialized terms and their definitions to aid your readers.

18. **Index**: With longer reports, you may want to include an alphabetical list of major topics, subtopics, and key terms, along with their page numbers. An index allows readers to quickly find information about specific topics.

Formal reports are often sent out for reading prior to meetings in which they will be discussed. In addition, reports are often sent out with a cover letter or transmittal letter, which identifies what is being sent, to whom, and by whom, as well as any information or content that should be highlighted for readers.

PROPOSALS

A proposal is a type of report that may be used internally or externally and is usually persuasive in nature because in a proposal you are asking someone to do something, whether it is a request to your manager for flexible scheduling, a bid for a job, a proposed policy change, or a solicitation for funds to renovate the employee break room. A proposal should have a clear, concise statement of purpose that tells the reader what you are proposing. It may follow the organizational pattern of a formal report and often will include a cost analysis and/or budget, as well as a work plan or timeline for the proposed action. Again, this type of report may include a cover letter or letter of transmittal.

BUSINESS PLANS

A particular type of proposal you may see in class assignments, as well as the real world, is the business plan. The business plan outlines an idea for a new business for the purpose of recruiting investors. It typically follows the format of the formal report. The body of the report may include the following types of information about the proposed business: mission/vision; background for the company, as well as the industry it will be competing in (industry analysis); products or services to be provided; market analysis; competition analysis; marketing strategy; operations plan, including the management team and its qualifications; development and/or workflow plan; and start-up and maintenance costs. In addition, a business plan might also include projected earnings, risks or possible problems, and an exit strategy for investors.

PRESENTATIONS

Business plans and proposals are often shared with colleagues and clients through formal presentations. Likewise, colleagues may share ideas at conferences and symposia organized by various disciplines or around topics of interest. These oral presentations are often accompanied by visual aids, such as a PowerPoint or Prezi presentation. In your classes, you may be asked to give an oral presentation in conjunction with turning in a project or report; these presentations may be for your classmates, the larger school community, or even for community and business partners. Presentations are organized much like written papers, with an introduction and statement of purpose; a body, which includes your main points and any evidence used to illustrate or support these points; and a conclusion, which may include recommendations for action. When your presentation includes the use of presentation software, there are some additional guidelines you should keep in mind:

- ❏ Use text sparingly.
  - » Use bulleted or numbered lists rather than complete sentences.

> » Include no more than 5–6 listed items per slide.

> » Use numbers for ranked or sequenced lists and bullets otherwise.

❏ Make your visuals consistent, using the same background and color scheme, font, size, and spacing across slides.

❏ To be sure the text is visible even at the back of the room, the font should typically be no smaller than 30 points, with the headings even larger. The contrast between the text and the background should be sharp to make it easier to read or view.

❏ Use graphs, charts, and other illustrations to clarify and simplify your message and add emphasis and interest. Do not overuse.

❏ Match your talk to your visuals. Develop clear transitions for yourself, so you'll keep your talk and your visuals in line with each other; clear transitions will also help your audience members keep pace with you.

Figure 6.1 CRAP Principles

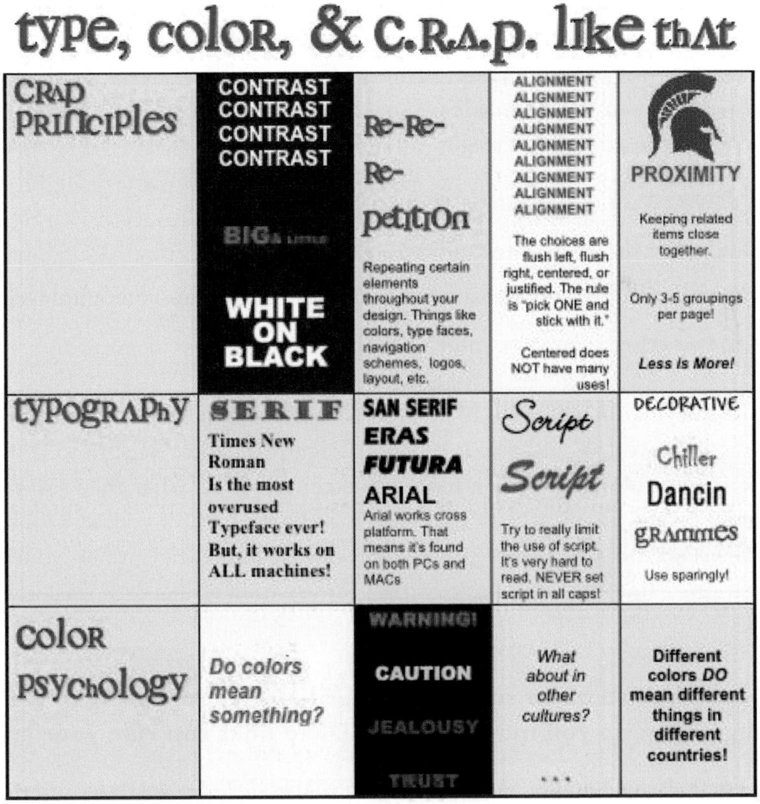

The CRAP principle concept was coined by author Robin Williams in her book *The Web Design Book for Non-designers.*
The study of typography is part of a 4-yr degree at some schools; as is Color Theory.
This handout is the BARE MINIMUM backgrounding for these concepts.

❑ Do not read the text on your visuals to your audience members.

❑ Bring a printout of your visuals with you and be prepared to move forward without the visuals if you need to. Technology doesn't always work, even when you have tested it and practiced with it beforehand.

Information might also be shared visually via a handout, brochure, or poster presentation; different venues or instructors might require different formats or leave the option up to you. With all presentations, it is important to follow published directions, including time limits and size requirements (36" x 48" is the typical poster size, for example, but larger sizes might be an option); you should also be prepared to answer questions from attendees.

Posters, handouts, and brochures are visual tools and should follow good design principles, such as the CRAP principles: contrast, repetition, alignment, proximity. See Figure 6.1.

DESIGNING AND WRITING FOR THE WEB

It is very important for most businesses to have a presence on the Web today, so web design and writing for the Web are important business writing skills to have. When designing and writing for the Web, you must consider your audience and purpose. Your answers to these questions will help you with your design:

❑ What do you want to happen on your website?

❑ How and when do you want people to access your site?

❑ How do you plan for your website to affect your business or your employees?

❑ How do you expect people to interact with your website?

Consider what information you want to include as well as how to organize it. Because websites are a visual medium, you should also use good design principles. Be sure to consider details such as background color; type color, font, and size; graphics (what they say, whether they enhance content or not, and how they affect site loading time); how your site looks and works in various browsers; and whether or not viewers always know they are on your site, (e.g., is your organization's name, logo, and basic contact information visible or at least accessible from every page?).

Regularly check to make sure all of your links work. The Web is an ever-changing entity, so you must keep up. Dead links can ruin your credibility.

Writing for the Web may include Web design, but it also includes writing content that will go on a site designed by someone else. You may be asked to write a description of your department, for example, or that report your team just completed may go on the company website as a downloadable attachment. You may become part of your workplace blog team, writing blogs on a regular basis about topics of interest to your website's target audience. In addition, many businesses now take advantage of the numerous social media sites that exist on the Web. You could be asked to post on your company's Facebook page, send tweets to its Twitter feed, upload images to its Flickr site, create an interest board related to your newest project on Pinterest, look for networking possibilities on LinkedIn, or create material to populate any number of social media sites related to your specific field or industry. As these various tools have different parameters and expectations, as well as different audiences, you will have to adjust your writing style for the audience and purpose of each, as well as the medium itself.

RÉSUMÉS AND COVER LETTERS

Your resumé is an overview of the education, skills, and experiences you will bring to a position. The typical entry-level resumé is one page, organized into major categories, and carefully designed. The visual impact of a resumé can affect the way it is read by a recruiter or potential employer, so use effective design skills. Pay attention to the arrangement of the text on the page, the use of white space, and your choice of font size and type. You will also want to use parallel lists, maintain consistent style, and make sure it is free of errors. Finally, in preparing your resumé, be sure to use a variety of strong action verbs. See Table 6.2 for suggestions.

Resumés may include the following types of sections. The job, your qualifications, and the field may determine which of these you include:

- ❏ Heading: Your address (both school and permanent if applicable), phone number(s), and professional e-mail address should be included.

- ❏ Objective: List the job title, type of experience, and tag line (fields and experts differ as to the importance of the objective on a resumé).

- ❏ Skills or Qualifications Summary: This is a type of overview of your resumé.

- ❏ Education: List the schools attended, degrees, subject areas, certifications, and special training, as well as the dates for each.

- ❏ Employment Experience: This information is usually presented in reverse chronological order, but it may also be listed by experience type. Include relevant internships, use action verbs, and focus on achievements when possible.

- ❏ Related Skills and Abilities: These include professional memberships, volunteer work, networks, publications, language and technology skills, writing abilities.

- ❏ Honors and Activities: This should be information that will enhance your appeal and should not duplicate information in other sections.

- ❏ References and Portfolios: This is a separate references page that includes the same header as your resumé. Be prepared to provide it when asked or during the interview process. Portfolios are usually provided upon request unless the job advertisement asks for them up front. Many professionals create online or e-portfolios so they can provide

TABLE 6.2

Action Verbs for Résumés

Analytical

analyzed	confirmed	estimated	negotiated	researched
ascertained	critiqued	evaluated	prescribed	scrutinized
assessed	deciphered	examined	prioritized	studied
compared	deliberated	forecasted	projected	substantiated
computed	determined	investigated	questioned	synthesized
concluded	diagnosed	measured	recommended	verified

Communication

addressed	communicated	explained	persuaded	reported
apprised	composed	informed	presented	spoke
authored	drafted	lectured	publicized	summarized
clarified	edited	marketed	queried	wrote

Creativity

brainstormed	designed	envisioned	illustrated	shaped
constructed	engineered	fabricated	produced	visualized

Initiative

accomplished	dedicated	implemented	launched	revamped
achieved	demonstrated	improved	minimized	revised
built	enriched	initiated	modernized	stimulated
coordinated	expanded	inspired	modified	suggested
created	expedited	introduced	multiplied	updated

Leadership

advised	delegated	empowered	guided	moderated
appointed	designated	enabled	hired	motivated
approved	directed	encouraged	influenced	recruited
authorized	elicited	facilitated	instructed	supervised
chaired	employed	founded	judged	trained

Organization

arranged	centralized	consolidated	organized	recorded
assembled	charted	correlated	planned	regulated
budgeted	classified	indexed	processed	scheduled
catalogued	compiled	orchestrated	purchased	tabulated

Problem Solving

aided	extracted	procured	rejuvenated	revived
alleviated	finalized	reconciled	relieved	settled
customized	generated	rectified	remedied	streamlined
debugged	invented	refined	retrieved	strengthened
extended	lightened	reinforced	revitalized	transformed

Teamwork

assisted	contributed	mediated	partnered	
collaborated	cooperated	participated		

SAMPLE RÉSUMÉ

nina elias

nina@e-mail.com
123.456.7899
123 Main St
Anytown, US 12345
anywebsite.com

learning

M.S. Information, Human Computer Interaction   Expected April 2013
University of Michigan - School of Information   3.91 GPA

B.A. Professional Writing, Design Specialization   May 2011
Michigan State University   3.94 GPA

working

User Interface Designer   September 2012 – Present
Linux Box   Ann Arbor, MI
- Conducted interviews and heuristic evaluation to learn about users
- Created and iterated on email archival & ediscovery software prototype

User Experience Research Intern   May 2012 – August 2012
T-Mobile USA   Bellevue, WA
- Conducted usability tests, heuristic evaluations, and competitive analyses on software and mobile
- Created wireframes, sketches, and mockups
- Presented findings and recommendations to stakeholders and product teams

User Experience Research Intern   August 2010 – January 2012
TechSmith Corporation   Okemos, MI
- Conducted usability tests on workflow concepts, software, and help documentation
- Conducted depth interviews, literature review and competitive analyses
- Collaboratively solved product issues through design studios and affinity walls
- Presented findings and recommendations using infographics, blog posts, and presentations

HCI Researcher   May 2010 – July 2010
Virginia Tech, Research Experience for Undergraduates in HCI   Blacksburg, VA
- Interviewed designers and researchers on design, reuse, and storyboarding processes
- Coded and analyzed interviews for inclusion in CHI 2011 paper

Art Production Intern   May 2009 – July 2009
Entertainment Publications   Troy, MI
- Created consumer materials using Adobe InDesign, Photoshop, and Illustrator

Writing Consultant   December 2008 – May 2011
Michigan State University, Writing Center   East Lansing, MI
- Presented workshops on effective PowerPoint presentations
- Assisted students with creating and editing patents, essays, websites, video projects, etc.

Technology Guide   August 2008 – May 2011
Michigan State University, College of Arts & Letters   East Lansing, MI
- Designed workflow, interface, and conducted usability tests on web applications
- Assisted staff through consultations, tech documentation, and workshops

volunteering

UX Research Intern, Prevent Child Abuse America   April 2012
Conducted competitive analysis and heuristic evaluation and presented findings to stakeholders

Web Designer, Lansing Give Camp   March 2010
Created mockups and IA for non-profits and coded front end in DotNetNuke

Designer, Information Technology Empowerment Center   September 2009 – June 2010
Crafted mockups and IA, assisted with tech workshops for children, customized Joomla theme

President, Spartan Web Authoring Team   May 2009 – May 2011
Used HTML, CSS, & Photoshop to create mockups for non-profit and student organizations
Planned and organized meetings, workshops, and speakers

Webmaster, Tower Guard Sophomore Honors Society   August 2008 – 2009
Volunteered 120+ hours on tests and schoolwork with disabled MSU students

ux skills
Affinity diagram
Competitive Analysis
Contextual Inquiry
Ethnography
Focus Groups
Heuristic Evaluation
Info Design
Info Architecture
Interviews
Persona creation
Prototyping
Sketching
Storyboarding
Survey design
Usability testing
Wireframing

tools
Axure
Balsamiq
CSS
Final Cut Pro
HTML
Illustrator
InDesign
JavaScript
jQuery
Morae
MS Office
MySQL
Omnigraffle
Ovo
PHP
Photoshop
Powerpoint

awards
2011 CHI paper

Most Outstanding
Graduating Senior
2011 nominee

courses
Contextual Inquiry
Database Design
Design of Complex
Websites
Evaluation of
Systems & Services
Fundamentals of
Human Behavior
Information
Architecture
Interaction Design
Market Research
Networked
Computing
Personal Informatics

the link in their résumé and make it easy to access. Portfolios should highlight your skills and give examples of your best work.

Also keep in mind the type of job for which you are applying. An applicant for a graphic artist job can take more liberties with résumé design than an applicant for an entry-level position at a conservative company. When hiring committees are reviewing applications, they are looking for people to eliminate, so you need to make a positive first impression.

Make sure your résumé is easy to scan, by the human eye as well as digital document scanners.

A résumé is usually accompanied by a cover letter or application letter. The application letter is where you sell yourself as the best applicant for the position, so it must be interesting and persuasive. Here you introduce yourself and your skills and explain why you are interested in the position, as well as how you are qualified for the position. You should give specific examples or highlight items from your résumé to demonstrate how you would be a good fit for the company or job. The application letter also provides an opportunity to request an interview. It is not a good idea to discuss salary or benefits in the application letter unless the job ad or description specifically asks you to.

Make the header on your application letter match the header on your résumé.

OTHER BUSINESS WRITING FORMS

Depending on the type of job you have or the company you work for, you may also write in many other forms. You may be asked to take minutes for meetings and distribute them to members in attendance as well as to those who couldn't be there. You may be asked to create or contribute to a company magazine or newsletter that is mailed out in hard copy or sent as an e-newsletter to people on your company's mailing list. You may find yourself creating forms to use in the office or send to clients. Likewise, you may have to write directions for goods and services or create manuals for products and procedures. In addition, if you find yourself in an internship, you may be asked to write daily or weekly logs and reflections, as well as summaries of what you've done and learned.

WRITING EFFECTIVELY IN BUSINESS
KNOW THE AUDIENCE(S) IN BUSINESS

People in business must write for a variety of audiences. Much of this writing is directed toward colleagues—bosses, employees, team members, project managers—people who are internal in the business. Likewise, much writing is directed outside the business, to past, present, or potential clients. People in business must communicate with others in their fields—industry experts, accreditation and licensing officials, professional colleagues, and competitors. Or they may be required to present at conferences or workshops, write journal or magazine articles, or share through newsletters, blogs, and websites. Additionally, they may need to communicate with more general, inexpert audiences through websites, blogs, newsletters, newspaper articles and editorials, and community talks or presentations. For these reasons, it is important to always know who you are writing for:

- ❑   Who are your primary readers?
- ❑   Who else might read your writing or listen to your presentation?
- ❑   What will the members of your audience already know about your topic?
- ❑   What will you need to define or explain?
- ❑   Will your audience be predisposed to agree or disagree with your point of view?
- ❑   What do you want this audience to do or believe?
- ❑   What kinds of evidence will be most convincing for this audience?

KNOW THE QUESTIONS TO ASK IN BUSINESS

As a student, your research questions or writing goals may be assigned to you by your instructor. Often, however, you will have to make a decision yourself about these questions or goals. You can begin your writing preparation by asking yourself what you want to know more about and what you need to understand better in order to complete the assigned task or goal. You should also think about how and where you can locate this information. Do you need figures and statistics that already exist in a government database, such as the Census Bureau? Do you need to conduct your own market tests, interviews, or client surveys? Do you need to research government regulations or material costs? Perhaps you will need to locate models that show you how employees in your company have successfully approached this type of writing in the

Did you know?

What social media users need to understand is that each social media channel attracts a unique audience, who will choose to communicate in a particular way, using various tools to carry on a Web conversation. If you are using any of the many available channels [e.g., Facebook, Twitter, Tweetdeck, Hoot Suite, Pinterest, LinkedIn], know who your audience is and with whom, in particular, you are conversing. Learn how to use the right method of delivery so that you can best relate and deliver a meaningful message, in a language they can understand.

• • •

"Target Your Messages: Know Your Audience." By Dawn Boshcoff. http://www.business2community.com/social-media/target-your-messages-know-your-audience-096776.

Did you know?

past. The type of writing required to achieve your communication goals should guide your research approach and topics.

KNOW THE KINDS OF EVIDENCE USED IN BUSINESS ARGUMENTS

Writers in the various fields of business use both quantitative and qualitative data in order to make arguments, support claims, and sell products. Both types of data come from primary research in the field or lab, as well as secondary research from other published resources. Common types of evidence used in business writing include facts and figures, examples, definitions, testimonies, and stories or narratives. Facts and figures, or quantitative data, are often presented as numbers within the text, or as a combination of numbers and visuals, such as charts and graphs in the text or in appendixes. You may need to present the methods you used to arrive at the numbers you present, including the mathematical formulas used or developed to test data, to look for or extend patterns, or to demonstrate causal relationships. Likewise, you may find it helpful or even necessary to use established statistical tests when presenting your quantitative data, so you should familiarize yourself with the computer software available at your institution or required in your field. Make sure your facts and figures are as up to date and accurate as possible.

The old business maxim that "what gets measured, matters" is overused but nonetheless powerful, especially when applied to corporate responsibility. When information and metrics are combined with disclosure and transparency, corporate posturing on issues that affect society can be quickly replaced with fact-based analysis and discussion. One example is Nike, Inc.'s published Corporate Responsibility (CR) Report for fiscal years 2007–2009. It's a slickly produced multimedia display of data and information . . .

Some critics of corporate responsibility reports believe they can't help but be self-serving. And, in fact, more companies are reporting. Sixty-six of the S&P 100 firms produced a formal sustainability report with performance data in 2008, a 35 percent jump from the 49 reports produced in 2007, according to a report from the Sustainable Investment Research Analyst Network (SIRAN), a working group of the Social Investment Forum (SIF). However, the SIRAN survey found that only six S&P 100 firms publish complete sustainability reports that meet the highest "A" level reporting standard set by the Global Reporting Initiative.

In the end, it's difficult to see how more reporting can't help, as long as it's done well. Nike's latest effort is a good example of how the process can lead to data being gathered, metrics developed and performance benchmarks set. The process grew out of Nike's public floggings in the 1990s, says CEO Parker, when "we learned to view transparency as an asset, not a risk."

• • •

"Nike: Corporate Responsibility at a 'Tipping Point'." By Michael Connor. http://business-ethics.com/2010/01/24/2154-nike-corporate-responsibility-at-a-tipping-point.

Qualitative data are non-numerical and may include testimonials from clients; comments from focus groups, interviews, and surveys; and stories and observations from employers and employees, clients or customers. Expert testimony often carries more weight with readers, so be prepared to explain your expert's credentials or qualifications. When possible, use multiple sources and types of evidence. You may often use a combination of both quantitative and qualitative data—for example, percentages that show how many customers say they are pleased with your services alongside sample comments from satisfied customers.

The most important question to ask is this: What kind of evidence is needed to support my claim or to make it persuasive to my intended audience? Of course, you must also present evidence in an ethical manner. Withholding evidence or not giving the full picture because you think it hurts your argument is unethical and presents inaccurate results; this misuse of data will be detrimental in the long run. In addition, you should make sure that the evidence used, no matter what kind, actually supports the claim you are making (avoid leaps in logic and inaccurate cause-and-effect arguments, for example).

KNOW THE WRITING AND STYLE CONVENTIONS IN BUSINESS WRITING

In the world of business, you only get one chance for a great first impression. The stakes are high—you are asking an investor for money, a customer for an order, or another executive for a partnership. Badly written letters, long rambling or emotional e-mails, or an obvious lack of spell-checking will brand you as a poor business risk before the message is even considered.

—Marty Zwilling, Cayenne Consulting
"Business Writing Style Is as Important as Content"

A good business writer communicates clearly, is aware of his or her audience, uses complete and thorough research (both primary and secondary), presents appropriate and accurate evidence for the goals of the writing, and uses the best format for the information and audience. To be a good business writer, you should accurately use the required documentation system and follow the basic tenets of all good writing—be organized, provide easy-to-read material, and make sure the material is grammatically correct. In addition, here are some specific conventions you may want to keep in mind when writing for business:

❏ Use short simple sentences.

❏ Use active voice. Also use verbs rather than nouns whenever possible.

Example:
The stockholders decided to change our organizational structure. Not, *The stockholders made a decision to change our organizational structure.*

❏ Write using second person or what some call the "you" viewpoint, which puts the reader's interests at the forefront. This point of view not only uses the words *you* and *your* to speak directly to the reader (the client or customer), it also stresses the benefit to the reader, not the company.

An exception here may be when you have bad or negative news. Since you want to avoid being accusatory with clients, using the "you" viewpoint may mean adopting a passive or indirect style.

For example: The budget should include matching funds from the agency (not, *Your budget does not indicate any matching funds from the agency***).**

❏ Use words and sentence structures that fit your audience and your communication format. The company's instant messaging system may allow for more informal communication between co-workers; this same style would be inappropriate for a letter going out to potential customers.

❏ Avoid biased language that may offend your readers and damage your credibility. Language that makes assumptions or is based on stereotypes about gender, ethnicity, age, mental or physical (dis)ability, or sexual orientation is not effective. Often differences among people are not relevant to the discussion, so avoid bias by not mentioning them. When the differences are relevant, research the accepted usage or the appropriateness of a term or expression. In addition, you can often avoid bias or awkward phrasing by using plural forms.

Example:
All employees should submit an evaluation form. Not, *Every employee should submit his or her evaluation form.*

See Table 6.3 for some common terms that have a preferred form of expression in business.

TABLE 6.3

Forms of Expression in Business	
Yes	**No**
chair, chairperson	chairman, chairwoman
police officer	policeman, policewoman
an employee with a disability	disabled employee
significant others welcome	spouses welcome

❏ Design your business communication effectively. Many types of communication have very specific and stylized forms such as letters, memos, and résumés. Likewise, with items such as brochures, newsletters, flyers, or even websites, the visual design of a document may be just as important as the written content. Design elements to consider and learn more about include the effective use of the following:

» White space: White space is used to frame the text and provide visual cues to the reader.

» Color: The colors themselves as well as their placement can be important as they are used to highlight items, emphasize material, organize material, and guide the reader.

» Font or typeface: Size, type, serif versus sans-serif, emphasis (underlining, italics, bold, and upper and lower case) can all affect readability and accessibility.

» Arrangement: Headings, headers, and footers, text justification, lists, and columns are all used to organize material on the page and help guide the reader through the document.

» Graphics: When integrating graphics, consider the proportion of image to text, the message or statement in the graphic, the graphic's connection to the text, the understandability of icons or global graphics, the purpose behind the graphic, and the relationship being shown in the graphic, as well as the words being replaced by the graphic.

1. **Graphics should always serve a specific function and should be as simple as possible.**
2. **Give each graphic a caption that clearly describes its content.**
3. **Figures and tables should be numbered chronologically below the graphic (e.g., Fig. 6-A, Fig. 6-B), and should be referred to in the text.**
4. **If your school, program, or company has a style guide, review it and use it.**

❏ Write effectively in collaborative groups. Many businesses operate through the use of project teams and working groups. This cooperative model may require you to research and write collaboratively. Such groups are designed to bring together multiple areas of expertise, experience, and viewpoints as well as to share the workload, often with a goal of shortening the time to completion. As part of a team, you will be expected to contribute your knowledge, meet your deadlines, and give feedback to your team members.

Your work will go more smoothly if you treat your teammates with respect, even when you disagree. Creative differences can lead to better outcomes if teams aren't hampered by bad tempers and hurt feelings.

❏ Be aware that many businesses operate in an international or global market, which means you may be writing for audiences with different rhetorical patterns, approaches to leadership, methods of persuasion, and styles of communication. They might even operate under different rules and regulations. In addition, you may be operating across technologies, general business practices, and time zones, as well as understandings of time.

KNOW THE APPROPRIATE DOCUMENTATION SYSTEM FOR BUSINESS WRITING

APA, the documentation style developed by the American Psychological Association, is often used in the social sciences and is the style most often used in business (see Chapter 12). It uses an author-date method of documentation for both its in-text citations and its references list at the end of the document. Putting the author's last name and the year of the publication in parentheses within the text as soon as the source is mentioned emphasizes the timeliness of the source and lends credibility to the writer. Some journals within the discipline of business may have their own documentation style guides, so always check to see what a particular publication says about how to prepare citations. In addition, in class you may be asked to use other guides such as MLA (the style guide of the Modern Language Association) or CMS (the *Chicago Manual of Style*). You should always follow the directions given. If none exist, use APA.

Content Strategy Report   1

CONTENT STRATEGY REPORT

Women's Center of Greater Lansing

By Whitney Orth, Callie Gesmundo, and Amy Miller

Introduction

This content strategy report is designed to provide the Women's Center of Greater Lansing with a clear understanding of the effectiveness of the content that is on the official website as well as strategies for improving and maintaining this content.

EXCERPT FROM A SAMPLE BUSINESS REPORT

Organization Background

The Women's Center of Greater Lansing is a private, nonprofit organization that provides services to women in the greater Lansing area. Its mission as an organization is to help women realize their potential. This is done by offering support groups, counseling services, and various workshops and seminars, all of which empower women to take hold of their lives and improve their current situation.

The Women's Center of Greater Lansing's website has two main objectives:

- to get public support; mainly through money donations, but also with volunteers and interns
- provide women in need of help with information about their organization, in hopes that the information will be useful, or that they will seek further help from the center.

Objective

The goal of this content strategy report is to provide the Women's Center of Greater Lansing with the resources needed to understand how the website can fulfill its objectives as effectively as possible.

Content Audit

Approach and Methods

A content audit of the current content on the Women's Center has been conducted. This means that all of the content on the website (links, pages, lists, widgets, pdfs) was recorded. This audit can be used to understand what content is currently on the website, and how the content is functioning in regards to the goals of the website.

The content audit was approached by dividing the website into twelve sections. Within each section the content was critically read and certain characteristics were analyzed—including layout, navigation, and, most importantly, whether or not the information displayed fit the organization and the website objectives.

In addition, the following characteristics of content were assessed and recorded:

- content type
- topic of the content
- who maintains the content
- date of creation

- date the content was last updated
- audience
- purpose of content
- if the content is redundant, trivial, or outdated
- any additional notes (mostly about the content and purpose not aligning, or serious problems with content that could not be discussed in any other section)

The audit spreadsheet is clearly labeled with each of these headings. The content is organized according to the page it is found on, and how deep content is within the site. For example, 1 would be the home page, 1.1 would be content on that homepage (1.1.1 would be a page that was linked to the homepage). The complete audit has been recorded on a spreadsheet and is included in Appendix 1.

Recommendations

Based on our research into the content that already exists on the website, as well as the research into the use of branding, there are several recommendations that we have proposed to make changes and additions to the website. These recommendations will act as a way to improve the function of the website, so that it will better fulfill the goals of the Women's Center of Greater Lansing. The recommendations are as follows:

- Move the website to a WordPress platform.
- Combine the News Release page with the Newsletter page.
- Restructure navigation of "Donate" and "Get Involved" Pages.
- Revise "About Us" and "Contact Us" Page.
- Combine all information about classes onto one page.
- Add a search function to the website.

In the following paragraphs, we have explained these recommendations in further detail.

Move the website to a WordPress platform

A majority of the areas on the website that are preventing the goals of the Women's Center from being accomplished seem to occur because of the current workflow. All of the content must be updated by one individual in charge of the site, because she is the only individual who has the knowledge to use the website program. This individual is only a volunteer, which makes it difficult to require her to complete all the necessary updates and website maintenance the center needs on a regular basis. To solve this issue, the quickest fix would be to move the website to a WordPress template.

On a website that is created using WordPress, a page can be updated without the use or knowledge of HTML or CSS. To add content to a page, an individual uses an interface that is like creating a blog post or using a word processor program like Microsoft Word. This means that anyone who has access to the WordPress account will be able to edit or upload content easily. Once this change has been made to the website, updates to the website could be made quicker, which would help to lessen the pattern of outdated content on the website, because updating would no longer require the expertise of only one individual. In addition, WordPress has something called Search Engine Optimization, which means WordPress inflates the amount of times the website appears as a search result by choosing "keywords" for the website pages based on the content within them.

Combine the News Release Page with the Newsletter Page

The current content on the "News Release" and "Newsletter" pages has not been updated frequently enough, and also the content is too similar and causes confusion about the purpose of each page. The purpose of both the "News Release" page and the "Newsletter" page are to advertise the exciting news and events that are going on in the Center. Because of this similarity in purpose, the two pages should be combined to create one. This would eliminate the confusion, as well as give the "News" section more information, so it will be updated more frequently.

The information presented in the news section should be made to further fulfill the website's mission of recruiting donations and acting as a resource for women in need. Simply looking at these current sections of the website, a user (either a potential donor or a client) would not know why this content is important, or if the information pertains to them. Providing a few brief bullet points of what was touched on within each update could help better explain the importance of each newsletter, and whether or not it pertains to a specific person. This would clean up the news section and emphasize important information covered by each piece of information, allowing users to more effectively find information that they want or need.

ACTIVITIES

Welcome to the Conversation

Discuss these questions with your classmates in class or via a class wiki or shared blog.

1. Business writing can be directed toward either internal or external audiences. What types of writing are for each type of audience? How are the goals for these audiences different? How are they the same?

2. How can writing have either a positive or a negative effect on your business?

3. How can you create a positive impression of your business on the Web? How is a Web audience for your business different from other audiences?

4. What are some key components to effective writing in business?

5. What are some common mistakes that may offend/alienate your audience in business writing?

Writing to Learn

1. **Oral draft**: As you pick a topic for a larger research paper or project, it can help you to also prepare an oral draft as you go. In this activity, present a five-minute talk to a small group of classmates about your project in progress. Your listeners should each ask you a question about your project after your talk, which you should be able to answer. Not only will this activity help you develop your research into a final draft, it also provides valuable practice in presenting your work.

2. **Project notebook**: As you work on research topics, keep an informal project notebook to help organize and guide your work. Here you can track the progress of your project from the invention or brainstorming level through to planning market studies, case reviews, and statistical research.

3. **Summaries**: As you review model business plans or marketing strategies, write a brief summary of each that describes the key elements.

Learning to Write

1. **Oral presentations**: This is the formal, full version of the practice oral draft you may have completed. Here you will present your researched business plan to an assigned audience of your colleagues. You must research and effectively analyze your audience to determine the best rhetorical choices for your presentation. Do not forget to use appropriate visual aids for the context. Also review this chapter and follow your instructor's guidelines for appropriate format and presentation conventions for your field.

2. **Memo**: Choose a topic that often causes personnel problems in your prospective career within business. How would management handle this issue effectively? What are the best practices according to the literature on this topic? After you have researched practical ways to handle this topic, write a memo that informs a hypothetical company of the issue and then persuades them to resolve it using your research as a guide.

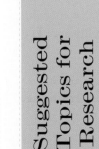

Suggested Topics for Research

1. What is the best social media platform for advertising, and why? Do certain products sell better to different social media demographics? Use primary and secondary sources to support your argument.

2. Develop a pitch for an American food company to establish restaurants in a developing nation. Be prepared to argue to the company why its products would do well in this emerging market, and why they should risk resources and reputation on a market with a possibly problematic economy.

READ MORE ABOUT IT

Alred, Gerald J., Charles T. Brusaw, and Walter E. Oliu. *The Business Writer's Handbook*. 9th ed. Boston: Bedford/St. Martin's, 2008. Print.

Evans, Poppy, and Mark A. Thomas. *Exploring the Elements of Design*, 2nd ed. Florence, KY: Delmar Cengage Learning, 2007. Print.

Freed, Richard, and Joe Romano. *Writing Winning Business Proposals: Your Guide to Landing the Client, Making the Sale, and Persuading the Boss*. New York: McGraw-Hill, 2003. Print.

Hall, Edward T. *Beyond Culture*. New York: Anchor Books, 1976. Print.

Hill, Charles L.W. *Global Business Today*. 7th ed. New York: McGraw-Hill, 2010. Print.

Krause, Jim. *Layout Index, Brochure, Web Design, Poster, Flyer, Advertising, Page Layout, Newsletter, Stationery Index*. Cincinnati: North Light Books, 2001. Print.

Lidwell, William, Kristina Holden, and Jill Butler. *Universal Principles of Design: 125 Ways to Enhance Usability, Influence Perception, Increase Appeal, Make Better Design Decisions, and Teach through Design*, Revised and Updated. Minneapolis: Rockport Publishers, 2010. Print.

McNeil, Patrick. *The Web Designer's Idea Book*. Vols. I and II. Palm Coast, FL: How Books, 2008 and 2010. Print.

Reynolds, Garr. *Presentation Zen: Simple Ideas on Presentation Design and Delivery*. Berkeley: New Riders P, 2008. Print.

University of Chicago Press Staff. *Chicago Manual of Style*. 16th ed. Chicago: U of Chicago P, 2010. Print.

Wilson, Kevin, and Jennifer Wauson. *The AMA Handbook of Business Writing: The Ultimate Guide to Style, Grammar, Punctuation, Usage, Construction, and Formatting*. New York: AMACOM, 2010. Print.

chapter 7

Writing in Education

HIGHER EDUCATION, COUNSELOR EDUCATION, EDUCATIONAL
LEADERSHIP, EDUCATIONAL PHILOSOPHY, EDUCATIONAL
TECHNOLOGY, PHYSICAL EDUCATION/KINESIOLOGY,
VOCATIONAL EDUCATION, RELIGIOUS EDUCATION, SECONDARY
EDUCATION, SPECIAL EDUCATION, AND ART EDUCATION

> *I believe that the community's duty to education is, therefore, its
> paramount moral duty. By law and punishment, by social agitation
> and discussion, society can regulate and form itself in a more or
> less haphazard and chance way. But through education society can
> formulate its own purposes, can organize its own means and resources,
> and thus shape itself with definiteness and economy in the direction in
> which it wishes to move.*
>
> —*John Dewey*

PURPOSES OF WRITING IN EDUCATION

The broad field of education covers many types of career and purpose, all with the central focus of teaching and assessment. Education uses a variety of research methods, both qualitative and quantitative, to analyze best teaching practices, assess teacher education, and create curricula. Writing in this discipline includes many different purposes, genres, and formats, each with their own style. The central focus of writing in any of these forms, however, is communication to audiences with an interest in education as a field or the results of active teaching or supervisory practice. The more specific purposes behind these communications may include providing information, making an argument, persuading people to agree or to act in a certain way, soliciting funds, or explaining behaviors, pedagogies, or areas for improvement. No matter what form you are using or what message you want to send, your writing will be more effective if it is clear and to the point and if it follows the conventions of the format you have chosen.

TYPES OF WRITING ASSIGNMENTS IN EDUCATION

The NCLB initiative is certainly not the first effort to apply scientific methods to educational practices. Since the beginning of formalized education, research has been used to help improve education and to determine how education works in a wide range of situations. Through scientific research, educators hope to obtain accurate and reliable information about important issues and problems that face the educational community.

—Marguerite Lodico et al

Writing in education often covers multiple genres and purposes, and the rhetorical components of audience and context determine how you should craft different pieces of writing. You will write lesson plans, which serve both as guides for your daily practice and as formal documentation that provides supervising administrators an insight into your teaching practices. Likewise, you may need to conduct a classroom observation for a practicum assignment or as part of your contribution to your department at school, but those observations could then lead you to develop a case study or a longer research paper to explore or argue for a certain theoretical construct or pedagogy. Education as a field is currently focused on accountability, meaning that schools are held accountable to state or federal guidelines and legislation regarding assessing and reporting student progress, generally via test scores. No Child Left Behind (NCLB) legislation of the first decade of the twenty-first century is still in place, although some provisions have been made by the Obama administration for flexibility in state school administration if certain criteria are met. However, throughout the education fields the emphasis on controlled, "scientific," measures of students' performance and progress remains. Being able to understand, design, write, implement, and interpret quantitative and qualitative research is necessary for all segments of the broader field of education.

LESSON PLANS

The goal of the lesson plan is to communicate a clear set of objectives and methods of assessing student performance. Usually lesson plans serve to inform multiple audiences. They are foremost geared to help you in planning and organizing your classes, but they are also often considered public documents. For example, if you teach in a public school, it is likely that your lesson plans will be subject to assessment by your supervisor or school board, depending on your location. Also, lesson plans are critical documents for teaching observations. Thus, while plans should be clear and concise enough for you to teach from them effectively, they must also be professional, grammatically correct, and fulfill all requirements of your instructor or employer. It is important that you follow the required format for these plans and clearly explain how your curriculum meets one or more requirements mandated for that course. Regulations vary by state, district, and grade level, so be sure you are using the correct standard for that educational context. Below are some general components for lesson planning, adapted from Madeline Hunter's Direct Instruction (DI) model. Note that not all lesson plans will use all of these components; rather, these are some general guiding principles for organizing a class session, and in turn, a lesson plan.

Box 7.1

General Components for Lesson Planning

- **Anticipatory set** (focus): an activity that prepares students for the main focus of the class session. This also includes the prerequisites the students will need to complete the day's work.

- **Purpose or Objective to lesson:** Be sure to state a complete objective, and match it to any required standards.

- **Input:** This is what the teacher will teach that students need to know.

- **Modeling:** This is how the teacher will show what the results of the activities should be.

- **Guided practice:** The teacher leads the students through the process.

- **Check for understanding**

- **Independent practice**

- **Closure:** Review of class session, or the wrap-up.

Adapted from Hunter, M. *Enhancing Teaching* 1994, pp 87–95

CURRICULUM GUIDES

A curriculum guide is a formal document that explains what should be taught in a certain context, why it should be taught, how it should be taught, and what adjustments may be made for different student populations. This general guide is tailored to specific pedagogical situations, and may be more general or more specific as needed. For example, one curriculum guide provides a specific curriculum for a standard high school algebra course. However, a curriculum written for an algebra course for advanced seventh graders might not have the same curriculum guide, as the implementation and assessment may need to change for the markedly different middle school population.

Often, curriculum guides are collaboratively written, as they are the product of a curriculum development committee. Regardless of whether they are written individually or collaboratively, certain key components should be considered, and the process of writing the guide should take many sources and opinions into account. Following is a standard process for writing these documents.

1. **Identify key issues and discipline trends in the content area and grade level.**

2. **Investigate the issues and needs involved. Specifically, what are the existing issues with program content, and what needs of the curriculum's community should be addressed?** This is often called a needs assessment, and it should account for variables such as teacher preparation, student and parent satisfaction, and test scores from previous curricula.

3. **Articulate curriculum philosophy, define goals, and develop and sequence objectives.** After developing a curriculum's philosophy, you should set the goals for the program, grade, or course should be set. After this basic framework, the

Did you know?

Bloom's Taxonomy

You are probably already familiar with the framework known as Bloom's Taxonomy, which many teachers use to guide their students through progressively difficult learning objectives. This hierarchical method provides an easy way to build on student knowledge. The full Taxonomy focuses on cognitive, affective, and psychomotor skills, but in many lesson plans your focus will be on cognitive skills, which are traditionally prioritized (and which are listed below). However, some educators argue for a more holistic approach to understanding cognition, and do not agree with a hierarchical view. Remember that your instructor or the specific needs of your classroom will dictate how you utilize the Taxonomy in your practice.

Cognitive:
1. Knowledge: recall facts, terms, concepts
2. Comprehension: interpretation, translation
3. Application: solve problems by applying knowledge
4. Analysis: understand components and find evidence to support generalizations
5. Synthesis: combine information to form a unique interpretation
6. Evaluation: judge information or validity based on internal evidence or external criteria

committee will develop curriculum objectives and sequence them appropriately. It is also important to address what resources are needed to implement the curriculum, and how the program might be assessed.

4. **Implementation.** After the curriculum guide is written, the committee ideally should monitor the curriculum's implementation. Do teachers understand and effectively employ the new curriculum?

5. **Evaluation.** Has this new curriculum proven successful? How is curriculum success measure, evaluated, or assessed? How should the curriculum be updated?

ASSESSMENT REPORTS

Assessment reports are comprehensive, well-written formal documents that explain the components of a student's psychological or psycho-educational evaluation. Within the entire field of education, these reports are used to guide instruction and to formulate plans for individual student progress. Within special education, these reports may also help guide treatments or advise caregivers. These reports influence decisions about the individual student on many levels, and may be considered legal documents, so it is vitally important that they communicate clearly for audiences including teachers, caregivers, parents, and administrators. The goals of these reports and these types of evaluations vary by individual case, but the general procedure is straightforward. The student will be referred to you for a specific reason or reasons, and then evaluated. After the evaluation, you will organize your data and answer the questions of the referral, including your recommendations for specific interventions. As part of this procedure, you will need to gather both qualitative and quantitative data, and from this data create a written comprehensive profile of the student in question. The types of data you focus on will depend on the type of assessment you are being asked to complete, and your professional area of expertise. Some of these reports will center on educational aspects, whereas other reports will cover psychological or behavioral issues, language or speech problems, or physical issues, which may be related to the student being differently-abled. In any type of report, however, you must write with an eye to your different audiences, and avoid heavy jargon or language that may obscure your message for non-specialists.

 You should always follow the directions given by your instructor.

CLASSROOM OBSERVATIONS (ANECDOTAL WRITING)

Throughout your training to teach or supervise teachers in any capacity, you will be required to conduct different types of classroom observations. You will also often be asked to complete observations in your chosen career or use these as qualitative research as part of research projects or assessments. Depending on the context, you may need to observe different things within the class, from student participation to teaching style or use of technology. You may also choose or be asked to conduct your observation from a specific theoretical framework, which will affect how you complete the observation and what you focus on. Generally, no matter the parameters of your observation, the language is formal and professional, and you should be objective in your observations. Your notes should be empirical, meaning that you observe the environment and take detailed, focused notes from which to later write your formal observation document. The key here is *focused*—make sure that you do not focus your comments on issues that are not important for evaluation purposes. For example, you may be evaluating a teacher's classroom management. In this case, it is appropriate to discuss class policies, and how the teacher responds to various situations that may arise. However, it is inappropriate to comment on clothing choices or hairstyles, unless these factors are somehow *directly* affecting the classroom components you're observing. A general observation procedure follows. Remember: your instructor may have different or additional requirements for you to follow.

1. **If necessary, make sure that you have received permission to conduct the observation.** If this observation is not one mandated for teacher evaluation, you may need to get permission from all involved teachers/staff, as well as students (or the student's guardians). If this is part of a research project, follow the IRB guidelines for your institution or your instructor's guidelines.

2. **Based on the requirements of the assignment, decide whether you are a participant or nonparticipant observer.** If you are a participant, consider how you will record your observations. Will you take short notes, or will you write up your notes after the observation? How will this affect your data? If you are a nonparticipant, how will you remain a nonparticipant? What will you do if students or teachers in the classroom try to ask questions or otherwise engage you during the class session?

3. **You can focus only on a few specific things in an observation.** If you have specific criteria to assess or questions to answer, focus your observations on those elements. Use the lesson plan and other ancillary documentation provided by the teacher to help focus your observations.

4. **Because of your limited time, keep your notes concise and empirically focused.** What is happening? What is being said? How are the participants reacting to each other and to class activities? If you are recording the session via video and/or audio, remember that these tools can influence the behavior of participants.

CASE STUDIES

A case study is an explanatory analysis of an educational situation. It presents a real-life scenario and seeks to recommend possible solutions to any problems found. Case studies can be either retrospective (reviewing historical evidence) or prospective, meaning criteria are established and cases that may meet these criteria are investigated. The case study will not only explain one specific case and its outcome, but often will also draw generalized, broader conclusions based on the case. The amount of research and theoretical analysis required for case study will vary, but conclusions about the educational situation under study should always be based on evidence. The case study typically includes the background or history of the person and situation, the empirical data gathered for the case, and the conclusions about possible interventions or pedagogical adjustments.

Case studies in education, much like classroom observations, are generally qualitative and ethnographic. They tend to focus on observations in a real setting with social interactions, and interpretations are formulated based on observations rather than through more scientific testing of a rigid hypothesis. This does not mean that numerical data and rigorous documentation are not necessary; rather, when you do a case study, you do a more holistic interpretation of all the data and examine the researcher's methodology in collecting and interpreting the evidence. Even with a focus on qualitative data, the case study is always firmly empirical, and relies on close observation and careful recording and analysis of data.

This is similar to conducting action research. Whereas action research studies an event or experimental situation created by the researcher to investigate an issue, case studies, like classroom observations, focus on someone else's situation.

JOURNAL WRITING

Teachers, administrators, and others working in education use journals for many purposes. Often, these journals chronicle how a class develops, or keep a record of teaching successes and areas for improvement. Generally they are more personal, reflective, and often recursive. Journals can also serve as a sounding board for you to work out your teaching philosophy or preferred pedagogy. Reflecting on your ongoing experiences as a teacher and your course readings will help you critically focus on your development as a teacher. These journals are not just a course or practicum requirement—even veteran teachers will often keep teaching journals to record, reflect, and continue to improve their teaching.

You may also need to keep a journal to record your observations in the field or to take notes during research. You can record nearly any relevant data in your journal, including details about your observations and questions you have as you teach or observe. Some journals should be more formal in language and approach, as required by your instructor. However, journals in their raw form tend to contain informal language, and more freedom of expression and reflection.

You might consider using a double-entry notebook that allows you to take data and observation notes on one side of the paper or in one column and then record your thoughts, reflections, or speculations on the other side.

REFLECTION PAPERS

Similar to journal writing, **reflection papers** focus on your personal reflection on some aspect of theory, your teaching practice, or critical literature in the field. This approach encourages writing as a means of reflecting critically on your reading and experiences in order to develop your philosophy of teaching. Often you will use this type of paper to analyze and react to a teaching event or situation. You will also use this type of paper to explore and analyze texts assigned to you by your instructor. These are not just documents focused on critical analysis, but are also by their nature connected to your personal beliefs and experiences. You will summarize and synthesize your chosen texts, and connect them to your experience or ideas about the topic. What do you agree with and disagree with, and why? Are these ideas logical, practical, and backed up with any evidence? How would you implement any of these ideas in your own practice? Even though reflective writing allows you to be more flexible in style, and use personal pronouns and more relaxed diction, try to remain professional in tone, if not also in language. Remember that you want to connect to your audience, who may not share your background or have had similar teaching experiences.

RESEARCH PAPERS

Research papers report original research, either conducted in practical settings, such as a classroom, or done by analyzing historical documents and data sets. While at the undergraduate level, you may be assigned a class observation, followed by a formal research paper assignment in which you investigate the specific pedagogical technique the teacher used, and assess the role of this pedagogy in the field. The research paper is a realistic exercise in learning how to communicate with your colleagues in your field, as you will return to this genre when writing in your professional life.

First, you must find a suitable research topic, often to fit specific parameters of an assignment. The possible areas of research are broad but are usually focused on direct experience, replicating previous research, or testing a prevailing or new educational theory. Possible topics could include developing new instructional methods for students having problems writing paragraphs, or for students with dyslexia. The possibilities are limited only by what you experience in the classroom or learn from your readings in the field.

All research papers across fields have similar basic structures, and in education, the paper is similar to those written in the social sciences and sciences. There are generally six sections that you will cover in a research paper, as explained below. Depending on the assignment, you may need to write an abstract of your paper, which is a short and concise summary of your research. You always include a references section or page at the end of any research paper.

1. **The Introduction introduces your readers to the problem or issue that you are investigating, explains why it is important to the field, and tells how you came to this topic.** It will need to draw the reader in, and then smoothly transition to

the literature review and theoretical background. Your tone should be formal and academic, and your treatment of the topic should remain serious; this writing style will help to convince your reader of your credibility.

2. **The Literature Review is your concise summary of the scholarly literature on the topic of your paper.** Here you will also analyze what is missing in the literature, and perhaps how your study fits into the field. This review also presents both the theoretical framework that supports your research and the methodology that you used in designing the study.

   Most sources used in these research papers are primary sources that detail empirical research. This means that the author of the primary source conducted research supported by data. Secondary research is also useful, but the more primary research you use, the more credible you appear as a researcher.

3. **The Methods section explains how you intend to carry out your research, and what limitations you may have in collecting your data.** You should explain exactly what methods and tools you use for data collection. It is important that you be as clear and specific as possible in this section, in order to demonstrate the validity of your research.

4. **The Results section explains your results from analyzing the data you collected, and explains any patterns you find in the data.** You may explain any quantitative or qualitative findings with charts, tables, or statistics. You do not interpret the data here or form your conclusion; this is done in the next section.

5. **In the Discussion section you focus on proving your argument using the evidence you have gathered.** You interpret and analyze your data, and then use it as support for your central argument and hypothesis. What is your finding? How does this affect how this issue is understood in the discipline, and how might it affect pedagogical practice? This section may require you to refer back to your literature review for additional research to support what your evidence has demonstrated.

6. **Your Conclusion summarizes your study, references all of the sections of your research paper, and reinforces how your work influences the field.**

You should never introduce new information in the conclusion.

POSITION PAPERS

In a position paper, you research an issue that is important to the field, and often controversial, then state and support your position on this issue. In professional practice, such papers are often collaboration in support of a specific "official" position. In these cases, position papers can be more public and formal documents, as they support the central goals or mission of an organization, school, or district. These papers also include a "call to action," asking the audience to agree with the authors' position and take steps to support the position and organization. As with other researched writing, it is vital that you support your claim with statistics and other primary research. Position papers are generally much more brief than other formal policy documents you may be asked to write, but this brevity helps to quickly inform the audience of the essentials needed to evaluate the author's position. Since this writing task is shorter than those you may be used to doing, it is even more important that you write concisely and to the point.

ANNOTATED BIBLIOGRAPHY

As part of your preliminary work on a research paper, particularly a literature review, you may be asked to write an annotated bibliography. An annotated bibliography will allow you to organize your source material for the topic of your research paper, and help you to synthesize, interpret, and add to the conversation on this subject in your field. Your document is organized like a bibliography, including the citations in the documentation style required. In this style of bibliography, however, you also add an annotation following each citation. These annotations may need specific information included as per your assignment, but you will generally include a summary of the text and an evaluation of or a reflection on the material.

To write the summary, think about the main idea or thesis of the text. What is the essay or book saying on the topic? How does it approach the topic? What should the reader take away from this text?

To write an evaluation, think about how the source covers the topic. Is it reliable? Biased? What kind of evidence is used in this source? Who is the intended audience?

The reflection is more personal. Is the source useful for your present research? How does it help you think about or shape your argument?

ELECTRONIC PORTFOLIOS

Teaching portfolios have been used in the field of education for many years, but more recent digital innovations in the past two decades have changed the nature of this important document. You may be asked to submit a portfolio of your collected work in order to pass a course or graduate from your program, and you will likely create a teaching portfolio to satisfy course requirements or to enter a career as a professional educator. Your teaching portfolio is not a static document; you will add to it, revise it, and reformat it as your career (and technology) progresses.

You will need to create or follow a specific set of criteria for selecting which documents you include in your portfolio. You will also frequently be asked to reflect on your portfolio, in which you will review your work and propose future work or improvement in certain areas represented in the portfolio.

Digital portfolios, or e-portfolios, have several advantages over paper portfolios. As this type of writing project often changes, a digital version allows for easier revision than a paper portfolio. Additionally, the use of features such as hyperlinks and video within the digital document or Web page allows a richer type of text. For example, if you prepare a lesson plan sample that includes state standards, you can include a hyperlink within the lesson plan that leads the reader directly to the state's official grade and course level standards. Likewise, if you are showcasing a particularly innovative unit on Internet videos, you can easily embed the videos or link to them on YouTube. New apps and other Web 2.0 tools have made the process of compiling your work and creating your e-portfolio easier. Not only does your work have the potential to reach a wider audience, you will also have experience to model for your students, who will likely be required to create their own e-portfolios, even at the elementary school level. You will need to consider the principles of good visual design, such as color choices, font, graphics, and how your portfolio appears across browsers or platforms. Keep your audience in mind, and create a formal and professional site or digital portfolio. If your portfolio is hosted in a public space (remembering the Internet is *always* a public space), you will especially want to ensure that it is reflective of your most professional work.

CONFERENCE PRESENTATION (ORAL OR POSTER FORMAT)

Throughout your courses and in your professional work, you will be asked to present your research and teaching or supervisory experiences to a variety of audiences. You may present to classmates, colleagues at your school, a school board or PTA, or at a national conference or organization meeting. Each of these audiences may require different styles and content of presentation, so be sure to take the time to analyze the audience and context when preparing your presentation. Most presentations you will do are oral, but you will frequently use visual aids to support your argument. You may also attend a poster session, where your visual aid will need to bear the weight of your argument.

Oral presentations are organized just like written research papers, with some important changes. First, since you are communicating orally and under a time constraint, it is necessary that you be concise in your language use. Do not overwhelm your audience with sentences that are overly long or convoluted. Also, remember that your audience needs the essential takeaways from your research. Reading too many complicated statistical formulas or long source quotes aloud will make it hard for your audience to follow your argument.

OTHER FORMS OF WRITING

Writing in the field of education is not limited to the discipline. Those in education are often, by the nature of their work, called on to communicate critical information to the public. You may write memos to public officials, letters to the editor, letters and evaluative documents for parents, websites, blogs, instructional videos, and other digital media sharing your curriculum or pedagogical ideas. And, in our increasingly Internet-focused world, you can expect most of these communications to have a digital dimension, including social media platforms such as Twitter, Reddit, and Facebook. You may also be required to create a class that is delivered purely via an online platform, such as Blackboard or Desire2Learn. The delivery of such courses is similar to creating other courses, but the digital platform allows and requires changes in the mode of delivery, including paying attention to visual construction and using media, hyperlinks, and other Web 2.0 tools to augment and communicate the material of the course.

WRITING EFFECTIVELY IN EDUCATION
KNOW THE AUDIENCE IN EDUCATION

Audiences for writing in the education field may include colleagues in the profession, including teachers, administrators, superintendents, academics, and scholars; the lay public; local, state, and federal government; private testing or assessment companies; and private granting agencies and foundations. Most writing that you will do on a daily basis will focus on formal writing that is intended for your classroom or your colleagues, from lesson plans and research papers to assessment reports. People in the education profession also create oral presentations for conferences and other venues, textbooks, pamphlets, and important messages about the importance of education through popular media. Based on your specific focus, you may also write for the government and private agencies that are monitoring or funding your work, corporate employers, or regulatory bodies, such as a county school board or the Department of Education. In every case, it is essential that you analyze your audience and write with their interests in mind:

❏ Who are your primary readers?

❏ Who else might read your writing or listen to your presentation?

❏ What will the members of your audience already know about your topic?

❏ What will you need to define or explain?

❏ Will your audience be predisposed to agree or disagree with your point of view?

❏ What kinds of evidence will be most convincing for this audience?

KNOW THE RESEARCH QUESTIONS TO ASK IN EDUCATION

As a student and as a professional, you will find that your research questions often spring directly from your work in the classroom. As a student, your instructor may assign your research questions or the conditions for your research.

Did you know?

There are several questions you can ask yourself to find an appropriate topic for research, including the following:

- How important is your question to the field?
- What is your rationale for pursuing this study?
- What population will you study, and why?
- Which variables will you take into account?

However, you may need to decide what research you want to pursue and how this research will impact your own growth as an educator.

Research topics might include studies of student populations across different schools, student responses to particular types of pedagogy, theoretical issues, and testing of assessments and interventions. The research question you decide on will form the basis for your project design and your final written product. Your research question is also your working hypothesis, the idea you will test through textual research and action research from your practice or observation; consequently, it will be described in your writing (see Table 7.1 for example).

TABLE 7.1

Research Questions	
What you want to know more about	**Your research question**
My students tend to become bored when I deliver course material only by lecture. Why? What other method could I use to engage them in the class?	How do teachers of a middle school physical science course improve student engagement through the technique of "flipping" the classroom?

KNOW THE KINDS OF EVIDENCE USED IN EDUCATION

Scientific educational research is defined as the application of systematic methods and techniques that help researchers and practitioners to understand and enhance the teaching and learning process.
— *Marguerite Lodico et al*

Researchers in education use quantitative and qualitative data to generate research questions and support their arguments. These types of data often come directly from the field, in the classroom or in observing a target population. While research can focus primarily on quantitative or qualitative approaches, a very effective process is "mixed-method" design, which calls for a mix of both quantitative and qualitative data sets. These research projects are systematic in their collection and evaluation of both kinds of evidence. Another common form of research in education is action research, which calls for you to examine an issue in your own teaching practice and school setting in order to fix what is problematic. This style, reminiscent of case studies and other writing discussed in this chapter, also calls for a mixed-methods approach, with both quantitative and qualitative data.

Research in the field of education uses two types of central reasoning, similar to how scientific research is structured across other fields.

❏ **Inductive reasoning calls for the researcher to observe a situation, look for patterns or themes, and then use this analysis to argue for a specific generalization** or conclusion about the subject under investigation. This type of reasoning is associated with qualitative research, which is when data is pulled from written or verbal narratives, such as classroom observations or student and teacher interviews.

Example:

After noticing that two science teachers have students who are performing at a higher level than other classes in the same grade level, you ask to observe their classes at different points through a unit. During the observation, you note that these teachers are team teaching, and have "flipped" their classes, putting the lectures and notes online for students to review at home, and spending valuable class time on active projects or experiments that illustrate the scientific principles under study. Your analysis leads you to argue that collaboration and the "flipping" pedagogical technique may be an important factor in increasing student involvement with curriculum, in turn resulting in better performance on assessment measures.

❏ **Deductive reasoning is similar to the reasoning used in traditional scientific research projects, and is based on the traditional scientific method.** This calls for the researcher to hypothesize based on a specific educational theory or a review of previous studies and then collect data to test the hypothesis. This is aligned with quantitative research, which focuses on data that can be interpreted numerically.

Example:

Paulo Friere's theory of critical pedagogy, which calls for educators to resist a "banking" model of education, may be used in advanced high school English curriculum to encourage active study of assigned texts in preparation for AP exams, and in turn influence students' scores. This will be done by allowing students to vote on choices of suitable texts to fulfill course and assessment goals, and then measuring changes in student scores on practice exams. (Note: this type of study would require some method of control, either with a control group of students to compare, and/or outside raters of the students' practice exams to avoid bias on the part of their teachers).

KNOW THE WRITING AND STYLE CONVENTIONS IN EDUCATION

If a man will begin with certainties, he shall end in doubts; but if he will be content to begin with doubts, he shall end in certainties.

—*Francis Bacon*

Writers in the education professions aim to communicate clearly, are aware of their audience, use complete and thorough quantitative and qualitative research, and utilize the format of each genre to highlight the most important aspects of the pedagogical or theoretical issues they are arguing for. Good writing in education follows the general basics of successful communication: effective organization, readability, correct grammar and mechanics, and adherence to the conventions of the chosen documentation style. There are also some specific conventions that you may want to follow as you write in education:

1. **When using qualitative or quantitative evidence, you should be as objective as possible in your collection and presentation of the data.** With qualitative data, it is important to remember how the human element affects how you handle the data. Because you are talking about your observations and interactions, many variables and variations exist and you will not be able to account for all of them, so it is important to use conditional terms as you talk about behaviors, motivations, and causes (e.g., *often* instead of *always*, *many* instead of *all*, the *participants* in this study rather than *students*).

Did you know?

Many theoretical frameworks or research paradigms form the basis for research in the broader field of education. Each approach has its central goals, which may or may not fit your research question. Here are some paradigms from which you may guide your work.

- Positivism/post-positivism
  There is one reality or best practice; objectivity in all data collection and analysis; focus on quantitative data.

- Interpretive/Constructionist
  There are multiple realities dictated by society; values and biases are acknowledged, interaction between you and subjects; focus on qualitative data.

- Emancipatory
  Multiple realities constructed by society, ethnic, gender, cultural, political values; interactive; knowledge is contextualized by social construction and historical value; both qualitative and quantitative data emphasized, with a focus on how different variables relate to oppression from outside forces. (Mertens, D. 1998, p. 8)

2. **Depending on the type of evidence and the method of data collection, you may decide to be objective (quantitative), or you might use first person and talk about yourself as a researcher or observer in the field.** Make sure you check with your professor about expectations and follow the examples set in the models you read and review for class. Particularly with documents such as reflections, lesson plans, and class observations, you will likely use the first person.

3. **If you are working from qualitative research, you will likely use direct evidence from research participants.** These may be quotes from interviews, observations, or survey responses. However, you should also explain in your own words how this data serves as evidence for your argument. Also, APA style calls for you to use the past

tense when citing others' work, as well as events that you have observed in a classroom setting.

4. Avoid biased language that may offend your readers and will damage your credibility. Language that makes assumptions or is based on stereotypes about gender, ethnicity, age, mental or physical (dis)ability, or sexual orientation is not effective. If one of these variables is part of your research, tread carefully and investigate the most appropriate way to address these aspects of your study.

5. Audience is very important to consider when communicating in education. If you are writing for a more formal audience of colleagues or professors, or in an official capacity, you should use the more formal terminology and language expectations of the discipline. However, when writing for a more general audience, such as a memo to parents or a newspaper article, you should thoroughly explain any theoretical constructs and terminology that you use.

 You should also avoid the other extreme of using overblown or pompous language that will make your writing harder to read and may alienate your reader.

KNOW THE APPROPRIATE DOCUMENTATION STYLE IN EDUCATION

APA, the documentation style developed by the American Psychological Association, is most often used in education (see Chapter 12). It uses an author-date method of documentation for both in-text citations and the reference list at the end of the document. Putting the author's last name and the year of the publication in parentheses within the text as soon as the source is mentioned emphasizes the timeliness of the resource and lends credibility to the writer. Some majors, areas of study, or journals within the discipline may have their own documentation style guides, so always check to see what is appropriate for your purposes or your assignment.

SAMPLE STUDENT POSITION PAPER

Resolving Teacher/Tutor Conflict Surrounding "Bad" Writing Assignments

Karen Wright

ABC University

English 6550

Instructor: Dr. Trixie Smith

December 6, 2004

Abstract

The purpose of this paper is to explore the conflict that often exists between writing teachers and writing center tutors surrounding so-called bad assignments. After two years in the classroom as a graduate teaching assistant, I returned to tutoring as part of the requirements for a Writing Center Theory course. Shortly into the semester, however, I found myself engaged in an unexpected conflict of tutor versus teacher. The trouble stemmed from tutor criticism of writing assignments and how that criticism affected my own assignment development. In this paper I reflect on my experiences in each role and conclude with a challenge to the basic structure of the typical tutoring session.

Resolving Teacher/Tutor Conflict Surrounding "Bad" Writing Assignments

Occupying dual roles of tutor and teacher was a schizophrenic experience. On one hand, I was becoming part of the writing center community again, but on the other hand, I was still in the teaching trenches. Most of the tutors were new, ambitious, idealistic, twenty-something graduate students. These tutors had a passion for theory; they absorbed and dissected the readings, extracting every possible meaning and seeking ways to apply the theories to our work in the writing center. Their enthusiasm was inspiring; however, from my view on the front line, I began to fear for the young recruits manning the writing center.

Rival Perspectives

The Tutors' View

Early discussions in the theory class focused on *student-centeredness*, the philosophy that students should have control over their own learning with instructors serving more as guides than wisdom-dispensing authorities. Our primary goal became ensuring student ownership. Linda K. Shamoon and Deborah H. Burns (2003) explain that the "tutor's mission is to help clarify what is in the text and to facilitate revision without imposing their own ideas or their own knowledge and, in so doing, without taking ownership of the text" (p. 177). We learned to identify ownership saboteurs, such as directive tutoring and faculty misperceptions of our work. We explored our own subject positions and how they might influence our sessions. Likewise, if we were to set aside our own agendas, then it was only logical that we must also disregard instructor agendas: "the student-text-teacher relationship complicates notions of ownership" (Gillespie & Lerner, 2004, p. 22). The more we learned, the closer we came to identifying our ultimate mission of serving writers—*students*—over serving faculty. Grounded in theory, the tutors became more confident in their understanding of what is best for students. Consequently, they became increasingly critical of instructors and particularly of what they deemed "bad" assignments.

The Teacher's View

The development of this critical community of writing assistants affected my teaching in conflicting ways. First, like my tutoring peers, I wanted to be student-centered; my students would have a voice. Second, the more the tutors blamed instructors for student problems in the writing center, the more indignant I became. Most of the tutors had not taught before, so they could not understand a teacher's perspective. Furthermore, when tutors assign all the blame to instructors, they completely excuse the failings of students *and* relinquish their own responsibility for helping the writers. Finally, when "bad" assignments began to dominate the conversations of tutors, I became downright paranoid about my own assignments. I regularly encouraged my students to go to the writing center, and I could not risk having a student show up with one of my assignment sheets only to have my peer judge it as "bad."

As it turns out, my effort to write good assignments completely undermined my goal to have a student-centered classroom. By trying to be absolutely clear and avoid tutor scrutiny, I gave more directions. The more directions I gave, the less freedom my students had to choose topics that were meaningful to them. The less freedom I gave to my students, the longer my assignment sheets grew. I realized I had a serious problem when my assignment sheet for Essay 4 filled two full pages—two full pages for a summary and response paper whose assigned length was only two and a half pages. I had become an ideal candidate for membership in AA (Assigners Anonymous).

Understandably, Essay 4 was an exercise in frustration. For the summary, I had provided four articles about the presidential election from which my students could choose. They balked at the limits imposed on them and tuned out my lengthy instruction. I was frustrated, too. The step-by-step instructions were intended to help them. Moreover, I had high hopes that the election would engage them, lead to self-discovery about issues that mattered to them, and inspire writing in their own empowered voices. However, when my students complained openly, I had to reexamine The Student-Centered Class That Wasn't. Consequently, I expanded the choice of topics, allowing students to write about any controversial essay they could locate on the Opposing Viewpoints database on our library's website. The students who chose topics other than the four articles I had provided wrote significantly better essays. Their average was an 83 and included the only two A's in the whole bunch, compared to a 77 average for the rest of the class, who had written about the articles I had selected.

I persevered through the Essay 4 writing process, but I was determined to not make the same mistake again. I thought carefully about what I wanted my students to accomplish in the next essay and arrived at about a half-page assignment with only two guidelines: 1) write an argumentative essay following the classical argumentative form; and 2) choose a topic not already addressed in a previous paper. I wondered how my peers back in the writing center might judge my assignment, but it did not matter. My students welcomed their freedom, and I felt good about empowering them through writing.

This Tutor's Experience

After realizing the serious implications of the "bad" assignment stigma on my teaching, I turned my attention to its effect on my tutoring. Close introspection revealed an uncomfortable paranoia there as well. Standard procedure had always dictated starting tutoring sessions with a review of the assignment sheet, but now I was examining them more closely than ever. Furthermore, I had adopted a checklist mentality, going between the student's essay and the assignment sheet to make certain that the teacher's expectations were met. *The teacher's expectations*. I had identified the problem.

By devoting excessive attention to the assignment, I was fostering a teacher-centered pedagogy, not the student-centered ideal that my colleagues and I had held up all semester. Furthermore, this was a center-wide problem. After all, it had been my classmates' scrutiny of assignments that had caused my own paranoia in the first place. And that paranoia had led to clinging more tightly to an authoritarian model of teaching. The teacher became a pervasive presence whom we all sought to please by interpreting and enforcing assignment expectations in every tutoring session.

The Broader Problem of the Assignment Sheet

Lack of Context

In reality, all assignment sheets are problematic when taken out of context. It is impossible for tutors to understand fully the assignments brought in to the center by tutees. We have not had the benefit of class lectures or discussions, nor are we privy to the readings leading up to the writing assignment. For example, one professor at my school assigns a series of sample descriptive essay readings to his students and then asks them to write an essay emulating one of the models. If one of his students shows up for a tutoring appointment with an assignment that says, "Write a 500-word essay in which you imitate the style of one of the assigned readings," the assignment-dependent tutor will be lost. What will likely happen is that the tutor will reschedule the appointment and send the student back to his or her professor to get more direction. In claiming an inability to help students, we shirk our responsibility to them and risk their not returning at all.

A Radical Proposal

This problem of so-called "bad" assignments must be addressed if we are to serve students, a purpose to which we profess. One remedy is simple: we could stop consulting assignment sheets altogether. [Collective gasp!] It sounds radical, but consider the benefits, especially for writing center administrators. As a representation of the instructor, the assignment sheet—the actual piece of paper—intrudes upon the session, causing discomfort for the tutee and undue stress on the tutor; this phenomenon naturally leads to tutor resentment. Gary A. Olson (1984) addresses this issue in "The Problem of Attitudes in Writing Center Relationships":

> The most serious attitudinal problem with tutors is animosity toward the methods
> or personalities of certain teachers who send students to the center…. They will
> object to his attitude, the way he teaches (or fails to teach) composition, his method
> or manner of evaluation, or a number of other traits. (p. 159)

Although the responsibility for controlling tutor attitudes is placed firmly on the director (Olson, 1984), a no-assignment-sheet policy could completely eliminate the (sometimes hostile) tension between faculty members and writing center staff. Disregarding the assignment sheet makes the teacher a non-issue; in fact, the identity of the instructor becomes unnecessary. Moreover, instructors could not accuse writing tutors of failing their students. The responsibility for success would lie completely with the student. We would have to trust the student's understanding of the assignment based on factors that we cannot possibly know, such as material covered in class and any verbal explanation of the essay assignment offered by the instructor. In this way, any flaw or lack of clarity in the assignment would be redirected back to the instructor.

Student-centeredness

In addition to facilitating harmonious departmental relations, taking the assignment sheet out of tutoring sessions would also promote the student-centeredness that we desire. The time spent reviewing the assignment sheet for the *instructor's* agenda would be allotted to the writer. Instead of considering what the instructor wants, we could focus on the needs of the student. Additionally, by silencing the instructor, we would emphasize the student's voice. In her article "The Writing Assignment: An Obstacle or a Vehicle?," Cheryl Sandford Jenkins (1980) argues that "[s]tudents may find a topic and a voice evolving from their speculative writing [freewriting] and should feel free to discuss the alternate subject, if they feel one emerging from the speculative paper even if it is different from the one assigned" (p. 68). When I assign an essay, I typically know what kind of writing my students will produce. Often, however, it is the student who submits something unexpected who delights me and earns the best grade. Students frequently know how they want to approach an assignment, and we should feel free to help them without constraints.

Critical Thinking

Despite adopting a student-centered, no-assignment-sheet policy, we can still expect students to come into the center seeking an interpreter for their assignments. Writing center maven Muriel Harris (1995) sees this type of translation as a means for students to enter the academic community:

> Misunderstanding the assignment happens with such astonishing regularity that we ought more properly to view it as part of the educational process—learning the language of academic communities, learning how to understand that language, and learning how to act on that understanding. (p. 39)

In situations where students request help in understanding assignments, tutors can readily assist, but a routine review of the assignment sheet is not necessary in every session.

Another approach to assignment sheets is to treat them as an opportunity to help students develop critical thinking skills. Deciphering an assignment can lead to an excellent brainstorming session. Emily Meyer and Louise Z. Smith (1987), authors of the influential book *The Practical Tutor*, stress helping tutees decode the language of assignments: "By identifying key concepts, noting imperatives, employing signal words, and analyzing the imperatives implied in practical interrogatives, [tutors] can help writers identify the important parts of writing assignments and can help writers think critically" (p. 79). In their sample essay question, "*On what grounds* can one *deplore* the bombing of Coventry *yet approve* the bombing of Dresden?" [emphasis theirs], Meyer and Smith (1987) explain that "'Grounds' are philosophical reasons, causes, and/or motives for actions, decisions, and/or beliefs" (p. 78). A tutor could use this definition to help the student develop an approach to the assignment. The student might begin by making a list to compare and contrast the reasons for bombing each city and then making a judgment between the two. This judgment would become his argument, which he would support with evidence from his comparison/contrast brainstorming (Meyer & Smith, 1987). In this scenario, the tutor is able to guide the writer without ever criticizing the clarity of the instructor's assignment, which would be counterproductive.

Conclusion

While teaching and tutoring during the same semester was strangely emotional and at times confusing, I am grateful for the ways in which each informed the other. I am a better teacher for my experience in the writing center and will be ever mindful of how my courses are centered in the future. Furthermore, as a future faculty member of some as-yet-unknown university, I will support the writing center, respect its staff, and exercise tolerance for well-intentioned tutors. My colleagues in the writing center truly care about students and preserving student ownership of papers, qualities that will serve them well when they move into the classroom as graduate teaching assistants next year. In the meantime, I caution them, and all tutors, to be aware of how their scrutiny of assignments is actually affecting their tutoring practices. Lastly, I urge them to be respectful towards faculty members because most tutors are teachers-in-training, and someday a graduate student might be criticizing their assignments.

References

Gillespie, P., & Lerner, N. (2004). *The Allyn and Bacon guide to peer tutoring*. (2nd ed.) New York: Pearson.

Harris, M. (1995). Talking in the middle: Why writers need writing tutors. *College English*, 57, 27-42.

Jenkins, C. S. (1980). The writing assignment: An obstacle or a vehicle?" *English Journal*, 69, 66-69.

Meyer, E., & Smith, L. Z. (1987). *The practical tutor*. New York: Oxford University Press.

Olson, G. A. (1984). The problem of attitudes in writing center relationships. In G. Olson (Ed.), *Writing centers: Theory and administration* (pp. 155-165). Urbana, IL: National Council for Teachers of English.

Shamoon, L. K., & Burns, D. H. (2003). A critique of pure tutoring. In C. Murphy & S. Sherwood (Eds.), *The St. Martin's sourcebook for writing tutors*. (2nd ed., pp. 174-190). Boston: Bedford/St. Martin's.

University of Mobile
School of Education
Lesson Plan

Date: December 4, 2012 Name: Tabitha Pierce
Size of Group: 30 Grade: Kindergarten Time Required: 45 minutes

A. Alabama Course of Study # and Standard:
#9) Identify seasons of the year.

B. Objective:
After learning about the seasons of the year, students will be able to describe each season with 90% accuracy.

C. Method of Assessing Objective:
Students will describe each season in their journal with 90% accuracy.

D. Orientation to the Lesson (Focus Attention/Motivate):
The teacher will show pictures from each season to prepare the students for the lesson.

E. Higher Order Thinking Questions (to be used in instruction):
1. What is the weather like in your favorite season?
2. How likely are you to wear your jacket during your favorite season?

F. Instruction:
1. Teaching/Develop the Lesson
a. The teacher will present each season and describe them.
b. The teacher will show students videos from each season.
2. Guided Practice
The students will dance out the seasons using props and noises.
3. Independent Practice
Students will describe each season in their journal and create an illustration of each season.

G. Materials/References/Technology:
Smart Board, journals, props, pictures, videos, music, crayons

H. Inclusion Modifications (as needed):
The teacher will help when needed.

I. Homework:
Students will share the dance they learned with friends or family.

Note: in APA format, a title page should be included

SAMPLE STUDENT REFLECTION PAPER

Revised Blog Article

A focal point of many writing center conversations is the unfortunate continuation of the "victim stance" that we have developed as part of our long struggle for legitimacy—and it's an issue I still see cropping up in articles I read out of writing center publications and texts. Take for example this quote from Derek Owens's "Two Centers, Not One" (2007): "Doesn't every unimaginative assignment that comes through the Writing Center door somehow, in some small way, undermine who we are, diminishing the talents of our staff?" (p. 153). What good does it do to prescribe such power and influence to professors, let alone the documents they create? How about this: "How can any of us expect part-time faculty who lack offices, office hours, benefits, and a living wage for their labor to excel at designing good assignments, or to keep up with advancements in writing pedagogy?" (p. 154).Yes, it may be 100% true that adjunct instructors face huge roadblocks to creating good work, but presenting it as a "losing battle" in the tone of a victim gets us exactly no-where.

Owens continues this problem by doing exactly what people in the victim state of mind do—assign blame. He blames reality TV, online shopping, and video games as being horrid distracters for students, keeping them from participating in the kinds of cultural interactions he believes they secretly desire, without ever once stopping to think that maybe the aforementioned activities are exactly the kind of culture these students want to participate in. Owens presents his notions of cultural activities as something more meaningful—literacy journals, poetry readings, film nights, etc—and I find myself asking, "Is that really culture?" Culture is anything but something specific, something preplanned and forced. Culture is an organic construction made through interaction, which I think the evolution of the Game Nights and Beer Rhetoric groups at our (the Michigan State University) writing center illuminates.

Now I certainly don't mean to say that the entirety of Owen's article is useless because he decided to play the victim card, only that it does reduce its usefulness. I believe this because coming from the place of a victim (something I've experienced a lot while battling with depression) automatically places you on the defensive, and being defensive reduces the amount of critical thinking you can accomplish, hindering your ability to overcome bias and keep an open mind, and increasing the likelihood that you will cling to your comfort zones and traditions and therefore work backwards instead of forwards.

[...]

I think it comes from the other angle entirely—one of offense instead of defense. This can be seen from her extensive discussion of "disruptive underlife," and more specifically, in her center's strategy of responding to reporting forms professors send them (which attempt to take control of the session) with forms of their own (p. 198). This tactic is beautiful to me—taking a potentially oppressive document and responding with a document of your own, critically constructed to throw its own weight around. But such offense can be potentially dangerous. The risk is that some people are going to find you offensive, and while I've never heard of any prescriptive documents coming into the center from professors (okay, yes, I guess assignment sheets technically count but that's a whole different kettle of fish), I might personally pause before sending back something that might be read as a big ol' F-You. However, I found myself enjoying the war Beech (2007) contends we should wage in the name of "impression management" (p. 199). The simple example of the higher/lower order concerns pyramid, even for someone as wary of those terms as I am, seems like a brilliant way to have our ideals, theories, and rationales right out there on the table and in the face of the uninitiated. Beech's general approach is something that I've struggled with considering, because though on one hand I absolutely love the bloody boldness of the whole thing, the question of whether such a strong aggressor stance will be any better at the end of the day then a weak victim stance nags me.

More personally troubling than either of these extremes, however, is the feeling I get from Neal Learner's "Writing Center Assessment: Searching for the 'Proof' of Our Effectiveness" (2003), a sense that went beyond victim into something that gave off the sense of Stockholm Syndrome-esque acceptance and assimilation. Now I know I'm going to be biased here because most quantitative data gives me the hibbie-jibbies, but to me this article went beyond enthusiasm for quantitative research to help fill in gaps of understanding and into championing the effectiveness of statistics solely because they are expected of us. I mean, I get it, we need to survive the budget cuts and the powers that be only speak in numbers, and I do believe that adding quantitative data to the soup will make it that much more hearty for the ravenous beasts of accountability. But should we be feeding them in the first place? Isn't the first step in stopping the coming tide of forced justification via spreadsheet to refuse to do just that, or from a less combative standpoint to use this conflict as an avenue to discuss what we mean by effective and find a place to come together?

Honestly, Learner's article seemed like its own slippery slope, beginning with a solid rationale about using and adapting qualitative data, then moving dangerously to suggesting that all writing centers should develop a unified set of standards (does no one remember to consider context?), and then finally just rolling around in a pit of insanity by stating,

"Perhaps even our long-standing attempts to escape the label of "remediation" can be reconsidered when we realize that working with the most underprepared writers allows for the greatest amount of development, a charge that few other campus entities embrace as fully as writing centers do" (2007, p. 72)

I don't mean to suggest that this isn't true, but rather that it comes off as sounding like we should go back to being remedial (or at least being labeled as such) so that we can attract more students who we can develop further (whatever the hell that means) than others so that our numbers will look good. Gross.

In contrast, I am intrigued by the focused discussion on location and political ramifications of space by Haviland and colleagues' "The Politics of Administrative and Physical Location." From my impressions of our space it really seems like we at MSU have done everything right in terms of where we are located and what departments we're attached to. I particularly liked the idea of a center as going not just beyond the specific text to the writer, but beyond the writer to the person. I feel like a greater connection with other support services might foster a more complete approach to some clients, though it could also create preconceptions and bias as well. The notion of ideas connecting our locations instead of sidewalks has also stuck with me, an ideal I think we accomplish when clients take the same piece of work to multiple locations. I was, however, disappointed that the logic jumped from

Online tutoring done using computers to computers replacing tutors—straight up-and-down technophobia at its worst.

Finally, I'd like to say that "Students as Stakeholders: Maintaining a Responsive Assessment" by Jennie Nelson and Diane Kelly-Riley raises a lot of important considerations about assessment stakeholders that are often forgotten, and I think for most centers those stakeholders are both the students and the consultants. We need to have a lot more input from our clients—as great as our focus groups in staff meetings can be, focus groups of clients are needed far more. This is particularly relevant when it comes to the assessment committees MSU has developed, where I think that there needs to be more input and consideration of consultants. All of our employees have the opportunity to serve on the committee if they care to do so, and thus the argument could be made that if you really care you've got your chance to do something. But as the article shows, stakeholders need a larger amount of consideration than that. With the exit surveys our assessments team uses, for example, the question was raised to me by several different employees about why it doesn't ask for the consultant's name. Even if consultant performance wasn't what was being considered, the data could have just been eliminated for certain analysis and thus still be worthwhile to collect for other considerations. Now I can think of several reasons why the committee doesn't ask for the consultant's name, but the more important point is that I don't know the real answer. Writing center assessment absolutely must be more transparent than that. I know it's an important part of assessment to not reveal exactly what you're going after so as to increase the usefulness of the data, but maybe we give that one a miss in the center. I think that we should work hard to make sure that as many people possible understand the reasons for why we assess the way we do and have had a chance to have a hand in the process apart from being a formal cog in the machine. The more you understand, the less you feel powerless, and the less you feel like a victim. And when it comes to real writing center progress, we just can't afford to act the victim any longer.

References

Beech, J. (2007). "Fronting our desired identities: The role of writing center documents in institutional underlife." *Marginal words, marginal work?: Tutoring the academy in the work of writing centers*. Eds. William J. Macauley, Jr. and Nicholas Mauriello. Cresskill, New Jersey: Hampton Press, Inc., 197–210.

Learner, N. (2003). "Writing center assessment: Searching for the 'proof' of our effectiveness." *The center will hold: Critical perspectives on writing center scholarship*. Eds. Michael A. Penberton and Joyce Kinkead. Logan, Utah: Utah State University Press, 58–73.

Nelson, J. and Kelly-Riley, D. (2001). "Students as stakeholders: Maintaining a responsive assessment." *Beyond outcomes: assessment and instruction within a university writing program*. Ed. Richard H. Haswell. Westport, Connecticut: Ablex Publishing, 143–159.

Owens, D. (2007). "Two centers, not one." *Marginal words, marginal work?: Tutoring the academy in the work of writing centers*. Eds. William J. Macauley, Jr. and Nicholas Mauriello. Cresskill, New Jersey: Hampton Press, Inc., 151–167.

ACTIVITIES

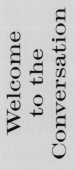

Welcome to the Conversation

Discuss these questions with your classmates in class or via a class wiki or shared blog.

1. Education uses different methods for writing that *assess* or *evaluate*. What types of writing perform these activities? Are some types considered more effective or reliable?

2. Who are some of the audiences for education writing? How do your rhetorical choices differ depending on the audience?

3. What are the differences between qualitative and quantitative data? How do you collect these data differently for different writing purposes?

4. What types of public writing might you be asked to do in education? How should you communicate your research to this audience?

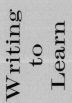

Writing to Learn

1. Write a letter to the editor of your local newspaper arguing for or against an issue affecting your local school district.

2. **Write a micro-theme**: write a one-page argument or explanation about the need for standardized testing in your field. Remember to include why it has been used (or not used), and the reason you agree or disagree with the effectiveness of standardized testing.

3. **Reading journal**: focus on three readings you've covered for class on the same topic. Respond to these readings with given guidelines, using the first person if instructed.

Learning to Write

1. **Annotated bibliography:** After you have chosen or been assigned a preliminary research topic, begin using your resources (Internet, database, library catalog searches) to compile a citation list of sources that you can use for your paper. Possible sources include books, book chapters, articles, essays, websites, government white or green papers, and other documents. After reading the sources, create a brief paragraph for each citation in which you summarize the source's thesis or argument, and evaluate the source. Is this information reliable? Is the author credible? How will this source help your research or argument?

2. **Position paper:** Using the most objective sources from your annotated bibliography, write a position paper that effectively argues your position on the research topic. Remember that the audience you choose for your position paper dictates the type of credible sources you should use to be persuasive.

Suggested Topics for Research

1. Based on course readings and your class discussions choose an educational theory or pedagogy that interests you and research how it has been used in previous studies. Have researchers found this pedagogy to be effective? In which educational contexts is this theory most effective, and why? Use evidence from these sources to support your evaluation and argument.

2. Using the theory you've chosen, design a targeted curriculum and **lesson plan** for the class you are visiting or will visit during your practicum or internship. Depending on how far you have progressed in your student teaching, ask your supervisor to observe you teaching the lesson you've created, and evaluate how you have applied the educational theory. You can then use a variety of sources, per your instructor's directions, to assess how your lesson did or did not meet instructional goals for the course. The primary sources could include student and teacher surveys, test scores, written responses, interviews, and other quantitative and qualitative measures.

READ MORE ABOUT IT

Faculty of Education and Social Work. "Advice on Academic Writing." November 2011. Web. 10 May 2013.

"Five Common Mistakes in Writing Lesson Plans." *Education Oasis*. 2005. Web.

Hunter, Madeline. *Enhancing Teaching*. New York: MacMillan, 1993. Print.

Klausmeier, Richard C. *Research Writing in Education and Psychology–From Planning to Publication: A Practical Handbook*. New York: Charles C. Thomas, 2001. Print.

Lichtenberger, Elizabeth O. et al. *Essentials of Assessment Report Writing*. Hoboken, NJ: Wiley & Sons, 2004. Print.

Lodico, Marguerite G., Dean T. Spalding, and Katherine H. Voegtle, *Methods in Educational Research: From Theory to Practice*. Hoboken, NJ: Jossey-Bass, 2006. Print.

Mertens, Donna M. *Research Methods in Education and Psychology*. Thousand Oaks, CA: Sage, 1998. Print.

Richards, Janet C., and Sharon K. Miller. *Doing Academic Writing in Education: Connecting the Personal and the Professional*. Mahwah, NJ: Lawrence Erlbaum Associates, 2008. Print.

Serdyukov, Peter, and Mark Ryan. *Writing Effective Lesson Plans: The 5-Star Approach*. Boston: Pearson, Allyn and Bacon, 2007. Print.

"Why Writing Matters in Teacher Education." *Saginaw Valley State University*. May 2007. Web. 10 May 2013.

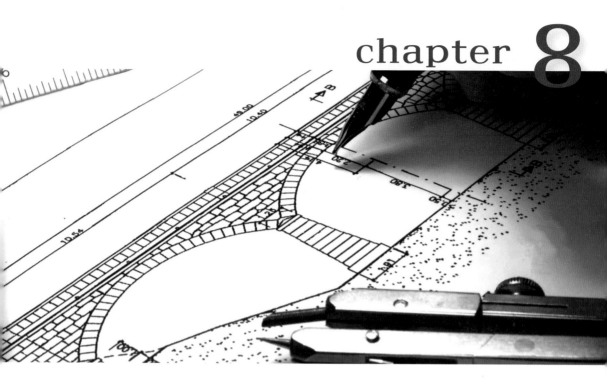

chapter 8

Writing in Engineering

As a practicing engineer, you will need to write reports, proposals, scientific papers, and electronic messages. Writing is perhaps the most important way in which you will convey your ideas to managers, other engineers, and customers. Your communication skills will therefore determine how successful you are as an engineer, perhaps even more so than your technical expertise!

—Electrical and Computer Engineering Department, University of Connecticut, Engineering Report Writing

Purposes of Writing in Engineering

No profession unleashes the spirit of innovation like engineering. From research to real-world applications, engineers constantly discover how to improve our lives by creating bold new solutions that connect science to life in unexpected, forward-thinking ways. Few professions turn so many ideas into so many realities. Few have such a direct and positive effect on people's everyday lives. We are counting on engineers and their imaginations to help us meet the needs of the twenty-first century.

—National Academy of Engineering

If you enjoy using your smartphone or driving your car, you can thank an engineer. If you have ever benefited from new medical advances or the latest computer technology, thank an engineer. But you may not know about innovations like these if they are not clearly communicated to the general public. In fact, we're more likely to hear about a lack of communication from engineers when something goes wrong, such as a rocket crash or a collapsing bridge. As the introductory quote reminds us, the primary aim of writing in engineering is to communicate your ideas to others: explaining facts, programs, directions, and so on to colleagues, clients, team members, agencies, or even society at large. Whether you are writing for peers who are familiar with the mathematical and scientific concepts being used or writing for a less informed general audience, you must create clear and concise prose that is easy to understand and follow. Colleagues who desire to replicate or expand on your work do not want to waste time muddling through jargon and dense sentences. Likewise, those following your instructions need them to be clear and concise. General readers of engineering reports and information want to be informed; unclear or confusing writing does not meet these goals. It's important that engineers at every level and in every field be able to communicate their ideas, plans, results, explanations, and innovations to others.

Types of Writing Assignments in Engineering

Many engineers and engineering students dislike writing. After all, don't we go into engineering because we want to work with machines, instruments, and numbers rather than words? Didn't we leave writing behind us when we finished freshman English? The blunt fact, however, is that to be a successful engineer you must be able to write (and speak) effectively. If you could set up your own lab in a vacuum you might be able to minimize your first hand communication with others, but all your ideas and discoveries would remain useless if they never got beyond your own mind.

— Beer and McMurray
A Guide to Writing as an Engineer

Writing in engineering can take many different forms. As mentioned previously, considerations of audience, purpose, and context or situation may determine the form you choose to compose your writing. Similarly, learning objectives, programmatic goals, and even accreditation requirements may affect the types of assignments you receive in class, just as various factors may influence what you are asked to create on the job.

The engineering report is the most common kind of writing completed by engineers on the job, but it is certainly not the only type of writing used. Memos and letters, lab or test reports, grant proposals, websites, blog entries, and newsletter and magazine articles are all frequently used. Likewise, technical writing, especially instructions and project specs, are also common. For those who teach engineering, the peer-reviewed journal article and the grant proposal are both used regularly. Keep in mind that the above is not an exhaustive list and that you may be asked to create other types of documents or communication; likewise, you may know of alternative forms that may be effective for your audience, purpose, and context—if so, you should discuss these alternative forms with your instructor.

ENGINEERING REPORTS

The final paper for a course is often the research report, which is designed to give you practice in communicating your findings with colleagues using one of the major genres of the field. Similar to report writing in the sciences more generally, the engineering report often follows the scientific method. An exception to this would be a report that follows the order in which the work or research was actually completed. Common parts of the engineering report include the following:

1.   **Title**: Title of work, names of contributors, date of submission.

2.   **Abstract or Executive Summary**: The abstract is typically 200–250 words summarizing the scope of the project and the main points or outcomes. The executive summary is typically one-tenth of the length of the full report and follows the order of the full report.

Look for the recommendations from the assignment or the requirements from the journal to know how long your abstract should be.

3.   **Introduction**: The introduction outlines the reasons for the project and any background needed to understand the project, including summaries of previous work on the topic, if applicable.

4. **Theory and Analysis**: This section explains any theory supporting the work being presented, which may include an overview of terms, concepts, formulas, test codes, and pertinent principles or laws at work. Some instructors may refer to this section as the *literature review*.

5. **Experimental Procedures**: Also known as the *Materials and Methods* section, this section explains what was done, how often, by whom, using what materials and measures. It may include graphs and charts to demonstrate methods.

6. **Results and Discussion**: In this section, you summarize your findings and any conclusions you have drawn from those findings. It often includes tables, graphs, charts, and other pictures to illustrate the results; in fact, graphical representation of data is encouraged. Discrepancies should be noted here, as well as the need for further tests. The discussion section should be linked back to the theory section, as the theory is used to explain the results from this particular study.

7. **Conclusions and Recommendations**: Conclusions must be linked directly to the data rather than formed from conjecture. As the researcher, you should show how you have arrived at the conclusions presented. More important are the recommendations from the study: How will or can this information be used? What are its implications? What further studies are needed? This section may also be titled *Implications and Further Research*.

8. **Acknowledgments**: Here you acknowledge all of those who have contributed to the project: fellow researchers, agencies that have provided data, access, or other support, funding entities, and any others who have contributed to the project.

9. **Bibliography**: This is a list of all resources used to complete the project, both those quoted and those referenced. You should follow the documentation format used in your field, in the journal, or as assigned by your professor.

10. **Appendix**: Any additional materials needed for a full understanding of the project should be placed here. Often long data tables are placed here so they don't interrupt the main text.

The engineering report varies in length depending on the type of project assignment, its complexity, and the requested materials. The report should use subheadings to guide the reader, as well as page numbers in headers or footers, which can also include a word or phrase referring to the section or subheading of the report.

Look for and follow the specific directions given for your report, whether they are dictated by the assignment, company policy, or government requirements.

LAB REPORTS

Just as the lab is designed to give you experience with various aspects of the research and design process, so, too, the lab report is designed to give you experience in communicating your process and results to a wider audience. The lab report is often a condensed version of the report paper. Like the report paper, it has the same main parts in the same order, so refer to the previous section for guidelines. Depending on the actual lab assignment, one section or another may be emphasized for the written paper. For example, many labs early in the semester are designed to acquaint students with lab equipment and methods of research; therefore, the Experimental Procedures section may receive the most attention in the write-up.

You should always follow the directions given by your instructor or the lab supervisor.

TECHNICAL WRITING

Engineers often write instructions, procedures, guidelines, and manuals, all of which fall under the label of technical writing. In the lab, office, or factory, they may work alone or with professional technical writers (those trained in writing, not engineering) to create these documents. The goal is to be clear and accurate while also being concise, because the general user won't read long pages of directions or guidelines. Here are some helpful hints to make your technical writing work for you and your readers:

1.   **Use numbers** to order the steps.

2.   **Use images or graphics** when appropriate to illustrate parts, to show how pieces fit together, or to showcase final products.

3.   **Use language** your reader can understand—no jargon or specialty words.

4.   **Add warnings** as appropriate and highlight these using different typography or color.

CORRESPONDENCE

Engineers write a wide variety of correspondence on the job, such as memos to supervisors, team members, and assistants and letters to clients, government agencies, and other corporations. They may also write progress reports, inquiries, petitions, and acknowledgments. These should always follow good business writing form (see Chapter 6 for additional instructions on letter and memo writing).

Intellectual Property Disclosures and Patent Office Applications

Because engineers often design or create new technologies and methods of doing or building, they also find themselves completing intellectual property disclosures and applying for patents to safeguard their work. Intellectual property disclosures explain where and how new inventions have been shared, such as at conferences, in published papers, and in lab demonstrations.

 Many colleges and universities, as well as businesses, have forms designed to help with intellectual property disclosures and/or patent applications. Your instructor may ask you to complete the form at your school in order to give you practice with this genre.

The disclosure statement is important to the patent application process because it helps establish originality and ownership. In the United States, inventors must file for a patent within one year of first disclosing a new invention. A patent application typically gives the background of an invention (the need for it, the process leading up to it) and then gives an overview of the actual invention and its uses; this description may contain images or graphics, mathematical or chemical formulas, and/or computer codes. Most patent offices also require an abstract and a title, both of which will aid in general searching.

 You may be asked to work with a lawyer or legal department to complete disclosure and patent paperwork.

Project, Research, and Grant Proposals

Project possibilities may come from a wide variety of places—businesses; governments; public needs; social, political, and environmental agencies; and even individuals. Likewise, research projects come from a wide array of requests and interests. All of these projects require financial support for lab space, equipment, supplies, and personnel, among other things. Projects may also be supported by grants, which again come from many different places, including government organizations/resources, private foundations, and corporate supporters. All of these proposals have a similar structure. The main difference is the intended audience.

In general, a proposal describes the work you will do on a project. It may give background information about the project, research questions or objectives, research methods or plan of action, a working timeline, and a list of materials (including personnel) needed to accomplish the project. If the proposal is unsolicited, you may first need to establish the problem or need for the proposed project before offering your solution.

When you are writing grant proposals, it is important to match your research to the purposes of the granting/funding organization. It will not matter how well-written your proposal is if you submit it to the wrong funding source. Once you have found the correct source, you will need to follow its proposal guidelines and directions carefully, using its directions or proposal form as the template for your submission. In fact, many agencies now provide their forms online, which forces you to fill in each of the categories and may limit word or character counts in each section.

Always keep your audience in mind as you write, explaining terms and concepts that your readers may not be familiar with. Many grant agencies also allow or even ask for tables, graphs, or other images that will help them visualize your working hypothesis. As you write, demonstrate how your proposed research fulfills the agency's goals or mission while also respecting your readers' expertise, experience, and knowledge of the field or topic. You should do a thorough investigation to tailor your proposal to the funder. And remember that a successful grant proposal is a persuasive argument. It should go without saying that your readers deserve a grant proposal that is clear, specific, and free of errors.

Consider collaboration when applying for a grant. Many grant funders want to see various departments, programs, disciplines, and organizations working together, so consider who might have similar or related goals and how you might work together to accomplish *all* **of your goals.**

LAB NOTES AND LOGS

In the field or the lab, scientists must record what they see or the results they get from experiments. Such notes are often recorded in notebooks, logs, or journals, which may be handwritten or recorded digitally on computers, tablets, or smartphones. Results may also be video recorded for later transcription and description. It is important that these notes be accurate and detailed since they will later be used to write up lab reports and research papers. You should include the date of the lab, all materials and equipment used, the procedures used, the results, calculations if applicable, and acknowledgments of help with the lab. You may also include your interpretations and conclusions. Many scientists develop their own short-hand methods of taking notes. As you begin this process, be sure to note what your abbreviations and symbols mean—make yourself a key or legend so your notes make sense when you come back to them. It is also important to rewrite messy and shorthand notes as soon as possible while the information is still fresh.

You might consider using a double-entry notebook that allows you to take lab data and observation notes on one side of the paper or in one column and then record your thoughts, reflections, and speculations on the other side.

CONFERENCE PRESENTATIONS (ORAL OR POSTER FORMAT)

Proposals are often shared with clients and colleagues through oral presentations. Likewise, new research is often shared with colleagues at conferences and symposia organized by various disciplines or around topics of interest. These oral presentations are often accompanied by visual aids, such as PowerPoint or Prezi presentations. Research might also be shared visually via a poster presentation. Different venues or instructors might require trifold posters or provide easels or bulletin boards for displaying large posters (36" x 48" is the typical size but larger sizes might be an option). In your classes, you may be asked to give an oral presentation in conjunction with turning in a written report or set of specifications, or you might be asked to share a poster presentation with the class or the larger school community. With all of these presentations, it is important to follow published directions, including time limits and size requirements for posters. You should also be prepared to answer questions from attendees.

Posters are visual tools and should follow good design principles, such as the CRAP principles: contrast, repetition, alignment, proximity. (See Chapter 6, Figure 6.1.)

OTHER FORMS OF WRITING

Depending on the type of job you have or the institution in which you use your science background and training, you may also write in many other forms. As an instructor, you may find yourself writing memos and letters to administrators, students, and parents, as well as creating lesson plans, assignments, and syllabi. You may write articles for alumni magazines and websites, or blog for the general public. If you run labs for schools and industries, you may find yourself writing reports to clients or bosses, using memos and letters to conduct business, making presentations to colleagues and buyers, crafting résumés and cover letters as you seek jobs and funding, and writing thank you notes to supporters. In today's Web 2.0+ world you may find that many, if not all, of these communications happen electronically through e-mails, text messages, blog posts, Twitter feeds, Facebook updates, YouTube videos, Pinterest boards, and various other social media platforms.

Did you know?

Many engineers find their way into politics, including two past presidents. "Civil Engineers are a good fit to solve the problems many cities are facing with aging infrastructure and infrastructure that has been outpaced by growth. I also think the analytical thinking which is part of an engineering background gives engineers an advantage in problem solving."

—Jeff Holtzinger
civil engineer and past
mayor of Frederick, Maryland

Writing Effectively in Engineering

Know the Audience in Engineering

Many people writing in engineering are writing for their clients and co-workers. They are writing a wide variety of documents as discussed above in order to communicate their proposals, projects, research, and other aspects of their work. Engineers may also be writing for government and corporate audiences, including employers, granting agencies, and regulatory agencies. It is important to always know who you are writing for:

❏ Who are your primary readers?

❏ Who else might read your writing or listen to your presentation?

❏ What will the members of your audience already know about your topic?

❏ What will you need to define or explain?

❏ Will your audience be predisposed to agree or disagree with your point of view?

❏ What kinds of evidence will be most convincing for this audience?

Know the Research Questions to Ask in Engineering

As a student, your research questions or the conditions for your research may be assigned to you by your instructor. Often, however, you will have to create your question on your own. One place to begin is by asking yourself what you want to know more about, what you want to understand better, or what assumptions you need to test. You may ask *how* questions or *why* questions. Your final research question will guide both your research design and your writing. The research question is also referred to as the *working hypothesis*. It is the idea you will systematically test or analyze through the research process and describe through the writing process. Table 8.1 illustrates how this process can be used to arrive at a viable research question.

Did you know?

Professionals trained as civil engineers design and plan roads, waterways, dams, and bridges. They also work on buildings, airports, and sewer systems. This type of engineering is one of the oldest engineering disciplines. Workers in this field keep track of issues like length of a project, design issues, costs, government regulations, and environmental issues like earthquakes and hurricanes. Civil engineers can be construction site supervisors, teachers, or city engineers, or they may hold jobs in design and research.

Other types of engineers include chemical, electrical, mechanical, aerospace, computer, and environmental engineers.

TABLE 8.1

Research Questions	
What you want to know more about:	**Your research question:**
Bridges continue to rust and decay and many will need to be rebuilt in the next few years. How can we build longer-lasting bridges?	What type of polymer materials are best suited for bridge building?
Is it possible to build bridges that can withstand natural disasters such as earthquakes and hurricanes? Would the use of flexible structures make bridges better able to withstand such disasters?	Which flexible structures are most viable for bridge building?

KNOW THE KINDS OF EVIDENCE USED IN ENGINEERING ARGUMENTS

Engineers use both quantitative and qualitative data in order to make arguments and support their claims; they also build and test prototypes. They use data from primary research in the field or lab, as well as secondary research from other published resources, especially when others detail what they have tried—what worked and what didn't. Data are often presented in mathematical and/or scientific formulas; this includes the presentation of statistics in the text as well as through graphs, charts, and tables. In your writing, you may need to present the mathematical formulas you developed to test data, look for or extend patterns, or demonstrate results. Likewise, you may find it helpful, or even necessary, to use established statistical tests when presenting your

Did you know?

We argue that the gap between empirical software engineering and software engineering practice might be lessened if more attention were paid to two important aspects of evidence. The first is that evidence from case or field studies of actual software engineering practice are essential in order to understand and inform that practice. The second is that the nature of evidence should fit the purpose to which the evidence is going to be put. One type of evidence is not per se better than another. For example, the evidence required to persuade a manager to change an aspect of practice might be totally different in nature from that required to deepen the academic community's understanding of such practice.

—J. Segal
"The nature of evidence in empirical software engineering." *Software Technology and Engineering Practice*, 2003.

quantitative data, so you should familiarize yourself with the computer software available at your institution or in your lab. Qualitative data may also be used in engineering because some experimental results must be described as well as measured. The most important question to ask is this: What kind of evidence is needed to test my claim or hypothesis? Your research should then be designed to help you accurately collect this type of data or evidence.

KNOW THE WRITING AND STYLE CONVENTIONS IN ENGINEERING

An effective writer in engineering communicates clearly, is aware of the audience, uses complete and thorough research (both primary and secondary), presents appropriate and accurate evidence for the study, and uses the best format for the information and audience. Good writing in engineering also follows the basic tenets of good writing in general: it is organized, easy to read, and grammatically correct, and accurately uses the required documentation system. In addition, here are some specific conventions you may want to keep in mind when writing about engineering:

❑ Use the terms and principles in the field in order to be understood. Avoid common or vernacular names, which may not be precise and can cause confusion. You should explain these engineering terms when writing for more general audiences.

　　» Follow disciplinary rules for the use of names and formulas such as those for species, genes, chemicals, proteins, and procedures.

　　» The use of abbreviations is common, but you should still write out the whole word or phrase the first time you use it, and put the abbreviation in parentheses. Then use the abbreviation consistently throughout the rest of the paper.

❑ Be as descriptive as possible so your reader can visualize the problem or solution, but avoid metaphorical language unless a comparison is used to make an abstract concept more concrete and thus more understandable.

❑ Use visuals strategically to illustrate points and present data—this includes the use of images, models, concept maps, photographs, tables, graphs, and charts.

Tables and figures should be numbered consecutively in separate series (e.g., Table 10.1, Table 10.2; Figure 10.1, Figure 10.2). Tables should have titles, and figures should have legends or keys. Both should be understandable apart from the text even though they should also be referenced in the text. Often images have captions to help readers make sense of what they are seeing.

❏ Every equation, table, or figure should be discussed in the text. It should also be labeled with an appropriate, descriptive caption.

❏ Equations should be set apart in the text for ease of reading as well as emphasis. Equations should also be numbered and then explained in the text following the equation.

TIP

Make sure all variables have been defined in the text.

❏ When listing equipment, give the manufacturer, model number, and serial number.

❏ Spell out numbers at the beginning of sentences or rephrase to move the number; spell out numbers 1–10 unless they are part of a series using Arabic numerals. Use the symbol ~ to mean "approximately equal to".

❏ Use headings and subheadings to divide your material into small, manageable chunks for the reader. These can also be used in your table of contents to guide your reader.

Did you know?

"Many engineers spend over 40 percent of their work time writing and usually find the percentage increases as they move up the corporate ladder."

—Beer and McMurray

❏ Pay attention to verb tense and be consistent. Studies already completed should be presented in past tense; studies being proposed (e.g., in a grant proposal) should be in future tense; conditions that presently exist should be discussed in the present tense. Some engineering style guides use passive voice (e.g., an experiment was conducted) while others use first person, active voice (e.g., we conducted an experiment). Check with your professor, your company style guide, or previous issues of the journal or magazine to help you decide which form is appropriate for your context and purpose, and then be consistent throughout the text.

❏ Rarely use direct quotes from source materials. Instead rely on summaries and paraphrases.

❏ Be as objective as possible, avoiding emotional words and phrasing that will bias or unduly influence the reader. This includes avoiding sexist language and gendered expressions in your writing.

Example:
The new equipment was tested by *firefighters* in three different precincts; rather than, The new equipment was tested by *firemen* in three different precincts.

KNOW THE APPROPRIATE DOCUMENTATION STYLE IN ENGINEERING

APA, the documentation style recommended by the American Psychological Association, and CMS, the documentation style outlined by the *Chicago Manual of Style*, are both used by engineers, depending on context. Likewise, many different areas or fields within engineering have their own documentation guides. For example, each of the groups or societies listed below has its own documentation style for use with its publications. These publications are widely read and published in by engineers.

> *IEEE: Electrical and Computer Engineering*
>
> *ACS: American Chemical Society*
>
> *MRS: Materials Research Society*
>
> *ASME: American Society of Mechanical Engineers*
>
> *BMES: Biomedical Engineering Society*

In choosing your documentation style, use the style required by your instructor or the journal to which you are submitting your paper, or consult the style set forth in your company's in-house style guide.

Note: in APA format, a title page should be included

SAMPLE STUDENT ECE 477 REVIEW PAPER

ECE 477-MICROELECTRONIC FABRICATION

Brent Woodman

Kunal Verma

Plasma Etching

Introduction

Plasma etching is a process used in PCB, semiconductor, and micro optical fabrication as an alternative to cheaper wet chemical etching techniques. The plasma etching process is a form of dry etching that uses neutral radicals and ions in plasma to bombard and remove the surface elements of a material. Plasma etching provides several advantages over wet chemical etching that have made it a popular technique for modern VLSI fabrication. In this report we will explain how plasma etching works and give a specific example of its use in micro-optics.

Theory

Plasma etching has become the standard etching method of industry over the past couple decades due to its ability to create high resolution features on the wafer. Like in wet etching, plasma etching requires application of a resist mask on the surface of the wafer prior to the etching stage. In most cases plasma etching provides better etching rates in the perpendicular direction, providing reduced undercut of the masked material. This is mostly due to the unique way plasma interacts with the etched material.

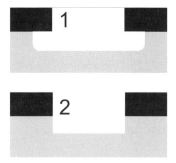

Figure 1: 1. Isotropic etch; 2. Anisotropic etch. [1]

When plasma is created in an etching chamber there are several control factors that are used to determine which of the free moving plasma particles will dominate the chemical reaction. In glow discharge applications where direct-current is applied to the plasma electrodes free radicals in the plasma cause isotropic bombardment of the material surface because of general particle dispersion. Figure 1.1 shows an isotropic etch profile. With reactive ion etching (RIE) an RF signal is applied to the plasma causing greater movement in plasma ions; larger molecules and free radicals are not able to move as fast as the ions and as a result do not contribute to the etching nearly as much as the ions. The influence from the directional magnetic field reduces deviation in ion movement, creating a much narrower dispersion than the larger particles in a glow discharge process. This creates an anisotropic profile with either no or minimal undercutting as seen in Figure 1.2.

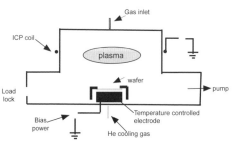

Figure 2: Schematic for a typical high-density etcher. [2]

ECE 477-MICROELECTRONIC FABRICATION

Brent Woodman

Kunal Verma

Implementation

The same basic layout for an etching chamber is used in both glow discharge and RIE devices. In Figure 2 above we see an example of an RIE system that uses inductively coupled plasma coils to create the plasma. A biasing voltage is also connected to the wafer platform in order to attract ions to the surface of the wafer. As ion bombardment of the wafer occurs it is important to note that there is constant gas flow in and out of the chamber. The gas flow rate in the system defines the chamber pressure which in turn controls the etch rate of the wafer material. The output pump removes reactant discharge from the wafer surface while the gas inlet provides the plasma gas source.

The RF signal in most commercial applications has been standardized by the FCC for a frequency of 13.56 MHz [4] although many manufacturers deviate from this operating frequency for specialized applications. Plasma etching machines are used for a variety of applications including semiconductor oxidation and etching, etching for SEM and TEM preparation, diffraction and refraction profiles on silica lenses, as well as etching for the creation of micro-electromechanical devices (MEMS). Control parameters for a plasma etch are determined by plasma species, gas intake, gas outtake, ion sheath thickness of the material surface, mean free path for particles in the chamber, pressure, and wafer temperature.

Figure 3: Plasma Quest ECR Etcher. [3]

With industry trends moving towards the production of smaller architectures and die sizes there is a need to create low pressure plasma systems for smaller pattern sizes. Scaling these pattern sizes requires higher selectivity between mask materials and etch materials in order to maintain anisotropy. Production time is always in need of reduction so increased etch rates are necessary to match with chip cost projections meaning that etch systems require higher density plasma. Lastly, in order to decrease costs further companies are using larger wafer sizes in production meaning larger diameter plasma with higher uniformity. These constitute the needs for the development of future plasma etching technologies. [9]

Application

With the ever increasing need for humans to have faster communication and simultaneous access to numerous resources the physical ability to move data is being taxed. Limitations on traditional analog and digital communication have forced the development of digital optical communication devices. In order to facilitate large bandwidth optical communication it is necessary to create and manipulate light on chip. According to Dr. Rüdiger Paschotta, the materials below are all direct band-gap semiconductor laser materials. They are more desirable for LASERs because they emit light more readily than indirect band-gap semiconductors. [5]

- GaAs (gallium arsenide)
- GaP (gallium phosphide)

ECE 477-MICROELECTRONIC FABRICATION

Brent Woodman

Kunal Verma

- AlGaAs (aluminum arsenide)
- GaN (gallium nitride)
- InGaAs (indium gallium arsenide)
- InGaP (indium gallium phosphide)
- GaInNAs (indium gallium arsenide nitride)
- InP (indium phosphide)

Once two or more of these semi-conductors are layered using epitaxy to create quantum wells, these layers can then be stimulated to emit photons with an electrical current. The wavelength of the light emitted is determined by the allowed energy levels of the individual semi-conductor. By changing the individual composition of the ternary and quaternary compounds the wavelength can be controlled. By creating an array of Lasers on chip all at different wavelengths once can create a discrete system of light over a very wide bandwidth. All of these can be transmitted over one fiber-optic cable and the individual data streams (wavelengths) can be de-muxed after transmission.

This de-muxing can be done on chip the method shown below in Figure 4. [7] The configuration of the de-muxer is a Rowland circle. The diffraction grating as well as the wave guides that serve as the single input and multiple outputs must be etched precisely using a plasma etching device. Also, the free propagation region needs to be etched out of the original wafer. The device takes advantage of the fact that the different wavelengths diffract at different rates. This results in the individual wavelengths being routed to individual wave guides out of the de-muxer.

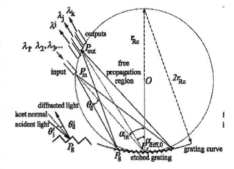

Figure 4: Optical de-muxer. [7]

The basic principle behind a wave guide is the same as a pipe full of water. Once you put the water into the pipe, it can only get out at one of the ends. The on chip wave guides do this same thing for light. This allows the integrated circuit chip designer to use waveguides as traces for routing the light on and off of the chip. Figure 5 is taken from Thomas et al. [8] and shows a "shallow feature [waveguide] through an epitaxial stack containing InGaAs, InP and InGaAsP etched at 180° C. Profile ~85°." This was created using an inductively coupled plasma (ICO) etch and an electro-static chuck.

Figure 5: Wave Guide. [8]

The shape and dimensions of the waveguide determine what and how well the light information is transmitted. Most importantly, the surfaces must be reflective to allow the light to propagate easily. This means using an etching process that results in smooth surfaces is paramount to creating on chip waveguides. As can be seen, the process resulted in very smooth surfaces.

In the article by Thomas et al., "It is shown that the combination of a high density inductively coupled plasma (ICP) and high temperature electro-static chuck (ESC) may be used for both shallow optical waveguides and for deep optical mirrors in InP-based epitaxial layers."

ECE 477-MICROELECTRONIC FABRICATION

Brent Woodman

Kunal Verma

References

(1) http://www.memsnet.org/mems/processes/etch.html
(2) http://www.laserfocusworld.com/articles/369345
(3) https://spf.stanford.edu/SNF/equipment/dry-etching/plasma-quest-ecr-etcher-pquest- contaminated/plasma-quest-ecr-etcher
(4) http://en.wikipedia.org/wiki/Plama_etching
(5) Paschotta, Dr. Rüdiger. "Encyclopedia of Laser Physics and Technology – semiconductor lasers, laser diodes." *RP Photonics Consulting – laser and amplifer design, nonlinear optics, fiber optics, fiber lasers and amplifers, ultrashort pulses, optoelectronics, consultant, training.* N.p., n.d. Web. 3 Nov. 2009. http://www.rp-photonics.com/semiconductor_lasers.html
(6) Yohji Fujii and Junichiro Minowa, "Optical demultiplexer using a silicon concave diffraction grating," Appl. Opt. 22, 974-978 (1983). *http://www.opticsinfobase.org.*
(7) Song, Jun, Sailing He, and Dongqing Pang. A MoM-based design and simulation method for an." *Optics Communications* 233-363-371 (2004): n. pag. Web 1 Nov. 2003.
(8) Thomas, DJ, YP Song, C Fragos, MM Bourke, and K Powell. "High Density Plasma Etch Processes for the Manufacture of." GaAs MANTECH unknown (2001): n. pag. *www.csmantech.org.* Web. 1 Nov. 2009.
(9) http://media.iupac.org/publications/pac/1996/pdf/6805x1011.pdf

SMART-PHONE CONTROL, DATA ANALYSIS 1

AN ENGINEERING PROJECT FOR MICHIGAN STATE UNIVERSITY'S ELECTRICAL AND
COMPUTER ENGINEERING SENIOR DESIGN CLASS, ECE 480

SMART-PHONE CONTROL,

DATA ACQUISITION

& ANALYSIS FOR ADVANCED SENSOR SYSTEMS

TEAM MEMBERS

NITIN ARORA

KENNETH HSU

ASHANTA MOSS

JEET PATEL

RAVI SINHA

PROJECT SPONSOR – CHRISTOPHER BALL

FACILITATOR – WEN LI

Executive Summary

Design Team 10's main project goal was to design a smart-phone application to replace the onboard central processing unit of an infrared spectroscopy sensor. Our project entitled "Smart-Phone Control, Data Acquisition and Data Analysis for Advanced Sensor Systems" is based on a transformational technology, and we used the current capability of smart-phones to create an Android application. This application exploits cutting-edge technologies and performs complex mathematical computations on a smart-phone. Advanced sensor systems that are able to utilize infrared spectroscopy to accurately analyze materials are currently commercially available. However, these units are large in size and are only suitable for fixed placement in laboratories. In order to address this limitation, Battelle has developed a line of infrared spectroscopy sensors that are both portable and accurate. One of the greatest hurdles facing Battelle in its development of these smaller sensors is the size and power consumption of individual components. Battelle sought to use a smart-phone to replace the onboard CPU thus both reducing power consumption and overall sensor size and weight. This is where our team has come in to help. We have created an Android application that performs all of the necessary FTIR computations. This will allow Battelle to reach their goal of further reducing the size of FTIR sensors.

Acknowledgements

This semester, Team 10 received support from many sources. We would like to sincerely thank everyone who aided in our project's success! First, we would like to thank our classmates for their thoughts and input, which helped us create the best application we could this semester. In addition, we would like to thank our facilitator Dr. Wen Li for all of her input, thoughts and assistance this semester. Whenever we needed her, she was always there to guide us. She was a great critic and only wanted the best for our team. Most importantly, we would like to thank our sponsors Dr. Ball and Battelle for their sponsorship and all that it entailed. He was always able to help and answer the many questions we had and was always prepared to give feedback to help us reach our goals. Without our sponsor and facilitator, our project would not have been as successful as it was. Thank you very much for all of your support and help throughout this semester Team 10 truly appreciates all you have done.

SMART-PHONE CONTROL, DATA ANALYSIS   4

Table of Contents

Chapter 1

Introduction

Battelle, a research and development organization that addresses the pressing needs of government and industry, is seeking to use the current smart-phone technologies to develop a new technology that will control the operations of advanced sensor systems. Smart-phones can potentially replace onboard, embedded systems. The systems that are currently in place have increased complexity, cost, size, and power constraints that could be cut down, or limited, by using a smart-phone. Our team has worked on creating an Android application to remotely control a stand-in sensor so that we can both evaluate how current devices perform at such a task and accurately measure the effects on the phone's resources, especially battery life, memory, and processing speed. In addition to the application, we aim to provide the sponsor with a comprehensive analysis of current smart-phones and their capabilities of transferring and analyzing complex data, as well as provide information on future advances in hardware and software that may have an impact on our applications functionality.

Background Information

The advanced sensor systems that are currently able to utilize infrared spectroscopy to accurately analyze materials are commercially available. However, these units are large in size and are only available for fixed placement in laboratories. In order to address this limitation, Battelle has developed a line of infrared spectroscopy sensors that are both portable and accurate. One of the greatest hurdles facing Battelle in its development of these smaller sensors is the size and power consumption of individual components. Currently, Battelle utilizes a full-featured onboard central processing unit (CPU) in each of their sensors. Battelle wishes to use a smart-phone to replace the onboard CPU thus both reducing power consumption and overall sensor size and weight. Smart-phones have reached a point in their development where they are capable of handling large amounts of data. Smart-phones have the ability to perform complex calculations on that data while presenting a user-friendly interface makes smart-phones an ideal solution for Battelle.

Objectives

The primary objective of our team was to assess the performance of smart-phone technologies as a replacement of CPUs in sensor systems. We broke down team goals down into three separate tasks:

1. Research smart-phones

    - Gather information on current and future smart-phone technologies.

    - Evaluate how a smart-phone's operating system and hardware affects the ability to process infrared spectroscopy sensor data.

2. Create a smart-phone application

    - Develop separate programs for communication, information processing, and user interface.

    - Simulate the applications on a PC to approximate the overall performance of the system.

3. Produce a working prototype

    - Integrate the applications into a smart-phone and assess different parameters such as power consumption, processing time, and transmission time.

    - Optimizing the performance parameters by altering the algorithms implemented in the applications.

Risk Analysis

The risks associated with this project differ with respect to the separate goals.

Smart-phone Analysis and Predictions:

- Some smart-phone producers may choose not to share all relevant information

- Lack of complete and accurate information may lead to an incomplete or inaccurate analysis

- Marketing strategies, government regulations, and unforeseen technological hurdles may alter future smart-phones in unforeseeable ways

Using Current Smart-phones to Control Sensor Systems:

- Current smart-phones may not be able to process raw sensor data quickly enough to be a viable replacement for onboard CPUs

- Battery life may be severely reduced as a result of the significant computational requirements

- The cost of smart-phones equipped with suitable processors may render their use economically infeasible

Today's Technology

In the Android phone market, there are so many different technologies. One of the biggest slogans out today is "There's an app for that." This is a big saying because everything is said to have an application that well perform anything necessary. Apple's iPhone started the slogan with their application store, but the Android market has caught up and has most, if not all, of the same programs. There are several applications in the Android market place that work on the same principles of converting from time domain to frequency domain using fast Fourier transform and doing a spectral comparison with the already installed library mainly using troughs and peaks. For example, the Shazam application works on the same principle as it identifies a song, by first collecting data then converting it to frequency domain and then comparing it with the already stored library. Because of course, "There's an app for that." Yet, our application introduces a new way to control complex sensors.

New Approach

Our team decided to take a new approach and broke our code into three different important aspects: comparison, spectra analysis and user interface. The concept that is unique to us is that we are trying to control sensors from a remote location, which gives our project a new level of difficulty. Our project was complex, as we first need to transfer data using Wi-Fi or Bluetooth and then perform Fournier transform to properly convert the data and the use spectra analysis, and compared the data. From here, we received a graph and a percentage of how well our data matches.

Chapter 5

Final Cost

Our project cost us $529, which was the cost of the Nexus S smart-phone. Other than that, we used an Android phone of one of our team member's to act as a stand-in sensor and all Google development kits were free too. The expected cost would be the same, as the only thing changing would be having an actual sensor in place of the second smart-phone, which is just acting as a dummy sensor.

Final Budget

Budget	Expenses
Google Android Development Phone	$529
Software Development Kit	$0
Stand-in Sensor (Android Phone)	$0
Total	$529

Schedule

A Gantt chart was created to keep our team goals and deadlines in order. We used the timeline to help us stay on schedule so that we knew where we stood in the project as well as how much time we had left to complete the project. The Gantt chart was divided into software and research; we also separated the time for presentations. We understood the importance of having good presentations as important as delivering a good project so that our audience would understand our project and how it could have an effect on our sponsoring company. In order to meet the deadlines we worked together. Communication was the key that helped our team pull everything together in a timely manner. Setting these deadlines gave us enough time at the end complete our project so that we had time to test and optimize our application to improve upon battery usage, power consumption as well as the speed and efficacy of our application. We attempted to get everything done a few weeks in advance so that we could a time cushion in case

of unexpected delays. The plan that we set was good because like most projects things do not go

according to plan. We ran into a few bumps along the way. We first encounter a problem getting

the Fournier transform to work properly, this pushed our timing back a few days. We also ran

into a problem combining all three parts of the code, which luckily was solved in one day.

Lastly, we ran into issues with comparison and the WiFi and Bluetooth and a few other minor

issues, which pushed our ending project end another week later. All in all, our project was

completed and optimized to the best of our teams ability.

Conclusion

Our project goal was to create a smart-phone application prototype that not only

introduces new technology to our company, but also works efficiently and effectively. To create

a functional prototype of our smart-phone application, our team applied the stages of the product

life cycle management and took into consideration the many different issues that could arise. By

acknowledging these potential issues that could affect our project, many problems were

addressed early on in our project. Using this method of planning, our team has been able to

effectively enhance our product to not only give the customer exactly what they asked for, but to

also provide an optimal working product. By doing this, our team may have facilitated the design

solution for a commercialized product, which in turn is a very exciting privilege for our sponsor

and us.

ACTIVITIES

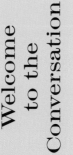

Welcome to the Conversation

Discuss these questions with your classmates in class or via a class wiki or shared blog.

1. What types of writing might you be asked to do in engineering? Who are the audiences for these different types of writing?

2. What are the differences between qualitative and quantitative data? What rhetorical purpose does each type of data serve?

3. Why does writing in engineering value objectivity? How can you achieve objectivity in your writing?

4. What are some ways you can be more precise in your writing to avoid confusion?

5. What are some important components to keep in mind when writing a proposal? Why are these components helpful?

Writing to Learn

1. **Problem analysis:** Your instructor will ask you and your classmates to create a hypothetical engineering problem. Then, each of you will select another's problem, and write an evaluation of the problem. Why is this issue considered a problem? What methods can be used to assess the issue? How can this problem be fixed? Who would provide funding to fix it?

2. **Oral draft:** As you pick a topic for a larger research paper or project, it can be helpful to also prepare an oral draft as you go. In this activity, present a five minute talk to a small group of classmates about your project in progress. Your listeners should each ask you a question about your project after your talk, which you should be able to answer. Not only will this activity help you develop your research into a final draft, it also provides valuable practice in presenting your work.

Learning to Write

1. **Jargon journal**: Although the most frequent type of writing you may do are engineering reports for an audience of your colleagues, you will also need to write for audiences who are unfamiliar with many engineering concepts. To learn how to address different audiences, create a jargon journal. Whenever you encounter jargon or terminology that only engineers understand, write an entry in your jargon journal which explains the jargon in lay terms.

2. **Field report**: As you begin to research in the field, you will want to learn accurate documentation for use in your career. From your field research, create a detailed field report that explains the reason for your research, your methodology, and your data, both quantitative and qualitative. This document can serve as a base from which to craft a longer engineering report.

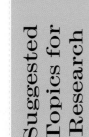

Suggested Topics for Research

1. The problems facing America's aging infrastructure are a routine issue discussed at all levels of government. You are tasked with researching a structure in your home city that is in need of repair or replacement. As an engineer, you must assess the structure and its context and complete an engineering report with your recommendations to solve the problem.

2. Your firm has asked you to research a new technique for developing a structural component. Research this technique and, using primary and secondary sources, explain the technique and evaluate whether or not your company should implement this new process.

 **READ MORE ABOUT IT**

Beer, David F., and David A. McMurray. *A Guide to Writing as an Engineer.* Hoboken, NJ: John Wiley & Sons, 1997. Print.

Mkandawire, Martin. *Ecowriting: Advice to ESL on Effective Scientific Writing in Environmental Science and Engineering.* New York: Nova Science Publishers. 2010. Print.

Silyn-Roberts, Heather. *Writing for Science and Engineering: Papers, Presentations and Reports.* Oxford, CA: Butterworth-Heinemann. 2000. Print.

chapter **9**

Writing in the Health Sciences

NURSING, HEALTH CARE MANAGEMENT, PUBLIC HEALTH,
NUTRITION SCIENCE, MEDICAL AND DENTAL ASSISTING,
RADIATION THERAPY, MEDICAL TECHNOLOGY,
PHARMACOLOGY TECH, AND VETERINARIAN TECH

*The only medicine for suffering, crime, and all other woes of mankind
is wisdom. Teach a man to read and write, and you have put into his
hands the great keys of the wisdom box.*

—Thomas Henry Huxley

PURPOSES OF WRITING IN THE HEALTH SCIENCES

Writing for the health sciences is geared toward accurate and clear communication to a variety of audiences and in multiple contexts. This type of science writing involves patient communication and education, accurate recording and reporting of vital health information, observation and experimentation with accompanying accurate explanations of scientific research, and the communication of both quantitative and qualitative data. The writing that those in the health professions do directly influences their environment in practical ways, even in the form of laboratory research, which is then used by those in the field to actively treat patients. Likewise, health writing is always influenced by the writer's environment—cultural assumptions and attitudes toward health and medicine, economics, insurance companies, drug manufacturers, and law—and, increasingly, by the effects of policy making at the state and federal legislative levels. Which types of quantitative observations, clinical research, and drug or treatment trials are investigated and grant-funded depend on these factors, all of which influence the types of treatment available to the public and the health messages disseminated to private and public sectors. The genres of writing in the health sciences span multiple platforms and media, from the more traditional scholarly research reports and case studies to digital writing such as public service announcements and instructional websites and videos. Each of these types of writing will call for different rhetorical approaches and styles, but as in all writing in the health professions, clear and concise prose is essential.

TYPES OF WRITING ASSIGNMENTS IN THE HEALTH SCIENCES

[M]any physicians claim that 90 percent of their job is communicating with the public in some way or representing themselves professionally through communication mechanisms. Much of their work in the office requires verbal skills (communicating with patients); however, medical professionals also spend many hours writing explanatory or educational materials, writing responses for inquiries from organizations, writing to receive reimbursement, writing to the administration at hospitals to request equipment or to establish their position on a controversial issue, and writing research papers and conference proposals to better their standing in the field. They write these documents themselves because they cannot trust someone else to represent them and their ideas accurately.

—Karl Terryberry

Writing in the health sciences covers many different genres and purposes. As mentioned previously, the rhetorical components of audience and context determine the types of writing you should create, both in the classroom and as part of a health care setting.

Many of the types of writing you may be asked to compose are discussed below, but there are types of writing which you may be asked to create that are not in this list or that combine multiple types of writing, such as in the field of public health, which often requires creative project design to communicate effectively with specific audiences. Often the ideas for research projects will arise naturally from possible new knowledge you gain in the classroom, the laboratory, or in clinical practice. Evidence-based practice is the guiding principle of much health writing, as often the best choices for patient care rely on putting the best available scientific research into practice.

 You should always follow the directions given by your instructor or the lab supervisor.

CASE STUDIES

Case studies ask you to describe specific cases that present a unique issue and outcome of interest to other practitioners. Patients are described in detail involving several measures with the purpose of documenting their conditions, pathologies, or effects of treatment or other interventions. Several components are necessary for this type of study, including extensive research and evidence for a certain issue or case. A conclusion is necessary to a case study, and it may generally show a correlation (or lack thereof) between variables. It may or may not, however, prove causation.

Most case studies you will be asked to write will focus on one patient's case and how treatment or intervention affected that patient's outcome, as well as how this particular case illustrates a larger principle in health or patient care. As usual in science writing, stick to relevant, objective information.

A case study generally includes a version of the following components:

- ❏ Introduction of the case
    - » Who is the patient and what is the problem?
    - » What is your argument/hypothesis?
- ❏ Pathophysiology
    - » What is the health issue/disease? How does it usually present?
- ❏ Patient History
    - » What are the patient's previous underlying health problems?

- » Has the patient had any previous procedures or surgeries? What interventions, including medication or lifestyle adjustments, have been given to this patient?

❏ Physical Assessment

- » The procedure for this will vary according to the specific field or purpose. For example, in nursing, the physical assessment usually entails a specific description of the patient's stats and cursory examination. For other health professionals, however, this may also include more intensive testing and physical examination.

❏ Treatments

- » Explain existing treatments the patient is receiving for the issue being examined, as well as other current treatments received for other health issues.

❏ Care Plan or Diagnosis

- » Explain both your diagnosis and your goal for further intervention.
- » Be sure to reference the literature to support your intervention plan.
- » Conclude this section by providing an evaluation of your results. Has the intervention worked? Has the patient's condition improved?

❏ Recommendations

- » What should the health care team and patient do in the future to improve the patient's outcome?

DIAGNOSES

The diagnosis is a type of writing you will most certainly be asked to complete in the health sciences field, and the form that it takes will change based on your specific field. Physicians will assess a patient and then write what most readers would understand as a "classic" diagnosis: the patient has a specific disease, ailment, or issue. Nurses, physical therapists, and technicians do not generally diagnose a patient like a physician but will instead identify a course of action to take, such as a treatment or intervention. For example, whereas a doctor may diagnose a patient as having high blood pressure and include a treatment, a nurse's diagnosis would state that a patient is at risk for various complications due to high blood pressure (the physician's diagnosis). The central focus of writing a diagnosis is to make a diagnostic statement. Depending on the type of diagnosis, different steps will lead up to the diagnostic statement, including analyzing the data, identifying the patient's normal functioning, and describing any current or possible dysfunction or disease process.

Importantly, nursing diagnoses differ in that they focus always on patient response, and they can vary as the patient responds to any intervention. In contrast, a physician's diagnosis tends to stay more uniform both across patients and during the process of the disease.

Box 9.1

Common Errors in Nursing Diagnoses

- Stating two problems in one diagnosis. Each separate problem should have its own diagnosis.

  Example: Pain and problems in self-perception following hysterectomy.

- Using medical diagnoses as nursing diagnoses. Nursing diagnoses focus on patient care; diagnosing medical problems is reserved for physicians.

  Example: Chronic sinusitis due to smoking.

- Relating one NANDA stem to another, including rewording a stem so that it appears to be different. This association leads to a faulty cause and effect.

- Causing legal or ethical problems. Diagnoses should be objective and free from bias.

  Example: Dehydration related to failure of nursing staff to change I.V. rehydration solution in a timely manner.

PATIENT CHARTS AND HISTORIES

During the course of a patient's treatment, one of the most important documents is the patient chart, also known as a patient history. These notes form a central tool for patient assessment and later documentation and research. Charts are the main written communication between a doctor and the hospital staff, and as such they are also important legal documents that protect the patients, physicians, staff, and facility. Charting requirements may differ at various facilities, but some general guidelines are recommended:

- ❏ Always write in ink, and write as legibly and accurately as possible.
- ❏ Never attempt to erase or otherwise destroy any entries. This is vitally important in case of litigation or other complications.
- ❏ Always include the date and time for each entry. Generally military time (24 hours) is used.
- ❏ Use only abbreviations that have been approved for that specific context.

Following these guidelines will ensure the clearest communication between all health care staff and will protect you as well as the patient receiving care. Various forms also may be included as part of the patient chart, such as consent forms, medication administration records (MAR), advance directives, and operating room records.

INSTRUCTION SHEETS

Instruction sheets and their accompanying care plans provide a patient with clear, focused directions for a treatment plan. Since the reader of this document is not a medical professional, it is important that the style be as clear and concise as possible, avoiding unessential jargon the reader may not understand.

Since these types of documents are necessary for a wide range of patients, try to avoid unnecessary abstractions, and keep the writing around a seventh grade level (or, about the level of a standard newspaper). Focus on just a few important concepts, and be sure to explain *why* a certain intervention is necessary. If you need to use a medical term that may be outside of a patient's knowledge, be sure to quickly define it. Bulleted lists are often easier for patients to follow, and graphics also can be added to aid comprehension.

RESEARCH PAPERS

Research papers present the results of original research, both quantitative and qualitative. This research might occur during a single experiment, over the course of a semester, or across multiple courses and semesters. This is a central genre in science writing, and it forms a foundation for communicating research in the health sciences. The research paper you may be assigned in class is very similar to a paper published in a professional journal. It allows you to practice communicating with fellow colleagues in the health sciences. You may be asked to design research that collects, synthesizes, and analyzes data, and to use the outcomes of this research to inform additional research, make correct choices in patient care, or effectively educate patients and other members of the public about a specific health issue. Be very specific when describing your methodology. Your colleagues need to know more than just a measurement; they also need to know the tools used to measure, as the reliability of a given tool is significant when replicating experiments or applying research to practice.

Sometimes your research project will need to take into account the expected behavior or outcome in a given situation. Be prepared to use your research to address this topic.

Qualitatively focused research papers can vary in format and scope; there is no single way to format and organize these types of papers. In this case, follow your instructor's directions for appropriate formatting.

Quantitative research focuses on implementing the principles of the scientific method to prove or disprove certain phenomena within a controlled experimental environment. In order for your research to follow the principles of scientific inquiry, your methods must be empirical and measureable. This means your experiment must be constructed and implemented to answer a specific research question and be free of biases. What distinguishes the scientific method from other investigative methods is that the results of the experiment should be self-evident.

The purpose of controlling the variables of an experiment is to ensure that any results can be reproduced in similarly controlled experiments. This moves a scientific experiment from simple inquiry to tested scientific theory. This objective attention to experimental control also helps to prevent personal biases on the part of the researcher. For example, you may expect a certain result after administering a new medication or implementing a novel procedure. However, this belief that an intervention will or must work may cause you to interpret the results as matching your belief, when in fact the results may actually indicate another outcome. Following the steps of the scientific method will safeguard against such problems.

Quantitative papers follow a traditional format based on the scientific method, which includes six sections in a specific order:

1. The **Abstract** is a concise, 250-word overview of the research paper. It provides the main points of your study, including brief statements about each of the six sections of the paper, the research question/hypothesis, the methods, the results, and the conclusion. Usually the abstract is written after the paper is complete, even though it is generally the first thing people read—either to decide whether your study is useful to them or to stay current in the field.

2. The **Introduction** serves many purposes for your reader, but its main role is to provide the context for your study. It includes a review of the scholarly literature that is relevant and explains why your research project is needed and important. It also shows how your project fits into existing research. The introduction is where you hook your reader and establish your own credibility as a researcher. This is also where you present your research question and your hypothesis, which you formulate based on the literature review and the parameters of your proposed experiment.

3. The **Materials and Methods** section details all of the essential information about the experiment's actual procedure: variables studied or taken into account, experimental controls, measurements and how they were taken, and other contexts and conditions of the study. It is important to be as clear and exact as possible with necessary details, so that the audience can replicate your research if desired. Generally, try to use generic names for materials, unless the brand names are essential for the study. When human subjects are involved, this section becomes more complicated, as humans are by their nature uncontrolled variables. However, you can account for all of the pertinent components/ features of your test subjects, which will aid in replication and verification of your experiment and results.

4. The **Results** section is a summary of your study's findings, focusing on trends or patterns in your data set. The results section may follow the order of your materials and methods section to make it easier for your reader to follow the whole study. Statistics, charts, tables, graphs, and other numerical data are given and explained in this section. The accompanying text should call attention to these visuals, but you do not need to repeat all of the information illustrated. This section is not where you should interpret your data or draw conclusions; rather, the focus here is on clear communication of actual experimental results.

5. The **Discussion** section is where you interpret your data, present your argument, and draw conclusions. You will need to support your argument with your data, and you will use your working hypothesis and the research from your introduction to bolster your conclusions. What is the most valid explanation for your results, and what does that mean for the subject of your study? How does your study fit into the context of previous work, and how does it affect the discipline? Are your findings consistent with those of previous studies, or do they show a different result? Have you proven something new or supplied a missing piece of information? Do your findings indicate the need for future studies?

6. The **References** section lists all sources used in the text and is formatted according to the style assigned by your instructor or the publication.

 Rely on your assignment sheet and instructor's guidance when determining the type of research you're being asked to do.

Lab Reports

The lab report is a concise record of an experiment or lab observation. It is a shorter version of a research paper, composed of the same six sections in the same order, (see the previous section for guidelines). Based on the actual assignment, specific sections may be emphasized for individual lab reports.

As discussed in the Research Papers section above, when writing lab reports for experiments dealing with human subjects or human/biological materials, it is vital that you be as detailed and observant of all variables as possible. Sometimes you may achieve a result that is unexpected, and—if you have not accounted for all of the aspects of the test subject that may affect the outcomes—you might misinterpret the data.

For example, suppose you are testing a new medication to aid weight loss. Out of 20 overweight patients who are given the medication, seven patients abruptly stop the trial because they report side effects such as dizziness, nausea, weakness, and increased thirst. If you have not recorded complete medical histories for these patients, you may not be aware that these seven subjects have diabetes, which affects how their bodies react to this type of medication. Without this information you might conclude erroneously that this medication is statistically unsafe for a general population, when really your results are only showing that it is unsafe for subjects who have pre-existing diabetes.

REVIEW PAPERS

In a review paper, you review a body of research, synthesize the findings, analyze and evaluate the studies, and then formulate conclusions. Multiple purposes may be served by this type of paper, including providing the audience with a clear summary of the current research on a topic, comparing related topics, and exploring new methodologies and theories. A review paper is similar to a literature review in that it is centered on a larger research question or problem, but it also presents an argument. It should be broad and detailed in scope, as it should identify and collect all of the major research previously done on a topic. It should always be organized with a clear central thesis. It is also important to include the purpose of the review, and whether such a review has been done previously (and if so, why it is being repeated); methodology used; conclusions about the subject, supported by evidence found during the course of the review; and a conclusion, which summarizes your findings and details the practical implications of your review. This paper should be appropriately cited and documented according to the documentation style assigned by your professor or called for in the publication.

CONFERENCE PRESENTATIONS (ORAL OR POSTER FORMAT)

Conferences are essential places for communicating research to colleagues, both within the discipline and across associated fields. Conference presentations typically are either oral with accompanying visuals, or poster presentations. A physician or nurse may read a paper sharing research results or participate in a panel debating an issue in the field. Visual aids might include PowerPoint presentations, video footage of a patient undergoing surgery or specific interventions, or an animation illustrating a new medical technique or procedure. Poster presentations can take various forms, with some conferences or instructors requiring different poster sizes or formats, from trifold to large posters on bulletin boards. These types of presentations are not limited to formal conferences, as your classes may require you to present your research to classmates or other colleagues on your campus. Thorough preparation is key: Make sure your oral presentations, visual aids, and posters conform to the guidelines of your discipline and the conference, and rehearse your speech so that it flows naturally. Finally, be prepared for a variety of questions from your colleagues.

 Posters are visual tools and should follow good design principles, such as the CRAP principles discussed in Chapter 6: contrast, repetition, alignment, proximity.

LAB NOTES OR LOGS

In order to write the most accurate research papers, it is essential that your lab notes include the details of your lab work, experiments, and observations with precision and care. Accuracy is key as these notes form the basis of your research papers and case studies, as well as other reports in which precise recording of data is required. Your record of the data should include all information necessary to complete the Methods and Materials and Results sections of your paper, including the dates and times of all important events and experiments in the lab; specifics about all materials and equipment used; procedures completed and techniques utilized; the results of any experiments and interventions; calculations; and acknowledgments of any other participants in the experiment, either as subjects or health care professionals. You can also begin to interpret the data and come to preliminary conclusions. If you decide to use shorthand terminology, make sure that you note all of the symbols or other codes that you use, so that you can later make a more meticulous transcription and ensure accurate reporting of the data and results. You may record these notes in a variety of ways, from handwritten notebooks to computer documents to video or audio recordings. Double-entry notebooks and traditional legal pads with large margins are two options that will enable you to record your notes as well as your thoughts on the data presented.

RESEARCH OR GRANT PROPOSALS

Knowing how to write an effective research or grant proposal is critical in the health sciences field because research requires money for equipment, space, supplies, and staff. The primary way to fund a project is via a grant. Governments, private and public foundations, corporations, and individuals can all make grants, and your research is more likely to be funded if it aligns with an organization's goals. Grants in the health sciences may include direct support for research projects, infrastructure improvements, fellowships for continued career development and education, and community outreach projects. In order for you to receive a grant, the organization must be convinced that your project will meet its expectations and be a wise use of the money. As with other formal writing, it is vital that you follow all research proposal guidelines exactly and be attentive to grammar, mechanics, style, and format.

You should always start with your research question, known as Specific Aims for many types of proposals. You must know *why* you are doing this research, *what* you hope to find out, and *how* you plan to study it before you can successfully write the rest of the proposal.

Since your readers will decide whether to fund your project based on your proposal, you must keep them in mind as you write. Explain any language or concepts they might not understand, and include any visuals (as allowed) that will help your readers better understand and evaluate your proposal. Your document, since it is a persuasive argument, should take into account the needs of the granting agency and respect its goals. You may have to complete additional research to ensure that your proposal will appeal to your readers.

Many funding agencies publish their own hints and tips for grant applications. You may also find examples of proposals from past award recipients on their websites. Make sure you read these models before you write your own proposal.

Unfortunately, when physicians think about medical writing, they have that mental image of scientific articles. However, that is only one part of medical writing in the life of a physician. Physicians (and medical students) need to learn medical writing for more reasons than that.

—Melnick

OTHER FORMS OF WRITING

Writing in the health professions is not limited to the discipline. Those in the health care field are often asked to communicate critical information to the public. As a health care professional, you can expect to write memos to public officials, letters to the editor, lab reports for authorities not familiar with your field, websites, blogs, and instructional videos, as well as fill out professional forms and documents for private practice. Particularly in the field of public health, you will need to write in genres that appeal to a targeted population, which may lead to surprising and unconventional choices for scientific writing—including public service announcements, radio spots, podcasts, YouTube video spots, or even animation. And, in our increasingly Internet-focused world, you can expect most of these communications to have a digital dimension, including social media platforms such as Twitter, Reddit, and Facebook.

WRITING EFFECTIVELY IN THE HEALTH SCIENCES

KNOW THE AUDIENCE(S) IN THE HEALTH SCIENCES

[W]riting in the field of Public Health involves assessing a problem and addressing it rhetorically through writing, [recognizing] that simply providing information may not persuade an audience to change its behavior, that it is necessary to assume a more nuanced writer identity in order to have an impact upon an intended audience, and that the assumption of this identity constitutes a performance.

—Clark and Fischbach

Audiences for health writing may include colleagues in the health professions, including physicians, nurses, public health officials, and other health care professionals; the lay public; local, state, and federal government agencies; and private agencies, insurance companies, and pharmaceutical companies. Most writing that you will do on a daily basis will focus on formal writing that is intended for colleagues, from charts, to research papers, to journal articles. Those in the health professions also write oral presentations for conferences and other venues, textbooks, pamphlets, and important health messages to be shared via popular media. Based on your specific focus, you may also be writing for government or private agencies that are monitoring or funding your work, corporate employers, and regulatory bodies, such as the

Food and Drug Administration or the Drug Enforcement Agency. In every case, it is essential that you analyze your audience and write with their interests in mind:

- ❏ Who are your primary readers?

- ❏ Who else might read your writing or listen to your presentation?

- ❏ What will the members of your audience already know about your topic?

- ❏ What will you need to define or explain?

- ❏ Will your audience be predisposed to agree or disagree with your point of view?

- ❏ What kinds of evidence will be most convincing for this audience?

KNOW THE RESEARCH QUESTIONS TO ASK IN THE HEALTH SCIENCES

As a student and as a professional, you will find that your research questions will often spring directly from your work in the field, clinic, or laboratory. As a student, you may be assigned research questions or the conditions for your research. In other cases, you may need to decide what research you want to pursue.

Research topics might include studies of patient populations or potential populations, patient responses to health problems and complications, theoretical issues, and the testing of assessments and interventions. The research question you decide on will form the basis for your

Did you know?

In selecting an appropriate topic for research, ask yourself the following questions:
- How important is your question to the field?
- What is your rationale for pursuing this study?
- What population will you study, and why?
- Which variables will you take into account?

project design and your final written product. Your research question is also your working hypothesis—the idea that you will test through research, clinical practice, or observation, and consequently describe in your writing (see Table 9.1 for example).

TABLE 9.1

Research Questions	
What you want to know more about:	**Your research question:**
I've noticed that many of my patients who are overweight into middle age tend to have diabetes, but they usually prefer medication to lifestyle changes.	Which lifestyle interventions succeed at preventing or reversing the course of type 2 diabetes in older populations?

KNOW THE KINDS OF EVIDENCE USED IN HEALTH SCIENCE ARGUMENTS

Scientists in the health profession use quantitative and qualitative data to generate research questions and support their arguments. These types of data often come directly from the field, either in clinical practice or in observing a target population. Quantitative data are often numerical and include statistics, charts, graphs, and other mathematical and scientific formulae. Accurate integration of numerical data will support your methods and help prove your results.

Did you know?

The Health Insurance Portability and Accountability Act (HIPPA) and the Patient Bill of Rights are important to consider, as they both protect patient rights and impact if and how health professionals write about patients and other aspects of their profession or future profession.

Qualitative data are non-numerical. For this reason, some believe these data are not as accurate since they rely on observation and description. However, qualitative data are important in many types of writing and research in the health sciences, particularly those projects focused directly on patient care and outcomes. With any sort of evidence, you must ask yourself whether or not it helps test or prove your hypothesis. What types of evidence are needed? To be effective, look for both types of evidence—both qualitative and quantitative—that will support and prove your research hypothesis.

KNOW THE WRITING AND STYLE CONVENTIONS IN THE HEALTH SCIENCES

I once heard a medical student claim that "writing has nothing to do with science." Of course, this is not true. No one would advance the profession if the results of research were not written and published. Ultimately, effective medical writing requires the same principles of logic, organization, clarity and precision that any science requires. Professionals of any kind must understand the importance of written communication and how it affects their status in the profession.

—Karl Terryberry

When writing in the health sciences, as in any other science, be precise and detailed. This is especially vital when you are writing direct-to-practice health care documents, such as charts and histories. Do not just state actions taken or other information vaguely, such as "changed I.V. fluid"; rather, record all relevant data that may be necessary to continue to evaluate and treat the patient, in this case which fluid was changed, the amount given, the time of the change, and why/on whose order the I.V. was changed. This preciseness also ensures readers that you are in compliance with care directives.

As with all science writing, objectivity is important. In your writing, remember to accurately and without bias observe your patient and precisely document your findings, keeping your own emotions from affecting your interpretation. Good writing in the health sciences demands an awareness of your audience, effective research, and careful choice of a format. In some cases, such as a public health message, appealing more directly to an audience's emotions may prove useful in getting your message across more effectively.

Good writing in any field follows the general basics of successful communication: it should be well organized, easy to read, logical, and grammatically and mechanically correct, and it should follow the conventions of the chosen documentation style. There are also some specific conventions that you may want to keep in mind as you write in the health sciences:

❏ Audience is very important to consider when communicating in the health sciences. If you are writing for more formal audiences of colleagues, professors, or in official capacities, you should use the scientific terms and principles of the field. However, when writing for a more general audience, such as in patient literature or digital sources of information, you should thoroughly explain these scientific terms and principles.

» Follow the disciplinary rules per context and audience when using names and formulae, such as those for genes, medications, proteins, and procedures.

» While it is common to use discipline-specific abbreviations, your writing may be read by an audience of practitioners from another discipline or a more general audience. You should still write out an entire word or phrase the first time that you use it, follow it with the abbreviation in parentheses, and then use this same abbreviation consistently throughout the paper, chart, or project.

❏ Generally, you should use a more formal and objective writing style, avoiding slang and contractions. However, in other types of writing, particularly as part of public health outreach, a more conversational style may be appropriate in order to reach target audiences.

 Avoid the other extreme of using overblown or pompous language that will make your writing harder to read and may alienate your reader.

❏ Use visuals strategically to illustrate points and present data. This includes the use of images, models, concept maps, photographs, tables, graphs, and charts.

 Tables and figures should be numbered consecutively in separate series (i.e., Table 9.1, Table 9.2; Figure 9.1, Figure 9.2). Tables should have titles and figures should have legends or keys. Both should be understandable apart from the text. Other images may have captions to help readers make the connection between the image and the text.

❑ Spell out numbers at the beginning of sentences or rephrase to move the number. Spell out the numbers 1–10 unless they are part of a series that is using Arabic numerals. (There is sometimes an exception to this if the number is part of a commonly accepted name for a disease or disorder, e.g., type 2 diabetes. Always consult the style guide or your instructor in these instances). Use the symbol ~ to mean "approximately equal to."

Example:
"The prevalence of hypertension in type 2 diabetes is higher than that in the general population, especially in younger patients. At the age of 45 around 40% of patients with type 2 diabetes are hypertensive, the proportion increasing to 60% by the age of 75."

Turner, R., Holman, R., et al. (1998) Tight blood pressure control and risk of macrovascular and microvascular complications in type 2 diabetes: UKPDS 38. *British Medical Journal*, pp. 703–713.

❑ Pay attention to verb tense and be consistent. Studies already completed should be presented in past tense; studies being proposed (e.g., in a grant proposal) should be in future tense; conditions that presently exist should be discussed in the present tense.

The sciences do not use the literary present tense that you may have been taught in a literature class. The literary present tense is reserved for fiction.

❑ Rarely use direct quotes from source materials; rely instead on summaries and paraphrases.

❑ In most health science writing, be as objective as possible, avoiding emotional words and phrasing that will bias or unduly influence the reader. This includes avoiding sexist language and gendered tropes in your writing. However, when writing materials to convince the public or another target audience to make lifestyle changes or adopt another health measure, it may be helpful for you to appeal to the *pathos*, or emotions, of your intended audience.

For example: You might encourage pregnant women to seek adequate prenatal care by presenting statistics of infant mortality rates, accompanied by pictures of healthy babies.

KNOW THE SPECIALIZED RESEARCH CONVENTIONS IN THE HEALTH SCIENCES

Research in the health sciences is generally empirical and often directly addresses outcomes of patient health, including not just the physical side of health, but the psychological and social aspects of health as well. Many research questions will focus on studying a specific variable or theory, which can then be applied in a practical setting. In outcomes-focused research, the patient is the first source: Is the patient satisfied with the results of a treatment or intervention? Has the patient's functionality or quality of life improved? When included as a part of evidence-based medicine, clinical research focuses directly on the treatments or interventions used by a health care provider for a particular patient or population.

Did you know?

The acronym PICO stands for the factors that a clinical research question should address in evidence-based medicine:
P : Patients/population
I : Intervention
C: Comparison/control
O: Outcome

You may be asked to conduct and write up several types of clinical research. Basic research calls for laboratory or field data to be used to influence theory. Applied research uses data to solve issues in practice. Translational research asks you to examine both how research influences practice and, in turn, how issues encountered in practice can lead to important research questions. These types of clinical research projects can also be categorized as experimental and observational, depending on the assignment and context.

KNOW THE APPROPRIATE DOCUMENTATION STYLE IN THE HEALTH SCIENCES

There are several documentation styles commonly used in the health sciences. APA, the documentation style of the American Psychological Association, is often used in writing specific to nursing, such as nursing case studies. CSE, the documentation style recommended by the Council of Science Editors, is also used by many in the medical fields. Occasionally, a journal will call for medical writing to be documented according to CMS, or the *Chicago Manual of Style* (see Chapter 12). However, many types of health writing and professional organizations also have their own documentation guides, such as that of the American Medical Association. CSE offers three different documentation options: the name-year option (also known as the "Harvard system"), which is similar to APA style (see Chapter 12), and two number formats—the citation-sequence option (also known as the "Vancouver system") and the citation-name option. You should use the style required by your instructor or the journal to which you are submitting your writing.

Note: in APA format, a title page should be included

SAMPLE STUDENT RESEARCH PAPER

PHYSICIAN-ASSISTED SUICIDE   1

Sean Hughes

Legalization of Physician-Assisted Suicide

Physician-assisted suicide (PAS) involves a physician writing a prescription for a lethal dose of medication at the request of a terminally ill patient. The debate over PAS is characterized by coancerns over its morality and the associated violation of medical ethics. The real debate, however, is centered on the questions of who should decide when and how death occurs and how society should react to requests for PAS. Because PAS involves a patient dying, some argue that physician involvement should be treated as a homicide and/or as a direct disregard for the sanctity of life. Others say that the physicians are simply acting in the best interest of the patient and respecting the sanctity of life by ensuring its quality. The ultimate question is whether or not PAS should be legalized, and it is this question that fuels the debate. In his article, "Opposing physician-assisted suicide: Good strategies and bad," Daniel Callahan (1999) argues that the answer is no. He discusses the common arguments against PAS before identifying what he believes to be the best argument supporting his position. This paper will argue in favor of PAS, examine his arguments opposed to legalization, and provide the counter-argument in support of legalization.

PAS should be legalized first and foremost because people should have the right to autonomy. Not being able to make rational decisions for ourselves robs us of our humanity, which is much more immoral than showing compassion to those who are suffering. Oregon is currently the only U.S. state where PAS is allowed by law. According to the annual report on the Oregon Death with Dignity Act (ODWDA), 96.6% of patients in 2009 expressed desire for autonomy/self-determination as their primary reason for requesting PAS (Dept. of Human Services [DHS], 2009). Terminal illnesses can wreak havoc on the body, resulting in a loss of control over many bodily functions. As this is the case, it's quite understandable that once in this situation, patients no longer have a desire to prolong life. As Margaret Battin put it, "The wise man . . . will always think of life in terms of quality, not quantity . . . whereas a prolonged life is not necessarily better, a prolonged death is necessarily worse" (as cited in Smith, 2007).

Opponents of PAS speak of respecting the intrinsic value of human life, yet the result of their opposition is people being forced to suffer unnecessarily. They don't simply ignore this suffering but rather suggest palliative care as an alternative. However, opponents of PAS can't ignore the cases where palliative care isn't enough. In Oregon, 91.5% of patients were enrolled in hospice care (the hallmark of palliative care) at the time of their request (ODHS, 2009). A much more effective way to protect the value of human life is to defend what makes us human—rationality—and allow terminally ill patients to use it to choose PAS and for physicians to respect those wishes without fear of legal prosecution.

Callahan begins by discussing Oregon's Death with Dignity Act. As no other state has followed suit in legalizing PAS, Callahan takes this as evidence that the nation as a whole disapproves of PAS. Emanuel (2002) reports that American public support ranges from about 30% to 65%, depending on how questions are phrased. He refers to the results as the Rule of Thirds: One-third of Americans always support PAS, one-third always opposes, and one-third are volatile.

Callahan next relays the most popular arguments against PAS, namely, that legalization will lead to abuse and victimization of the poor and weak (by pressuring them to request PAS before they're ready), and legalization is simply society forsaking patients' dignity by setting aside their legitimate needs (e.g., pain control). However, Callahan does not think these are strong arguments on the part of the opposition. First, he predicts that middle/upper class patients are the most at risk because they care most about maintaining dignity and control. This has indeed been confirmed in Oregon, where 98.3% of PAS patients in 2009 were white, 98.7% had health insurance, and most were well-educated (DHS, 2009). This is not, however, evidence of abuse of that group. Rather, this should be taken as evidence of success, as the group who might seem to care most about maintaining control and claiming their right to autonomy are the patients who are taking advantage of the option for PAS. To the second point, Callahan responds that the Oregon law, rather than causing society to forsake patients' dignity, is actually allowing patients to forsake their own dignity. In the eyes and minds of these patients, however, disease is forsaking their dignity and death redeems it.

Next, Callahan discusses the Oregon law itself, writing, "the Oregon law is a badly written law . . . open to serious abuse" (Callahan, 1999). First of all, interpretation of the law is the job of judges. In *Gonzales v. Oregon* (2006), the Supreme Court upheld the ODWDA. Second, an entire section of the law is devoted to safeguards, written in specifically to prevent abuse. These include the following requirements: three separate requests from the patient; confirmation that the patient is terminally ill and will die in six months, that the patient is making a rational and informed decision (by two unrelated witnesses who are not beneficiaries of the patient's estate or life insurance), and that their decision is not being unduly influenced by depression; and a waiting period of 15 days between the request and receipt of the prescription to allow them time to change their mind. Further, the law explicitly states that failure to comply with any of the safeguards will constitute a Class A felony (ODWDA § 3, 1997). The law is clearly written and ensures the right to autonomy, while protecting patients from abuse as well as physicians who choose to help from fear of the law.

Perhaps realizing this, Callahan states that arguments relying on the existence of abuse (called slippery slope arguments—event A will lead to consequence B) are a "bad gamble." Margaret Battin (2000) agrees and expresses frustration that the slippery slope is the central argument of opponents of legalization because of its inherent weaknesses (one-sided, given undue weight, only sound when data supports). The data reported in Oregon over the last 10 years do not support the argument in this situation, which Callahan was afraid would happen.

Callahan (1999) advised his readers to stick with the strongest argument opposing PAS, that the practice is intrinsically wrong because it constitutes social legitimization of suicide as an escape from suffering and perverts long-standing medical traditions. The first part only matters when taken in slippery slope form (legalization will lead to an increase in suicide because people perceive it to be the socially accepted solution). Stevens (2006) reported that many Oregon physicians speak of feelings of isolation and that they are afraid to talk about their involvement, fearing ostracism and disapproval from others. This hardly suggests that society is legitimizing PAS, despite it being legal in Oregon, and it certainly does not suggest social legitimization of suicide (without the help of a doctor). Further, the suicide rate among Oregonians aged 10–24 decreased from 1997 to 2005 from 10 per 100,000 to 9 (DHS, 2006). Ganzini and Dahl (2008) describe the reaction of family members to patients' decisions, stating that even the most avid opponents try their best to support the patient because they choose to respect their autonomy. Thus, it's more accurate to say that society is legitimizing autonomy, not suicide. Additionally, 85% of Oregon psychologists approve of PAS (Ganzini & Dahl, 2008). Since they treat clinical depression, it is unlikely they would approve of PAS if they noticed a significant increase in attempted or completed suicides among their patients.

Callahan's (1999) second reason for arguing the intrinsic evils of PAS is that it perverts long-standing medical traditions. Based on the Hippocratic Oath, doctors are supposed to be healers, not killers. However, the Hippocratic Oath has changed significantly over time. For example, the Oath used to outlaw surgery. Smith (2007) argues that the "First, do no harm" clause is virtually impossible because doctors would be prohibited from most of their job. Essentially, its end justifies the means. That is, painful, invasive surgery is acceptable because it's helpful and life-saving in the long run. PAS should be viewed similarly, as death is the ultimate end of pain and suffering.

Callahan (1999) mentions the psychological burden placed on doctors because PAS involves violation of this oath. Many doctors in Oregon believe assisting patients in dying is the right thing to do, which overrides any feelings of discomfort (Ganzini & Dahl, 2008). Some feel PAS has made them better doctors as it forces them to have important discussions with patients, causing them to rethink their own values (Stevens, 2006). Additionally, it drives them to come up with alternative treatments and seek education/ training on palliative care methods (Ganzini & Dahl, 2008). Third, it causes them to question their treatments and why they failed (Smith, 2007). Overall, legalization of PAS has changed medicine in a positive way, driving the advancement of better end-of-life care and treatments in general. Physicians seem to realize this; many report that despite the emotional drain, the experience had an overall positive effect on them as doctors (Ganzini & Dahl, 2008).

Callahan (1999) ends by contending that the debate should continue on moral/ ethical grounds because there is no legal remedy. This is his most disconcerting argument, especially considering the debate is over legalization. The Supreme Court decided there was no federal remedy, ruling unanimously that the constitution neither allows nor prohibits PAS (*Washington v. Glucksberg*, 1997). This only means it's the job of the states, a job that is far from impossible. It is much more unlikely this debate will be resolved morally, as Emanuel's Rule of Thirds holds even in terminally ill patients and their caregivers, whose support of PAS matches the national average (Emanuel, 2002). This suggests that two-thirds of Americans are set in their moral beliefs concerning PAS.

Beyond that, Callahan's argument is designed to recruit for the "against" side so they can win the fight against the "for" side. He claims the "PAS is intrinsically wrong" argument is best because it's the one argument opponents of *legalization* can't be swayed from. This approach can only lead to a place where discussion is frozen and compromise is impossible. Margaret Battin (2000) expresses frustration at the "for-and-against" nature of the PAS debate. She argues this structure is okay only when a debate is in infancy (Battin, 2000). The PAS debate needs to be refocused on finding compromise rather than being hung up on irresolvable moral issues. While I strongly believe in the legalization of PAS, and respect that Callahan strongly believes the opposite, resolution and compromise are better than the war he is advocating.

References

Battin, M. (2000). On the structure of the euthanasia debate: Observations provoked by a near-perfect for-and-against book. *Journal of Health Politics, Policy, and Law*, 25, 415–430.

Callahan, D. (1999). Opposing physician-assisted suicide: Good strategies and bad. *Commonwealth*, 126, 7–9.

Department of Human Services. (2006). *Oregon Youth Suicide Facts*. Center for Health Statistics, Portland, Oregon.

Department of Human Services. (2009). *Eleventh Annual Report on Oregon's Death with Dignity Act*. Office of Disease Prevention and Epidemiology, Portland, Oregon.

Emanuel, E. (2002). Euthanasia and physician-assisted suicide. *Archives of Internal Medicine*, 162, 142–153.

Ganzini, L. & Dahl, E. (2008). Physician-assisted suicide in Oregon. In D. Birnbacher & E. Dahl (Eds.), *Giving death a helping hand.* (pp. 67–75). Champaign, IL: Springer Science+Business Media.

Gonzales v. Oregon, 546 U.S. 243 (2006).

Oregon Death with Dignity Act of 1997. Or. Rev. Stat. 127.800–97 § 3 (1997). Retrieved from http://www.oregon.gov/DHS/ph/pas/ors.shtml.

Smith, S. (2007). Some realism about end of life: The current prohibition and the euthanasia underground. *American Journal of Law and Medicine*, 33, 1–26.

Stevens, K. (2006). Emotional and psychological effects of physician-assisted suicide and euthanasia on participating physicians. *Issues in Law and Medicine*, 21, 187–200.

Washington v. Glucksberg, 521 U.S. 702 (1997).

Note: in APA format, a title page should be included

SAMPLE STUDENT REVIEW PAPER

David Carr

NSC 495 Section 2

The Challenges and Application of Induced Pluripotent Stem Cells

Introduction

Stem cells are found in all multicellular organisms and are defined by their ability to differentiate into multiple cell types and self-renew (divide and form two identitcal undifferentiated stem cells thereby maintaining the stem cell pool) (Reya et al., 2001). Stem cells can be characterized based on the number of different tissue types that they can form. This is called cellular potency. As organisms develop, their cells gradually lose potency and become differentiated. The fertilized egg and zygote have the potential to form an entire organism and are called "totipotent." Embryonic stem cells (ESCs), which are found in the inner cell mass of the blastocyst, can form all of the cells found in the three germ layers (i.e., ectoderm, mesoderm, and endoderm) and are referred to as "pluripotent." Stem cells found in adult tissues (i.e., hematopoietic stem cells) can give rise to only a limited number of cells and are called "multipotent" (Stadtfeld and Hochedlinger, 2010).

Induced pluripotent stem cells (iPSCs) are produced by "cellular reprogramming" of fully differentiated somatic cells back to a pluripotent state. iPSCs are an appealing research tool because they can form any cell in the body (just like ESCs) but do not raise the same ethical issues as ESCs. Further, because they are derived from adult tissues it is possible to obtain cells for therapy directly from the patient in question, eliminating the need for immunosuppression and the possibility of tissue rejection (Nishikawa, et al., 2008). iPSCs have the potential to be an invaluable tool for medical research and patient specific cell therapy. There remain many challenges in the path towards use of iPSC technology for medical treatment and other scientific applications. However, the potential benefits of iPSCs make any challenges well worth overcoming.

Generation of iPSCs

iPSCs were first generated from mouse fibroblasts (Takahashi and Yamanaka, 2006). This technology was then used to generate iPSCs from human fibroblasts (Takahashi et al., 2007). The researchers selected 24 genes associated with the maintenance of pluripotency in ESCs and, using retroviral gene transduction, introduced these genetic factors into a culture of mouse fibroblast cells. After several weeks of culturing, colonies of cells resembling ESCs in their morphology, expression of cell markers, gene expression, promoter methylation, differentiation potential, and ability to form teratomas were observed. By selectively withholding certain factors in subsequent experiments, it was determined that only four of the original 24 factors were critical for induced pluripotency (Oct3/4, Sox2, Klf4, c-Myc) (Takahashi and Yamanka, 2006). Using these four reprogramming factors, the same research group was able to generate iPSCs from human fibroblasts with similar results. PCR of the genomic DNA showed that the iPSCs displayed integration of the four retroviral vectors (Takahashi et al., 2007).

Challenges of iPSCs

These initial experiments demonstrated the ability to reprogram differentiated adult cells back to a pluripotent state. Since these studies, other researchers have been able to replicate these same results. The techniques described above represent the standard techniques currently used for iPSC generation. These techniques are not yet applicable to widespread medical research, or to human stem cell therapy. Several problems with the methods need to be solved.

Current methods of iPSC induction involve retroviral integration of the required gene factors. This current strategy poses two problems. First, the necessary reprogramming factors have oncogenetic potential (Seifinejad, et al., 2010). Any cell forced to express higher levels of these genes may have an increased risk of tumor formation. Chimeric mice, grown from the injection of iPSCs into blastocysts, showed a high rate of tumor formation. Of the 17 chimeric mice, 16 had tumors, and three of them had multiple tumors. Examination of the tumor cells showed high levels of retroviral c-Myc expression, while normal cells showed lower levels (Okita et al., 2007).

Second, viral integration is believed to occur randomly in the genome. This could lead to the inactivation of an important gene, the activation of the nearby oncogene, or inactivation of a tumor suppressor (Seifinejad, et al., 2010). Taken together, it is clear that viral integration is not an appropriate method for the induction of iPSCs for therapy.

Fortunately, studies reveal that retrovirally-transduced genes are commonly silenced during iPSC induction (Okita et al., 2007). This indicates that viral integration is not essential for the generation of iPSCs, and that the necessary changes in gene transcription are induced by transient expression of the four reprogramming factors before the silencing occurs. With this in mind, several researchers have attempted to generate iPSCs using other delivery methods for the genes. iPSCs have been generated with the use of non-integrating adenoviral vectors and endonuclease mediated excision of integrated transgenes (Seifinejad, et al., 2010).

Recently, it was shown that iPSCs can be induced without the use of any genetic factors. Rather than using transcription of the delivered genes to increase protein expression, Zhou et al. (2009) delivered the protein products of the four gene factors directly into the cell. Previous studies had shown that certain short peptide sequences could be taken up by the cell. The proteins Oct4, Sox2, Klf4, and c-Myc were conjugated to a cell penetrating protein. Transient addition of these conjugates to the growth media led to generation of iPSCs. This significant advance provides an additional benefit because it does not involve the use of any genetic material, which eliminates the risk of unintentionally altering the target cell genome during iPSC induction (Zhou et al., 2009).

Other studies have produced iPSCs using other chemical compounds (mostly inhibitors of DNA modification proteins) and microRNAs, which are important regulators of gene expression during development. However, most of these alternative methods result in very low reprogramming efficiency and the inhibition of enzymes modifying DNA and chromatin could introduce other undesirable genetic changes (Stadtfeld, and Hochedlinger, 2010). The multitude of different approaches that have produced iPSCs, using both genetic and non-genetic approaches, offers the possibility of combining various methods to create the most effective approach to introduce each reprogramming factor into the cell. Further, analysis of the resultant iPSCs for signs of oncogene expression or other genetic abnormalities could help to improve safety.

In addition to tumor formation caused by viral integration of the oncogentic transgenes, undifferentiated pluripotent cells themselves also form tumors. When pluripotent cells are introduced into a host they form a particularly aggressive tumor called a teratoma. iPSCs must be partially differentiated before being introduced into the organism (Seifinejad, et al., 2010). Therefore any applicable stem cell therapy will require a method to identify and eliminate undifferentiated cells from the culture.

Therapeutic Possibilities

iPSCs are an important advance in the field of stem cell research. They offer many of the same potential benefits of ESCs (due to the fact that both cell types are pluripotent) without the political and ethical issues. The most widely publicized therapeutic application of iPSCs is cell therapy. iPSCs are especially promising in this regard in that they can be derived from the patient's own tissue, thereby eliminating the possibility of immune rejection (Nishikawa, et al., 2008).

The most straightforward type of cell therapy involves the replacement of damaged cells. Differentiated cells (i.e., skin cells) would be taken from the patient and treated to become iPSCs at which point they can be re-differentiated into the necessary cell type. This type of therapy could be used to treat muscle damage, replace cardiac muscle or neurons after a heart attack or stroke, or, specifically, for the treatment of the diseases type 1 diabetes mellitus, Parkinson's disease, and amyotrophic lateral sclerosis (Seifinejad, et al., 2010).

In an important proof of concept iPSCs were differentiated into neuronal precursors and injected into the brains of embryonic mice. Histological examination after birth showed extensive migration of the iPSCs and differentiation into multiple cell types. Electrical recordings showed that the iPSC-derived neurons were synaptically integrated among other neurons and could propagate an action potential. This study further explored the potential applications of iPSCs by attempting to treat a rat model of Parkinson's disease (Wernig, et al., 2008). Parkinson's disease is caused by the death of dopamine-releasing neurons in the substantia nigra, causing insufficient dopaminergic input to the striatum (Sultzer, 2007). iPSCs were differentiated in culture to form domaminergic neurons. These cells were grafted into the striatum of rats with chemically induced Parkinson's disease. A behavior test was performed pre-graft and four weeks post-graft to measure any changes in behavior. In this test, rats were injected with amphetamines in one side of their brain. This is known to cause ipsilateral movement bias in rats with model Parkinson's disease, but does not affect movement in healthy rats. One group of rats with model Parkinson's disease received a iPSC-derived dopaminergic neuron graft and another group did not. Rats receiving the graft showed marked improvement in their movement bias compared with the rats not receiving a graft. Further, rats receiving the graft displayed high density of dopaminergic neurons in the substantia nigra (Wernig, et al., 2008).

This study shows the promise and (relative) simplicity of using stem cells to treat diseases or conditions caused by cell loss. The integration of the neurons was surprisingly efficient and very promising, but whether this same type of integration occurs in other tissues is largely unknown. The researchers also noted signs of teratoma formation in the brains of grafted rats, indicating contamination of undifferentiated iPSCs. After the introduction of a sorting system, the number of contaminating cells was reduced, and there were no signs of teratoma formation eight weeks following a graft (Wernig, et al., 2008). No doubt more research is needed to explore the most effective way to reduce or eliminate contamination with undifferentiated cells.

A second type of cell therapy involves the genetic modification of iPSCs before transplantation. This type of therapy could be used to treat or correct conditions caused by simple, known genetic polymorphisms or mutations (i.e., sickle cell anemia, Huntington's disease). This strategy involves using differentiated cells from the patient to produce iPSCs which can be treated to correct the genetic abnormality, differentiated, and then introduced into the patient.

Using this strategy, Hanna et al. (2007) were able to treat genetically modified mice who were given the human genes for sickle cell anemia. These mice showed similar symptoms and pathology to humans with sickle cell anemia, including elongated RBCs, decreased urine production (due to reduction of renal medullary blood flow as a result of RBC sickling in the renal tubules), and decreased RBC count. Researchers generated iPSCs from tail fibroblast cells taken from the diseased mice. The normal hemoglobin gene was introduced into the iPSCs by homologous recombination, and then the cells were differentiated in vitro to form hematopoietic stem cells (HSCs). These HSCs were introduced into the mice and various measurements were taken before and after treatment and compared to a control group receiving no cell therapy. The results showed that all of the normal pathological symptoms seen in sickle cell anemia were improved in mice receiving treatment. Mice receiving the iPSC-derived HSCs showed improved symptoms for the duration of the study (three months post-treatment). Importantly, no mice displayed any evidence of tumor formation, however, the possibility of tumor formation; after the study ended cannot be ruled out (Hanna, et al., 2007). This study displays another example of iPSC-derived cell differentiation in vivo and the maintenance of a HSC pool for an extended period of time, indicating physiological functioning of the iPSC derived cells.

A second application of iPSCs, distinct from cell therapy, involves the concept of disease modeling. This approach involves identifying a patient with a disease to be studied (such as type 1 diabetes mellitus or Parkinson's disease, which involve specific known cell types, and a possible genetic origin), inducing differentiated adult cell samples to become iPSCs, and then differentiating the iPSCs into the cell type of interest for that particular disease. This would allow researchers to study any differences between these types of cells in those afflicted with the disease compared to other individuals. It could also allow researchers to watch the progression of the disease in a controlled environment in the laboratory (Nishikawa, et al. 2008).

Recently, a study has shown, for the first time, the ability of iPSCs to model the pathology of a disease. Motor neurons were generated from iPSC cells derived from fibroblasts taken from a human patient with spinal muscular atrophy (SMA). SMA is caused by a mutation in the SMN1 gene and results in decreased levels of SMN protein and the resulting degeneration of motor neurons. iPSC cells were differentiated into motor neurons and compared to the differentiation pattern of a control patient. Results showed that the iPSC cells derived from the SMA patient could initially produce motor neurons at a comparable level to the control; however, after a time the number of motor neurons in the control exceeded that in the SMA patient, a pattern similar to that seen during disease progression (Elbert, et al., 2009). The ability of iPSCs to model a disease in culture could provide a powerful tool for scientists attempting to study many types of diseases. It could allow for the observation of the progression of disease in specific cell types, without interference of the many other cells found in vivo, and could allow for the determination of the role that each cell plays in creating a disease phenotype.

Conclusion

iPSCs are produced by genetic reprogramming of somatic cells back to a pluripotent state. Due to their potential to differentiate into any cell in the body and the possibility of creating patient-specific treatments, iPSCs have become a cutting edge area of stem cell research. A number of challenges in the current method of producing iPSCs will have to be overcome before they can be applied to human therapies. However, the incredible therapeutic and scientific potential of iPSCs make this a worthwhile problem to face. iPSCs have been implicated for use in direct cell replacement therapy, genetically modified cell replacement therapy, and disease modeling, with each area showing promising results in early proof-of-concept experiments. Future research in this area should be aimed at developing a standard procedure to generate iPSCs to improve the safety and reduce the cost of their production, in an attempt to make iPSC therapy a realistic treatment for many diseases.

References

Elbert A., Yu J., Rose F. Induced pluripotent stem cells from a spinal muscular atrophy patient. *Nature*. 2009: 457: 277–281

Hanna J., Wernig M., Markoulaki S., et al. Treatment of sickle cell anemia mouse model with iPSC cells generated from autologous skin. *Science*. 2007: 318: 1920–1923

Nishikawa S., Goldstein R., Nierras C. The promise of human induced pluripotent stem cells for research and therapy. *Nature Reviews*. 2008: 9: 725–729

Okita K., Ichisaka T., Yamanaka S. Generation of germline-competent induced pluripotent stem cells. *Nature*. 2007: 448: 313–318.

Reya T., Morrison S., Clarke M., et al. Stem cells, cancer, and cancer stem cells. *Nature*. 2001: 414: 105–111.

Seifinejad A., Tabebordbar M., Baharvand H., et al. Progress and promise towards safe induced pluripotent stem cells for therapy. *Stem Cell Reviews and Reports*. 2010: 6: 297–306.

Stadtfeld M., Hochedlinger K. Induced pluripotency: history, mechanisms, and applications. *Genes & Development*. 2010: 24: 2239–2263.

Sulzer D. Multiple hit hypothesis for dopamine neuron loss in Parkinson's disease. *Trends in Neuroscience*. 2007: 30: 244–250.

Wernig M., Zhao J., Pruszak J. Neurons derived from reprogrammed fibroblasts functionally integrate into the fetal brain and improve symptoms of rats with Parkinson's disease. 2008: 105: 5856–5861.

Yao S., Sukonnik T., Kean T., et al. Retroviral silencing, variegation, extinction and memory are controlled by a dynamic interplay of multiple epigenetic modifications. *Molecular Therapy*. 2004: 10: 27–36.

Zhou H., Wu S., Joo J.Y., et al. Generation of induced pluripotent stem cells using recombinant proteins. *Cell Stem Cell*. 2009: 4: 381–384.

ACTIVITIES

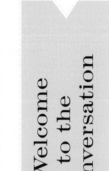

Welcome to the Conversation

Discuss these questions with your classmates in class or via a class wiki or shared blog.

1. Who are some of the nonprofessional audiences intended for health sciences writing? How should your rhetorical choices change for these different audiences?

2. Contrary to what you may have expected, research and writing in health doesn't just include quantitative data. What types of qualitative data might you include in certain writing activities?

3. Your career in the health sciences will often require you to communicate with the public on various levels about different health issues. How would your communication differ in the following contexts?
    - Creating a website that informs Americans about liver disease.
    - Filming and narrating a YouTube video that teaches other professionals (or any YouTube audience) about a technique, such as drawing blood, cleaning an abrasion, or how to perform CPR.
    - Writing a radio PSA encouraging listeners to get screened for HIV.

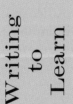

Writing to Learn

1. **Discussion blog**: Either in your individual blog or a class blog, write a post that summarizes a discussion from class. Then, in your post, evaluate the discussion, and pose at least two follow-up discussion questions.

2. **Outline**: After your class has reviewed a particular case, list your response to the case in a linear, organized outline. What are the essentials of the case? What treatments or interventions were used? Were these the correct ones to use? Would you have handled the case differently? Why? How?

3. **Progress report**: As you work on your longer research project, you may be asked at intervals to report your progress. Describe briefly where you are in your project and what your next steps will be. Be concise, but also be very specific with details that are essential to evaluating your process.

1. **Grant proposal**: In your coursework, you have encountered many unresolved problems, diseases, and other health issues that require research or action to solve or treat. Write a proposal that explains the problem, hypothesize a possible solution, and request funding to experiment or gather data to find an answer. Follow the guidelines in this chapter and per your instructor to format this document. You may need to analyze your target funding agency in order to create the most convincing proposal.

2. **Popular article**: You have been asked to write an article for *CNN.com* about an important health issue facing American women. You should inform your audience about this issue from your professional perspective, but the information you present must be understandable to the typical reader for this website.

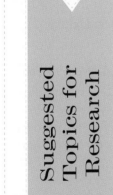

1. In your practicum or course work, you have encountered cases that interested you, either in how they were assessed or how they were handled. Research some case studies that are similar to a case you have seen. What does this literature review tell you and your colleagues about the preferred treatment for this particular set of symptoms, disease process, or complication?

2. What is the most pressing health problem in the world today? Research the secondary literature to decide, and then design a qualitative or quantitative research project that will collect primary evidence to prove your assertion. What do others in your field think? Colleagues in the health professions? Where are the highest mortality rates? What are the causes of this health problem and how might they be eliminated or changed?

READ MORE ABOUT IT

Clark, Irene L., and Ronald Fischbach. "Writing and Learning in the Health Sciences: Rhetoric, Identity, Genre and Performance." *The WAC Journal* 19 (2008): 15–28. Print.

Heifferon, Barbara A. *Writing in the Health Professions*. White Plains, NY: Pearson Longman, 2005. Print.

"How to Write Easy-to-Read Health Materials." *Medline Plus*. U.S. National Library of Medicine. 13 Feb. 2013. Web. 20 Feb. 2013. Web.

Oermann, Marilyn H., and Judith C. Hays. *Writing for Publication in Nursing*. New York: Springer Publishing, 2010. Print.

"Medical Writing." The Purdue Online Writing Lab. Purdue U. 25 Jun. 2012. Web. 15 Feb. 2013.

Melnick, Arnold. *Medical Writing 101: A Primer for Health Professionals*. Bloomington, IN: Authorhouse, 2006. Print.

Portney, Leslie G., and Mary P. Watkins. *Foundations of Clinical Research: Applications to Practice*. 3rd ed. Upper Saddle River, NJ: Pearson Prentice Hall, 2009. Print.

Straus, Sharon E., Scott Richardson, Paul Glasziou, R. Brian Haynes. *Evidence-based Medicine: How to Practice and Teach It*. 4th ed. Edinburgh: Churchill Livingstone, 2005. Print.

Terryberry, Karl. *Writing for the Health Professions*. Clifton, New York: Delmar Cengage Learning, 2005. Print.

"Writing in Nursing." *The Purdue Online Writing Lab*. Purdue U. n.d. Web. 15 Feb. 2013.

chapter 10

Writing in the Sciences

Biology, Chemistry, Geology, Earth Science, Meteorology, and Physics

Had there been a newspaper in the early days of humankind, the discovery of fire would have received front-page coverage. If television had existed, news anchors would have attempted to articulate what the discovery really meant to the common cave dweller. And CNN would have gone on and on for days about the latest breaking developments, mostly consisting of reports of charred meat and singed fingers. But at that time, of course, there was no need for newspapers, Fred Flintstone notwithstanding. Society was small, and almost everyone would have had some exposure to the science of fire-making.

Today, however, society is large and scientific experiments across the world are carried out by people who are usually hidden from public view. So much of what scientists do affects our daily lives, yet most people remain largely unaware of how scientists use their (mostly public) funding, and how their work affects them. Good science writing helps us understand what scientists around the world are up to.

—Anton Holland
Eureka! The Importance of Good Science Writing

PURPOSES OF WRITING IN THE SCIENCES

As with any discipline, the primary aim of writing in the sciences is to communicate: to explain concepts, explore theoretical principles and approaches, report and interpret the results of research and experimentation, argue for various hypotheses, and share information. Science has a profound influence on our lives. It helps us with everyday decision making such as how to dress for the weather or what food choices to make to remain healthy. It also helps with policy making, city planning, and curriculum choices. However, this influence works both ways. Scientists are influenced by the dominant culture in which they participate: The beliefs and assumptions of this culture affect the questions scientists ask, the circumstances in which they operate, and the types of research that get funded. According to Thomas Kuhn, these guiding cultural assumptions form the paradigms of the field and are the basics of a science education. These paradigms specify rules and conventions, including the guidelines for writing in the field—and scientists do a lot of writing.

Written texts such as peer-reviewed journal articles are the most common way scientists share their work with each other. Magazine and newspaper articles, popular books, and textbooks are other methods for sharing findings with the general public. Scientists may also use websites, databases, blogs, and other formats to communicate. When writing in the sciences, whether you are writing for peers who are familiar with the scientific concepts or writing for a less-informed general audience, you must create clear and concise prose that is easy to understand and follow. Colleagues who desire to replicate or expand on your research do not want to waste time muddling through dense sentences. Likewise, general readers of scientific writing want to be informed, and possibly even entertained; unclear or confusing writing does not meet these goals.

TYPES OF WRITING ASSIGNMENTS IN THE SCIENCES

Writing is the most important means for communicating scientific work. Research and publication complement teaching and training, clinical service and patient care. There are many reasons for writing, one of the most important of which is the inherent training undertaken to better appreciate and evaluate the published work of others.

—W.C.G. Peh
"Scientific writing and publishing: Its importance to radiologists"

Writing in the sciences can take many different forms. As mentioned previously, considerations of audience, purpose, and context or situation may determine the form in which you choose to compose. Similarly, learning objectives, programmatic goals, or even accreditation requirements may affect the types of assignments you receive in class, just as various factors may influence what you are asked to create on the job. Below are some common types of writing assignments you may see, but keep in mind that this is not an exhaustive list and that you may be asked to create other types of documents or communication. Likewise, you may know of alternative forms that may be effective for your audience, purpose, and context. If so, you should discuss these alternative forms with your instructor.

Research Papers

Research papers report the findings of original research conducted in the lab or in the field. At the undergraduate level, this research may happen in a single lab experiment (see the lab report on **page 283**) or it may occur over a semester or two. The final paper for a course is often the research paper, which is designed to give you practice in communicating your findings with colleagues using one of the major genres of the field. The research paper assigned in a class is much like the research report prepared by a scientist for publication in a journal, whether the scientist is working in a university or a commercial lab.

The research paper generally follows a specific structure that is designed to follow the scientific method. This format includes six sections: (1) Abstract or Summary, (2) Introduction, (3) Materials and Methods, (4) Results, (5) Discussion, and (6) References (Literature or Works Cited).

1. **The Abstract is a brief overview of the entire research paper.** Usually about 250 words, it gives the main points of the study, including the study's objective/hypothesis, the methods, the results, and the conclusion. The Abstract is usually written last, even though it is the first thing most people read (and sometimes the only thing people read to stay current or to evaluate usefulness).

2. **The Introduction gives readers the context for your study:** the relevant existing literature, the need for the study and how it fits into what has already been done, and the importance, or "so what," of your particular research. The Introduction is the place where you draw your reader in. It is also the place where you define your credibility as a writer and researcher, showing that you have done your homework.

3. **The Materials and Methods section is also important for context and for establishing credibility.** Here you explain your exact methods for data collection: the experimental controls in place, variables studied, measurements taken, how the measurements were taken, and conditions of the study. The reader should be given enough information to replicate your study. When describing materials, give as much information as possible using generic names; use brand names only when necessary.

4. **The Results section should summarize your findings, drawing attention to trends or patterns in the data.** This section illustrates and/or explains the findings with details, statistics, charts, tables, graphs, and other images. Often the Results section follows the same logical order used in your Materials and Methods section so it will be easy for the reader to follow. You do not need to repeat in writing the full information illustrated through visuals, but you should call attention to these visuals by referencing them in the text. The Results section is not the place to interpret or draw conclusions about what the data implies.

5. **The Discussion section is where you interpret your results and present your argument about what the data show.** This is the place to draw conclusions and support them with the data from the research. Here you refer back to the significance of your research and your working hypothesis. What is the most reasonable explanation for your findings? What does this mean for the phenomenon being studied? What does it mean for the discipline? How does your study fit with other scientists' work? For example, are your findings consistent with other studies or do they show that something was missing in previous studies? Do your findings indicate the need for further investigation? The Discussion section often integrates references to other studies and findings as well (many of which you will want to mention in the Introduction).

6. **The References section lists all sources used in the text and follows whichever citation format has been requested by your instructor or the publication venue.**

LAB REPORTS

The lab report is often a condensed version of the research paper. Like the research paper, it has all six parts in the same order, so refer to the preceding section for guidelines. Depending on the actual lab assignment, one section or another may be emphasized for the written paper. For example, many labs early in the semester are designed to acquaint students with lab equipment and methods of research; therefore, the Methods and Materials section may receive the most attention in the write-up.

You should always follow the directions given by your instructor or the lab supervisor.

REVIEW PAPERS

A review paper is a synthesis of research on a particular topic or set of related topics; it has much in common with a literature review but also presents a critical argument. A review paper may be written with a variety of goals in mind: to synthesize information on a topic in order to show a need for proposed research, to give an historical perspective, or to compare and contrast related topics. It may be a way to advocate for new approaches or theories, introduce interdisciplinary possibilities, or evaluate various methods of approaching or researching a topic. Because a review paper can be written for a variety of purposes and audiences, it has no specific required length but should be well organized with a clear thesis or stated research question. You may find headings or subheadings useful for organizing your review, but they should be informative and to the point, as well as parallel in structure. Likewise, you may find that visual aids can help readers understand the connections you are making and the argument you are advancing. In addition, you should carefully document all sources used in your review with the citation system required by your assignment or the journal style guide. This type of paper may also be referred to as a *thesis-driven paper*.

CONFERENCE PRESENTATIONS (ORAL OR POSTER FORMAT)

New research is often shared with colleagues at conferences and symposia organized by various disciplines or around topics of interest. A scientist might read a copy of a written research paper in order to share preliminary results of research or extend a conversation about ongoing projects. These oral presentations are often accompanied by visual aids, such as a PowerPoint or Prezi presentation. Research might also be shared visually via a poster presentation. Different venues or instructors might require trifold posters or provide easels or bulletin boards for displaying large posters (36" x 48" is the typical size but larger sizes might

Figure 10.1 Creating Effective Posters

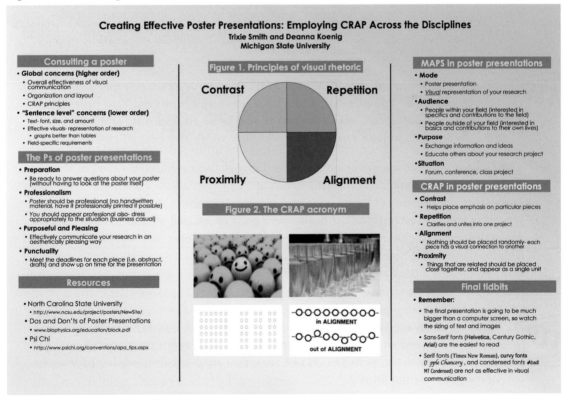

be an option). In your classes, you may be asked to give an oral presentation in conjunction with turning in a written research paper, or you might be asked to share a poster presentation with the class or the larger school community. With all of these presentations, it is important to follow published directions, including time limits and size requirements for posters. You should also be prepared to answer questions from attendees. In addition, poster presentations should follow good design principles (see Figure 10.1).

Posters are visual tools and should follow good design principles, such as the CRAP principles: contrast, repetition, alignment, proximity (See Chapter 6, Figure 6.1).

RESEARCH AND GRANT PROPOSALS

Research that involves experimentation is the primary tool of many scientists. This type of research requires financial support for lab space, equipment, supplies, and personnel. For many scientists, grants are the method for supporting such research. Grants may come from government organizations, private foundations, or corporate supporters. It is important to match your research to the purposes of the funding organization. It will not matter how well-written your proposal is if you submit it to the wrong funding source. Once you have found the correct source, you will need to follow its proposal guidelines/directions carefully, using its directions or proposal form as the template for your submission (in fact, many agencies now provide their forms in an online format, which forces you to fill in each of their categories and may limit word or character counts in each section).

Your grant proposal should always start with your research question, which is referred to as Specific Aims in many types of proposals. You must know *why* you are doing this research, *what* you hope to find out, and *how* you plan to study it before you can successfully write the rest of the proposal.

Always keep your audience in mind as you write, explaining terms and concepts that your readers may not be familiar with. Many grants allow or even ask for tables, graphs, or other images that will help the reader visualize your working hypothesis. As you write, demonstrate how your proposed research fulfills the agency's goals or mission while also respecting your readers' expertise, experience, and knowledge of the field or topic. You will have to do some additional research in order to tailor your proposal to the funder. Remember that a successful grant proposal is a persuasive argument. Your readers deserve a grant proposal that is clear, specific, and free from errors.

Many funding agencies publish their own hints and tips for grant applications and may post examples of proposals from past award recipients on their websites. Make sure you read these models before you write your own proposal.

Lab Notes and Logs

In the field or the lab, scientists must record what they see or the results they obtain from experiments. Such notes are often recorded in notebooks, logs, or journals, which may be handwritten or recorded digitally on computers, tablets, or smartphones. Results may also be video recorded for later transcription and description. It is important that these notes be accurate and detailed since they will later be used to write up lab reports and research papers. You should include the date of the experiment, all materials and equipment used, the procedures used, the results, calculations if applicable, and acknowledgments of help with the lab. You may also include your interpretations and conclusions. Many scientists develop their own shorthand methods of taking notes. As you begin this process, be sure to note what your abbreviations and symbols mean. Make yourself a key or legend so your notes make sense when you come back to them. It is also important to rewrite messy or shorthand notes while the information is still fresh.

You might consider using a double-entry notebook that allows you to take data and observation notes on one side of the paper or in one column and then record your thoughts, reflections, and/or speculations on the other side.

Other Forms of Writing

Depending on the type of job you have or the institution or industry in which you use your science background and training, you may also write in many other forms. As a teacher or professor, for example, you may find yourself writing memos and letters to administrators, students, and parents, as well as creating lesson plans, assignments, and syllabi (see Chapter 7 Writing for Education). In many industries and corporations, you may need to write reports for shareholders and investors, write briefs for government agencies and lobbyists, write articles for company magazines and websites, or compose blogs for the general public. The geologist may be writing field reports, and the chemist creating warning signs for the lab or directions on how to use equipment. The meteorologist may be composing public service announcements for extreme weather warnings as the physicist designs a workshop for elementary kids aimed at keeping kids interested in the sciences. Again, depending on the type of job you have, you may find yourself writing reports for clients or bosses, using memos and letters to conduct business, making presentations to colleagues and buyers, and writing thank you notes to supporters (genres discussed in Chapter 6 Writing For Business). Likewise, as you seek jobs and funding, you will be crafting résumés and cover letters and possibly putting together a portfolio. In today's Web 2.0+ world you may find that many, if not all, of these communications happen electronically through e-mails, text messages, blog posts, Twitter feeds, Facebook updates, YouTube videos, Pinterest boards, and various other social media sites.

WRITING EFFECTIVELY IN THE SCIENCES
KNOW THE AUDIENCE IN THE SCIENCES

Many people writing in the sciences are writing for their colleagues in order to expand scientific knowledge and continually advance our understanding in every scientific discipline from biology and chemistry to physics and geology. They are writing journal articles to be read by other scientists and students, presenting their findings at conferences, publishing textbooks for students at a variety of school levels, and sharing scientific principles in popular magazines and books. Scientists may also write for government and corporate audiences, including employers, granting agencies, and regulatory agencies such as the Environmental Protection Agency or the Food and Drug Administration. It is important to always know who you are writing for:

Did you know?

Successful science writers have come from the ranks of both science and journalism majors in college, with each gaining the complementary knowledge and skills necessary for a successful career. For example, science majors must learn
the reporting and writing skills necessary to pursue a story, and journalism majors must understand scientific concepts and terms and the scientific method.

–Council for the Advancement of Science Writing

- ❑ Who are your primary readers?
- ❑ Who else might read your writing or listen to your presentation?
- ❑ What will the members of your audience already know about your topic?
- ❑ What will you need to define or explain?
- ❑ Will your audience be predisposed to agree or disagree with your point of view?
- ❑ What kinds of evidence will be most convincing for this audience?

KNOW THE RESEARCH QUESTIONS TO ASK IN THE SCIENCES

As a student, your research questions or the conditions for your research may be assigned by your instructor. Often, however, you will have to develop your research questions on your own. One place to begin is by asking yourself what you want to know more about, what you want to understand better, or what assumptions you need to test. You may ask *how* questions or *why* questions. Your final research questions will guide both your research design and your writing. The research question is also referred to as the *working hypothesis*. It is the idea you will systematically test or analyze through the research process and describe through the writing process. Table 10.1 illustrates how this process can be used to create a viable research question.

TABLE 10.1

Research Questions	
What you want to know more about:	**Your research question:**
There are so many kinds of suntan lotion out there I don't know what to buy, but I really don't want to get burned when I go to the beach for spring break.	Is SPF 65 more effective at preventing sunburn than SPF 50?
MTA3 plays an important role in the pluripotency of mice ES cells; however, the role of MTA3 in induced pluripotency of human iPS cells is still unknown. Therefore, we want to determine the functional requirement for MTA3 in iPS cell generation.	Is MTA3 required in iPS cell generation?

KNOW THE KINDS OF EVIDENCE USED IN SCIENCE ARGUMENTS

Scientists use both quantitative and qualitative data in order to make arguments and support their claims. Both types of data come from primary research in the field or lab, as well as secondary research from other published resources. Quantitative data are presented in numbers and scientific formulas; this includes the presentation of statistics in the text as well as through graphs and charts. In your writing, you may need to present the mathematical formulas you developed to test data, look for or extend patterns, or demonstrate results. Likewise, you may find it helpful, or even necessary, to use established statistical tests when presenting your quantitative data, so you should familiarize yourself with the computer software available at your institution or in your lab. Qualitative data are non-numerical; because they rely on descriptions, many scientists find qualitative data less accurate or rigorous than quantitative data. However, both types have their place in the lab and in the field. Some experimental results must be described as well as measured. The most important question to ask is this: What kind of evidence is needed to test my claim or hypothesis? Your research should then be designed to help you accurately collect this type of data or evidence.

Did you know?

Forensic science, first made famous in popular television by *Quincy, M.E.*, and then later glamorized through shows such as *CSI* and *NCIS*, relies on both physical and biological evidence. Physical evidence refers to anything that is nonliving and may include trace and impression evidence—specifically, fingerprints, footprints, tire tracks, fibers, dirt and minerals, paint, and other building materials. Biological evidence comes from living beings and includes body fluids (e.g., blood, feces, urine, saliva, vomit), hair, and animal and insect evidence.

KNOW THE WRITING AND STYLE CONVENTIONS IN THE SCIENCES

Reading, writing, and science are, or should be, inseparable. Many of the process skills needed for science inquiry are similar to reading skills, and when taught together reinforce each other. Examples of skills in common are predicting, inferring, communicating, comparing and contrasting, and recognizing cause and effect relationships. In language as well as science learning, students analyze, interpret and communicate ideas. These are skills needed to evaluate sources of information and the validity of the information itself, a key factor for scientifically literate citizens.

—Science Magazine

Good science writers communicate clearly, are aware of their audience, use complete and thorough research (both primary and secondary), present appropriate and accurate evidence for the study, and use the best format for the information and audience. Good writing in the sciences also follows the basic tenets of good writing in general, so it is organized, easy to read, grammatically correct, and accurately uses the required documentation system. In addition, here are some specific conventions you may want to keep in mind when writing about science:

❑ Use the terms and principles of the field in order to be understood; avoid common or vernacular names, which may not be precise and can therefore cause confusion. You should explain these scientific terms when writing for more general audiences.

» Follow disciplinary rules for the use of names and formulas such as those for species, genes, chemicals, proteins, and procedures.

» The use of abbreviations is common, but you should still write out the whole word or phrase the first time you use it, followed by the

Did you know?

Illustrations have historically been a part of scientific writing and this "pictorial rhetoric" offers its own story to accompany that of the alphabetic text. These illustrations serve a variety of functions: charts usually summarize and compare data; graphs offer analyses by showing patterns and relationships; images may demonstrate layers or connections, while photographs may provide snapshots of points in time, giving a visual of the field or a point in an experiment. "Illustrations that offer data with clarity and elegance are a unique type of achievement—creative, efficient, even a source of delight."

—Scott L. Montgomery,
The Chicago Guide to Communicating Science

abbreviation in parentheses. Then use the abbreviation consistently throughout the rest of the paper.

❑ Use a more formal objective writing style rather than a conversational style. Avoid slang and contractions as well as metaphorical examples.

You should also avoid the other extreme of using overblown or pompous language that will make your writing harder to read and possibly alienate your reader.

❑ Use visuals strategically to illustrate points and present data. This includes the use of images, models, concept maps, photographs, tables, graphs, and charts.

Tables and figures should be numbered consecutively in separate series (e.g., Table 10.1, Table 10.2; Figure 10.1, Figure 10.2). Tables should have titles, and figures should have legends or keys. Both should be understandable apart from the text. Other images may have captions to help readers make sense of what they are seeing.

❑ Spell out numbers at the beginning of sentences or rephrase to move the number. Spell out numbers 1–10 unless they are part of a series that is using Arabic numerals. Use the symbol ~ to mean "approximately equal to."

Example:
Of the 83 species of freshwater fish in southeastern Australia, half migrate at least once as part of their life cycle. Four notable long distance swimmers are the Mary River cod (30km), silver perch (570km), Murray cod (1,000km) and the golden perch, which has been recorded swimming a staggering 2,300km.

Fairfull, S. and Witheridge, G. (2003) Why Do Fish Need to Cross the Road? Fish Passage Requirements for Waterway Crossings. NSW Fisheries, Cronulla, 16 pp.

❑ Pay attention to verb tense and be consistent. Studies already completed should be presented in past tense; studies being proposed (e.g., in a grant proposal) should be in future tense; conditions that presently exist should be discussed in the present tense.

Science does not use the literary present tense that you may have been taught in a literature class. The literary present tense is reserved for fiction writing.

❑ Use direct quotes from source materials sparingly. Instead, rely on summaries and paraphrases.

❑ Be as objective as possible, avoiding emotional words and phrasing that will bias or unduly influence the reader. This includes avoiding sexist language and gendered expressions in your writing.

Example:
talking about eggs as passive and sperm as aggressive because of cultural notions about female and male roles in reproduction and in human culture

❑ Avoid anthropomorphizing objects, giving human feelings or actions to nonhuman beings, or giving sensory experiences to inanimate objects.

Example:
"The Praying Mantis has lived among us for centuries. Their beauty and mystique stirs our curiosity. Long and slender, quick yet graceful they stand on top of the insect world as regal creatures of the fields even in all their many colors of camouflage."

From http://www.theprayingmantis.org/

KNOW THE APPROPRIATE DOCUMENTATION STYLE IN THE SCIENCES

CSE, the documentation style recommended by the Council of Science Editors, is typically used by biologists, chemists, and those in many medical fields. However, many fields also have their own documentation guides, including the American Chemical Society and the American Medical Association. CSE offers three different documentation options: the name-year option, which is similar to APA style (see Chapter 12), and two number formats, the citation-sequence option and the citation-name option. You should use the style required by your instructor or the journal to which you are submitting your paper.

CMS (see Chapter 12), or the Chicago Manual of Style, is used by many journals, including some scientific journals, so you may need to be familiar with this documentation style as well.

Did you know?

For many years, it was believed that science writing needed to be presented in third person with passive constructions in order to appear more objective. However, many fields now encourage the use of the first person in order to avoid awkward passive constructions and unclear writing. The use of first person also acknowledges the fact that experiments in the lab and in the field are actually conducted by people—researchers—who may affect the outcomes.

SAMPLE STUDENT LAB REPORT

Investigating the Properties of Skeletal Muscle Using the Gastrocnemius Muscle from Leopard Frog

David Carr, Chelsea Reynolds, and Jillian Reed

Dept. of Physiology, Michigan State University
31 March 2011

Skeletal Muscle 2

ABSTRACT

Skeletal muscle is a type of striated muscle associated with voluntary movement. The organization of skeletal muscle into sarcomeres and motor units gives it several distinct physiological characteristics. In this experiment we isolated the gastrocnemius muscle from leopard frogs and, using a force transducer and exogenous electrical stimulation, we attempted to determine several properties of the muscle including the threshold stimulus, maximal stimulus, and the effect of muscle length on contraction among others.

INTRODUCTION

Skeletal muscle is a type of striated muscle associated with the somatic nervous system. Contraction of skeletal muscle is induced by release of acetylcholine by motor neurons associated with the motor endplate, which activates nicotinic acetylcholine receptors. Subsequent release of $Ca2+$ from the sarcoplasmic reticulum (SR) allows for the association of myosin and actin and the resulting "power stroke" (PSL 475L Lab Manual 2010). While a muscle is at rest a molecule known as troponin blocks the myosin binding site on the actin molecule. Calcium binds to troponin and induces a conformation change that causes it to shift positions and expose the myosin binding site. This allows the power stroke to occur. Therefore, the contraction of a muscle requires the presence of calcium. Provided there is no further stimulation of the muscle, the calcium is pumped back into the SR and the troponin again prevents the association of actin and myosin (Squire 2010). This provides a basic explanation of the process of excitation-contraction coupling, which can be complicated by the degree and frequency of muscle stimulation.

The basic unit of skeletal muscle is called a sarcomere, which consists of overlapping myosin and actin filaments. These sarcomeres are arranged in parallel to form individual muscle fibers. A motor unit consists of a motor neuron and all of the muscle fibers that it innervates. Because each muscle fiber contracts in an all-or-nothing manner, changes in overall muscle tension are achieved by changing the number of motor units that are activated; that is, increasing muscle tension is achieved by activating a greater number of motor units while decreasing muscle tension results from the activation of a lesser number of motor units.

These characteristics of skeletal muscle including its organization into sarcomeres and its innervations as motor unit give it several noted physiological properties including single twitch contractions, tetanus contractions, and a relationship between muscle length and contraction strength.

By applying electrical stimulation in vitro, we can mimic an action potential coming from the central nervous system and cause contraction of the muscle. In this experiment we isolated the gastrocnemius muscle from leopard frogs and applied electrical stimuli to study the above mentioned characteristics of skeletal muscle.

METHODS

Leopard frogs were anesthetized using tricaine methanesulfonate before being euthanized by double pithing. The skin was cut completely around the body of the frog just under the front limbs. The skin was then pulled down over the pelvis and then the feet resulting in a skinned frog from the upper limbs down. From this point on amphibian Ringer's solution was used regularly to keep the tissue moist. Each leg was cut free from the hip joint as close to the head of the femur as possible. The gastrocnemius muscle was identified and all other muscles were removed from the leg. Then, the Achilles tendon was cut free from its distal attachment, and the tibia and fibula were cut just below the knee. This left the gastrocnemius muscle attached proximally to the femur, and free at its distal end. Both legs were prepared in this fashion. One leg was placed into the force transducer and the other was stored in amphibian Ringer's solution until it was needed.

Before setting up the muscle in the apparatus a known weight of 150 grams was hung from the hook and the deflection was noted. This allowed us to calibrate the transducer and calculate the actual force of muscle contraction.

The force transducer consisted of a femur clamp to hold the femur in place and a hook attached to the actual transducer. The femur was placed in the femur clamp and the hook was pushed through the Achilles tendon. This setup was adjusted so that the muscle was under slight tension. Two wires attached to a Grass stimulator were wrapped around each end of the muscle to allow stimulation.

To determine the threshold stimulus required for contraction, we delivered single pulses lasting 5 mSec at increasing voltages. Beginning at 0.1 volts we delivered single stimuli 8-10 seconds apart, increasing the voltage by 0.1 volts until contraction was observed. The first voltage that resulted in deflection from our baseline was noted as the threshold stimulus. After reaching threshold we continued to increase the voltage, this time in increments of 0.2 volts, again inducing single stimuli in 8-10 second intervals until increases in voltage no longer resulted in increased amplitude of contraction. The voltage at which this occurred was noted as the maximal stimulus. Following this, we induced single twitches in the muscle by applying single stimuli to the muscle at the maximum stimulus voltage.

Next, using a stimulus intensity roughly 80% of the maximum, we applied two pulses in succession so that the second stimulus occurred during the relaxation phase of the first contraction. This allowed us to observe wave summation.

To study the properties of muscle tetanus we applied a repeat stimulus at the maximal stimulus level, increasing the pulse frequency by 1 pps from a starting frequency of 2 pps. This was done until the contractile response resulted in a graph that was nearly a straight line indicating that the muscle was in a state of sustained contraction. This state was maintained for 3 minutes before removing the stimuli. The muscle was allowed to recover for 3 minutes and this process was again repeated until the induction of muscle tetanus, noting any changes in amplitude between the two trials.

Following this second trial, the first gastrocnemius muscle was discarded and the second one was inserted into the force transducer set-up. The femur was inserted into the femur clamp and the Achilles tendon was hooked onto the transducer. However, in this case, this was done without any tension in the muscle at all. The length of the muscle from its origin at the knee joint to the point where the needle pierced the tendon was measured and recorded as the resting muscle length. The stimulator was set to deliver maximal stimulus and five contractions were elicited at three second intervals. Using a micrometer, the muscle was stretched one millimeter and this procedure was repeated. This process was continued until the tension reached the measurement limits of the load cell.

RESULTS

Calibration using the 150 gram weight resulted in a deflection amplitude of 2 mV.

DISCUSSION

Our results showed that increasing the strength of electrical stimulation resulted in an increased strength of contraction in a graded fashion. This result can be explained by the organization of skeletal muscle into motor units. Each motor unit itself contracts in an all-or-nothing fashion, however, increasing the strength of electrical stimulation results in the activation of a greater number of motor units. As a result, the muscle as a whole shows a greater degree of contraction. This physiological organization gives the body a great deal of control over skeletal muscle contractions allowing changes in the number of motor units activated to have a direct graded response on the degree of skeletal muscle contraction.

We also found that repeated stimulation of the muscle at a sufficient number of stimulations per second (10 pps) resulted in muscle tetanus, a condition where the muscle was in a state of constant contraction. This condition results from the build-up of calcium in the cytoplasm above a concentration sufficient to allow the maximum number of myosin binding sites to be exposed. During a normal muscle "twitch", calcium is released from the SR which causes movement of troponin and exposes the binding site for mysin on the actin filament. The amount of calcium released determines the number of binding sites exposed and the strength of contraction. During muscle tetanus, the action potentials are continually causing calcium release from the SR faster than it can be pumped back in. This causes the number of available cross-bridge sites to increase continuously until all of the sites are available and the muscle remains maximally contracted.

However, after remaining under tetanus for an extended period of time, we found that the degree of muscle tension started to gradually decrease. This result can be explained by skeletal muscle fatigue. Skeletal muscle fatigue is a decrease in performance due to prolonged or repeated use of a muscle (Allen et al. 2008). A variety of factors have been implicated in their contribution to muscle fatigue including depletion of cellular ATP and creatine phosphate levels, inhibition of calcium release from the SR, and decreased sensitivity of troponin to calcium (Allen et al. 2008). All of these mechanisms are related in that sustained muscle contraction and the resulting physiological changes (i.e., increased cytosolic calcium, increased ATP turnover) cause a resulting decrease in the ability of the muscle to undergo further contraction. Interestingly, researchers have been unable to find a solid link between lactic acid and muscle fatigue. Historically, it was believed that the accumulation of lactic acid was the major cause of muscle fatigue, however, researchers have found that lactic acid seems to have minimal deleterious effects on muscle fatigue and may even provide other beneficial effects (Allen et al. 2008).

Cited References

1. PSL 475L Capstone Laboratory in *Physiology Laboratory Manual*. 2010. Michigan State University.

2. Vander A, Sherman, J. 1998. *Human Physiology: The Mechanisms of Body Function* (7th Ed.). New York: McGraw-Hill Companies, Inc.

3. Squire, J. 2010. Muscle Contraction: Regulation. In: *Encyclopedia of Life Sciences*. Hoboken: John Wiley & Sons.

4. Allen, D, Lamb, G, Westerblad, H. 2008. Skeletal muscle fatigue: Cellular mechanisms. *Physiology Reviews*. 88: 287-332.

Note: in CSE format, a title page should be included

Antibiotics   1

Antibiotics as Growth Promotants

This paper is designed to examine and discuss the effects of sub-therapeutic levels of

antibiotics in feed on growth promotion in livestock; the use of sub-therapeutic levels of

antibiotics in livestock feed helps producers have a better product to sell due to increased growth

of the animals, reduced animal disease, reduced feed costs and reduced drug costs. This is a

common practice among producers to increase the growth rate of their livestock, ultimately

improving feed to gain ratio of the animals and thus, higher profits for the producers. However,

it comes under much scrutiny by the media and general public due to concerns of antibiotic

resistance and antibiotic residues found in the animal products. With the multitude of benefits, it

seems contradictory that antibiotic growth promoters would be so frowned upon. A large portion

of the problem is a misunderstanding of growth promoter use and its associated problems.

Sub-therapeutic levels of antibiotics have been used as growth promoters since the 1950s

(Page 2006). They are used as a feed additive in livestock species such as beef and dairy cattle,

swine and poultry. They function by reducing or eliminating microbial populations in the gut

that are potentially harmful to the health of the animal. Doing this allows for increased growth

rates because the animal can put its energy toward growing instead of fighting off a bacterial

infection. Antibiotics fed at such small levels do not pose as many problems as therapeutic

levels of antibiotics with regards to withdraw times and discarded milk. The prevalence of use is

mainly concentrated within the swine and poultry industries. However, it is also used somewhat

in the beef and dairy industries. The majority of studies on the benefits of antibiotics on growth

> This thesis-driven research paper reviews key arguments for and against the use of antibiotics to promote growth in livestock. While the author looks at both sides of the issue, his thesis indicates that he is in favor of their use.

promotion are done exclusively in swine and poultry (Alexander et al. 2008). In all studies,

regardless of species, improvements in growth rates were found to be statistically significant.

Average daily gain rates range from 4-8% across all species. However, ADG was not

equal across all phases of growth, indicating that there is an ideal time period to use antibiotics as

growth promotants (Page 2006). Even without an ideal time period the results are irrefutable;

sub-therapeutic levels of antibiotics in feed are efficacious in promoting growth. A main benefit

of this increased growth is the increased profits for producers. Since antibiotic growth promoter

(AGPs) improve the feed to gain ratio, producers can save vast amounts of money on feed cost

alone. With the other added benefits such as reduced animal disease and reduced waste,

producers can have much larger profit margins than those producers not using AGPs (Page

2006).

With the multitude of benefits from using AGPs, there should be no concerns with the

usage. However, in the past decade there have been growing concerns with AGP usage. The

main concern is antibiotic resistance. Several of the antibiotics used as AGPs are also used in

humans to treat bacterial infections (Alexander et al. 2008). A significant portion of this concern

stems from the ability of antibiotic resistant bacteria to be transferred from animals to humans.

In an effort to reduce antibiotic resistance, the European Union banned the use of most AGPs by

1999. Recent consumer concerns are a significant contributor to the push toward a ban in the

United States (Chesson 2006). It is not clear as to whether AGP use is actually a significant

contributor to antibiotic resistance.

A study performed in Canada by Alexander et al. (2008) found evidence that AGP use

does not contribute as much as originally believed. Upon testing fecal samples, many of the

cattle shed antibiotic resistant bacteria prior to receiving AGPs. Two different diets were set up;

The author mentions antibio[tic] growth promoter[s] indicates the abbreviation for these in parenthe[ses] (AGPs), and then uses the abbreviation for t[he] rest of the paper.

a grain-based diet and a silage based diet. They were fed common AGP feed additives over a period of 200 days. Upon collecting samples throughout the trial, the cattle fed grain-based diets had consistently higher amounts of antibiotic resistance than both the silage fed and control group. This led them to conclude that diet most likely contributes to antibiotic resistance. They concluded that environmental factors need to be taken into consideration when evaluating how much AGP use is involved in antibiotic resistance.

If a ban were to occur in the United States, producers would have to find alternate methods of improving animal performance. An increasingly popular area of research in animal science is new products that can compete with the growth rates achieved by AGPs. Studies performed in both swine and poultry found products that show improvement in growth, but many of these products do not compare to the growth rates seen with AGPs. A study performed by Khosravi et al. (2008) examined three different products as possible replacements for AGPs in poultry. These products are propionic acid, protexin, and nettle extract. Both the propionic acid and the pronexin significantly increased the body weight gain throughout the duration of the study. Birds given propionic acid weighed 2400.79 g by the end of the study, and birds given protexin weighed 2339.16 g. The control birds weighed 2273.24. That is a 5.6% and 2.9% increase respectively, when compared with the control. However, the results were not directly compared to the growth rates associated with AGP use. The nettle extract did not show a significant improvement. A study performed by Pettigrew (2006) examined different feed additives for swine. These products were spray-dried plasma, conventional egg products, immune egg products, milk protein products, acids, lactose mannan oligosaccharide, zinc and copper. If they did compare, the products were often costly. Several of the products had to be administered at levels that exceeded the recommended amounts. This raises concerns with

The author draws upon a number of different studies to make his argument; he summarizes their findings and indicates his sources through in-text citations and then a References list at the end.

toxicity and the environment. Products such as copper and zinc in swine are excreted in high

levels. This becomes a problem because pig manure is often used to fertilize crops. The high

levels of copper and zinc in the manure can lead to a build-up of these compounds in the soil.

Research in this area has a long way to go before finding a product with the same caliber as

AGPs.

At this time, a ban in AGP usage would be devastating for some producers, and

potentially harmful to consumers. A study performed by Cox (2006) analyzed the risk to

humans if virginiamycin use were to be banned in poultry. Using risk analysis techniques, Cox

found that human Campylobacter cases would increase by 6991 cases a year, and result in 0.54

more deaths, bringing the total up to 730.54 possible deaths per 2.5 million Campylobacter cases.

Though that may not be a large increase in illnesses, the cost associated with the increase may be

problematic. Also, that is only the increase in poultry. The study did not take into account the

illness that would arise from consumption of other animal products. One conclusion from this

study is that the costs from disease and treatment that would be caused by the disuse of AGPs

exceeds the cost of possible antibiotic resistance from use of AGPs.

The benefits of AGP use far outweigh the costs. Increased growth rates benefit the

producers with higher profits and more product to sell. AGP use benefits the animal by better

health and welfare through reduced disease. Thus far, no product exists on the market that

functions in a similar way to AGPs that elicits the same increase in growth rate at an affordable

price. The problem of antibiotic resistance also is not very clear. Though AGP use may increase

it slightly, at this time it appears that AGPs do not contribute a noteworthy amount to resistance.

However, more research is needed in that area to confirm how much it does contribute. Overall,

AGPs should continue to be used for their benefits since the costs are limited or nonexistent.

Notice how the author points out a limitation of the study he is referencing. This acknowledgement is important for the author's credibility with the reader.

The author's last paragraph summarizes the various arguments presented and restates his thesis that AGPs should be used because their benefits outweigh their costs.

Cited References

1. Alexander, T. W., Yanke, L. J., Topp, E., et al. 2008. Effect of subtherapeutic administration of antibiotics on the prevalence of antibiotic-resistant Escherichia coli bacteria in feedlot cattle. Applied and Environmental Microbiology 74 (14): 4405-4416.

2. Chesson, A. 2006. Antimicrobial growth promoters: where do we go from here? Wageningen, The Netherlands: Wageningen Academic Publishers, 69-79.

3. Cox, T.2006. Antimicrobial growth promoters: where do we go from here? Wageningen, The Netherlands: Wageningen Academic Publishers, 107-122.

4. Khosravi, A., Boldaji, F., Dastar, B., et al. 2008. The use of some feed additives as growth promoter in broilers nutrition. International Journal of Poultry Science 7 (11): 1095-1099.

5. Page, S.W. 2006. Antimicrobial growth promoters: where do we go from here? Wageningen, The Netherlands: Wageningen Academic Publishers, 19-42.

6. Pettigrew, J. E.2006. Reduced use of antibiotic growth promoters in diets fed to weanling pigs: dietary tools, Part 1. Animal Biotechnology 17 (2): 207-215.

ACTIVITIES

Welcome to the Conversation

Discuss these questions with your classmates in class or via a class wiki or shared blog.

1. What types of qualitative data might you use in science writing? Why are quantitative data used more often than qualitative?

2. Who are the public and government audiences of science writing? How should you change the way you present your evidence and support to meet the needs of these audiences?

3. What types of informal writing will you do in science classes? How will these informal writing activities translate to the field?

4. What are some ways that you can be more precise in your writing to avoid confusion?

Writing to Learn

1. **Discourse analysis**: In order to understand how to write in different genres and formats, it is important to analyze models of writing in these different contexts. Pick two formal assignments you have to write this semester, and analyze the conventions and formats in the documents. Are there any components which you don't understand? How will you change your writing process to fit these modes of discourse?

2. **Problem analysis**: Your instructor will ask you and your classmates to create a hypothetical science problem. Then, each of you will select another's problem and write an evaluation of the problem. Why is this issue considered a problem? What methods can be used to assess the issue? How can this problem be fixed? Who could (and would) provide funding to fix it?

Learning to Write

1. **Journal article**: Following the list of approved topics, experiments, or field research topics, research an issue in your field. You will want to gather primary and secondary sources. Then, following the format guidelines in this chapter and supplied by your instructor, write a research paper that meets all of the parameters for a journal article in your field. Remember that your colleagues in the field expect formal, professional writing and reporting of your results.

2. **Lab report**: As you conduct experiments in your courses, you will need to keep a detailed, precise, and understandable journal. You will use your notes to create a formal lab report that details all of the pertinent information necessary to understanding and replicating your work in the lab. Be sure to follow your instructor's guidelines exactly. Scientists rely on the expected formats to deliver information succinctly.

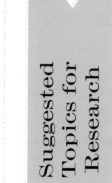

Suggested Topics for Research

1. You have encountered various interesting results in your lab experiments this year. Pick one of these experiments and brainstorm how you could use different variables to obtain new data. Plan an experiment around these new variables, and create a research paper using the guidelines in this chapter from your results.

2. Pick a controversial topic in your field. Research the various sides of the topic in the literature, analyze these previous studies, and then formulate a researched argument for your interpretation of the topic.

 **READ MORE ABOUT IT**

Blackburn, Thomas R. *Getting Science Grants: Effective Strategies for Funding Success.* San Francisco: Jossey-Bass, 2003. Print.

Council of Science Educators. *Scientific Style and Format: The CSE Manual for Authors, Editors, and Publishers.* 7th ed. Wheat Ridge, CO: CSE, 2006. Print.

Friedland, Andrew J., and Carol L. Folt. *Writing Successful Science Proposals.* 2nd ed. New Haven, CT: Yale UP, 2009. Print.

Kuhn, Thomas. *The Structure of Scientific Revolutions.* 3rd ed. Chicago: U of Chicago P, 1996. Print.

McMillan, Victoria E. *Writing Papers in the Biological Sciences.* 4th ed. Boston: Bedford/St. Martin's, 2006. Print.

Martin, Emily. "The Egg and the Sperm: How Science Has Constructed a Romance Based on Stereotypical Male-Female Roles." *Signs* 16 (Spring 1991): 485–501. Print.

Montgomery, Scott L. *The Chicago Guide to Communicating Science.* Chicago: U of Chicago P, 2002. Print.

Peh, W.C.G. "Scientific Writing and Publishing: Its Importance to Radiologists." *Biomedical Imaging and Intervention Journal* 3.3. 2007:e55. Print.

Penrose, Ann M., and Steven B. Katz. *Writing in the Sciences: Exploring Conventions of Scientific Discourse.* 2nd ed. New York: Pearson/Longman, 2004. Print.

Reynolds, Garr. *Presentation Zen: Simple Ideas on Presentation Design and Delivery.* Berkeley: New Riders P, 2008. Print.

Richards, Anne. "Argument and Authority in the Visual Representations of Science." *Technical Communication Quarterly* 12.2 (Spring 2003): 183–206. Print.

Schimel, Joshua. *Writing Science: How to Write Papers That Get Cited and Proposals That Get Funded.* New York: Oxford UP, 2011. Print.

University of Chicago Press Staff. *The Chicago Manual of Style.* 16th ed. Chicago: U of Chicago P, 2010. Print.

chapter 11

Writing in the Social Sciences

ANTHROPOLOGY, ARCHAEOLOGY, COMMUNICATION STUDIES, ECONOMICS, LINGUISTICS, POLITICAL SCIENCE, PSYCHOLOGY, SOCIOLOGY, AND SOCIAL WORK

In immortalizing our words, we take a central risk—that our words will be used to represent us as a whole, to be misused, misrepresented, and when we're gone, to be left undefended.

Therefore, it is imperative that when we write, we consider each word and craft each sentence with caution. To satisfy this imperative in science requires an uncommon combination of humility (because you could be wrong) and hubris (because you think you're right). It is almost impossible to identify the value or significance that a work will have in the longer term—the accumulation of knowledge over time will provide the best assessment of a work's significance. Only time will tell.

−Charles Limb
"Why I Write"

PURPOSES OF WRITING IN THE SOCIAL SCIENCES

The term *social science* is a broad disciplinary label for a wide variety of fields or majors that examine people and their behaviors, either individually or in groups. The discipline draws on research methods from the hard sciences as well as more humanities-based approaches, often using a combination of the two. Consequently, writing in the social sciences takes on a wide variety of formats and purposes. As with other majors, the one purpose these different forms all have in common is communication. It might be the psychologist writing patient notes, the archeologist writing an article for a museum's magazine as the museum sets up an exhibit of recent findings, the sociologist reporting on television viewing patterns, the economist making recommendations to a governmental policy organization, or the anthropologist writing a grant proposal, to name a few examples. The more specific purposes behind these communications may include providing information, making an argument, persuading people to agree or to act in a certain way, soliciting funds, or explaining behaviors, treatments, or possible outcomes. No matter what form you're using or what message you want to send, your writing will be more effective if it writing is clear and to the point and if it follows the conventions of the format you have chosen (or been assigned). From short memos and chart notes to lengthy reports and proposals, from field notes to blogs, you want your writing to be understood, and this chapter is designed to help you achieve that goal.

TYPES OF WRITING ASSIGNMENTS IN THE SOCIAL SCIENCES

Beyond the purpose of testing students' mastery of course material, we found two other purposes for writing in the social science classes we visited. In a few classes professors trained students to write like professionals in a discipline; in other classes, professors followed the liberal arts tradition of asking students to explore questions presented by the subject matter of the course.

—Faigly and Hansen

Writing in the social sciences takes on many different forms, depending on major, audience, purpose, and context. Similarly, learning objectives, programmatic goals, instructor experience, and even accreditation requirements may affect the types of assignments you receive in class, just as various factors may influence what you are asked to create on the job. Following are some common types of writing assignments you may see, but keep in mind that this is not an exhaustive list and that you may be asked to create other types of documents or communication. Likewise, you may know of alternative forms of communication that may be effective for your audience, purpose, and context—if so, you should discuss these alternative forms with your instructor.

REVIEW OR SOCIAL ISSUES PAPERS

A review paper is a synthesis of research on a particular topic or set of related topics. It has much in common with the literature review section of a larger research paper but also presents a critical argument. In the social sciences, the review paper is often an argument about a particular social issue. Such a paper may be written with a variety of goals in mind: to show a need for proposed research, to give an historical perspective on an issue, or to compare and contrast related topics. It may be a way to advocate for new approaches or theories, introduce interdisciplinary possibilities, or evaluate various methods of approaching or researching a topic. Your professor may also refer to this essay as a *thesis-driven paper* or *research paper* since it is forming an argument. Take for example, the topic of family. According to *The Sociology Student Writer's Manual*, social issue papers may focus on this kind of issue in a variety of different ways:

❑ **A definitional focus:** What is the traditional family and how does it differ from other forms of family organization?

❑ **A geographical focus:** What is family life like in Concord, New Hampshire? Is it different from family life in Papua, New Guinea?

❑ **An historical focus:** How has the traditional family changed over time?

❑ **A systems focus:** How does the traditional family as an American institution interact with other basic systems or institutions in society, such as churches, schools, or government agencies?

❑ **An interaction focus:** What are the roles played in the family? What social, economic, political, or environmental forces affect these roles?

❑ **A future focus:** What does the future hold for the family? What conclusions can be projected from what you have learned about the issue?

Keep in mind that the review paper does not just summarize source material on a topic. It is a place to be analytical and show off your critical thinking and writing skills. You should analyze your resources for author bias or slanted points of view. Also, consider the arguments in the texts: Are they well supported? Does the evidence make sense? Does the evidence really show what the argument claims? Does the theoretical model fit the argument? Has the theoretical model been used appropriately? Has the author fully used the theoretical model, or has she selected only those parts that fit her claims? Asking these critical questions of the resource texts will help you develop your own point of view and argument. See the Sample Student Review Paper on page 312.

TIP

Think critically about your own writing as well as the resource texts you use in your review essay.

One particular type of review paper students are often asked to write is the annotated bibliography. An annotated bibliography gives writers an opportunity to collect information on a given subject, helping them see where their own ideas might fit into a given conversation on a topic. Each entry in an annotated bibliography includes two parts: (1) the bibliographic citation, following the documentation style assigned, and (2) the annotation, which may vary in length and purpose. Annotations usually include a summary of the text being read and then an evaluation of the text or a reflection on the text.

❏ To write the summary, think about the main idea or thesis of the text. What is the essay or book saying about the topic? How does it approach the topic? What should the reader take away from this text?

❏ To write an evaluation, think about how the source covers the topic. Is it reliable? Unbiased? What kind of evidence is used in this source? Who is the intended audience?

❏ The reflection is more personal. Is the source useful for your present research? How does it help you think about or shape your argument?

Because a review paper can be written for a variety of purposes and audiences, it has no certain length but should be well organized and include a clear thesis or stated research question. In addition, your thesis must be supported by relevant data that are considered appropriate in the social sciences and show evidence of critical thinking. You may find headings or subheadings useful for organizing your review, but they should be informative and to the point, as well as parallel in structure. Likewise, you may find that visual aids can help readers understand the connections you are making and the argument you are advancing. Finally, you should carefully document all sources used in your review paper with the citation system required by your assignment or the journal style guide.

RESEARCH PAPERS

Research papers report the findings of original research—research conducted in the field or possibly in the lab. At the undergraduate level, this research may happen in a single lab experiment or may occur over a semester or two. For example, an anthropology class may include an assignment to conduct a mini-ethnography for a day, observing a particular subculture or environment; a sociology class may send students out to conduct interviews on an issue such as dating practices; or students in a psychology class may survey students' learning styles. This research will usually lead to some type of final product. For a school course, this final product is often the research paper, which is designed to give you practice in communicating your findings with colleagues and in practicing one of the major genres of the field. The research paper assigned in a class is much like the research report a social scientist writes for a journal, whether the researcher is working in a university or elsewhere.

The research paper generally follows a specific structure that is much the same as the structure used with research papers in the sciences. This format usually includes six sections: (1) Introduction, (2) Literature Review, (3) Materials and Methods, (4) Results/Findings, (5) Discussion, and (6) Conclusion. The paper may also include an abstract, which is usually about 250 words, and it should definitely include a References section at the end of the paper.

1. The **Introduction** gives readers the context for your study and typically includes the statement of the problem. It should lead into the literature review and theoretical framework. The Introduction is the place where you draw your reader in. It is also the place where you define your credibility as a writer and researcher.

2. The **Literature Review** gives an overview of the literature on the problem or topic being researched. It often points out gaps in the literature, which can help you identify the need for a study. The review shows how the study fits into what has already been done and the importance—the "so what" or "who cares"—of your particular research. Or perhaps it demonstrates why you care about the topic or research. It also gives the theoretical framework for the study and the way it has been designed.

3. The **Materials and Methods** section is also important for context and for establishing credibility. Here you explain your exact methods and tools for data collection: the sample used, the variables tested, and the data collection methods employed, such as interviews, surveys, and observations. The reader should be given enough information to fully understand the validity of your study.

4. The **Results/Findings** section should summarize your findings, drawing attention to trends or patterns in the data. This section illustrates and/or explains the findings with details, examples, stories, statistics, charts, tables, graphs, and other images. Often the Results section follows the same logical order used in your Materials and Methods section so it will be easy for the reader to follow. With some shorter reports, the methods and results sections are reported together. You do not need to repeat in writing the full information illustrated through visuals, but you should call attention to these visuals by referencing them in the text. The Results section is not the place to interpret the data or draw conclusions about the data and its implications.

5. The **Discussion** section is where you interpret your results and present your argument about what the data show. This is the place to discuss the implications of the data and support them with evidence from the research. Here you refer back to the significance of your research and your working hypothesis. What is the most reasonable explanation for your findings? What does this mean for the issue being studied? What does it mean for the discipline? How does your study fit with other researchers' work? For example, are your findings consistent with other studies, or do they show that something was missing in previous studies? Do your findings indicate the need for further investigation? What are the limitations of your study? The Discussion section often integrates references

to theories as well as other studies and findings (including those mentioned in the introduction). This is the place where your argument is showcased and reinforced.

6. The **Conclusion** section pulls together all of the parts of the study, summarizing the study and its implications.

 You should never introduce new information in the conclusion.

IRB Proposals

A second assignment related to research in the social sciences is the writing of an IRB proposal. Institutional Review Boards are designed to oversee research that involves human subjects, which is very common in the social sciences. IRBs are usually interdisciplinary committees at colleges and universities, as well as other research facilities. Their goal is to make sure subjects are treated fairly and ethically and that the benefits of the study outweigh its risks. The goal of an IRB proposal assignment is usually to familiarize students with the policies and procedures of the IRB so they'll be successful with such proposals down the road, including the completion of required forms such as those needed for informed consent. Often students must take the required training at their institutions in order to be IRB certified. Then they have to follow the IRB procedures in place—completing the required forms, submitting all requested materials, and answering any questions from the review board or the instructor filling this role for the class. If students are going to complete the proposed research, they may be asked to submit the proposal to the actual IRB at their institution.

Research and Grant Proposals

Social science research often requires financial support—money for supplies and equipment, researchers' and participants' time, space, and other needs. For many social scientists, grants are the mechanism for supporting such research. Grants may come from government organizations/resources, private foundations, or corporate supporters. It is important to match your research to the purposes of the granting/funding organization. It will not matter how well written your proposal is if you submit it to the wrong funding source. Once you have found the correct source, you will need to follow its proposal guidelines/directions carefully, using its directions or proposal form as the template for your submission (in fact, many agencies now provide their forms in an online format, which forces you to fill in each of their categories and may limit word or character counts in each section).

You should always start with your research questions or specific aims. You must know *why* you are doing this research, *what* you hope to find out, and *how* you plan to study a particular phenomenon before you can successfully write the rest of the proposal. This will help you formulate your working hypothesis, which is the specific question you are seeking to answer with your research. Also of key importance in the social sciences is your data analysis plan, which shows how you plan to analyze your data and how such analysis will prove (or disprove) your hypothesis. As mentioned previously, keep your audience in mind as you write, explaining terms and concepts that your readers may not be familiar with. Many grants also allow or even ask for tables, graphs, or other images that will help the reviewers visualize your working hypothesis. As you write, demonstrate how your proposed research fulfills the agency's goals or mission, while also respecting your readers' expertise, experience, and knowledge of the field or topic. You will have to do some additional research in order to tailor your proposal to the funder. And remember that a successful grant proposal is a persuasive argument. Your readers deserve a grant proposal that is clear, specific, and free from errors.

Many funding agencies publish their own hints and tips for grant applications and may post examples of proposals from past award recipients on their websites. Make sure you read these models before you write your own proposal.

FIELD NOTES AND LOGS

In the field, social scientists must record their observations or results from various research methods. Such notes are often recorded in notebooks, logs, or journals, which may be handwritten or recorded digitally on computers, tablets, or smartphones. Field notes may include written descriptions, sketches or drawings, photographs, overheard conversations and comments, as well as interview responses. Some observations may also be video or audio recorded for later transcription and description. Field notes are both descriptive and reflective, and it is important that these notes be accurate and detailed since you will later use them to write up your research. You should include the dates and times of the observations, and what/ who you see and hear, including participants' behaviors and conversations, background events, and other relevant data. Likewise you should include any thoughts, questions, or conjectures that occur as you are making your observations. If the information is relevant, record materials, equipment, and the procedures used, the results, calculations or early analysis if applicable, and acknowledgments of help with the research. You may also include your working interpretations and conclusions. Many social scientists develop their own shorthand methods of taking notes. As you begin this process, be sure to note what your abbreviations and symbols mean—make yourself a key or legend so your notes make sense when you come back to them. Similarly, rewrite messy or shorthand notes while the information is still fresh.

You might consider using a double-entry notebook that allows you to take data and observation notes on one side of the paper or in one column and then record your thoughts, reflections, and/or speculations on the other side.

CASE STUDIES AND TREATMENT PLANS

In majors such as psychology and social work, you may be asked to write a case study or a treatment plan. Generally, a case study is an in-depth analysis of a person. You may be given a scenario to work from, asked to analyze a person in the news, or assigned a character in a movie to write about. In more advanced classes, you may work with actual clients in a lab or study. The amount of research and theoretical analysis required for the assignment will vary, but conclusions about the person under study should always be based on presented evidence, not conjecture. The case study typically includes the background or history of the person and problem, the diagnosis of the problem, and the planned intervention. Sometimes you will be asked to write up only the planned intervention, otherwise known as the treatment plan. The treatment plan should delineate specific, realistic, and measurable goals as well as specific incremental steps for achieving these goals. Treatment plans often include a time frame for accomplishing each step toward the goal.

PRESENTATIONS

Research results are often shared with classmates, colleagues, and clients through formal presentations. Likewise, colleagues may share ideas at conferences and symposia organized by various disciplines or around topics of interest. These oral presentations are often accompanied by visual aids, such as a PowerPoint or Prezi presentations. In your classes, you may be asked to give an oral presentation in conjunction with turning in a project or report. These presentations may be for your classmates, the larger school community, or even for community partners. Presentations are organized much like written papers with (1) an introduction and statement of purpose, (2) the body of the presentation, which includes your main points and any evidence used to illustrate or support these points, and (3) your conclusion, which may include recommendations for action. When your presentation includes the use of presentation software, there are some additional guidelines you should keep in mind:

- ❏ Use text sparingly.
  - » Use bulleted or numbered lists rather than complete sentences.
  - » Include no more than 5–6 listed items per slide.
  - » Use numbers for ranked or sequenced lists, and bullets for other lists.
- ❏ Make your visuals consistent. Use the same background and color scheme, font, size, and spacing across slides.
- ❏ Choose a font no smaller than 30 points, with the headings even larger, so that the text will be visible even from the back of the room. The contrast between the text and the background should be sharp to make it easier to read or view.
- ❏ Use graphs, charts, and other illustrations to clarify and simplify your message and to add emphasis and interest. Do not overuse.

❏ Match your talk to your visuals. Develop clear transitions for yourself, so you'll keep your talk and your visuals in line with each other. These transitions will also help your audience members keep up.

❏ Do not read the text on your visuals to your audience members.

❏ Technology doesn't always work, even when you've tested it and practiced with it beforehand. Bring a printout of your visuals with you and be prepared to move forward without the visuals if you need to.

TIP

Do not stand in front of your audience and simply read your slides to them. Think of your slides as an outline that you are filling in with your presentation.

Information might also be shared visually via a handout, brochure, or poster presentation. Different venues or instructors might require different formats or leave the option up to you. With all of these presentations, it is important to follow published directions, including time limits and size requirements (36" x 48" is the typical poster size, for example, but larger sizes might be an option). You should also be prepared to answer questions from attendees.

TIP

Posters, handouts, and brochures are visual tools and should follow good design principles, such as the CRAP principles: contrast, repetition, alignment, proximity (See Chapter 6, Figure 6.1)

DESIGNING AND WRITING FOR THE WEB

It is very important for most fields and majors to have a presence on the Web, so web design and writing for the Web are important writing skills to have. When designing and writing for the Web, it is again important to consider your audience and purpose. Your answers to these questions will help you with your design:

❏ What do you want to happen on your website?

❏ How and when do you want people to access your site?

❏ How do you plan for your website to affect your clients or your employees?

❏ How do you expect people to interact with your website?

You should also consider what information you want to include as well as how to organize it. Because websites are a visual medium, you should also use good design principles. Consider details such as background color; type color, font, and size; graphics, including what they say, whether they enhance your message or not, and how they affect site loading time; how your site looks and works in various browsers; and whether or not viewers always know they are on your site (e.g., whether your organization's name, logo, and basic contact information is visible or at least accessible from every page).

TIP Regularly check to make sure all of your links work. The Web is an ever-changing entity, so you must keep up. Dead links can ruin your credibility.

Writing for the Web may include web design, but it also includes writing content that will go on a site designed by someone else. You may be asked to write a description of your department, for example, or the report your team just completed may go on the organization's website as a downloadable attachment. You may become part of your workplace blog team, writing blogs on a regular basis about topics of interest to your website's target audience. In addition, given the prevalence of social media outlets, many researchers and organizations now take advantage of the numerous social media sites to further their work. You could be asked to post surveys on a Facebook page, send Tweets to your organization's Twitter feed, upload images to a Flickr site, create an interest board related to your newest project on Pinterest, look for networking possibilities on LinkedIn, or create material to populate any number of social media sites related to your specific area of study or industry. As these various tools have different parameters and expectations, as well as different audiences, you'll have to adjust your writing style for the audience and purpose as well as the medium.

OTHER FORMS OF WRITING

Depending on the type of job you have or the type of institution in which you use your social science background and training, you may also write in many other forms. As an instructor or professor, you may find yourself writing memos and letters to administrators, students, and parents, as well as creating lesson plans, assignments, and syllabi (see Chapter 7 Writing for Education). You may write articles for alumni magazines and websites, or blog for the general public. You may conduct research on social patterns for an industry, such as music listening patterns for radio advertisers or buying patterns for department stores. If so, you may find yourself writing reports to clients or bosses, using memos and letters to conduct business, and making presentations to colleagues. You may also find yourself writing briefs for government agencies, designing public service announcements, creating handouts for the general public on a certain topic, or even creating information videos or podcasts. You may also need to craft resumes and cover letters as you seek jobs and funding, as well as write thank you notes to supporters. In today's Web 2.0+ world, you may find that many, if not all, of these communications happen electronically.

Did you know?

According to the U.S. Office of Personnel Management, there are more than 50,000 jobs with the federal government requiring a social science background. The top three agencies with such jobs are the Department of Veteran Affairs, the Department of Defense, and the Department of Justice. These include jobs in intelligence, social work, and social sciences broadly defined.

http://www.makingthedifference.org/federalcareers/socialsciences.shtml.

Some organizations in the social sciences provide suggestions for writing effectively in a particular field. See Box 11.1 for some writing tips from the American Anthropological Association.

Box 11.1

Writing Tips from the Writers Circle of the American Anthropological Association

The American Anthropological Association is a group designed to engage the public on topics of central importance to anthropology through the publication of op-ed pieces, short magazine articles, and other short pieces in a variety of local, regional, and national media outlets.

- We want to come across as capable and well educated, and we don't want to insult our readers' intelligence; but we don't want them to feel it's a chore to wade through our writing.

- Address topics that prospective readers will find interesting.

- Try to lead off with something that will catch their interest and conclude by stating forcefully and succinctly the main point that you want them to remember after they put down the paper.

- Use vivid examples, especially near the start, to bring alive your theoretical or methodological points.

- Use ordinary, straightforward English, avoid jargon, and use short, declarative sentences. Be concise.

- When you think you've accomplished this, ask someone outside your field (WAY outside your field) to read it and give feedback

http://www.aaanet.org/resources/AAA-Writers-Circle.cfm.

WRITING EFFECTIVELY IN THE SOCIAL SCIENCES
KNOW THE AUDIENCE IN THE SOCIAL SCIENCES

Many people writing in the social sciences are writing for their colleagues—their classmates, their fellow researchers, their employers and employees, and their team members and project managers. Likewise, social scientists are writing to patients and clients—past, present, and potential. They may also be communicating with others in their discipline—industry experts, government leaders, accreditation and licensing officials, and professional colleagues. They may be presenting at conferences or workshops, writing journal or magazine articles, or sharing through newsletters, blogs, and websites. These same social scientists may be communicating with more general, inexpert audiences through their websites and blogs, newsletters, newspaper articles and editorials, and community talks or presentations. As a social scientist, you always need to know who you are writing for:

- ❏ Who are your primary readers?
- ❏ Who else might read your writing or listen to your presentation?
- ❏ What will the members of your audience already know about your topic?
- ❏ What will you need to define or explain?
- ❏ Will your audience be predisposed to agree or disagree with your point of view?
- ❏ What do you want this audience to do or believe?
- ❏ What kinds of evidence will be most convincing for this audience?

KNOW THE QUESTIONS TO ASK IN THE SOCIAL SCIENCES

As a student, your assignment or research question may be assigned to you by your instructor. Often, however, you will have to formulate your research questions or goals for yourself. Typically, the social sciences ask *how* and *why* questions. One place to begin is by asking yourself what you want to know more about and what you need to understand better in order to complete an assigned task or goal. Starting with your own day-to-day life and interests will help you ask more interesting and useful questions. Preliminary research of existing literature may help you narrow and refine your questions. Find out what has already been said on your topic, where there are holes in the research, and perhaps where you disagree with what has already been said. Talking with others about your topic will also help; classmates, writing center consultants, and your professor are all good resources for helping you focus your research. Your final product and communication goals should guide your research approach and topic.

KNOW THE KINDS OF EVIDENCE USED IN SOCIAL SCIENCE ARGUMENTS

After you've formed your research questions, you'll want to think about how you can collect the information you need to answer the questions you have posed. As one instructor puts it, "You need to know how to marshal your evidence." Social scientists use both primary and secondary research and types of evidence. Primary research tools include interviews, focus groups, surveys, and observations. Perhaps you need to interview friends about local sports clubs or family members about holiday traditions. You may want to conduct surveys about students' study habits or spending habits. Perhaps you could use a focus group to learn more about why gamers prefer certain games over others. You might use observations to study a particular time and space, such as your local writing center for a day or parent behavior in the mall over the weekend. In many majors, social scientists choose to supplement the stories and first hand experiences they collect (i.e., their qualitative data) with quantitative data.

Statistics and figures, or quantitative data, are often presented as numbers within the text or as a combination of numbers and visuals, such as charts, graphs, and tables in the text or in appendixes. You may need to present in your writing the methods you used to arrive at the numbers you are presenting, including the mathematical formulas used or developed to test data, to look for or extend patterns, or to demonstrate causal relationships. Likewise, you may find it helpful, or even required, to use established statistical tests when presenting your quantitative data, so you should familiarize yourself with the computer software available at your institution or required in your field, such as SPSS in psychology and social work and Stata in economics. Make sure your secondary data sources are as up to date as possible and that your statistics are as accurate as possible.

In some disciplines, researchers and experts take sides on which is the best method for research in the field, qualitative versus quantitative. As Faigley and Hansen explain, "In anthropology, for example, physical anthropologists write articles that resemble those of natural scientists while cultural anthropologists sometimes write essays that resemble those of literary scholars" (140). The same is true with majors such as psychology and linguistics, which are often divided along clinical and cultural lines.

When possible, use multiple reliable sources and types of evidence in order to triangulate your data and validate your arguments for your readers. You may often use a combination of both quantitative and qualitative data—for example, percentages that show how many students play intramural sports alongside interview responses from students who play an intramural sport. The most important question to ask (and answer) is this: What kind of evidence is needed to support my claim or to make it persuasive to my intended audience? Of course, you must also present evidence in an ethical manner. Withholding evidence or not giving the full picture because you think it hurts your argument is unethical and presents inaccurate results. This misuse of data will be detrimental in the long run. In addition, you should make sure that the argument you present is clear and logical and is actually supported by the evidence.

KNOW THE WRITING AND STYLE CONVENTIONS FOR SOCIAL SCIENCE WRITING

Good writers in the social sciences communicate clearly, are aware of their audience, use complete and thorough research (both primary and secondary), present appropriate and accurate evidence for the goals of the writing, and use the best format for the information and audience. Good social science writing also follows the basic tenets of all good writing, so it is organized, easy to read, grammatically correct, and accurately and correctly documented. In addition, below are some specific conventions you may want to keep in mind when writing for the social sciences:

❑   Be as objective as possible in your presentation of evidence. Because you are talking about human behaviors, many variables and variations exist and you will not be able to account for all of them. Therefore it is important to use conditional terms as you talk about behaviors, motivations, and causes (e.g., *often* instead of *always*, *many* instead of *all, the participants in this study* rather than *students*).

» Some majors such as psychology ask you to use the passive voice in order to keep the researcher/observer out of the text (e.g., No significant increase in aggressive driving was observed, rather than, *I observed no significant increase in aggressive driving.*)

❑ Other majors such as communication studies may ask you to use first person and to talk about yourself as a researcher in the field. Make sure you check with your professor about expectations and follow the examples set in the models you read and review for class.

❑ You will often use quotes from research participants, also referred to as informants, subjects, or even research partners, as evidence in your papers. These may be quotes from interviews, observations, or survey responses. However, you should also explain in your own words how these statements provide evidence for your argument.

People say and argue things. Books, articles, or even quotes do not. Likewise, the data or the evidence may indicate something. Be precise with your attribution. For example, *Leibowitz (2008) has argued that gephyrophobia, the fear of bridges, is related to other types of panic disorders.* **(Not:** *This essay shows that gephyrophobia, the fear of bridges, is a panic disorder.***)**

❑ Always link your evidence, whether participant quotes, statistical data, or secondary sources, to your main argument or thesis. Guide your reader through your argument.

❑ Avoid biased language that may offend your readers and damage your credibility. Language that makes assumptions or is based on stereotypes about gender, ethnicity, age, mental or physical (dis)ability, or sexual orientation is not effective. In the social sciences, various identity markers may be the very subject you are writing about, making it even more important to be precise with your language and to not make assumptions about groups of people based on these various markers. Look into accepted usage or the appropriateness of a label, term, or expression. In addition, you can often avoid bias or awkward phrasing by using plural forms (e.g., All employees should submit an evaluation form, rather than, *Every employee should submit his or her evaluation form*).

KNOW THE APPROPRIATE DOCUMENTATION SYSTEM FOR SOCIAL SCIENCE WRITING

APA, the documentation style developed by the American Psychological Association, is most often used in the social sciences (see Chapter 12). It uses an author-date method of documentation for both its in-text citations and its reference list at the end of the document. Put the author's last name and the year of the publication in parentheses within the text as soon as the source is mentioned; this emphasizes the timeliness of the source and lends credibility to the writer. Some majors, areas of study, or journals within the discipline may have their own documentation style guides, so always check to see what is appropriate for your purposes or your assignment.

Some organizations in the social sciences provide writing tips so that their members might better achieve their goals. See Box 11.2 for writing tips provided by the National Association of Social Workers (NASW).

Box 11.2

Writing a Letter to Your Member of Congress

Personal letters from constituents can be powerful. Personal letters show that you really care about the issue. Fax or e-mail the letter. Postal mail to the U.S. Congress has slowed down considerably after increased security. You can still mail a letter, but you will need more lead time for delivery. Never underestimate the power of a constituent's letter.

NASW provides prewritten letters that you can modify and send to your members of Congress. If you do not know your members of Congress, we can help you find them as well.

To make your letter effective:

- **Keep it short.** Be concise and limit your letter to one or two pages.
- **Use the appropriate address and salutation.** Use the correct title, address, and salutation, and remember to use spell check after completing your letter.

- **Identify yourself.** Let your legislator know that you are a constituent, a social worker, and a member of the National Association of Social Workers.
- **Be polite.** Like most of us, legislators will respond better to positive communication. Start by recognizing their support on other legislation.
- **Explain your position.** Talk about how the legislation has affected you or the people you serve. Include the NASW recommendations in your letter.
- **Ask for a response.** Be clear about what you would like your legislator to do—for example, vote for a piece of legislation, co-sponsor legislation, or offer an amendment—and request a reply to your letter.
- **Establish yourself as a resource.** You are an expert in your field and can offer to provide additional information regarding the field, the issue, and the effect of proposed legislation.
- **Write legibly.** Handwritten letters can be as persuasive as typed letters, but your handwriting must be legible. Generally, writing in a professional capacity related to your employment lends credibility. If your letter is part of a letter-writing campaign, a handwritten letter gives the appearance of a grassroots "ordinary citizen" communication, rather than a communication from a "special interest group."

National Association of Social Workers

A Model Project, Presented with Permission of the Author

MOVING ON UP:
(AGENCY WITHIN THE AFRICAN AMERICAN FAMILY)
William T. Langford IV

Sociology 351

MOVING ON UP   1

We are trying to retell History, as seen from below. We do not talk over society's head; we do

not speak as conquerors of History; rather, in keeping with the nature of our profession, we are

notoriously on the side of the losers, of those who are marginalized or excluded from society.

-Günter Grass

A comprehensive understanding of the African American family structure

requires an analysis of the sum of the structural limitations (Garcia, 2000; 99) that

ultimately determine that structure; among them: Diaspora, slavery, and ethnic

discrimination to name a few. The single-parent structure of slave families was (in

part) the result of the forced separation of spouses through sale to other plantations

(Zinn, 2005; 82), a reality beyond their control. Today, African American households

experience what is often referred to as an "epidemic" of unstable, matriarchal families.

This view, needless to say, fails to give sympathy or attention to the *response* of

African American families to the structural factors that result in "deviant" (meaning

non-nuclear) familial structures. New sociologists, however, are beginning to "analyze

family life as a positive adaptation to social conditions" (Zinn, 2005; 82). That is to say, credit is being given to the resilience of African American families in responding to (the setbacks of) slavery, unequal pay for equal work, discrimination in housing and employment, and so on. African American families have been *extremely* effective in exercising agency to see to it that they regain what they have been denied, and inch ever closer to stability and prosperity.

In order to understand ethnic-family agency, we must understand the immediate threats facing it. Detroit, MI, for example, has a population that is eighty-two percent African American. Thirty-two percent of these individuals live below the poverty level (U.S Census Bureau, 2005-2007). According to the 2000 U.S Census, in Washington, D.C, 88% of single-parent homes are those of African Americans. Single-parent households headed by women are *considerably* more likely to live in poverty than their male-headed counterparts. This trend is known as the *feminization of poverty* (Zinn, 2005). In Washington, twenty-five percent of children live in single-parent households. Eighty-eight percent of foster children living in single-parent homes, however, are black (Racial Disproportionality in Washington State, 2007).

The African American family is not without agency. African American families have responded to familial difficulties by developing *strategies* (Zinn, 2005; 176) to aid in providing educational and financial prosperity, and emotional support to their members. The *other-mothering* process as outlined by Karen Cage (Cage, 1997; 25) is such a strategy. Other-mothering strengthens the family unit by looking to the extended family for support. This process is akin to the *compadrazgo* system used by Latino families (Gordon; 1998). African Americans have also exercised their agency via the founding of groups like the Youth and College Division of the NAACP (NAACP Youth And College Division, 2009). The formation and patronage of groups like the NAACP reflects the reality that African American families are *not* passive victims of the structural limitations they have faced historically; rather, they are actively involved in restructuring their community in an effort to right the pressures they face. If the

African American community continues to rally around its support groups, augment family structures to suit their needs, and promote the values of familial responsibility and education, there is no reason why African American families cannot (in the *next* ten years) continue to close the gaps of America's socio-economic inequalities.

As the African American family continues to exercise agency to combat the structural limitations of today and the historical limitations of the past, new trends in family structure may arise. Increased community and familial input in educational programs within the African community has the potential to increase overall academic achievement of Blacks as well as the general attitude toward minority students in America. This increased academic success may have the impact of increasing the number of African Americans who are able to complete a degree at a four-year institution. Only eleven percent of Detroiters have achieved at least a bachelor's degree (Census, 2005-2007). There is a direct correlation between the completion of a degree and increased financial security. Financial worries, according to *Diversity in Families*, are some of the leading causes of marital stress (Zinn, 2005). As African Americans become more financially stable, one can infer the African American family structure will begin to become more nuclear. Financial wellness, as supported through a communal interest in education helps lessen the stress on parents in raising their children, and thus, on a husband and wife relationship as a whole. This could serve to lessen divorce rates, keeping more African American families intact in a nuclear manner. Each bit of agency on the part of African American families, be it within education, emotional support, financial support, political action, etc., aids in the restructuring of their future family structure. In ten years, the African American family will see increased stability and surely a more nuclear structure, if present trends continue.

MOVING ON UP   4

References

Cage, Karen I. (1997) African American Other-mothering in the Urban Elementary
   School. *Urban Review*, Volume 29, p25-39.

Deller, Bill. (2000) *The Destruction and Recreation of Community*. The Nation
   Company, L.P. http://ethicalpolitics.org/blackwood/bill02.htm.

Garcia, Mario (Ed.). Bridging Cultures. September 30, 2009. Kendall Hunt Pub. Co. (July
   2000).

Gordon, Marshall. "compadrazgo." A Dictionary of Sociology. 1998. Retrieved October
   06, 2009 from Encyclopedia.com: http://www.encyclopedia.com/doc/1O88-
   compadrazgo.html

NAACP Youth And College Division. *Mission and Objectives*. Retrieved October 6,
   2009. http://www.naacp.org/youth/college/mission/index.htm

Racial Disproportionality in Washington State. (June 2007). Retrieved October 1, 2009,
   from http://www.dshs.wa.gov/pdf/ca/dispro_Exec_Summary.pdf.

U.S. Census Bureau, 2005-2007 American Community Survey. "Detroit City,
   Michigan". Retrieved October 8, 2009 from http://factfinder.census.gov/
   servlet/ACSSAFFFacts?_event=Search&geo_id=&_geoContext=&_street=&_
   county=Detroit&_cityTown=Detroit&_state=04000US26&_zip=&_lang=en&_
   sse=on&pctxt=fph&pgsl=010.

Zinn, Maxine Baca & Eitzen, D. Stanley & Wells, Barbara. *Diversity in Families*, 7th
   Edition. Allyn & Bacon; 7th edition (2005).

Kimberly Tweedale

Paper Abstract and Annotated Reference List

May 24, 2011

Abstract

This research paper will examine the etiology of childhood and adolescent disordered eating. Abnormal eating is a problematic behavior that can affect people across gender lines, socio-economic classes, and ages. However, certain groups, particularly adolescent girls, develop eating disorders at higher rates than the rest of the population. Several theories have been articulated to explain why individuals develop abnormal eating patterns; additionally, the risk factors that are associated with eating disorders have been a topic of research in the field of psychology during the last decade. This paper will look critically at several of these research studies to determine the strengths and weaknesses within their various methodologies and how each study contributes to a more comprehensive understanding of the etiology of disordered eating.

References

Jackson, T., & Chen, H. (2011). Risk factors for disordered eating during early and middle adolescence: Prospective evidence from mainland Chinese boys and girls [Electronic version]. *Journal of Abnormal Psychology*, 120(2), 454-464. Despite evidence that sociocultural and psychological factors contribute to disordered eating, researchers have yet to examine the extent to which putative risk factors influence vulnerability for girls versus boys within and across phases of adolescence, particularly in non-Western cultures. In this study, early and middle adolescent samples from China (N = 2,909) completed measures of eating disorder pathology and putative risk factors at baseline and were reassessed 12 months later. Among both younger and older girls, elevations in appearance-focused interactions with friends, negative affect, and body dissatisfaction predicted increases in symptomatology at follow-up. In contrast, there was more discontinuity in risk factors relevant to samples of boys. Although media and friendship influences contributed to later disturbances among early adolescent boys, psychological factors, including body dissatisfaction and negative affect, had stronger effects in the multivariate model for older boys. Implications of finding are discussed in relation to adolescent development and a Chinese cultural context.

This study is one of the only available that looks at the risk factors for disordered eating among both boys and girls. This article can provide evidence that risk factors vary among different populations, and additional research could clarify why these differences are present.

Klump, K. L., Suisman, J. L., Burt, S. A., McGue, M., & Iacono, W. G. (2009). Genetic and environmental influences on disordered eating: An adoption study [Electronic version]. *Journal of Abnormal Psychology*, 118(4), 797-805. Twin studies indicate significant genetic, but little shared environmental, influences on eating disorders. However, critics argue that study limitations constrain the conclusions that can be drawn. Adoption studies avoid many of these limitations, but to date, no adoption studies of eating pathology have been conducted. The current study was the first adoption study to examine genetic/environmental effects for disordered eating. Participants included 123 adopted and 56 biological female sibling pairs. Disordered eating (i.e., overall eating pathology, body dissatisfaction, weight preoccupation, binge eating) was assessed with the Minnesota Eating Behaviors Survey (Klump, McGue, & Iacono, 2000; von Ranson, Klump, Iacono, & McGue, 2005). Biometric model fitting indicated significant genetic influences (59%–82%) on all forms of disordered eating, with nonshared environmental factors accounting for the remaining variance. Shared environmental factors did not contribute significantly to any disordered eating symptom. Our findings bolster those from twin studies and provide critical evidence of significant genetic effects on disordered eating symptoms.

This study provides valuable heritability measures from both twin and adoption study methodologies. It examines the biological and genetic factors that can play a role in the development of disordered eating. Like most studies within the field, the population for this study was restricted to adolescent girls, which is a limiting factor in the results.

Mash, E. J. & Wolfe, D. A. (2010). Eating disorders and related conditions. In Abnormal child psychology (4th ed., chap. 13). Belmont, CA: Wadsworth Publishing.

This chapter gives an overview of the topic of disordered eating. It discussed various patterns of disordered eating and the risk factors, developmental causes, treatments, and diagnostic criteria associated with these patterns. The information from this chapter will provide background information on the history of disordered eating and the way it is traditionally studied and understood.

McVey, G. L., Pepler, D., Davis, R., Flett, G. L., & Abdolell, M. (2002). Risk and protective factors associated with disordered eating during early adolescence [Electronic version]. The *Journal of Early Adolescence*, 22(1), 75-95.

Risk and protective factors associated with disordered eating were examined among 363 girls grades 7–8. The variables included self-report ratings of competence and of the importance of physical appearance and social acceptance by peers, self-oriented and socially prescribed perfectionism, negative events, and parental support. In a multivariate regression analysis, low competence in physical appearance, high importance of social acceptance, high self-oriented perfectionism, and low paternal support were correlated significantly with reports of high levels of disordered eating. The negative influence of low physical appearance competence on disordered eating was attenuated for those girls who placed low, as compared with high, levels of importance on physical appearance. Paternal support was found to have a protective function in regard to disordered eating for those girls who experienced high, as compared with low, levels of school-related negative events. Implications for school-based prevention strategies are discussed.

This study examines both risk factors and protective factors of disordered eating, allowing more comparisons between etiology research and treatment research. Like most other studies, this article focused solely on adolescent girls. However, the methodology was simple and effective enough to be replicated with broader populations in the future.

Stice, E., Presnell, K., & Spangler, D. (2002). Risk factors for binge eating onset in adolescent girls: A 2-year prospective investigation [Electronic version]. *Health Psychology*, 21(2), 131-138.

Because little is known about the predictors of binge eating (a risk factor for obesity), a set of putative risk factors for binge eating was investigated in a longitudinal study of adolescent girls. Results verified that binge eating predicted obesity onset. Elevated dieting, pressure to be thin, modeling of eating disturbances, appearance overvaluation, body dissatisfaction, depressive symptoms, emotional eating, body mass, and low self-esteem and social support predicted binge eating onset with 92% accuracy, Classification tree analysis revealed an interaction between appearance overvaluation, body mass, dieting, and depressive symptoms, suggesting qualitatively different pathways to binge eating and identifying subgroups at extreme risk for this outcome. Results support the assertion that these psychosocial and biological factors increase risk for binge eating.

This study looked specifically at predictors of binge eating rather than disordered eating in general. The study identified risk factors that are similar to other studies of disordered eating in adolescent girls. This implies that the etiology of disordered eating may depend more on the population being studied than the symptoms that are observed.

Stice, E., Shaw, H., Burton, E., & Wade, E. (2006). Dissonance and healthy weight eating disorder prevention programs: A randomized efficacy trial [Electronic version].

Journal of Consulting and Clinical Psychology, 74(2), 263-275.

In this trial, adolescent girls with body dissatisfaction (N = 481, M age = 17 years) were randomized to an eating disorder prevention program involving dissonance-inducing activities that reduce thin-ideal internalization, a prevention program promoting healthy weight management, an expressive writing control condition, or an assessment-only control condition. Dissonance participants showed significantly greater reductions in eating disorder risk factors and bulimic symptoms than healthy weight, expressive writing, and assessment-only participants, and healthy weight participants showed significantly greater reductions in risk factors and symptoms than expressive writing and assessment-only participants from pretest to posttest. Although these effects faded over 6-month and 12-month follow-ups, dissonance and healthy weight participants showed significantly lower binge eating and obesity onset and reduced service utilization through 12-month follow-up, suggesting that both interventions have public health potential.

This study investigated the link between the risk factors, prevention, and treatment of disordered eating. The results confirm that reducing risk factors through treatment can reduce onset of disordered eating symptoms. These risk factors were determined by previous studies of adolescent girls, and the treatment protocols were developed for this same population. These findings imply that risk factors particular to a certain population need to be identified in order to effectively treat that population.

Striegel-Moore, R. H., & Bulik, C. M. (2007). Risk factors for eating disorders [Electronic version]. *American Psychologist*, 62(3), 181-198.

The authors review research on risk factors for eating disorders, restricting their focus to studies in which clear precedence of the hypothesized risk factor over onset of the disorder is established. They illustrate how studies of sociocultural risk factors and biological factors have progressed on parallel tracks and propose that major advances in understanding the etiology of eating disorders require a new generation of studies that integrate these domains. They discuss how more sophisticated and novel conceptualizations of risk and causal processes may inform both etiology and intervention efforts.

This literature review does a thorough job of identifying shortcomings in the current research on disordered eating. In particular, few studies have integrated biological and environmental risk factors into a single study, and very few studies have examined how environmental factors could affect men and women differently. There is also little cross-cultural research on risk factors for disordered eating. These are areas that need to be explored further in order to fully understand the etiology of disordered eating.

Wilksch, S. M., & Wade, T. D. (2010). Risk factors for clinically significant importance of shape and weight in adolescent girls [Electronic version]. *Journal of Abnormal Psychology*, 119(1), 206-215.

The objective of the current study was to conduct a longitudinal study of adolescent girls to determine how temperament, attitudes toward shape and weight, life events, and family factors might contribute to the growth of clinically significant importance of shape and weight, assessed using the Eating Disorder Examination (EDE). Time 1 data were available from 699 female twins (M age = 13.96 years) and 595 parents, and approximately 1.15 years later (Time 2) the twins completed the EDE again (M age = 15.10 years). Twins were treated as singletons in the analyses. Time 1 importance of shape and weight was a significant predictor of Time 2 lifetime disordered eating behaviors. Seven Time 1 variables were significant univariate predictors of Time 2 importance of shape and weight. In multivariate analyses, fathers' sensitivity to reward was the only significant predictor of growth of Time 2 importance of shape and weight. Some support was found for established risk factors of disordered eating risk, while the multivariate analyses highlight the importance of developing conceptualizations of eating disorder etiology beyond the individual level.

This study takes risk factor research a step further by looking at risk factors for clinically significant importance of shape and weight, an established risk factor for developing disordered eating in adolescent girls. This demonstrates the depth of the current research for a single population while other populations have been virtually ignored. However, this is one of the only studies that looks simultaneously at biological and environmental risk factors and asks questions about the relationship between these variables.

ACTIVITIES

Welcome to the Conversation

Discuss these questions with your classmates in class or via a class wiki or shared blog.

1. Who are some of the nonprofessional audiences for writing in the social sciences? How should your rhetorical choices differ depending on the audience?

2. What are some key components to effective writing in the social sciences?

3. How can your writing in the social sciences have either a positive or negative effect on your society?

4. What are some common mistakes that may offend or alienate your audiences?

Writing to Learn

1. **Annotations:** This is a preliminary step in writing annotated bibliographies and research papers. As you locate source material or you are assigned readings by your instructor, read the source and write an annotation evaluating it. Your annotation may include a summary of the text, as well as your evaluation and how you see this source helping your research.

2. **Letter:** Write a letter to the editor of a popular magazine in your field arguing against the ideas in an article from a previous issue. As this is more public writing, keep your audience in mind as you explain your side of this professional issue.

Learning to Write

1. **Casebook:** Similar to an annotated bibliography or a literature review, a casebook requires you to review a set of cases (studies) or problems that support your position on an issue. This paper will require you to gather research on your topic and synthesize the information from your sources to best argue for your side.

2. **Project proposal:** Write a proposal to a federal grant agency that explains how you plan to organize and manage your project. This will require you to research model proposals and follow the conventions of your field and the granting agency.

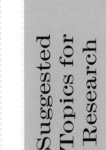

Suggested Topics for Research

1. Research the factors that may have led to the 2007 Great Recession, and pick one discrete topic to research. As part of your research and argument, decide how this topic factored into the market turn and whether there was historical precedent. Then, argue for an appropriate course of action to prevent this factor from causing this type of incident again.

2. Locate a subculture on your campus, and develop a research plan to observe its members in order to prove or disprove a theory about this subculture. Based on your instructor's guidance, you may choose to observe this community either as part of it (ethnographically) or as an outside observer. Then, combined with your secondary research, use your primary research to craft an argument about this subculture.

READ MORE ABOUT IT

Betts, Katherine, Karen Farquharson, and Anne Seitz. *Writing Essays and Research Reports in the Social Sciences*. New York: Cengage, 2005. Print.

Becker, Howard S. *Writing for Social Scientists: How to Start and Finish Your Thesis, Book or Article: Second Edition*. Chicago: University of Chicago Press, 2007. Print.

Beebe, Linda. *Professional Writing for the Human Services*. Washington DC: NASW Press, 1993. Print.

Faigley, Lester, and Kristine Hansen. "Learning to Write in the Social Sciences." *College Composition and Communication*. May 1985. 140–49. Print.

Hurt, Christine. *Researching and Writing in the Social Sciences*. Boston: Allyn and Bacon, 1996. Print.

Johnson, William A., Jr., Richard P. Rettig, Gregory M. Scott, and Stephen M. Garrison. *The Sociology Student Writer's Manual*. 6th ed. Upper Saddle River, NJ: Prentice Hall, 2010. Print.

Making the Difference. Social Sciences Jobs in the Federal Government. March 2009. Web. 12 July 2012.

Staines, Gail M., Katherine Johnson, and Mark Bonacci. *Social Sciences Writing: Research, Writing and Presentation Strategies for Students*. Lanmah, MD: Scarecrow Press, 2008. Print.

"Writing in the Social Sciences." *The Purdue Owl Online Writing Lab*. 2013. Web. 14 July 2013.

chapter 12

Documentation Styles
Across the Curriculum

MLA

When you do research to find supporting evidence for your ideas or arguments, you need to credit your outside sources. Depending on what type of essay you are writing or which type of course you are writing for, you will need to choose a documentation style and continue with that style for the entire essay. Two of the most common styles, especially for freshman and sophomore students, are MLA (Modern Language Association) and APA (American Psychological Association).

If you write in composition, language, linguistics, and literature courses, you will often be asked to use documentation guidelines created by the Modern Language Association (MLA). The MLA Handbook for Writers of Research Papers, in its seventh edition, provides a full description of the conventions used by this particular community of writers. Updates to the MLA Handbook can be found at www.mla.org.

MLA guidelines require that you give both an in-text citation and a Works Cited entry for any and all sources you use. Using accurate in-text citations helps guide your reader to the appropriate entry in the Works Cited. For example, the in-text citation given below in parentheses directs the reader to the correct page of the book listed in the Works Cited.

In-text citation

The beam of a bridge can be made simply (Cortright 2).

Entry in Works Cited

Cortright, Robert S. *Bridging the World*. Wilsonville, Oregon: Bridge Ink Publishing, 2003. Print.

This section provides a general overview of MLA documentation style and an explanation of the most commonly used MLA documentation formats, including a few significant revisions since the previous edition of the MLA guidelines.

Using MLA In-Text Citations

In-text citations (also called parenthetical citations) point readers to where they can find more information about your researched supporting materials. When you use MLA documentation style, you need to indicate the author's last name and the location of the source material (page or paragraph number). Where this in-text information is placed depends on how you want to phrase the sentence that is summarized, paraphrased, or quoted. Be sure that the in-text citation guides the reader clearly to the source in the Works Cited, where complete information about the source is given.

The following are some of the most common examples of parenthetical citations.

1. Author's name in text

When using a parenthetical reference to a single source that is already named in the sentence, put the page number in parentheses at the end of the sentence before the period. Note that the period goes after the parentheses.

Jean Holder (2010) discusses the problems associated with owning airlines in Jamaica: "We don't want to burn bridges" (63).

2. Author's name in reference

When the author's name is not included in the preceding sentence, put the author's last name and the page number in parentheses at the end of the sentence before the period. Note that there is no comma between the name and date in an MLA parenthetical reference, and also note that the period comes at the end of the sentence after the parentheses.

There are potential issues associated with owning airlines in Jamaica (Holder 63).

3. No author given

When a work has no credited author, use a clipped version of the work's title.

> In a recent *Time* article, a list of 15 most popular bridges locates 10 bridges in the United States ("Popular Bridges").

4. Two or three authors given

When you use a source that was written by two or three authors, use all the names in the text of the sentence or in the citation.

> The Golden Gate Bridge is "unquestionably an American icon" (McDonald and Nadel 7).

> According to Proske and van Gelder, "bridges, as physical features, already existed for millions of years, created from geological formations by wind and water" (1).

5. Four or more authors given

MLA documentation style offers a choice when an item to be cited has four or more authors. You can either name all the authors or include only the first author's name followed by et al. (Latin for "and others").

> A variety of groups have been working together to "bridge the science and practice of the field of bereavement" and to use dialogue to close the divide between the two (Neimeyer, Harris, Winokuer, Thornton).

> A variety of groups have been working together to "bridge the science and practice of the field of bereavement" and to use dialogue to close the divide between the two (Neimeyer, et al.).

6. Authors with the same last names

If your source material includes items by authors who happen to have the same last name, be sure to use each author's first name or initial in the parentheses.

> The history of bridges stretches back to the 13th century BC (S. Jones 63).

> Bridges can occur in nature (B. Jones 114).

7. Encyclopedia or dictionary unsigned entry

When you use an encyclopedia or dictionary to look up a word or entry, be sure to include the word or entry title in the parenthetical entry.

> According to *The Oxford English Dictionary*, the card game of Bridge was first referenced in the 1800s ("bridge").

8. Lines of verse (plays, poetry, or song lyrics)

For plays, give the act, scene, and line numbers that are located in any edition of the play. Separate the act, scene, and line numbers with periods. For example, the quotation below comes from *Much Ado About Nothing*, Act I, Scene 1, lines 255 and 256. The MLA also advises using this method with biblical chapters and verses. Be sure, though, that the sequence goes from largest unit to smallest unit.

> Don Pedro responds to Claudio by saying, "What need the bridge much broader than the flood?/The fairest grant is the necessity" (1.1.255-256).

Use a slash (/) to signify line breaks when you quote poetry or song lyrics, and put line numbers in the in-text citation instead of page numbers.

> Simon and Garfunkel famously sang about friendship, "I'm on your side/When times get rough/And friends just can't be found/Like a bridge over troubled water/I will lay me down" (5-9).

9. Indirect quotation

When you use a quotation of a quotation—that is, a quotation that quotes from another source—use the term "qtd. in" to designate the source.

> Smith has said, "I have always had an affinity toward bridges" (qtd. in Jones, par. 8).

USING LONG OR BLOCK QUOTATIONS

Long or block quotations have special formatting requirements of their own.

1. Block quote of prose

If you quote a chunk of prose that is longer than four typed lines, you are using what is called a block quotation. Follow these MLA guidelines for block quotations:

1. If introducing the block quotation with a sentence, use a colon at the end of the sentence.

2. Begin the quotation on a new line.

3. Do not use quotation marks to enclose the block quote.

4. Indent the quote one inch from the left margin, but use the same right margin as the rest of the text.

5. Double space the entire quotation.

6. Put a period at the end of the quotation, and then add the parenthetical citation.

In an interview, Bridges explained:

> A large part of acting is just pretending. You get to work with these other great make-believers, all making believe as hard as they can. What I learned most from my father wasn't anything he said; it was just the way he behaved. He loved his work so much that, whenever he came on set, he brought that with him, and other people rose to it. (72)

2. Block quote of poetry, drama, or song lyrics

For songs and poems, be sure to give line numbers rather than page numbers and to use the original line breaks.

> Simon and Garfunkel famously sang about the power of friendship:

> I'm on your side
> When times get rough
> And friends just can't be found
> Like a bridge over troubled water
> I will lay me down (5-9).

ADDING OR OMITTING WORDS IN A QUOTATION

1. When adding words to a quotation, use [square brackets] to point out words or phrases that are not part of the original text.

> Original quotation: "When we entered the People's Republic of China, we noticed that the bridges were unique."

> Quotation with added word: She said, "When we entered the People's Republic of China, [Dunkirk and I] noticed that the bridges were unique" (Donelson 141).

You can also add your own comments inside a quotation by using square brackets. For example, you can add the word *sic* to a quotation when you know that there is an error.

> Original quotation: "When we entered the People's Repulic of China, we noticed that the bridges were unique."

> Quotation with added comment: She said, "When we entered the People's Repulic [*sic*] of China, we noticed that the bridges were unique" (Donelson 141).

2. Omitting words in a quotation

Use an ellipsis (. . .) to represent words that you deleted from a quotation. The ellipsis begins with a space, then has three periods with spaces between them, and then ends with a space.

> Original quotation: "As it stretches across the Golden Gate from San Francisco to Marin County, the bridge, with its suspended arc and majestic towers, dominates but does not overpower its natural setting."

> Quotation with words omitted in middle of sentence: Donald McDonald and Ira Nadel, authors of *Golden Gate Bridge: History and Design of an Icon*, remark, "As it stretches across the Golden Gate from San Francisco to Marin County, the bridge . . . dominates but does not overpower its natural setting" (6).

If you omit words at the end of a quotation from a source and the sentence has a parenthetical citation at the end, use an ellipsis with no space before the ellipsis, then the quotation mark with no space before it, and then the parenthetical before ending the sentence with a period.

> Original quotation: "As it stretches across the Golden Gate from San Francisco to Marin County, the bridge, with its suspended arc and majestic towers, dominates but does not overpower its natural setting."

> Quotation with words omitted at end of sentence when there is also a parenthetical at the end of the sentence: Donald McDonald and Ira Nadel, authors of *Golden Gate Bridge: History and Design of an Icon*, remark, "As it stretches across the Golden Gate from San Francisco to Marin County, the bridge, with its suspended arc and majestic towers, dominates but does not overpower. . ." (6).

CITING ONLINE SOURCES

In the MLA documentation style, online or electronic sources have their own formatting guidelines since these types of sources rarely give specific page numbers.

The MLA recommends that you include in the text, rather than in an in-text citation, the name of the person (e.g., author, editor, director, performer) that begins the matching Works Cited entry. For instance, the following is the recommended way to begin an in-text citation for an online source:

> In a review of the film *Bridge to Terabithia*, Catsoulis says that the acting is "spectacular and the characters are enchanting" (par. 8).

If the author or creator of the website uses paragraph or page numbers, use these numbers in the parenthetical citation. If no numbering is used, do not use or add numbers to the paragraphs, pages, or parenthetical citation.

When the website does not number paragraphs:

> In a review of the film *Bridge to Terabithia*, Catsoulis says that the acting is "spectacular and the characters are enchanting."

When the website numbers paragraphs:

> In a review of the film *Bridge to Terabithia*, Catsoulis says that the acting is "spectacular and the characters are enchanting" (par. 8).

GENERAL FORMATTING GUIDELINES FOR THE MLA WORKS CITED

If you cite any sources within a paper, be sure to include a Works Cited at the end of the paper. Here are some general formatting guidelines to follow when setting up a Works Cited.

1. Put the Works Cited at the end of your paper as a separate page.

2. Use one-inch margins on all sides.

3. Include any header used for the paper on the Works Cited.

4. Center the title Works Cited at the top of the page, using no underlining, quotation marks, or italics.

5. Place the first line of each entry flush left with the margin. Indent any additional lines of the entry one-half inch (or one tab).

6. Double-space the entries in the Works Cited; don't add any extra spaces between entries.

7. Alphabetize the Works Cited. Use the first major word in each entry, not including articles such as *a, an,* or *the,* to determine the alphabetical order. If the cited source does not have an author, alphabetize by using the first word of the title of the source.

8. Put author's last name first (e.g., Ebert, Roger). Use this reverse order (last name, then first) only for the first author's name. If there is more than one author, follow the first author's name with a comma, and add the other author names in the order of first then last names (e.g., Ebert, Roger, and Gene Siskel).

9. Use hyphens in place of the author's name for the second and subsequent works by the same author. Alphabetize the titles, use the author's full name for the first entry, and then use three hyphens to replace the author's name in all entries after the first.

10. Capitalize all words in titles except for articles, conjunctions, and short prepositions. Always capitalize the first word of a subtitle.

11. Use quotation marks for titles of shorter works, including articles, book chapters, episodes on television or radio, poems, and short stories.

12. Italicize the titles of longer works, including album or CD titles, art pieces, books, films, journals, magazines, newspapers, and television shows.

13. Give the edition number for works with more than one edition (e.g., *MLA Handbook for Writers of Research Papers*, 7th edition).

14. Use the word *Print* after print sources and *Web* for Internet or Web sources.

FORMATS FOR PRINT SOURCES

1. Books (includes brochures, pamphlets, and graphic novels)

Author's Name. *Title of Book*. Place of publication: Publisher, date of publication. Print.

> Holder, Jean. *Don't Burn our Bridges: The Case for Owning Airlines*. Jamaica: University of West Indies Press, 2010. Print.

2. Books with two or more authors

A comma is used between the author names, even if there are only two authors.

First Author's Name, and second Author's Name. *Title of Book*. Place of publication: Publisher, date of publication. Print.

> Dupre, Judith, and Frank O. Gehry. *Bridges: A History of the World's Most Famous and Important Spans*. New York: Black Dog & Leventhal Publishers, 1997. Print.

3. Two books by the same author

Use three hyphens and a period in place of the author name in the consecutive entries. Be sure the entries are in alphabetical order.

> McCullough, David. *The Epic Story of the Building of the Brooklyn Bridge*. New York: Simon & Schuster, 1983. Print.

> ---. *The Path Between the Seas: The Creation of the Panama Canal, 1870-1914*. New York: Simon & Schuster, 1978. Print.

4. Anthology or collection

Editor's Name(s), ed. *Title of Book*. Place of publication: Publisher, date. Print.

> Hummel, Heather, ed. *Bridges: An Anthology*. New York: PathBinder Publishing, 2008. Print.

5. Work within an anthology

Author's Name. "Title of Work." *Title of Anthology*. Ed. Editor's Name(s). Place of publication: Publisher, date. Pages. Print.

> Schwartz, Susan E.B. "Gracie's First Multi-Pitch." *Bridges: An Anthology*. Ed. Heather Hummel. New York: PathBinder Publishing, 2008. 1-6. Print.

6. Article in a scholarly journal

Author's Name. "Title of the Article." *Journal Title* vol. number (date of publication): pages. Print.

> Adam, M.D., and J.P. Hayes "Use of Bridges as Night Roosts by Bats in the Oregon Coast Range." *Journal of Mammalogy* 81.2 (2000): 402-407. Print.

7. Article in a scholarly journal that uses only issue numbers

Author's Name. "Title of the Article." *Journal Title* issue number (date of publication): pages. Print.

> Clark, Robert. "A Tale of Two Bridges: Dangerous and Still Standing." *Leadership and Management in Engineering* 4 (Oct. 2008): 186-190. Print.

8. Article in a newspaper

Author's Name. "Title of Article." *Newspaper Title* Day Month Year: pages. Print.

> Note: When citing English language newspapers, use the name on the masthead but be sure to omit any introductory article (*New York Times*, not *The New York Times*).

> Maeder, Jay. "In the Naming of a Bridge, a Lesson in Democracy Foiled." *New York Times* 18 Feb. 2011: 26. Print.

9. Article in a magazine

Author's Name. "Title of Article." *Magazine Title* Day Month Year: pages. Print.

> Note: Use the day only if the magazine is published on a weekly or bi-weekly basis.

> Bukota, George. "Big Bridges; Local Spans Expanding and Receiving Facelifts." *Northwest Construction* 1 May 2004: 25. Print.

10. Review

Reviewer's Name. "Title of Review." Rev. of Title of Work, by name of author (editor, director, etc.). Journal or Newspaper Title Day Month Year: pages. Print.

Holden, Stephen. "That Beautiful but Deadly San Francisco Span." Rev. of *The Bridge*, by Dir. Eric Steel. *New York Times* 27 Oct. 2006: E11. Print.

11. Article in a reference book

Author's Name. "Title of Article." *Title of Reference Book*. Ed. Editor's Name. Location: Publisher, date. Pages. Print.

"Bridge." *New American Webster Handy College Dictionary*. Ed. Philip D. Morehead. New York: Signet, 2006. 99. Print.

12. Religious works

Title of Work. Ed. Editor's Name. Place of publication: Publisher, date. Print.

Zondervan NIV Study Bible. Fully rev. ed. Ed. Kenneth L. Barker. Grand Rapids, MI: Zondervan, 2002. Print.

FORMATS FOR ONLINE SOURCES

1. Web publications

Author's Name (if author given). *Name of Page*. Name of institution or organization associated with the website. Date of posting/revision. Web. Date of access.

Services Locator. United States Post Office. 2010. Web. 9 Feb. 2010.

2. Article on a website (including blogs and wikis)

Author's Name. "Article Title." *Name of website*. Name of institution or organization associated with the website. Date of posting/revision. Web. Date of access.

Note: If no author's name is given, begin the citation with the article title.

"Building Big: Bridge Basics." PBS. 2001. Web. 9 Feb. 2012.

Lamb, Robert and Michael Morrissey. "How Bridges Work." *HowStuffWorks.com*. 1 April 2000. Web. 9 Feb. 2012.

3. Online newspaper or magazine

Author's Name. " Title of Article." *Newspaper Title.* Day Month Year: pages. Web. Date of access.

Eckholm, Erik. "Covered Bridges, Beloved Remnants of Another Era, Were Casualties, Too." *The New York Times* 2011: A20. Web. 9 Feb. 2012.

4. Online journal article

Author's Name. "Title of Article." *Title of Journal* Vol. Issue (Year): pages. Web. Date of access.

Adam, M.D. and J.P. Hayes. "Use of Bridges as Night Roosts by Bats in the Oregon Coast Range." *Journal of Mammalogy* 81.2 (2000): 402-407. Web.

5. Article from an online service, such as General One- File or LexisNexis

Author's Name. "Title of the Article." *Journal Title* vol. issue (Date of publication): pages. Name of database or other relevant information. *Access Provider.* Web. Date of access.

Starossek, Uwe. "Avoiding Disproportionate Collapse of Major Bridges." *Structural Engineering International* 19.3 (2009): 289-97. *ProQuest.* Michigan State University. Web. 9 Feb. 2012.

6. Article from an online reference work

Author's (or editor's) Name. "Title of Article." *Title of Reference Work.* Location, Date of publication (Day Month Year). Web. Date of access (Day Month Year).

Alder, Phillip and Albert H. Morehead. "Bridge." *Encyclopedia Britannica,* 2012. Web. 2 Feb. 2012.

FORMATS FOR OTHER COMMONLY USED SOURCES

1. Television or radio program

"Title of Episode or Segment." *Title of Program or Series.* Name of network. Call letters and city of the local station (if applicable). Broadcast date. Medium of reception (e.g., Radio, Television). Supplemental information (e.g., Transcript).

"Lost and Found." *Nash Bridges.* CBS. WSFO, San Francisco, CA. 19 Sept. 1997. Television.

2. Sound recording

Artist/Band. "Song Title." *Title of Album*. Manufacturer, year of issue. Medium (e.g., Audiocassette, CD, Audiotape, LP, Digital download).

Simon & Garfunkel. "Bridge over Troubled Water." *Bridge over Troubled Water*. Columbia Records, 1969. LP.

3. Film

Title. Dir. Director's Name. Perf. Actor's Name(s) (if relevant). Distributor, year of release. Medium.

Quake Proof: Building the Perfect Bridge. Dir. Dylan Weiss. Ex. Prod. Milt Weiss. Cry Havoc Productions, 2006. Film.

4. Advertisement

Name of product, company, or institution. Advertisement. Publisher date of publication. Medium of publication.

SunChips. Advertisement. *Newsweek* 15 Jan. 2010: 33. Print.

SunChips. Advertisement. NBC. 15 Jan. 2010. Television.

Note the difference in how the citations for print and television advertisements are formatted.

5. Painting, sculpture, or photograph

Artist's Name. *Title*. Creation date (if known). Medium of Composition. Name of institution that houses the work or the individual who owns the work, City.

da Vinci, Leonardo. *Mona Lisa*. c. 1503-6. Oil on Poplar. Louvre, Paris.

6. Interview

Interviewee's Name. Descriptive Title of Interview (e.g., Personal, Telephone, Webcam). Date of interview.

Elbow, Peter. Interview. 1 Jan. 2009.

7. Lecture, speech, address, or reading

Author's Name. " Title of Speech." Relevant information of where speech was given. Date of presentation. Descriptive label (e.g., Lecture, Speech, Address, Reading).

Gibson, Denise D. "Building Bridges: Professional Development Advising Teams." Annual Meeting of the Association of American Medical Colleges, Kansas City, MO. 25 Mar 1999. Address.

SAMPLE WORKS CITED USING MLA

Following is an example of how a completed Works Cited would look at the end of your paper.

Works Cited

Besner, Hilda F., and Charlotte I. Spungin. *Training for Professionals Who work with Gays and Lesbians in Education and Workplace Settings*. Washington D. C.: Accelerated Development, 1998. Print.

Condon, Frankie. "Beyond the Known: Writing Center and the Work of Anti-Racism." *The Writing Center Journal* 27.2 (2007): 19-38. Print.

Fletcher, Anne C., and Stephen T. Russell. "Incorporating Issues of Sexual Orientation in the Classroom: Challenges and Solutions." *Family Relations* 50.1 (2001): 34-40. Print.

Hanks, Janet and Frances Heller. "After the Sock Factory: Collaboration between Generations in the Writing Center." *Inquiry* 4.2 (1999): 62-68. Web. 21 April 2010.

Konstant, Shoshanna Beth. "Multi-sensory Tutoring for Multi-Sensory Learners." *The Writing Lab Newsletter* 16.9/10 (1992): 6-8. Print.

Martin, Patricia Yancey. "'Said and Done' versus 'Saying and Doing': Gendering Practices, Practicing Gender at Work." *Gender and Society* 17.3 (2003): 342-66. Print.

Miritello, Mary. "Teaching Writing to Adults: Examining Assumptions and Revising Expectations for Adult Learners in the Writing Class." *Composition Chronicle: Newsletter for Writing Teachers*. 9.2 (1996): 6-9. Web. 25 April 2010.

Villanueva, Victor. "Blind: Talking about the New Racism." *The Writing Center Journal* 26.1 (2006): 3-19. Print.

Wall, Vernon A., and Nancy J. Evans. *Toward Acceptance: Sexual Orientation Issues on Campus*. Alexandria: American College Personnel Association, 2000. Print.

APA

If you write an essay in the social sciences, you will usually be asked to use documentation guidelines created by the American Psychological Association. *The Publication Manual of the American Psychological Association*, in its sixth edition, provides a full description of the conventions used by this particular community of writers. Updates to the APA manual can be found at www.apastyle.org.

This section provides a general overview of APA documentation style and an explanation of the most commonly used APA documentation formats.

USING APA IN-TEXT CITATIONS

In-text citations (also called parenthetical citations) point readers to where they can find more information about your researched supporting materials. In APA documentation style, the author's last name (or the title of the work if no author is listed) and the date of publication must appear in the body text of your paper. The author's name can appear either in the sentence itself or in parentheses following the quotation or paraphrase. The date of publication can appear either in the sentence itself, surrounded by parentheses, or in the parentheses that follow the quotation or paraphrase. The page number always appears in the parentheses following a quotation or close paraphrase.

Your parenthetical citation should give enough information to identify the source that was used for the research material as the same source that is listed in your References list. Where this in-text information is placed depends on how you want to phrase the sentence that is summarized, paraphrased, or quoted. Be sure that the in-text citation guides the reader clearly to the source in the References list, where complete information about the source is given.

The following are some of the most common examples of in-text citations.

1. Author's name and date in reference

When making a parenthetical reference to a single source by a single author, use parentheses to enclose the author's last name + comma + year of publication. Note that the period is placed after the parenthetical element ends.

> When a teenager sleeps more than 10 hours per night, it is time to question whether she is having significant problems (Jones, 1999).

2. Author's name and date in text

In APA, you can also give the author's name and date within the sentence; write the author's full name and the date of the publication in parentheses.

> Jean Holder (2010) discusses owning airlines in Jamaica.

3. Using a partial quotation in text

When you cite a specific part of a source, give the page number, using p. (for one page) and pp. (for two or more pages).

> Jean Holder (2010) discusses the problems associated with owning airlines in Jamaica: "we don't want to burn bridges" (p. 63).

4. No author given

When a work has no credited author, use the first two or three words of the work's title or the name that begins the entry in the References list. The title of an article or chapter should be in quotation marks, and the title of a book or periodical should be in italics. Inside the parenthetical citation, place a comma between the title and year.

> In a recent *Time* article, a list of the 15 most popular bridges in the world locates 10 bridges in the United States ("Popular Bridges," 2010).

5. Two to five authors given

When you use a source that was written by two to five authors, you must use all the names in the citation. For the in-text citation, when a work has two authors, use both names each time the reference occurs in the text. When a work has three to five authors, give all authors the first time the reference occurs in the text, and then, in subsequent citations, use only the surname of the first author followed by *et al.* (Latin for "and others") and the year for the first citation of the reference in a paragraph.

> The idea that "complexity is a constant in biology" is not an innovative one (Sole & Goodwin, 1997, p. 63).

The last two authors' names in a string of three to five authors are separated by a comma and an ampersand (e.g., Jones, Smith, Black, & White).

> A variety of groups have been working together to "bridge the science and practice of the field of bereavement" and to use dialogue to close the divide between the two (Neimeyer, Harris, Winokuer, & Thornton, 2011, p. 3).

6. Six or more authors given

When an item to be cited has six or more authors, include only the first author's name followed by et al. (Latin for "and others"). Use this form for the first reference of this text and all references to this text after that. Note: be sure, though, to list all six or more of the authors in your References list.

In Hong Kong, most of the signs on bridges are in Chinese and English; however, once you are in mainland China, English is rarely found on bridge signs, except in tourist areas (Li, et al., 2007).

7. Authors with the same last names

If your source material includes items by authors who happen to have the same last name, be sure to use each author's initials in all text citations.

The history of bridges stretches back to the 13th century BC (S. Jones, 1999, p. 63).

Bridges can occur in nature (B. Jones, 2003, p. 114).

8. Encyclopedia or dictionary unsigned entry

When you use an encyclopedia or dictionary to look up a word or entry, be sure to include the word or entry title in the parenthetical entry.

According to *The Oxford English Dictionary*, the card game of Bridge was first referenced in the 1800s ("bridge," 2001).

9. Indirect quotation

When you use a quotation of a quotation—that is, a quotation that quotes from another source—use "as cited in" to designate the secondary source.

Smith has said, "I have always had an affinity toward bridges" (as cited in Jones, 1990, p. 64).

10. Personal communication

Personal communications—private letters, memos, non-archived e-mails, interviews—are usually considered unrecoverable information and, as such, are not included in the References list. However, you do include them in parenthetical form in the text, giving the initials and surname of the communicator and providing as exact a date as possible.

A. D. Smith (personal communication, February 2, 2010)

J. Elbow (personal interview, January 6, 2009)

USING LONG OR BLOCK QUOTATIONS

Long or block quotations have special formatting requirements of their own. A prose quotation that is longer than 40 words is called a block quotation. Follow these APA guidelines for block quotations.

1. If introducing the block quotation with a sentence, use a colon at the end of the sentence.

2. Begin the quotation on a new line.

3. Do not use quotation marks to enclose the block quote.

4. Indent the quote five spaces from the left margin, but use the same right margin as the rest of the text.

5. Double space the entire quotation.

6. Indent the first line of any additional paragraph.

7. Put a period at the end of the quotation, and then add the parenthetical citation.

In an interview, Bridges (2007) explained:

> A large part of acting is just pretending. You get to work with these other great make-believers, all making believe as hard as they can. What I learned most from my father wasn't anything he said; it was just the way he behaved. He loved his work so much that, whenever he came on set, he brought that with him, and other people rose to it. (p. 72)

ADDING OR OMITTING WORDS IN A QUOTATION

1. When adding words in a quotation, use [square brackets] to point out words or phrases that are not part of the original text.

> Original quotation: "When we entered the People's Republic of China, we noticed that the bridges were unique" (Donelson, 2001, p. 141).

> Quotation with added word: She said, "When we entered the People's Republic of China, [Dunkirk and I] noticed that the bridges were unique" (Donelson, 2001, p. 141).

You can also add your own comments inside a quotation by using square brackets. For example, you can add the word *sic* to a quotation when you know that there is an error.

> Original quotation: "When we entered the People's Repulic of China, we noticed that the bridges were unique" (Donelson, 2001, p. 141).

> Quotation with added comment: She said, "When we entered the People's Repulic [*sic*] of China, we noticed that the bridges were unique" (Donelson, 2001, p. 141).

2. Omitting words in a quotation

Use an ellipsis (. . .) to represent words that you delete from a quotation. The ellipsis begins with a space, then has three periods with spaces between them, and then ends with a space.

> Original quotation: "As it stretches across the Golden Gate from San Francisco to Marin County, the bridge, with its suspended arc and majestic towers, dominates but does not overpower its natural setting" (McDonald & Nadel, 2008, p. 6).

> Quotation with words omitted in middle of sentence: Donald McDonald and Ira Nadel, authors of *Golden Gate Bridge: History and Design of an Icon*, remark, "As it stretches across the Golden Gate from San Francisco to Marin County, the bridge . . . dominates but does not overpower its natural setting" (2008, p. 6).

If you omit words at the end of a quotation, and that is also the end of your sentence, you should use an ellipsis plus a period with no space before the ellipsis or after the period. Use an ellipsis only if words have been omitted.

> Original quotation: "As it stretches across the Golden Gate from San Francisco to Marin County, the bridge, with its suspended arc and majestic towers, dominates but does not overpower its natural setting" (McDonald & Nadel, 2008, p. 6).

> Quotation with words omitted at end of sentence: Donald McDonald and Ira Nadel, authors of *Golden Gate Bridge: History and Design of an Icon*, remark, "As it stretches across the Golden Gate from San Francisco to Marin County, the bridge, with its suspended arc and majestic towers, dominates but does not overpower. . . ." (2008, p. 6).

CITING ONLINE SOURCES

In the APA documentation style, online or electronic sources have their own formatting guidelines since these types of sources rarely give specific page numbers.

The APA recommends that you include in the text, rather than in an in-text citation, the name of the person that begins the matching References list entry. If the author or creator of the website uses paragraph or page numbers, use these numbers in the parenthetical citation. If no numbering is used, do not use or add numbers to the paragraphs, pages, or parenthetical citation.

When the website does not number paragraphs:

> In a review of the film *Bridge to Terabithia*, Catsoulis says that the acting is "spectacular and the characters are enchanting."

When the website numbers paragraphs:

> In a review of the film *Bridge to Terabithia*, Catsoulis says that the acting is "spectacular and the characters are enchanting" (para. 8).

GENERAL FORMATTING GUIDELINES FOR THE APA REFERENCES LIST

If you cite any sources within a paper, be sure to include a References list at the end of the paper. Below are some general formatting guidelines to follow when setting up a References list.

1. Put the References list at the end of your paper as a separate page.

2. Use one-inch margins on all sides.

3. Include any header used for the paper on the References page.

4. Center the title References at the top of the page, using no underlining, quotation marks, or italics.

5. Place the first line of each entry flush left with the margin. Indent any additional lines of the entry one-half inch (or one tab) to form a hanging indent.

6. Double-space the entries in the References list; do not add any extra spaces between entries.

7. Alphabetize the References list. Use the first major word in each entry, not including articles such as *a*, *an*, or *the*, to determine the alphabetical order. If the cited source does not have an author, alphabetize by using the first word of the source's title.

8. Put the author's last name, first initial, and middle initial, if given (e.g., Ebert, R.). If a work has more than one author, invert all the authors' names, follow each with a comma, and then continue listing all the authors, putting a comma and ampersand (, &) before the final name (e.g., Ebert, R., & Siskel, G.).

9. Arrange two or more works by the same authors in the same name order by year of publication.

10. Capitalize only the first word in a title and a subtitle unless the title or subtitle includes a proper noun, which would also be capitalized.

11. Do not use quotation marks for titles of shorter works, including articles, book chapters, episodes on television or radio, poems, and short stories.

12. Italicize the titles of longer works, including album or CD titles, art pieces, books, films, journals, magazines, newspapers, and television shows.

13. Give the edition number for works with more than one edition [e.g., Publication manual of the American Psychological Association (6th ed.)].

14. Include the DOI (digital object identifier), a unique alpha-numeric string assigned by a registration agency that helps identify content and provides a link to the source online. All DOI numbers begin with a 10 and contain a prefix and suffix separated by a slash (for example, 10.11037/0278-6133.27.3.379). The DOI is usually found in the citation detail or on the first page of an electronic journal article near the copyright notice. See example on the following page.

Indexing Details

Title:
An Ability Traitor at Work: A Treasonous Call to Subvert Writing From Within.

Authors:
Holbrook, Teri[1] tholbrook@gsu.edu

Source:
Qualitative Inquiry; Mar2010, Vol. 16 Issue 3, p171-183, 13p

Document Type:
Article

Subject Terms:
*DISABILITIES
*QUALITATIVE research
*MANAGEMENT science
*WRITING

Author-Supplied Keywords:
assemblage
disability
multimodal writing

NAICS/Industry Codes:
541930 Translation and Interpretation Services

Abstract:

In questioning conventional qualitative research methods, St. Pierre asked, "What else might *writing* do except mean?" The author answers, it oppresses. Co-opting the race traitor figurative, she calls on qualitative researchers to become "ability traitors" who interrogate how a valuable coinage of their trade— the written word—is used to rank and categorize individuals with troubling effects. In this article, she commits three betrayals: (a) multigenre *writing* that undermines the authoritative text; (b) assemblage as a method of analysis that deprivileges the written word; and (c) a gesture toward a dis/comfort text intended to take up Lather's example of challenging the "usual ways of making sense." In committing these betrayals, the author articulates her "traitorous agenda" designed to interrogate assumptions about inquiry, power, equity, and *writing* as practice-as-usual. [ABSTRACT FROM AUTHOR]

Copyright of Qualitative Inquiry is the property of Sage Publications Inc. and its content may not be copied or emailed to multiple sites or posted to a listserv without the copyright holder's express written permission. However, users may print, download, or email articles for individual use. This abstract may be abridged. No warranty is given about the accuracy of the copy. Users should refer to the original published version of the material for the full abstract. (Copyright applies to all Abstracts.)

Author Affiliations:
[1]Georgia State University

ISSN:
10778004

DOI:
10.1177/1077800409351973

Accession Number:
47934623

Database:
Academic Search Premier

View Links:
Find Fulltext

Formats for Print Sources

1. Books (includes brochures, pamphlets, and graphic novels)

Author's last name, Author's initial of first name. (Year of publication). *Title of book.* Place of publication: Publisher.

> Holder, Jean. (2010). *Don't burn our bridges: The case for owning airlines.* Jamaica: University of West Indies Press.

2. Books with two or more authors

A comma is used between the author names, even if there are only two authors.

First Author's Last name, First author's Initial of first name, & Second author's Last name, Second author's Initial of first name. (Year of publication). *Title of book.* Place of publication: Publisher.

> Dupre, J., & Gehry, F. (1997). *Bridges: A history of the world's most famous and important spans.* New York: Black Dog & Leventhal Publishers.

3. Two books by the same author

Be sure the entries are in sequential time order with earliest date first.

> McCullough, D. (1978). *The path between the seas: the creation of the Panama Canal, 1870-1914.* New York: Simon & Schuster.

> McCullough, D. (1983). *The epic story of the building of the Brooklyn Bridge.* New York: Simon & Schuster.

4. Anthology or collection

Editor's Last name, Editor's Initial of first name. (Ed). (Year of publication). *Title of book.* Place of publication: Publisher.

> Hummel, H. (Ed.). (2008). *Bridges: An anthology.* New York: PathBinder Publishing.

5. Article in a scholarly journal without DOI (digital object identifier)

Include the issue number if the journal is paginated by issue. If there is no DOI available and the article was found online, give the URL of the journal home page.

Author's Last name, Author's Initial of first name. (Year of publication). Title of the article. *Journal Title, volume number* (issue number), pages. URL (if retrieved online).

Adam, M.D. & Hayes, J.P. (2000). Use of bridges as night roosts by bats in the Oregon coast range. *Journal of Mammalogy*, 81(2), 402-407. Retrieved from E-Journals database.

6. Article in a scholarly journal with DOI (digital object identifier)

Author's Last name, Author's Initial of first name. (Year of publication). Title of the article. *Journal Title, volume number* (issue number), pages. DOI:

Clark, R. (2008). A tale of two bridges: dangerous and still standing. *Leadership and Management in Engineering, 4*, 186-190. DOI: 10.1061/(ASCE)1532-6748(2008)8:4(186)

7. Article in a newspaper

Use p. or pp. before the page numbers in references of newspapers.

Author's Last name, Author's Initial of first name. (Year of publication, Month and Date of publication). Title of article. *Newspaper Title*, pp. page numbers.

Maeder, J. (2011, February 18). In the naming of a bridge, a lesson in democracy foiled. *The New York Times*, p. 18.

Note: If the newspaper article appears on discontinuous pages, be sure to give all the page numbers, separating them with a comma (e.g., pp. A4, A10, A13–14).

8. Article in a magazine

Author's Last name, Author's Initial of first name. (Year of publication, Month of publication). Title of article. *Magazine Title, volume number* (issue number), pages.

Bukota, George. (2004, May). Big bridges; local spans expanding and receiving facelifts. *Northwest Construction, 13*(11), 25.

Note: Use the day only if the magazine is published on a weekly or bi-weekly basis.

9. Review

Be sure to identify the type of work being reviewed by noting if it is a book, film, television program, painting, song, or other creative work. If the work is a book, include the author name(s) after the book title, separated by a comma. If the work is a film, song, or other media, be sure to include the year of release after the title of the work, separated by a comma.

Reviewer's Last name, Reviewer's Initial of first name. (Year of publication, Month and Date of Publication). Title of review [Review of the *Title of work*, by Author's Name]. *Magazine or Journal Title*, *volume number* (issue number), pp. page numbers. DOI number (if available).

Holden, S. (2006, Oct. 27). That beautiful but deadly San Francisco span. [Review of the film *The Bridge*, 2006]. *The New York Times*, pp. E11.

11. Article in a reference book

Author's Last name, Author's Initial of first name. (Year of publication). Title of chapter or entry. In A. Editor (Ed). *Title of book* (pp. xx-xx). Location: Publisher.

Jones, A. (2006). Bridge. In P. Morehead (Ed.). *New American Webster Handy College Dictionary* (pp. 99). New York: Signet.

FORMATS FOR ONLINE SOURCES

1. Website

The documentation form for a website can also be used for online message, blog, or video posts.

Author's Last name, Author's Initial of first name (if author given). (Year, Month Day). *Title of page* [Description of form]. Retrieved from http://www.xxxx

United States Post Office (2010). United States Post Office Services Locator [search engine]. Retrieved from http://usps.whitepages.com/post_office

2. Article from a website, online newspaper, blog, or wiki (with author given)

Author's Last name, Author's Initial of first name. (Year, Month Day of publication). Title of article. *Name of webpage/Journal/Newspaper*. Retrieved from http://www.xxxxxxx

Catsoulis, J. (2007, February 16). Bridge to Terabithia: Transcending pain, a friendship fed on imagination. *The New York Times*. Retrieved from http://movies.nytimes. com/2007/02/16/movies/

3. Article from a website, online newspaper, blog, or wiki (with no author given)

Title of article. (Year, Month Day of publication). *Name of webpage/Journal/Newspaper*. Retrieved from http://www.xxxxxxx

> Building Big: Bridge Basics. (2001, October). PBS. Retrieved from http://www.pbs. org/wgbh/buildingbig/bridge/basics.html

4. Online journal article

The reference for an online journal article is set up the same way as for a print one, including the DOI.

Author's Last name, Author's Initial of first name. (Year of publication). Title of the article. *Journal Title, volume number* (issue number), pages. doi:xxxxxxxxxxx

> Clark, R. (2008). A tale of two bridges: dangerous and still standing. *Leadership and Management in Engineering*, 4, 186-190. DOI: 10.1061/(ASCE)1532-6748(2008)8:4(186)

If a DOI is not assigned to content you have retrieved online, use the home page URL for the journal or magazine in the reference (e.g., Retrieved from http://www.xxxxxx).

> Adam, M.D., Hayes, J.P. (2000). Use of bridges as night roosts by bats in the Oregon coast range. *Journal of Mammalogy 81*(2), 402-407. Retrieved from http://www. asmjournals.org/

5. Article from an online service, such as General One- File, LexisNexis, JSTOR, ERIC

When using APA, it is not necessary to include database information as long as you can include the publishing information required in a normal citation. Note: this is quite different from using MLA documentation, which requires full information about the database.

6. Article in an online reference work

Author's Last name, Author's Initial of first name. (Year of publication). Title of chapter or entry. In A. Editor (Ed). *Title of book*. Retrieved from http://xxxxxxxxxx

> Alder, P. & Morehead, A. (2012). Bridge. *Encyclopedia Britannica*. Retrieved from http://www.britannica.com/EBchecked/topic/79272/bridge

FORMATS FOR OTHER COMMONLY USED SOURCES

1. Television or radio program (single episode)

Writer's Last name, Writer's Initial of first name. (Writer), & Director's Last name, Director's Initial of first name. (Director). (Year). Title of episode [Television/Radio series episode]. In Executive Producer's name (Executive Producer), *Title of show*. Place: Network.

> Cruse, C. (Writer), Cruse, C. (Creator), & Nimoy, A (Director). (1997). Lost and found [Television series episode]. In C. Carter (Executive Producer), *Nash Bridges*. San Francisco, CA: CBS.

2. Sound recording

Writer's Last name, Writer's Initial of first name. (Copyright year). Title of song. [Recorded by Artist's name if different from writer]. On *Title of album* [Medium of recording]. Location: Label. (Date of recording if different from song copyright date).

> Simon, P. (1969). Bridge over troubled water. [Recorded by Paul Simon and Art Garfunkel]. On *Bridge over troubled water* [LP]. Location: Columbia Records.

3. Film

Producer's Last name, Producer's Initial of first name. (Producer), & Director's Last name, Director's Initial of first name. (Director). (Year). *Title of film* [Motion picture]. Country of Origin: Studio.

> Weiss, M. (Producer), & Weiss, D. (Director). (2006). *Quake proof: building the perfect bridge* [film]. USA: Cry Havoc Productions.

4. Painting, sculpture, or photograph

Artist's Last name, Artist's Initial of first name. (Year, Month Day). *Title of material*. [Description of material]. Name of collection (if available). Name of Repository, Location.

> Gainsborough, T. (1745). *Conversation in a park*. [Oil painting on canvas]. Louvre, Paris, France.

5. Personal interview

Unlike MLA documentation, personal interviews and other types of personal communication are not included in APA References lists. Be sure to cite personal communications in the text only.

6. Lecture, speech, address, or reading

Speaker's Last name, Speaker's Initial of first name. (Year, Month). Title of speech. *Event name.* Lecture conducted from Sponsor, Location.

Gibson, D. (1999, March). Building bridges: professional development advising teams. *Annual meeting of the Association of American Medical Colleges.* Address conducted from Kansas City, MO.

SAMPLE REFERENCES LIST USING APA

Following is an example of how a completed References list would look at the end of your paper.

References

Jackson, T., & Chen, H. (2011). Risk factors for disordered eating during early and

   middle adolescence: Prospective evidence from mainland Chinese boys and girls

   [Electronic version]. *Journal of Abnormal Psychology, 120*(2), 454-464.

Klump, K. L., Suisman, J. L., Burt, S. A., McGue, M., & Iacono, W. G. (2009).

   Genetic and environmental influences on disordered eating: An adoption study

   [Electronic version]. *Journal of Abnormal Psychology, 118*(4), 797-805.

Mash, E. J. & Wolfe, D. A. (2010). Eating disorders and related conditions. In

   Abnormal child psychology (4th ed., chap. 13). Belmont, CA: Wadsworth

   Publishing.

McVey, G. L., Pepler, D., Davis, R., Flett, G. L., & Abdolell, M. (2002). Risk and

   protective factors associated with disordered eating during early adolescence

   [Electronic version]. *The Journal of Early Adolescence, 22*(1), 75-95.

Stice, E., Shaw, H., Burton, E., & Wade, E. (2006). Dissonance and healthy weight

   eating disorder prevention programs: A randomized efficacy trial [Electronic

   version]. *Journal of Consulting and Clinical Psychology, 74*(2), 263-275.

Striegel-Moore, R. H., & Bulik, C. M. (2007). Risk factors for eating disorders

   [Electronic version]. *American Psychologist, 62*(3), 181-198.

Wilksch, S. M., & Wade, T. D. (2010). Risk factors for clinically significant importance

   of shape and weight in adolescent girls [Electronic version]. *Journal of Abnormal

   Psychology,* 119 (1), 206-215.

CMS

Instructors in a wide variety of disciplines may require you to use documentation guidelines created by the University of Chicago Press. *The Chicago Manual of Style* (CMS), in its 16th edition, provides a full description of the conventions used by this particular community of writers. Updates to the Chicago manual can be found at www.chicagomanuelofstyle.org.

Chicago documentation style uses two different systems: the notes-bibliography system (NB) is usually used by those in literature, history, and the arts; the author-date system, which is similar in content but different in form, is often used by the social sciences, particularly history.

When using NB, each time a source is used you must have a note (endnote or footnote). Footnotes are listed at the bottom of each page and endnotes come at the end of the document. The first time a source is used, a full citation must be included in the note (author's full name, title of document, relevant publication information). The next time that source is used in the document, a shorter version of the citation is needed. If a source is cited with the same page numbers more than twice in a row, each consecutive citation should read "Ibid." If the source is the same but the page number is different, use: "Ibid., new page numbers".

When using the author-date system, each time a source is used you must have an in-text citation. The author's last name (or the title of the work, if no author is listed) and the date of publication must appear in the body text of your paper. The author's name can appear either in the sentence itself or in parentheses following the quotation or paraphrase. The date of publication can appear either in the sentence itself, surrounded by parentheses, or in the parentheses that follow the quotation or paraphrase. The page number(s) always appears in the parentheses following a quotation or close paraphrase.

Your parenthetical citation should give enough information to identify the source that was used for the research material as the same source that is listed in your References list. Where this in-text information is placed depends on how you want to phrase the sentence that is summarized, paraphrased, or quoted. Be sure that the in-text citation guides the reader clearly to the source in the References list, where complete information about the source is given.

The following are some of the most common examples of Note and Bibliography entries.

Formats for Print Sources

1. Books (includes brochures, pamphlets, and graphic novels)

Footnote or Endnote (N):

> 1. Firstname Lastname, *Title of Book* (Place of publication: Publisher, Year of publication), page number.

> 1. Jean Holder, *Don't Burn our Bridges: The Case for Owning Airlines* (Jamaica: University of West Indies Press, 2010), 43.

Bibliography entry (B):

> Lastname, Firstname. *Title of Book*. Place of publication: Publisher, Year of publication.

> Holder, Jean. *Don't Burn our Bridges: The Case for Owning Airlines*. Jamaica: University of West Indies Press, 2010.

2. Books with two or more authors

N:

> 1. Judith Dupre and Frank O. Gehry, *Bridges: A History of the World's Most Famous and Important Spans*. (New York: Black Dog & Leventhal Publishers, 1997), 122.

B:

> Dupre, Judith, and Frank O. Gehry. *Bridges: A History of the World's Most Famous and Important Spans*. New York: Black Dog & Leventhal Publishers, 1997.

3. Translated work with one author

N:

> 1. Tadaki Kawada, *History of the Modern Suspension Bridge*, trans. Richard Scott (Virginia: American Society of Engineers, 2010), 156.

B:

> Kawada, Tadaki. *History of the Modern Suspension Bridge*. Translated by Richard Scott. Reston, Virgina: American Society of Engineers, 2010.

4. Article in a scholarly journal

Citations for journal articles should include author's name, title of document, journal title, and issue information (volume, issue number, month, year, page numbers). Retrieval information and date of access are required for online documents.

N:

>   1. Robert Clark, "A Tale of Two Bridges: Dangerous and Still Standing," *Leadership and Management in Engineering* 4, no. 3 (2008): 186.

B:

>   Clark, Robert. "A Tale of Two Bridges: Dangerous and Still Standing." *Leadership and Management in Engineering* 4, no. 3 (2008): 186–194.

5. Article in a scholarly journal online

Online journal articles are cited the same as printed articles with one addition: online articles need to include either a DOI or URL.

N:

>   1. M. D. Adam and J.P. Hayes, "Use of Bridges as Night Roosts by Bats in the Oregon Coast Range," *Journal of Mammology* 81, no. 2 (2000): 402–407.

B:

>   Adam, M.D., and Hayes, J.P. "Use of Bridges as Night Roosts by Bats in the Oregon Coast Range." *Journal of Mammalogy* 81, no. 2 (2000): 402-407. Accessed January 7, 2012. http://www.asmjournals.org/.

6. Article in a newspaper

In the names of newspapers, the word *the* is left out of the citation. Include the city of publication for less well-known newspapers. Headlines can be written either with all the major words capitalized or with just the first word and proper nouns capitalized (the first option is recommended).

N:

>   1. Jay Maeder, "In the Naming of a Bridge, a Lesson in Democracy Foiled," *New York Times*, (NY), Feb. 18, 2011.

B:

>   Maeder, Jay. "In the Naming of a Bridge, a Lesson in Democracy Foiled." *New York Times*, (NY), Feb. 18, 2011.

7. Article in a magazine

Include author, article title, magazine name, date, page number.

N:

> 1. George Bukota, "Big Bridges; Local Spans Expanding and Receiving Facelifts," *Northwest Construction*, May 2004, 25.

B:

> Bukota, George. "Big Bridges; Local Spans Expanding and Receiving Facelifts." *Northwest Construction*, May 2004.

FORMATS FOR ONLINE SOURCES

1. Web Sources

N:

> 1. Firstname Lastname, "Title of Web Page," *Publishing Organization or Name of Website*, publication date and/or access date, URL.

B:

> Lastname, Firstname. "Title of Web Page." *Publishing Organization or Name of Website*, publication date and/or access date, URL.

2. Article from a website with author and date

N:

> 1. Jeannette Catsoulis, "Bridge to Terabithia: Transcending Pain, a Friendship Fed on Imagination," *New York Times*, last modified February 16, 2007, http://movies.nytimes.com/2007/02/16/movies/.

B:

> Catsoulis, Jeannette. "Bridge to Terabithia: Transcending Pain, a Friendship Fed on Imagination," *New York Times*, last modified February 16, 2007. http://movies.nytimes.com/2007/02/16/movies/.

3. Article from a website with no author or date given

N:

> 1. "Building Big: Bridge Basics," PBS, accessed February 2, 2012, http://www.pbs.org/wgbh/buildingbig/bridge/basics.html.

B:

"Building Big: Bridge Basics." PBS. Accessed February 2, 2012. http://www.pbs.org/wgbh/buildingbig/bridge/basics.html.

FORMATS FOR OTHER COMMONLY USED SOURCES

1. Television, Film, or Radio Program

N:

     1. Group, Composer, or Performer, *Title*, Medium, Recording Company or Publisher, Catalog Number, Year of Release.

B:

Group, Composer, or Performer. Title. Medium. Recording Company or Publisher, Catalog Number. Year of Release.

N:

     1. "Lost and Found," *Nash Bridges*, CBS, San Francisco, CA: CBS, September 19, 1997.

B:

"Lost and Found." *Nash Bridges*. CBS. San Francisco, CA: CBS, September 19, 1997.

2. Lecture, speech, address, or reading

These citations usually include information including location and date of the meeting, and the sponsoring organization.

N:

     1. Denise Gibson, "Building Bridges: Professional Development Advising Teams," (presentation, Annual Meeting of the Association of American Medical Colleges, Kansas City, MO, March 1999).

B:

Gibson, Denise. "Building Bridges: Professional Development Advising Teams." Presentation at the Annual Meeting of the Association of American Medical Colleges, Kansas City, MO, March 1999.

SAMPLE REFERENCES LIST USING CMS

Following is an example of how a completed References list would look at the end of your paper.

Bibliography

Boquet, Elizabeth. "Disciplinary Action: Writing Center Work and the Making of a Researcher." In *Writing Center Research: Extending the Conversation*, edited by Paula Gillespie, Alice Gillam, Lady Falls Brown, and Byron Stay, 23-38. Mahwah, NJ: Lawrence Erlbaum, 2002.

Carino, Peter. "Writing Centers and Writing Programs: Local and Communal Politics." In *The Politics of Writing Centers*, edited by Jane Nelson and Kathy Evertz, 1-14. Portsmouth, HN: Heinemann, 2001.

Geller, Anne Ellen, Michele Eodice, Frankie Condon, Meg Carroll, and Elizabeth H. Boquet. *The Everyday Writing Center: A Community of Practice*. Logan: Utah State UP, 2007.

Grimm, Nancy. *Good Intentions: Writing Center Work in Postmodern Times*. Portsmouth, NH: Boynton/Cook, 1999.

Nicolas, Melissa. "Why There is No 'Happily Ever After': A Look at the Stories and Images That Sustain Us." In *Marginal Words, Marginal Work?: Tutoring the Academy in the Work of Writing Centers*, edited by William J. Macauley, Jr. and Nicholas Mauriello, 1-17. Cresskill, NJ: Hampton Press, 2007.

Singh-Corcoran, Nathalie. "You're Either a Scholar or an Administrator, Make Your Choice: Preparing Graduate Students for Writing Center Administration." In *(E)Merging Identities: Graduate Students in the Writing Center*, edited by Melissa Nicolas, 27-18. Southlake, TX: Fountainhead Press, 2008.

Welch, Nancy. "Playing with Reality: Writing Centers After the Mirror Stage." *College Composition and Communication* 51 no. 1 (1999): 51-69.

Index

W